EXPERIMENTAL RESEARCH DESIGNS IN SOCIAL WORK

EXPERIMENTAL RESEARCH DESIGNS IN SOCIAL WORK

Theory and Applications

BRUCE A. THYER

Columbia University Press
New York

Columbia University Press
Publishers Since 1893
New York   Chichester, West Sussex
cup.columbia.edu

Library of Congress Cataloging-in-Publication Data
Names: Thyer, Bruce A., author.
Title: Experimental Research Designs in Social Work : theory and
    applications / Bruce A. Thyer.
Description: 1 Edition. | New York, NY : Columbia University Press, 2023. |
    Includes index.
Identifiers: LCCN 2022047190 | ISBN 9780231201162 (hardback) | ISBN
    9780231201179 (trade paperback) | ISBN 9780231553964 (ebook)
Subjects: LCSH: Social service—Research. | Experimental design. |
    Research—Methodology.
Classification: LCC HV40 .T51376 2023 | DDC 361.3/2—dc23/eng/20220929
LC record available at https://lccn.loc.gov/2022047190

Cover design: Elliott S. Cairns
Cover image: Benjamin Chee Chee, *Learning*. Reproduced with permission
    from the administrator of the estate of Benjamin Chee Chee.

Felix, qui potuit rerum cognoscere causas

(Fortunate, who was able to know the causes of things)

—Virgil, *Georgics*, Book 2, Verse 490

CONTENTS

NOTE TO THE READER

An up-to-date appendix of experiments in social work can be found at the book's page within the Columbia University Press website.

FOREWORD

BY GAIL S. STEKETEE, PHD, LCSW

Dean Emeritus, Boston University School of Social Work

Social work research to advance both social policy and social work practice knowledge is a fairly recent phenomenon in the history of social work, which dates back to the late 1800s. Not yet thirty years old, the Society for Social Work and Research was founded in 1994 to advance social work research in the United States. Its success in doing so is evident in its increasing membership and attendance at its annual convention, as well as in its leadership by well-recognized academic and industry researchers. Other North American social work organizations have also advanced social work research, among them the St. Louis Group of social work programs, primarily located in research 1 universities, including the Group for the Advancement of Doctoral Education in Social Work, which serves as an umbrella for social work doctoral programs that train researchers and academics, and the Council on Social Work Education, which offers a forum for research presentations on social work education at its annual program meeting.

However, despite the profession's professed scientific basis, relatively few studies have examined the effectiveness of social work practices and programs. Published social work research has often focused on social policy using large sample data collected in survey studies. In contrast, experimental designs comparing one intervention or social program with others are less common, especially when compared to the studies published in psychology journals.

My professional upbringing in social work research parallels Dr. Thyer's. We were both trained in mental health research groups populated by psychologists and psychiatrists, he at the University of Michigan in Ann Arbor and I at

Temple University in Philadelphia. Our highly interdisciplinary experiences in the late 1970s and early 1980s facilitated a solid understanding of experimental designs as applied to behavioral health problems and interventions. We began to understand the complex experimental controls needed to evaluate whether one intervention worked better than another, under what conditions, and for whom. Those were exciting times in the development of social work research, as increasing numbers of doctoral students were beginning to receive solid research training.

The mental health world on the East Coast at the time was dominated by adherents to psychodynamic models and therapies, and there were few behavioral theorists and experimental psychiatric researchers, so I had limited exposure to experimental research during my MSW training at Bryn Mawr's Graduate School of Social Work and Social Research. But that had changed by the time I returned for my PhD education eight years later. My research training commenced two years into my first job in a family service agency when I began to attend research talks in the Behavior Therapy Unit at Temple University. The BTU, as we called it, was directed by Dr. Joseph Wolpe, a South African psychiatrist whose research on animals helped inform his studies of people with anxiety disorders. He had assembled a team of clinical and counseling psychologists, psychiatrists, and psychiatric nurses interested in the treatment of anxiety and related mental health problems. Also in Philadelphia, at the University of Pennsylvania, was Aaron T. Beck, a psychiatrist whose theories and research on cognitive therapy for depression were garnering increasing attention among mental health professionals. Several fine clinical psychologists were also actively engaged in research in Philadelphia—Martin Seligman, Paul Crits-Christoph, Jacques Barber, Richard Heimberg, Robert DeRubeis, and Philip C. Kendall, to name just a few—which had become a fertile environment in which to conceptualize and study mental health problems.

Along with interdisciplinary colleagues at the BTU, I loved being part of experimental studies in which we were evaluating the effectiveness of a new behavioral treatment for obsessive-compulsive disorder (OCD) called exposure and response (ritual) prevention (ERP). Treating one of the last few participants in Dr. Edna Foa's pre–post experimental design was a highlight and helped established my career as an academic researcher. My client was a surgical resident in training whose increasing OCD contamination fears had stopped his career in its tracks. Our ERP treatment protocol, designed specifically to address his fears and rituals, proved so successful in just a few weeks that my client was able to resume his training and qualify for practice as a surgeon. He was elated, as was I. That experience established my interest in OCD and related disorders, as well as my commitment to test theories and improve treatment outcomes through research. I became hooked on experimental research as we compared different intervention components to evaluate a hypothesized model of how OCD symptoms operated and what would reduce their emotional (anxiety, guilt) and behavioral (obsessive thoughts, compulsive rituals) intensity.

Since then, I've also joined colleagues in experimental research to understand the role of thoughts and beliefs in intensifying and maintaining OCD symptoms. The rewards of this work have been the excitement of generating new knowledge, albeit in small steps, toward understanding people's problems and identifying strategies to effectively address them. There are also challenges. When research results do not fit the hypotheses, it is very tempting to explain away negative results rather than face facts and figure out where the thinking may be off track. Recently, my colleague Dr. Randy Frost and I were sure that providing guidance for making decisions about discarding would be helpful to people with hoarding problems. But it wasn't. In fact, it led to less discarding than simply asking them to talk aloud about the items in question. In retrospect, it is not surprising that people who hoard often react negatively to efforts by others to guide them toward discarding, contrary to any motivation to discard they may have had at the outset. On the other hand, talking about their collected items offers an opportunity to consider their meaning, potentially opening the door to a decision not to keep them. Humans and their motivations are complex, so it is hardly surprising that some hypotheses will not be supported, hopefully leading to better theories and practices down the road.

While my background is in behavioral health research, studying the causes of and treatments for such problems, experimental research is of course broadly applicable to social work practice, as Dr. Thyer's book clearly shows. Indeed, the range of experimental research spans the study of psychotherapies, biological and health interventions, family intervention programs, and community-wide efforts and social programs to effect positive change. Methods of assessment and the nature of problems of all types lend themselves to experimental study. There are few areas of social work in which experimental designs are not useful to inform practitioners, instructors, researchers, and administrators. Kudos to Dr. Thyer for undertaking this impressive effort to articulate and illustrate how to advance the science and practice of social work in all its forms.

PREFACE

If there's a book that you want to read, but it hasn't been written yet, then you must write it.

—Toni Morrison

Preparing a preface is one of the most enjoyable tasks of being an author. By this time, the book is completed, or nearly so. Although the tedium of correcting your book's page proofs lurks on the horizon, the prospect is so distant, often some months into the future, that one anticipates with hand-rubbing satisfaction an interlude without the harpies of unfinished composition hovering overhead. Perhaps there will be some free time for recreation and relaxation, but more likely the time will be filled by catching up on other long-deferred scholarly tasks.

Why did I undertake the writing of this book? As a recently discharged army veteran when I began my master of social work (MSW) studies at the University of Georgia (UGA) in March 1977, I came across the writings of social work professors Joel Fischer and Steven P. Segal, both of whom had independently tracked down and critiqued the experimental studies on what was called social casework available at the time. What they found was a shockingly small number of published randomized experiments whose authors largely concluded that social work was ineffective or, in some cases, actively harmful to clients. In fact, there was very little credible evidence that social work was a useful profession. These compendia of conclusions created something of a furor in the social work literature of the day, a furor with three ramifications. The first and positive one was to recognize the existence of this gap in evaluation research more clearly. This realization enhanced our efforts to use controlled experiments to evaluate not amorphous services (whatever it was the caseworkers were doing) but more structured interventions, practices that lent themselves to being operationalized (i.e., described in a standardized manner that facilitates replication by others and adoption within the practice community). As a result of this initiative, there now exist hundreds of published treatment manuals describing how psychotherapy should be conducted for a wide variety of therapies, including even psychoanalysis. Another consequence was for social work researchers to focus more narrowly on circumscribed client problems that could be more reliably and validly measured. There are now thousands of rapid assessment instruments that clients can complete to facilitate more precise measurements of their situation. Asking a client how they are feeling is good, akin to a physician measuring a patient's temperature by placing her hand on the patient's forehead. Using a reliable and valid scale that is completed by a client is even better, as it helps quantify their feelings, just as a thermometer permits a more precise measurement of a fever. These three steps—facing the problem of the lack of evidence that what we did was helpful, describing services more specifically, and defining outcomes more concretely—constituted progress within the profession and made possible the more effective use of experimental designs. Because of this, beginning in the 1980s, the number of papers published annually describing experimental studies in social work increased and seemed to report more positive outcomes.

But there was another, less sanguine, response to the assessments of Fischer and Segal, and that was to shrug off the older studies with negative results and to promote the claim that randomized experiments were much too blunt an instrument to effectively assess the subtle effects of social casework. Criticisms were raised about the ethics of randomized experiments, the applicability of their findings to everyday practice, their supposed impracticalities and difficulties, and their origins in outmoded philosophies of science. There is a word for this perspective, and that is "nihilism": the abandonment of the position that the methods of science can uncover truth, or even that objective truth exists to be discovered.

I kept abreast of this literature over the years, as I completed my MSW and began doctoral studies at the University of Michigan, then as now, home to one of the most rigorous social work programs in the world. During my MSW and PhD studies I was exposed to little formal course content involving the value, design, and conduct of experimental studies and regularly heard faculty and graduate students disparage the value or practicality of experimental studies applied to social work practice. Survey research was then the vogue. After working as a clinical social worker for several years during and after my PhD studies, I got licensed and began my academic career as an assistant professor at Florida State University (FSU), followed by a lengthy stint back at UGA and then a return to FSU, where I have been since 2002. Throughout my career I have been fortunate enough to regularly teach social work research courses across the curriculum, including bachelor of social work (BSW) and MSW introduction-to-research courses, MSW courses on the evaluation of clinical practice and on program evaluation, and a PhD seminar on preparing systematic reviews. This necessitated my staying abreast of research developments in our field.

In 1991 I founded a peer-viewed journal, *Research on Social Work Practice* (*RSWP*), produced by Sage Publications, and continue to edit this now highly regarded journal, which focuses on social work intervention studies. My thirty-plus years of editing *RSWP* have given me a firsthand appreciation of the breadth and depth of high-quality social work research being conducted by scholars around the world and given me the opportunity to process hundreds of randomized experiments evaluating social work outcomes. Over the years I have also edited and authored a number of books on social work research, including one titled *Quasi-Experimental Research Designs*. In this book I described the strengths and limitations of quasi-experimental studies (studies involving two or more groups *not* composed on the basis of random assignment) and many published social work studies involving this approach. I presented the simpler designs and examples first and slowly progressed to describing the more complex ones. I was happy with this book, and after its publication in 2012 I began to toy with the idea of writing something comparable on the use of true experimental methods in social work research. To my knowledge no social work books exclusively devoted to the topic of experimental research yet existed, with the fine exception of *Randomized Controlled Trials: Design and Implementation for Community-Based Psychosocial Interventions* by Solomon, Cavanaugh, and Draine. But I thought it had some limitations. It focused solely on community-based clinical trials, but experimental methodology has much broader applications than that narrow scope, vignette studies for example. It also paid scant attention to the value of posttest-only studies, investigations lacking formal pretest assessments of client functioning that rely instead on the magic of random assignment procedures to ensure the equality of the two or more groups in a study.

Over the years I began to informally collect hard copies of true experiments published by social workers, and as this stack grew from a single folder to several stuffed file drawers, I decided to attempt a bibliography of such works. I combined this with an introductory essay on the value of experiments and how the very existence of hundreds of such studies was an effective refutation to critics who claimed that experimental research was somehow inappropriate for our field. I published this essay and bibliography (covering publications from 1949 to 2013) in 2015 and, having been bitten by the collecting bug, continued to locate additional studies published during and before 2013 and those published in later years. This mania has continued to the present. I then determined to try to provide an overview of the principles, history, ethics, designs, and applications of experimental designs, a lengthier exposition than my early book on quasi-experiments.

Aside from a couple decades of a priori brooding and ruminating, the actual process of intermittently writing the present work took about three years, aided by a one-semester sabbatical provided by FSU. This book is composed of two major parts: the text itself and the expanded bibliography. I make no claim that my bibliography is inclusive of all published experiments authored or coauthored by social workers, but it is a good start. I am always finding both old and new publications that merit inclusion. Our field's experiments are published across hundreds of outlets, most outside the narrow range of disciplinary social work journals. We often coauthor our work as part of interdisciplinary teams of practitioners and academics. Most journals do not list the authors' degrees or programs. The interventions delivered by social workers are multitudinous, micro and macro, and the psychosocial problems and environmental and health conditions we try to help people overcome have a range that boggles the imagination. A large number of medications and somatic, spiritual, and alternative therapies are now being evaluated by professional social workers, in addition to the more traditional psychosocial and policy interventions that form the mainstay of the field. This renders the task of locating *all* social worker–authored experiments an impossible one (at least with my skill set). But the bibliography has grown from about 744 citations as of 2013 to more than 1,000 by 2023. Near my office computer I have hung a framed print of a painting made in 1657 by Ambroise Fredeau titled *The Blessed Guillaume de Toulouse Tormented by Demons*. The poor guy is trying to attend to his book while evil creatures clutch his throat and claw his neck in an effort to distract him. At times while composing this work, I would glance up at Guillaume and experience twinges of empathy. Look up the title of this painting on Google to see what I mean.

My hope is that this book on the real-world use of experimental research designs by social workers will drive another nail into the coffin containing the dusty bones of antiexperimentalists. The proper point of view, from my perspective, is that social work research should embrace all methodologies that help us come into contact with nature's truths. And truths there are indeed. Social work practices, programs, and policies can be helpful or harmful, so we need to know what their effects really are, and experiments are one tool that can be extremely helpful in determining this. Note, however, that saying experimental designs are a good methodology does not belittle the valuable role of other approaches. In fact, experiments have significant limitations for their use in social work research. They are not particularly helpful in creating new theories or deriving hypotheses from these theories, for example. What experiments *are* particularly good at is testing hypotheses derived from theory and other sources. The research method should suit the question at hand. If a social worker is conducting descriptive research, correlational investigations, opinion surveys, needs assessments, a client satisfaction study, or risk assessments, for example, experimental designs are relatively useless and should not be used. They are not the *best* research method in such instances. They are not even a *good* research method. And the vast majority of social work research does *not* call for the use of experimental designs. But when one is faced with the task of empirically determining the effects of our policies and practices on objective aspects of people's lives, then true experimental methods have a clear and valuable role. Given the more than one thousand published experiments completed by social workers, it would be foolish to deny this. But there are other tools, such as quasi-experimental designs, interrupted time-series designs, natural experiments, and within-subject or single-system research designs, that may be better suited.

While attempting to rank or rate research *methods* in terms of their value (some have claimed that randomized controlled trials are the best method), the endeavor to rate various research *purposes* is even more contentious. For example, it is said that the purpose of qualitative research is to understand the lived experiences of others, usually social work clients but sometimes also caregivers, administrators, practitioners, or other groups. The purpose of randomized experiments is to try to make causal inferences about the effects of social work interventions or about the factors that influence decision-making. I am not at all bashful in asserting that evaluating the impacts of treatments and the success (or failure) of policies and practices is *much* more important to the profession and society. Contemporary social work smiles approvingly on studies intended to try to *understand* what it means to a homeless person to be without shelter or what it means to a victim of intimate partner violence to be abused. I prefer and more highly value empirical investigations to try to *prevent* or *stop* homelessness or intimate partner violence, research that aims to *help* people, not just understand their points of view better. For this purpose, true experimental designs can be extremely helpful: to our clients, to our societal credibility, and to our claim of being a science-based profession. To me this is obvious, but while writing this preface I looked up the last three issues of the major journals published by the National Association of Social Workers (*Social Work*, *Social Work Research*, and *Health & Social Work*) and found not one experimental study. I think it is clear that the profession's research priorities are out of alignment with what society actually needs. I hope that by demonstrating via this book that social work experiments are common, can be conducted ethically, cover a wide array of interventions, and are used with participant populations all over the world, reflecting diverse psychosocial issues and health conditions, that others within the discipline, including graduate students, will be encouraged to undertake similar investigations.

I am deeply indebted to a large number of people who for the past forty years have helped bring about this book. I have had three fabulous deans, Charles Stuart and Bonnie Yegidis at UGA and Jim Clark at FSU, who all largely allowed me to develop my professional career. The large number of past and current social workers who have authored experimental studies over the past seventy years have always been a source of inspiration by enabling me to read and learn from their efforts. These people are far too numerous to list, but their names appear frequently in the bibliography. An academic and personal relationship I particularly treasure is that with John and Lois Ann Wodarski. John was already well known as a scholar when I met him in 1978 when he arrived at UGA as I was departing for Michigan. Nine years later he recruited me back to Georgia from FSU, using methods akin to those employed by Svengali with Trilby. It was a good move. John and I have coauthored and coedited various professional articles and books, and for the past seven years we have coedited the *Journal of Evidence-Based Social Work*. Lois Ann is also an accomplished scholar with many articles and grants in the field of nutrition to her credit, and the Wodarski and Thyer families have traveled together on numerous vacations. I could not ask for better or more generous friends. My four adult children are all now graduated from university with an assortment of degrees, well launched into careers and relationships of their own, and I am most proud of them. They too have been a major source of inspiration to my career path and a great source of personal joy. More recently a new muse came into my life in the form of Laura C. Nugent. Words cannot express how instrumental she was through her love and encouragement (and editing) in helping me finish this book. Last, I gratefully acknowledge the thousands of undergraduate, graduate, and doctoral students I have been privileged to teach over the years. Robert Heinlein said, "When one teaches, two learn," and that has certainly been true in my case. Of particular note are the twenty-three PhD students for whom I have served as major professor. What a privilege it has been to work with them and to be regularly introduced to new fields of social work practice over the years. My gratitude to all of these individuals for helping shape me.

Bruce A. Thyer
Florida State University
Tallahassee, Florida

EXPERIMENTAL RESEARCH DESIGNS IN SOCIAL WORK

CHAPTER 1

WHY DOES SOCIAL WORK NEED EXPERIMENTAL DESIGNS?

All life is an experiment. The more experiments you make the better.

—Ralph Waldo Emerson

The profession of social work is thriving. The number of professionally trained social workers, people with a bachelor's or master's degree from a program accredited by the Council on Social Work Education (CSWE), is going up, driven in part by the widespread availability of jobs and by the growing number of accredited degree programs. The past twenty years have seen the revival and growth of the practice doctorate, the doctor of social work (DSW) degree (Thyer 2015), alongside the more slowly increasing number of PhD programs in social work (CSWE 2021). President Biden nominated a number of professionally trained social workers to fill important senior federal positions administering various national social welfare, social care, and health organizations with billions of dollars in their budgets. And a number of MSWs serve in the U.S. House and Senate. The clinical arm of the discipline, the largest branch of social work, is legally regulated in all fifty states and in some territories, with robust laws governing both title protection and practice. We can legally diagnose mental disorders in most states, and in many, admit people to hospital for mental health evaluations. Federal, state, and private insurance programs recognize social workers as health-care providers whose services are reimbursable. This status promotes the employment of social workers within agencies and the growth of private sector social work. We have a strong accreditation body and a number of professional membership organizations whose interests are so diverse that there is an association that is a good match for almost every practitioner, educator, and researcher. We have a comprehensive code of ethics, a wide array of academic and practice journals, and generally congenial relationships with sister disciplines such as psychology, psychiatry, marriage and family therapy, behavior analysis, mental health counseling, and nursing. In many meaningful ways we have responded well to the challenge placed before us by Abraham Flexner ([1915] 2000), who proclaimed at one of our national conferences that we were not yet a true profession because our knowledge was mostly borrowed from other fields. All seems well.

But something of a specter haunts the field, and that is the question, What good do we do? Do all the services that we provide, ranging from the one-to-one delivery of various psychotherapeutic modalities in office-based private practice by individual clinical social workers to nationwide programs of social welfare intended to improve the health and well-being of millions of people in North America actually result in demonstrable improvements in the human condition? This is an important issue that strikes at the heart of the rationale for the existence of the profession. To the dispassionate observer, the evidence in favor of the effectiveness of social work is surprisingly weak, relative to the vast resources expended in social care programs. This is not to say that social work does not work. As we shall see, in many instances it decidedly does have demonstrated value. But many large and crucial areas of practice are not well researched, meaning we cannot authoritatively assert that some services are effective—or that they are not effective. As MacDonald (1966, 188) noted, "We do not have good scientific proof of effectiveness. On the other hand we also lack good scientific proof of ineffectiveness." But the comfort provided by asserting that "the absence of evidence is not evidence of absence" is rather lukewarm and unlikely to persuade hard-hearted politicians looking for an excuse to save dollars in federal and state budgets. In other areas of the field considerable research has been conducted, and the available evidence seems to show that many social work programs and practices are ineffective. And in the worst case, some psychosocial interventions provided by social workers have been shown to be harmful, up to and including leading to the death of clients. Lest you think this latter claim is an exaggeration, I suggest reviewing Blenkner, Bloom, and Nielsen (1971), an experimental evaluation of intensive social worker services provided by MSWs compared to treatment as usual, conducted with geriatric clients in Cleveland, Ohio, in the 1960s. The experiment lasted one year, after which results were monitored over several years. It was hoped that the clients who received assistance from the professionally trained MSWs would have better outcomes than those who received treatment as usual. In fact, the experimental group appeared to decline more than the comparison group. At a five-year follow-up, it was found that more members of the experimental group had died than those in the control group. In other words, it seemed clear at follow-up that the receipt of MSW-delivered casework resulted in people dying. However, it was later determined that this pattern of excess mortality was attributable to the people assigned to the experimental group being referred to nursing home care to a greater extent than those in the control group and that those in the nursing homes were dying in greater numbers than those who were not.

At the level of individual practice, we can learn from the tragic case of Candace Newmaker, a ten-year-old girl who did not get along well with her adoptive mother. Her adoptive mother took her to a number of therapists, who determined that Candace suffered from a variety of conditions and provided several treatments, including trials of several medications. Candace eventually ended up in the care of two MSWs who prescribed a rigorous course of "holding therapy," which culminated in a session of simulated "rebirthing." This approach was based on a nonempirically supported version of attachment theory. Candace was wrapped tightly in a flannel blanket and had pillows placed atop, which the therapists then pressed against. Candace was told to wriggle free (supposedly simulating the birthing process). For forty minutes she begged to be released, saying she could not get free, while she choked and screamed. For the final minutes she was silent and unmoving. When at last unwrapped, her heart had stopped, and her lips and fingers were blue. She was brain-dead and officially pronounced dead the next day, after twenty hours of breathing only with the assistance of a mechanical ventilator. The two therapists were convicted of reckless child abuse leading to death and served prison time. Mercer, Sarner, and Rosa (2003) describe this tragic story in detail.

Are these two instances typical of programs promoted by social workers? No. But similar examples of harmful therapies can unfortunately be found among the practices of related health-care professions, such as clinical psychology and psychiatry (e.g., Dawes 1994; Johnstone 1989; Ross and Pam 1995; Stuart 1970; Valenstein 1986). Shocking examples like this leave us with the question of how we can determine if a treatment is helpful, of no benefit, or harmful. And that is the subject of this book: how experimental research designs can be a genuinely useful research method of determining the effectiveness of psychosocial treatments used by social workers. As we shall see, experimental research studies are used not only to evaluate the potential of various psychotherapies with individual clients but also to evaluate the use of medications for neurodiverse people (those with so-called mental illnesses) or people with clearly biologically based medical conditions. Clinical trials also measure the effectiveness of somatic therapies, social work interventions for groups of clients, interventions used in couples therapy, methods intended to produce organizational change, community interventions, and even large-scale social and health programs such as Medicaid. Experimental studies can also be used to evaluate different forms of social work assessment and professional educational practices. These are weighty issues of concern to both members of the profession and the general public.

Some social workers have suggested that if we do not undertake more work to develop a stronger empirical foundation for our profession, we may face an erosion of the great gains we have already made. A few members of the field have predicted a decline in the support of our profession's services, given the lack of forthcoming studies clearly demonstrating that what we do actually helps people (e.g., Fischer 1976; Brewer and Lait 1980; Lymbery 2019). In the United Kingdom, the field of social work most akin to clinical social work in the United States was known as psychiatric social work. However, over the past few decades it has declined to the point of invisibility since the government decided that these services were not useful. Jansen foresaw the end of psychiatric social work, writing in 1972, "Psychiatric Social Work as a profession with its tradition, training and culture rooted in the Hospital Services, will in all probability cease to exist. . . . Now the profession has received its death sentence as surely as if the Judge had donned his black cap, or a lethal dose of radiation had penetrated its ranks, for the malady will only slowly become apparent" (647–48). Almost fifty years later, Henning (2018) confirmed Jansen's prediction, lamenting, "The end of specialist PSW training has, arguably, seen a loss of influence for social work in the mental health field. . . . Having exclusively mental-health-based placements is no longer an option for the vast majority of UK social work students" (253). Similarly, family home visiting as a program of prevention and intervention for children at risk of abuse used to be almost the exclusive province of social workers. Now a substantial amount of this type of work is assigned to nurses, as this profession has undertaken a series of well-designed randomized experiments demonstrating that children and families benefit from home visits by nurses (e.g., Holland et al. 2018; Olds et al. 2014). Although there is currently no credible evidence showing that home visits by nurses produce better outcomes than similar visits by social workers, the evidence gathered by the nursing profession is substantially stronger than that for social work visits, so it is understandable that more of this work is now being done by nurses.

Before delving into the details of randomized experiments and their benefits, let's examine what exactly is meant by the terms "social work" and "social work services." I have examined these topics before (Thyer 2002, 2015), and they are not quite as simple as they seem.

What Is Social Work?

To answer this question, we can turn to *The Social Work Dictionary* (Barker 2014): "Social work 1. The applied science of helping people achieve an effective level of psychosocial functioning and effecting societal changes to enhance the well-being of all people. . . . 2. Social work is the professional activity of helping individuals, groups or communities enhance or restore their capacity for social functioning and creating societal conditions favorable to this goal" (401). Each state or territory that licenses clinical social work has its own definition. Florida's is typical:

> (8) The "practice of clinical social work" is defined as the use of scientific and applied knowledge, theories, and methods for the purpose of describing, preventing, evaluating, and treating individual, couple, marital, family, or group behavior, based on the person-in-situation perspective of psychosocial development, normal and abnormal behavior, psychopathology, unconscious motivation, interpersonal relationships, environmental stress, differential assessment, differential planning, and data gathering. . . . The purpose of such services is the prevention and treatment of undesired behavior and enhancement of mental health. The practice of clinical social work includes methods of a psychological nature used to evaluate, assess, diagnose, treat, and prevent emotional and mental disorders and dysfunctions (whether cognitive, affective, or behavioral), sexual dysfunction, behavioral disorders, alcoholism, and substance abuse. The practice of clinical social work includes, but is not limited to, psychotherapy, hypnotherapy, and sex therapy. The practice of clinical social work also includes counseling, behavior modification, consultation, client-centered advocacy, crisis intervention, and the provision of needed information and education to clients.
>
> (Florida Legislature 2022b)

Note the insistence in both definitions that social work is based on science. This feature helps distinguish our field as a profession from philanthropy and other forms of charitable giving. Efforts to provide "social work" not grounded in behavioral science cannot be called professional. The comprehensive definitions of social work given here are broad, so much so that in terms of both methods (e.g., psychotherapy, family therapy) and clientele (e.g., individuals, families), clinical social work is difficult to distinguish from the practice of related disciplines. For example, examine the definitions for some other mental health professions found in box 1.1. There is little to wonder why members of the public are often confused about the distinctions among members of these professions and why some label themselves with the generic term "psychotherapist."

Box 1.1 Selected Definitions of Mental Health Fields Outside Social Work

Marriage and Family Therapy

"The use of scientific and applied marriage and family theories, methods, and procedures for the purpose of describing, evaluating, and modifying marital, family, and individual behavior, within the context of marital and family systems" (Florida Legislature 2022b).

Mental Health Counseling

"The use of scientific and applied behavioral science theories, methods, and techniques for the purpose of describing, preventing, and treating undesired behavior and enhancing mental health and human development" (Florida Legislature 2022b).

Psychology

"The observations, description, evaluation, interpretation, and modification of human behavior, by the use of scientific and applied psychological principles, methods, and procedures, for the purpose of describing, preventing, alleviating, or eliminating symptomatic, maladaptive, or undesired behavior and of enhancing interpersonal behavioral health and mental or psychological health" (Florida Legislature 2022a).

The American Psychological Association says that "psychologists are scientists who use data collected both in the laboratory and in non-laboratory settings to find answers to complex individual and social issues. They study ways to help people overcome health and developmental challenges or circumstances, to understand how groups function, and to make technology and people work better together. They use their research to improve lives all around the world. While they traditionally study and treat individuals with mental and emotional problems, psychologists also work with people to help them change behaviors that are having negative effects on their physical health" (APA 2013).

Psychiatric Mental Health Nursing

"Psychiatric mental health registered nurses work with individuals, families, groups, and communities, assessing their mental health needs. . . .

Psychiatric mental health advanced practice registered nurses (PMH-APRNs) offer primary care services to the psychiatric-mental health population. PMH-APRNs assess, diagnose, and treat individuals and families with psychiatric disorders or the potential for such disorders using their full scope of therapeutic skills. ... PMH-APRNs often own private practices and corporations as well as consult with groups, communities, legislators, and corporations. ... Advanced practice registered nurses (APRN) earn master's or doctoral degrees in psychiatric-mental health nursing. APRNs apply the nursing process to assess, diagnose, and treat individuals or families with psychiatric disorders and identify risk factors for such disorders. They also contribute to policy development, quality improvement, practice evaluation, and healthcare reform" (APNA 2022).

We social workers have something of a problem in that the types of services we provide are also delivered by members of a number of other professions. We cannot claim uniqueness in this regard. We address a diverse clientele in a variety of ways. We work with individuals, couples, families, and communities, and our work can even inform policy. All mental health professions require at least a master's degree (professional psychology and psychiatry require a doctorate) and suitable state licensure. Studies comparing the effectiveness of clinical outcomes for psychotherapy services provided by individuals with a master's degree versus a PhD usually fail to find meaningful differences, much to the dismay of those with doctoral degrees. Treatment outcomes obtained by psychotherapists with different master's degrees are essentially the same as well (e.g., Rubin and Parrish 2012). And there is some evidence that practitioners with bachelor's degrees or even paraprofessional credentials can be as effective as therapists with master's degrees (Fals-Stewart and Birchler 2002; Montgomery et al. 2010; Seligman 1995; Stein and Lambert 1995).

One fascinating study was conducted by Strupp and Hadley (1979), who recruited a sample of highly experienced doctoral-level psychotherapists and a demographically similar sample of PhD-level college professors lacking professional training in psychotherapy. Each "therapist" was assigned to treat fifteen male college students with problems related to anxiety or depression. Valid measures of mental health were taken before treatment, immediately after treatment was terminated, and at a follow-up point. The individuals in each group received a total of seventeen to eighteen hours of therapy delivered in twice-weekly sessions. The results? "Patients undergoing psychotherapy with college professors showed, on the average, quantitatively as much improvement as patients treated by experienced professional psychotherapists" (Strupp and Hadley 1979, 1134).

Another interesting area to consider is the self-help phenomenon, with emerging literature available on outcomes associated with the use of self-help manuals, computer-assisted therapy, and self-help smartphone apps. Psychotherapy delivered through asynchronous texts between a client and a licensed clinical social worker is also becoming popular. The use of some such self-help methods has been shown to be followed by client improvements and, in a few cases, tested and found to be equivalent or superior to face-to-face counseling with a licensed psychotherapist. This is good news for clients: Effective resources for relief from problems such as depression, anxiety, obsessive-compulsive disorder, substance abuse, and obesity are available at low cost. But such findings also accentuate the need for professional social workers to develop a stronger research base to provide empirical evidence that their services are valuable and effective and enhance well-being.

What Is Social Work Practice?

Because defining social work itself poses problems in terms of establishing a discipline-unique method of practice, clientele, and body of knowledge, describing what is meant by "social work practice" poses its own issues. *The Social Work Dictionary* (Barker 2014, 403) provides little help with its tautological definition: "the use of *social work knowledge* and *social work skills* to implement society's mandate to provide social services in ways that are consistent with social work values" (emphasis in the original). Elsewhere I have described the formidable obstacles to defining and locating social work knowledge and the factual information, empirical research, practice methods, theories, and conceptual models unique to our field, originating solely within our ranks (Thyer 2013). Most theories and models found in our textbooks originated outside social work (a few exceptions are solution-focused brief treatment, narrative therapy, and task-centered practice), and the interventions we employ are widely used throughout the helping professions and were mostly developed by others (Brandell 2021; Turner 2017). The person-in-environment perspective, often said to be the centerpiece of our conceptual framework, did not originate in social work and is widely used in other domains, such as family systems theory and applied behavior analysis. Our ethical foundations are also widely shared. Those who contend otherwise, that we are somehow unique in our value base, are usually unaware of the extent to which other disciplines' codes of ethics mirror ours, especially in supposedly hallmark features such as a particular concern for helping historically oppressed groups, helping those who have been victims of discrimination, and the promotion of social justice

(Bhuga 2016; Johnson et al. 2014; Pearson 2012; Watson 2019). All helping professions' codes of ethics and internal standards share similar concerns.

When others have grappled with the important issues of defining social work, social workers, and what social work practice and research are, the quest for answers that are unique to social work has gotten bogged down, and practical if academically unsatisfying definitions have resulted. In her article "But What Is Social Casework?" (1971), Hartman draws the following conclusion: "Because people who define themselves as caseworkers define the practice so differently and because no one has been elected to determine the definition, I assume that we can all carve out our area and practice it, teach it, and write articles about it as long as the community, clients, universities, and editors will support us" (419). You can almost see her shrugging in a resigned manner as she wrote this.

In 1972 Steven P. Segal prepared a review article on the outcomes of social work treatments in an outpatient setting. Among the screening criteria used to include or exclude studies is his definition of a social worker: "The *technologists* in this review are primarily social workers who have received master's training in a graduate school of social work" (Segal 1972, 3, emphasis in the original). In other words, he looked not at *what they did* but *who provided* the services and with what credentials. On the first page of his article, he states his view: "I know of no study of outcome with respect to social work therapeutic interventions with both an adequate control group design and positive results" (Segal 1972, 3). And he found little to change his position following his review: "The evidence with respect to the effectiveness of social work therapeutic interventions remains equivocal. The trends in the data, however, point strongly in the negative direction" (Segal 1972, 15).

When Joel Fischer similarly searched the literature in the early 1970s for credible outcome studies on social casework ("Many social workers consider social casework to be synonymous with *clinical social work* practice" [Barker 2014, 396, emphasis in the original]), he too was struck by the difficulties in defining the field. In his 1973 paper, "Is Casework Effective? A Review," he writes, "In a most general sense, then, casework could be defined—at least for the purpose of reviewing studies that evaluate casework—as the services of professional caseworkers" (Fischer 1973, 6). He stuck with this view in his later book-length treatment of the topic, writing, "Social casework then appears to be more of a professional designation than one which describes either a specific theory or method of specific techniques of practice" (Fischer 1976, 10), and arriving at a pragmatic definition: "Social casework is defined in this book as *the services provided by professional caseworkers*" (11, emphasis in the original). Similar to Segal's approach, social workers were said to be people who had earned an MSW degree from a program accredited by the CSWE. The CSWE did not define those who had earned a BSW as social work professionals until after Fisher wrote his book, but presumably Fischer's definition could now be expanded to anyone with a social work degree, whether a BSW, MSW, or doctorate. Fischer noted some advantages of such a wide if ambiguous definition. The scope of practice of social workers is genuinely very broad, so a narrower definition would exclude the practice activities of a good many members of our profession. The work of the former U.S. senator Barbara Mikulski, MSW, who served for many years and promoted social welfare programs, the current U.S. senator (as of the time of this writing) Kyrsten Sinema, MSW, and the American civil rights leader and former executive director of the National Urban League, Whitney Young, MSW, come to mind, as does the work of the well-known financial adviser Suze Orman, BSW, who helps people get out of debt and promotes prudent investing. Our field is broad indeed.

Fischer went on to note that "the definition of casework as the services of professional caseworkers is an attempt to reflect the realities of social casework practice. It assumes that casework is not a unitary or homogeneous phenomenon; it includes under its scope whatever services the professionals involved in a given project or study deemed appropriate, and hence, recognizes the necessity of individualizing services; and it provides the broadest possible base for drawing conclusions about the effectiveness of professional casework, no matter what techniques or methods are used in providing casework services" (1976, 13).

The wide and expanding scope of social work practice has been recognized for a long time, which also militates against coming up with a more precise definition. In 1925 Washington said, "The trained social worker is prepared to find and expects to find social work extended from year to year to include activities that formerly were not considered social work at all" (169). In 1949 a review of two books based on papers read at a conference sponsored by the Columbia University School of Social Work and the Community Service Society of New York was published in the *Journal of Consulting and Clinical Psychology*. The author wrote, "[The two books] show how closely psychology and social work have drawn together in recent years as each has moved toward the other's position in emphasis on theory and service. Even much of their research becomes indistinguishable, as social and clinical psychology acquire social workers' broad cultural frame of reference, and social work acquires the former's refinements of technique" (Staff 1949, 385). Two years later, the noted social work experts Hollis and Taylor said, "Social work and social workers should be looked upon as evolving concepts that are yet too fluid for precise definition" (1951, 51).

The first issue of the then new National Association of Social Workers' journal, *Social Work*, contained a sociological analysis of the state of social work practice. In that piece, Eaton notes that "in a report prepared for the Bureau of Labor Statistics, social workers were found to be doing almost anything that aimed at helping people with social, economic, psychological, and educational problems. They were engaged in 145 different vocational functions but had no exclusive jurisdiction over any of them" (1956, 11). At about this time the CSWE published a monograph titled *Social Science in the Professional Education of Social Workers*, which claims, "In defining the focus of direct practice . . . we have not defined what the social worker does. This is, as all social workers know, difficult to agree upon" (Coyle 1958, 17).

Subsequent to Segal's (1972) and Fischer's (1973, 1976) reviews of outcome studies on social work, Lynn Videka-Sherman (1988) conducted the first meta-analysis of social work outcome studies (a meta-analysis is used to parse out possible effects of treatments across studies) and used the following as her criterion for study inclusion: "1. The practitioners were social workers (BSW, MSW or doctorate) or an interdisciplinary team that included social workers" (Saunders 1986, 3); this was essentially the same standard as that used by Segal and Fischer.

This definitional ambiguity should not be a source of alarm, as it is not uncommon. In trying to arrive at a definition of social work science, the social work faculty members Mor Barak and Brekke fell back on a familiar approach, saying, "Social work science is what social work scientists do" (2014, 620). In sociology we learn that "sociology is what sociologists teach" (Kennedy and Kennedy 1942, 661). Similarly, the American Psychological Association (APA) defines a psychologist as someone with a degree in psychology: "A doctoral-level psychologist holds a PhD, PsyD or EdD in psychology from a regionally accredited institution" (APA 2012). The APA contends that people with master's or bachelor's degrees in psychology are not considered psychologists and that psychology "is a diverse discipline, grounded in science, but with nearly boundless applications to everyday life" (APA 2020). Diverse indeed!

Sometimes when discussing the problem of defining social work, social work practice, and social worker, I ask my students what medical doctors can do that no other professionals can. I get answers like prescribe medicine, diagnose diseases, and perform surgery. I reply that dentists, osteopaths, and podiatrists can do all these things, too, and that nurses and physician assistants can do some of them. I ask the same about lawyers and get responses like prepare wills, argue in court, and file lawsuits. I point out that people can prepare their own wills using online software and defend themselves in court and that non-lawyers can sue people. Permeable disciplinary boundaries are common across professions and should not give rise to alarm. We have plenty of evidence of our independent professional status—features such as strong legal regulation, public sanction, insurance reimbursement, and the ability to work in private practice—so much so that even though we may be unable to pin down an exact definition of who we are and what we do, we are in good company.

To be clear, then, for the purposes of this book, a social worker is defined as someone with a degree in social work, whether a bachelor's, master's, or doctorate. Other degrees do not matter as long as the person has at least one social work degree. Thus, someone with a BSW or MSW *and* a PhD in, say, sociology, education, or psychology, is, for our purposes, considered a social worker. And social work practice is simply what people with social work degrees do. While these definitions are not completely satisfactory, until resolutions to the issues of defining these terms are found, they are what we will use in this book.

Concern with Causation

Throughout our history we can find statements that a good heart and good intentions are not a sufficient justification for doing social work. While a kind heart and noble intentions are of course prerequisite for good practice, it is equally important that the results obtained from social work programs, policies, and practices benefit clients and the public and that the potential harms of a given service do not outweigh the benefits. The history of social work, and of the other human services, is replete with examples of well-intended practices that ultimately turned out to be ineffective, socially unjust, or even harmful. Psychiatry has its history of lobotomies and false claims about the effectiveness of psychotropic medications; psychology has its history of phrenology and assistance in the torture of detainees at the Guantanamo Bay detention camp, and social work has its history of orphan trains, complicity in Japanese internment camps in the United States during World War II, and support of involuntary sterilization programs early in the last century.

Given that clinical social workers make up the largest segment of the profession and that the major intervention licensed clinical social workers provide is psychotherapy, it is alarming that there is considerable evidence that psychotherapy can produce harmful effects (Grunebaum 1986; Lilienfeld 2007). It is regrettable that social work as a practice is rife with individuals who practice ineffective, pseudoscientific, and sometimes harmful therapies (Thyer and Pignotti 2015; Holden and Barker 2018). This is due in part to the unwillingness of the major professional associations and state licensing boards to take proactive steps to discourage social workers from providing therapies that are unvalidated (i.e., not supported by evidence) or invalidated (i.e., with evidence demonstrating ineffectiveness). The only treatments explicitly prohibited by the National Association of Social Workers and some states' licensing laws are conversion or reparative therapies; that is, efforts to change someone's sexual orientation from gay to straight (NASW 2015). Thus, one can Google "LCSW" (licensed clinical social worker) and "tarot" and find social workers using tarot cards in their professional practice with clients. Similar searches will find licensed clinical social workers offering to heal clients with crystals or to help them obtain guidance from the spirits of the dead. And virtually nothing is being done to prohibit such practices. No wonder Specht and Courtney (1994) labeled such members of the profession "unfaithful angels."

Knowing that social work services have the potential for both good and bad results has led some members of the field to explore the actual outcomes of social work services. This was seen as crucial very early in our history. Take for example the plea made by Richard Cabot in his presidential address at the fifty-eighth annual meeting of the National Conference of Social Work in 1931:

> I appeal to you, the social workers of this country. . . . Measure, evaluate, esti-
> mate, appraise your results, in some form,—in any terms that rest upon some-
> thing beyond assertion, and "illustrative cases." State your objectives and how
> far you have reached them. . . . Let enough time elapse so that there may be
> some reasonable hope of permanence in the results which you state. . . . Try to
> separate what you did from what other forces or agencies did. . . . The greatest
> value of all this, I believe, will not be a comparison of worker with worker, or
> of agency with agency, but an evaluation of one method against another. . . .
> Out of such evaluations will come, I believe, better service to the client.
>
>   (450–51)

Cabot raised several important issues in these remarks. One was the neces-
sity of obtaining empirical data on client outcomes and of going beyond the level of clinical anecdote to do so. He talked about the need for measurable objectives and for a follow-up of sufficient duration to ascertain the durability of any improvements. He also clearly thought it was a good idea to compare methods of social work practice against each other to determine whether one yielded superior outcomes. And he cited a pragmatic reason for us to be concerned with attempting to demonstrate positive results: "Those who support our social agencies, by subscription or by taxation, need to be convinced that our clients are on the whole so much benefited by our efforts that it is right and reasonable to continue the expenditure of money for this purpose, rather than to use it for, say, better college education or better public health" (Cabot 1931, 442). Also in this prescient speech he acknowledged that many factors influence our clients, which we must try to control for when attempting to determine the effectiveness of our services. He even alluded to the importance of comparison or control groups: "Pending the much-desired epoch when we shall control our results by comparison with a parallel series of cases in which we did nothing, we must admit that we may not be responsible for either our successes or our failures" (Cabot 1931, 448). Given the time, it was remarkable to recognize that we needed to compare the results of the clients we treated with those of a similar group who did not get treatment to truly ascertain the

effects of social work services. Also impressive was his contention that positive evaluations will lead to improved services and client outcomes.

Several issues were embedded in Cabot's talk. One involved the importance of determining the status of clients after treatment. Some rudimentary steps had been taken along these lines at the time. Glueck and Glueck (1930) published a follow-up study completed five years after about five hundred young people labeled juvenile delinquents had been treated, and Theis (1924) followed up on the status of almost eight hundred adults who had been in foster care when they were young. These were good efforts for their time, but Cabot knew that these studies had shortcomings. No measures of psychosocial functioning had been taken prior to treatment, the outcome measures were usually subjective and weak, the follow-up periods were not long enough, and there were no comparison groups of equivalently troubled youth who did not receive social work care. Essentially Cabot was urging the profession not only to document client status after receiving services but also to document changes (ideally improvements) in such functioning, and eventually to try to determine whether these changes had been *caused* by social casework.

Early social workers, as much as their contemporary ones, were also much concerned with trying to determine the causes of psychosocial dysfunction. Wayland (1894), for example, said, "The charity that is informed by wisdom looks first of all to *causes*" (265, my emphasis). Although the multiplicity of causal factors giving rise to psychosocial problems was well recognized, there was little doubt that causes indeed there were and that scientific methods had the potential to be valuable in determining these. Statistics were recognized as a valuable tool for understanding causation: "To get some hint of the *causes* of the changes going on all about, he must understand what correlation is, he must study the degree of association of variables one with another. It is about the only hope we have about learning cause and effect relations in human affairs" (Hewes 1930, 29, my emphasis). Jaggers and Loomis (2020) recently reiterated this point. As statistical methods became more refined and applicable to human affairs, their importance became more appreciated: "The discovery of association may provide insight into *cause-effect relationships*, on which all science is built" (Miller 1960, 171, my emphasis). One effort to define social casework bluntly stated as an operating assumption, "Cause and effect relationships exist. Behavior, as well as other natural phenomena, is caused and not happenstance" (Cockerill et al. 1952, 6). Claiming that *all* science is built upon establishing cause-and-effect relations may be too strong a position for many philosophers of science, but few such philosophers or social workers would deny that discovering valid causal relationships is important in many science-based disciplines.

Determining causation is also relevant in the etiologies of psychiatric conditions (Lowery 1949; Burns 1966; Saari 1994), as well as other issues of problematic behavior such as domestic violence and child abuse and forms of criminality such as theft (Wootton 1959). However, it may not always be possible to determine the causes of a client's problem. Sometimes the clinical situation demands that we begin prevention or treatment services right away, regardless of the causes of the problem; for example, in cases of domestic violence, child abuse and neglect, and suicidality. On a larger scale, we can begin investigating the effectiveness of social work interventions targeting a particular problem prior to understanding the causes of the problem. This is actually the common scenario. We have few science-based etiological explanations for most diagnoses found in the *Diagnostic and Statistical Manual of Mental Disorders* (DSM; currently in a revised fifth edition, DSM-5-TR), and the causes of larger-scale issues such as racism, poverty, and social injustice also continue to elude us. But this does not preclude efforts to intervene. And some scholars have criticized a perceived overemphasis on determining cause prior to intervention. For example, Cabot said, "To look for the 'cause' of what is characteristic in a person's life, his opinions, his total behavior, is as much of a wild goose chase as to look for perpetual motion" (1931, 439). The misidentification of causes can also be harmful, as we shall see.

Finding the Causes of Problems

Social workers have two focuses in terms of causation. One is uncovering the presumptive causes of psychosocial dysfunction, mental illnesses, and larger societal-level problems. This is an evolving process. Initial conceptualizations of the causes of something are revised as these early views are found to be incorrect, sometimes discarded, and often replaced with new theories. One example of this process is the disorder labeled schizophrenia. Preprofessional ideas of the causes of what we now call schizophrenia involved supernatural concepts such as demonic possession or witchcraft. Later came biological theories, such as physical lesions in the brain (Griesinger 1867); dysfunctional ovaries that needed to be removed (Thiery 1998); sexual complexes centered in the nose that required cauterization, as speculated by Freud (Young 2002); undetected infections in tooth cavities requiring extraction (Cotton 1922); and more recently the theory of chemical imbalances in the brain (Whitaker 2015), all now known to be false and largely discarded. The notion upon which Alcoholics Anonymous is based—that alcoholism is caused by an inherited allergic reaction to small amounts of alcohol, which causes an irresistible craving for more—has also been found to be false (Sobell, Sobell, and Christelman 1972). Nota bene: The truth or falsity of a given theory upon which a therapy is based has no direct bearing on the effectiveness of the therapy. The theory of Alcoholics Anonymous says little about the value of its twelve-step program of recovery. The geocentric theory of the universe (that the earth is the center of things) works well for explaining many astronomical phenomena like eclipses, even though that theory is wrong and has been replaced by a heliocentric (sun-centered) theory, which does a better job. Many treatments established as effective were originally based on theories now known to be false. After decades of chasing largely biologically based theories of the etiologies of so-called mental illnesses, our profession widely embraced psychodynamic theories in all their varieties. The theory of the emotionally distant "refrigerator mother" as the cause of autism has been shown to be incorrect, as have psychodynamic theories of the etiology of same-sex attraction (Lorand and Balint 1956; Wasserman 1960). However, psychodynamic theory remains a powerfully influential perspective within clinical social work (Thyer 2017).

The rejection of etiological theories on the basis of credible empirical data showing them to be incorrect is a form of *progress* in our scientific understanding and practice. Because the theories I have just mentioned have been proved to be false, healthy ovaries are no longer being removed or nasal passages burned, teeth are not being extracted in the name of mental health treatment, gay men are no longer subjected to electric shocks as a form of aversive conditioning, and children are no longer taken from their homes and placed in institutions to distance them from supposedly pathogenic parents. Although these egregiously false treatments have largely been deleted from contemporary practice, many fringe therapies continue to survive, and new ones emerge, some of which are practiced by LCSWs. State licensing boards and professional associations tolerate these fringe practices in a way that ill serves the public, taking action only when a Candace Newmaker is killed or the large and influential community of LGBTQ+ social workers lobbies to have conversion therapy declared unethical. Apart from these few conspicuous examples of treatments considered beyond the pale, when it comes to therapies, as Cole Porter wrote, almost *Anything Goes!*

Social Work Interventions as a Cause of Change

The second focus social workers have with regard to causation is on trying to determine whether social work treatment is *responsible* for any improvements or deterioration observed in clients. In everyday practice with real social work practitioners serving real clients in real agencies, this is exceedingly difficult to do. Such efforts involve two major sequential tasks. The first is to see whether clients have changed (i.e., improved or deteriorated). In the early years of our field, studies were undertaken in which clients were simply asked by their social caseworkers if they had improved, and some method was undertaken to try to quantify these self-reports. One way to do so is to report the percentage of clients who said they had improved, not improved, or declined follow-ing casework. A caseworker with a substantial number of clients reporting improvement was judged to be doing a good job, and an agency could claim the same if a substantial majority of its clientele made the same claim. Another approach is to ask caseworkers for their professional judgments regarding their clients' improvement, perhaps using a similar metric (i.e., improved, not improved, or worse off). An improvement upon using only one approach is to use both methods: asking the clients and asking the caseworkers, perhaps at discharge. For children, caseworkers or the agency could ask the parents or caregivers for their impressions. This was the approach used in Theis's (1924) report, for example.

Perhaps you can see some problems with using client self-reports, caseworker assessments, or parents' judgments as the primary indicator of a treatment's effectiveness. Are the people reporting outcomes judging changes accurately? Can you see why a caseworker might tend to overestimate the improvement shown by their clients? It would be a strong individual indeed who accurately reported that their clients had not gotten any better, perhaps after months of therapy sessions. Can you see why a client or parent's judgment could also be biased? After all, many are likely to have attended numerous counseling sessions, perhaps paying fees, and to have devoted much time to traveling to and from a social worker's office. It is easy to see how clients or parents might overestimate improvements, whether consciously or unconsciously. The pos-sibility of overestimating improvements may be related to what the social psy-chologist Leon Festinger (1957) labeled the over-justification effect, observed when people report more value or enjoyment in having engaged in an activity simply because of the efforts they devoted to that activity. The over-justifica-tion effect is but one example of a possible confounding factor in accurately reporting treatment effectiveness. Other events in clients' lives over the course of treatment may be responsible for changes apart from treatment influences themselves.

In the landmark social work experiment reported in *Girls at Vocational High* (Meyer, Borgatta, and Jones 1965), the social workers who provided the case-work services reported positive and optimistic improvements among the young women in the experimental treatment condition; yet according to the more objective indicators of outcome, the treated participants improved no more than those randomly assigned to the control condition. It is through examples like this that we can see that relying solely on client self-reports or clinician judgments may not allow for the most accurate assessment of a treatment's success. This is not to say that these more subjective indicators should not be used in outcome studies, only that they should be paired with more objective measures, such as observations of client behavior, reports of thoughts, or physi-ological measurements (e.g., drug test results in substance abuse services).

The late psychologist Scott Lilienfeld and his colleagues (Lilienfeld et al. 2014) published a brilliant paper titled "Why Ineffective Psychotherapies Appear to Work: A Taxonomy of Causes of Spurious Therapeutic Effectiveness." We will be examining some of these causes later in this book, when we address what are called threats to internal validity. Suffice it to say, determining whether real changes occurred among our clients is difficult, and establishing that any such changes were caused by our interventions is more difficult still.

In the famous study by Glueck and Glueck (1930), it was found that 20 percent of the cases of juvenile delinquents could be considered treatment successes, and 80 percent were said to be failures. The problem with judging results like this is that there is nothing to compare the results to. If someone tells me at the end of a University of Michigan football game against Ohio State University that Michigan scored thirty-six points, I do not know if that is a good result (Michigan won!) or a bad one (Michigan lost!) because of the lack of comparison. If 20 percent of youth treated in a reformatory are considered successes, I do not know if this is a good or bad outcome. To assess this, I would need results for a similar comparison group of young people labeled juvenile delinquents who had received no treatment. If the untreated youth were found to have only a 5 percent success rate over the same period of time, that initially dismal-appearing 20 percent would look pretty good. But if the untreated teens showed a 40 percent success rate, it would seem that the reformatory treatment actually induced a higher rate of adult criminality, the exact opposite of its intended purpose. So, clearly, to help us determine if a given treatment causes an observed outcome, we need some sort of comparison.

In research projects on the outcomes of social work, it is usually considered desirable to have some valid measures of client functioning *before* we begin an intervention. When we have these, we can compare them with similar measures made after treatment is completed, which can help us to determine whether change occurred. For example, knowing that at the end of a weight loss program, our clients weigh on average 138 pounds tells us little. But if we also know that before treatment, they weighed on average 155 pounds, we can legitimately claim that members of the group lost an average of 17 pounds. This is change in the desired direction and for most people would be seen as a meaningful weight loss. Similarly, if a group of clients with depression began treatment with a mean score on the Beck Depression Inventory of 52 points and ended treatment three months later with a mean score of 20 (higher scores indicate more severe depression), the loss of 32 points posttreatment would be seen as an improvement. However, knowing that obese clients lost an average of 17 pounds following treatment or that clients with depression showed a 32-point reduction in depression score does not prove that the respective treatment worked. There is a big difference between saying, "*Clients showed improvement following treatment*" and claiming, "*Treatment caused the clients to improve.*"

In a study lacking a comparison group who did not receive treatment, making the second claim is usually not justifiable because of all the other potential influences operative in our clients' lives. The resolution of a contentious presidential election could be one, as could seasonal changes (e.g., emerging from a severe winter into spring), a pandemic, or an economic contraction. A real-life positive example of such a phenomenon has been labeled the Obama Effect, which was observed across the country following President Obama's first election as president (Marx, Ko, and Friedman 2009).

Another important factor in studies evaluating change, as well as those attempting to determine whether changes were caused by the treatment, is the legitimacy of the outcome measures. It should be evident that a self-report measure alone can be problematic. For example, asking clients in treatment for alcoholism if they had had anything to drink during the past week would obviously not be a very credible measure of treatment success, owing to the possibility that they might deny drinking or that alcohol poses a problem for them. Asking pedophiles if they had been thinking of having sex with children would be equally liable to result in strong denials, as would asking the perpetrators of domestic violence if they had struck their partner recently. A blood alcohol test might be a more legitimate outcome measure to evaluate the treatment of people with alcoholism than client self-report. As we shall see, the selection of one or more outcome measures is a prerequisite to undertaking a scientifically legitimate study of social work practice and is also essential in studies attempting to see if a treatment caused any evident improvements.

Social work research covers a wide array of purposes and methodologies, and some research approaches are better for some purposes than others. One can undertake purely descriptive studies, attempting to gain an accurate picture of some client population or of the nature and extent of some psychosocial problem. *Hull-House Maps and Papers* (Hull-House 1895) provides an early example of this type of study undertaken in Chicago. Each home in a Chicago neighborhood was visited, and recordings were made of the number of residents, their race and ethnicity, and the presence or absence of indoor plumbing and utilities such as electricity and gas. This information was displayed on a map, providing concurrent qualitative and quantitative information about the city's residents and living conditions. A Google search will bring up examples of such maps. The U.S. census is another example of descriptive research. The field of descriptive psychopathology examines selected characteristics of people sharing a psychiatric diagnosis. Thyer et al. (1985) retrieved age-of-onset information from several hundred patients diagnosed with DSM-3 anxiety disorders in part to see if this differed among people with different anxiety disorders; for example, those with a simple phobia versus those with agoraphobia. There were no hypotheses to be tested or correlations to be performed. A sizable amount of social work research is purely descriptive. Charles Darwin came up with his revolutionary theory of evolution via natural selection only after spending four years collecting and describing specimens of plants and animals from all over the world. He then examined and ruminated over his descriptive research collections, not conceiving of his theory until some years after he returned home. This process illustrates how descriptive research can help generate other forms of research and theory.

Correlational research is more sophisticated than descriptive research, as it examines associations between two or more variables statistically. For example if an experienced child protective services worker made the clinical observation that many of the abusive mothers she saw spent a great deal of time alone caring for their children with little adult contact throughout the day, she might be motivated to begin a systematic assessment of time spent alone and the intensity of abuse by looking at client records. If, through agency records, she found that abuse intensity was statistically significantly correlated with the length of time mothers were alone during the day, she could publish her findings in a professional journal. Readers might be motivated to replicate her study to see if the same association was found among their agencies' clientele. If it were, and a number of similar findings were obtained at agencies across the country, with different type of clients, then a valid risk factor could emerge that might be of clinical value. A theory might develop postulating that socially insular mothers are at greater risk of abusing their children. Then, someone might conceive of an intervention aimed at reducing this risk by arranging for mothers to spend more time in the company of other adults (e.g., through mothers' clubs or play dates in public parks or libraries) or arranging for them to have more time on their own (e.g., by providing child care services at local churches). Such potential outcomes illustrate the value of correlational research.

If a program intended to reduce the social insularity of abusive mothers were created, social workers could obtain data on episodes of abuse in the months prior to beginning the program and obtain the same data while the program was in place. This would be seen as a simple type of evaluative research: trying to see if clients show improvement following receipt of an intervention. If it was found that indicators of abuse had decreased following the establishment of a program for abusive mothers, it would not be correct to say that the program had "worked" or caused the reduction in risk of abuse, but it would be legitimate to say that following participation in the program, the risk of abuse had been reduced. If, in turn, this positive finding were replicated across other agencies and types of clientele, the stage might be set for conducting a more sophisticated study, perhaps one involving implementing the intervention at one agency but not at another similar one in the same town to see if the risk of abuse declined among clients of the agency implementing the program but *not* among clients of the other agency. If this outcome were found, then replication studies and longer-term follow-ups would be needed, with the goal of eventually being able to conclude that yes, this program *does* reduce the risk of abuse. This scenario illustrates how social work research can be cumulative, with simple early studies justifying more complex investigations later on.

There are many other forms of research methods of course. Surveys remain a popular way to investigate things in social work and are now easier to administer with the rise of online platforms that allow respondents to complete surveys via computer, rather than pencil and paper. The online platform Mechanical Turk greatly facilitates recruiting large numbers of survey respondents for social work researchers (Chan and Holosko 2016). And, as we shall see, surveys are one method of conducting true experiments in the field of social work. Qualitative methods such as in-depth interviews, focus groups and Delphi studies, ethnographic investigations, and historical analyses are all good ways to learn about the inner lives of people, such as social work clients, and how they feel about the services they received, for example. Add to the mix research methods such as needs assessments, cost–benefit analyses, instrument validation studies, theory development, cost-effectiveness studies, oral histories, and policy analysis, and it is easy to see how the general topic of social work research can be perceived as overwhelming or intimidating to many social workers. Some comfort may be gleaned by realizing that most social work researchers tend to focus their careers on particular fields of practice and methodologies. Just as few practitioners proclaim expertise in solving all clinical problems, few social work researchers are masters of all approaches to research methodology. Just as specializing in practice (e.g., trauma-informed care of abused children) enables one to build stronger practice knowledge and skills in a particular area, specializing in certain forms of research inquiry makes the process of being a "social work scientist" more feasible.

Box 1.2 Selected Quotes on the Central Importance of Evaluation Research

"The third type of research, evaluative studies of welfare programs and the activities of practitioners, are the most important of all" (Angell 1954, 169).

"The function of research in a helping profession is to provide a body of verified knowledge directed towards increasing and extending the effectiveness of service to client and community" (SWRG 1955, 33).

"Social work is not a science whose aim is to derive knowledge; it is a technology whose aim is to apply knowledge for the purpose of control. Therefore, on the research continuum social work research falls neared to

(continued on next page)

(*continued from previous page*)

the applied end, because of its purpose of practical knowledge" (Greenwood 1957, 315).

"Evaluation and client feedback are not only necessary for effective service delivery, but are an ethical requirement of the profession. Systematic methods must be developed to assess whether social workers are helping, harming, or doing nothing for the people they serve" (Rosenberg and Brody 1974, 349).

"Social work has no more important use of research methods than the assessment of the consequences of practice and policy choices. . . . Small scale agency-based studies are worthwhile if they succeed in placing interest of effectiveness at the center of agency practice and when they create a critical alliance between practitioners and researchers" (Mullen 1995, 282–83).

"Studies are needed on the effectiveness of psychosocial intervention, including interventions previously tested under ideal controlled conditions, in real-world health care systems" (Ell 1996, 589).

"Research on actual service interventions is the critical element in connecting research to the knowledge base used by professional practitioners. . . . The issue now is one of developing investigations of social work intervention initiatives, studies that go beyond descriptive and explanatory research" (Austin 1998, 17, 43).

"We need to establish a research agenda for social work . . . and intervention studies must be high in priority to such an agenda" (Rosen, Proctor, and Staudt 1999, 9).

Building upon the quotes from Richard Cabot cited earlier in this chapter, I would like to make the case that evaluation studies of the outcomes of social work practice are one of the most valuable forms of research inquiry to be undertaken by social workers. Box 1.2 provides the opinions of various social work authorities pronounced over the decades since Cabot's admonition. Among the points made is that evaluation research, focusing on actual client outcomes, is a very, and perhaps the most, important type of research social workers can undertake. Social work is an applied profession, not an academic science, and we typically pursue knowledge not for knowledge's sake but to move us in the direction of being more effective practitioners for our clients. To be sure, the findings of basic science research sometimes yield practical and useful applications, but the closer we remain tied to applied issues, the more we are adhering to social work's primary mission. Evaluation studies are one form of hypothesis testing, designed to assess whether a clear directional hypothesis can be corroborated. In this case, we wish to test the hypothesis that clients receiving a given treatment improve. Or we may more ambitiously test the hypothesis that clients receiving a new experimental treatment will improve more than clients who receive standard care. The importance of hypothesis testing within social work, more rigorously accomplished by conducting experimental studies, was noted by MacDonald (1957): "Except as hypotheses are systematically tested, the process of research—that is the application of scientific method—is essentially incomplete. Relatively few such studies have been made in social work. Exploratory and descriptive studies are necessary antecedents to hypothesis-testing, but they fail in this purpose unless they are planned with this end in view and with reference to other studies" (491). This is a strong perspective, and one on which many social and behavioral scientists disagree, but this disagreement stems in part from one's disciplinary perspective. Some fields, such as sociology, are largely content with research describing and explaining human phenomena, but more applied fields such as social work, professional psychology, marital and family therapy, and mental health counseling have a much more activist and pragmatic focus: the *improvement* of the human condition. By themselves, descriptive, correlational, and theoretical types of research do not move us much in this direction, unless the findings from such studies lead to methods of intervention. If they do, then these methods need to be evaluated, usually by hypothesis testing; that is, through experimental studies. Social work is not alone among the applied sciences in having something of a divergence of views on research methodology. Kerlinger noted,

> We need to know that two strong tendencies seem to exist among behavioral researchers: one toward experimental research and one toward non-experimental research. We have the individual who says that most behavioral research should be experimental and then the individual who says that experiments are absurd. Perhaps half the research in psychology and education, and most of the research in sociology and anthropology, is non-experimental. Some psychological, sociological and educational researchers even say that the most important and interesting research problems do not lend themselves to an experimental approach. Ideally, we should, whenever possible, approach research problems and test research hypotheses both experimentally and non-experimentally. Whenever an independent variable can be manipulated, an experimental approach can and should be used.
>
> (1973, 346)

It seems obvious that the social work researcher should use whichever methodological approach will provide credible answers to their research question. For example, some approaches (e.g., qualitative methods) are better for obtaining information that *develops* hypotheses. Experimental research is not very good at this. Other approaches are better at *testing* hypotheses, once they have been formulated. Qualitative research is not very good at this (Thyer 2013). Advocates of specific research methods are best served by using their preferred approaches, publishing the results, and letting readers determine the value of their findings. There is no point in experimentalists, for example, criticizing those who use nonexperimental methods, or vice versa. Most investigatory methods have their merits, under certain circumstances, just as hammers and saws have different functions. A saw is pretty useless at driving nails, and hammers are not an efficient tool to cut wood. But when it comes to rigorously testing hypotheses pertaining to the effectiveness of social work practices, experiments have much greater value than most other methods of investigation.

Evaluating our own practice outcomes is baked into the very soul of our field, as exemplified by our code of ethics, which contains hortatory statements such as the following:

5.02 Evaluation and Research

(a) Social workers should monitor and evaluate policies, the implementation of programs, and practice interventions.
(b) Social workers should promote and facilitate evaluation and research to contribute to the development of knowledge.
(NASW 2017)

Note that this passage does not say "social work *researchers*." It says "social workers," which includes those with BSWs, MSWs, and doctorates alike. So not only is doing evaluation research ethical but the code also states that it *should* be done.

One writer cited in box 1.2 promotes the value of small-scale evaluation studies conducted in real-world agencies, and others stress the importance of replicating the results of intervention studies under carefully controlled conditions in the real-world agencies in which they are ultimately intended to be used. When a researcher or research team wishes to evaluate a promising treatment, they take steps to maximize the likelihood that a true effect can be found by controlling for factors that might cloud the issue. For example, study therapists could be well trained in an experimental therapy and perhaps be LCSWs or licensed in some other mental health field. They could be supervised by highly trained clinical experts who would observe their delivery of treatment, either live or via video recording. This supervision would ensure that the therapists were delivering the new treatment effectively and not deviating from their "script." The study could involve the use of a treatment manual or experimental protocol to ensure that the clients are receiving the treatment as it is intended to be given. Efforts could be made to ensure that clients fully engage in treatment, for example by providing reminders to attend sessions (e.g., via automated messaging, emails, or phone calls), as well as bus or taxi fare. If the therapy is intended to treat a given disorder, let's say bipolar disorder, inclusion and exclusion criteria are likely to be used in recruiting participants to obtain as homogeneous a sample as possible of people who meet the DSM-5 criteria for bipolar disorder. The researchers could ensure these criteria were applied appropriate by having expert diagnosticians conduct screening interviews, rather than relying on diagnostic appraisals in clients' records made by previous clinicians of unknown expertise. This selection process would likely mean excluding potential participants with a concurrent diagnosis of another serious mental disorder (e.g., schizophrenia), those judged to be at high risk for suicide, and those with a concurrent substance use disorder. At the extreme, the researchers might choose to test the new therapy only among people of a single gender or race. These steps are all taken to ensure that people who genuinely meet the DSM-5 criteria for bipolar disorder are included and that people with highly complex needs are not. It is easier to initially determine if a proposed treatment for bipolar disorder works if the people it is tested on represent true cases of the disorder without complicating features. Tightly controlled outcome studies of this type have been called *efficacy trials* and are intended to determine whether a new treatment works under ideal conditions. If such trials reflect positive outcomes, then replication studies should occur under conditions increasingly resembling the real world of actual therapy. In the real world, therapists' backgrounds may be more diverse, the clients more heterogeneous, and the supervision less rigorous. And the physical settings where therapy is delivered may vary, for example local community mental health clinics as opposed to a university hospital's outpatient psychiatric treatment facility. These types of studies are called *effectiveness trials*, and any new therapy should be rigorously tested in this way, proving to work under real-world conditions, before widespread adoption is advocated. Social work agencies, and clinics with large numbers of LCSWs are ideal sites to conduct effectiveness trials, since these settings reflect the real-world conditions under which most mental health care is delivered. The term "field experiment" has long been used to describe the conduct of effectiveness trials. For example, the social worker Edwin J. Thomas said, "The field experiment is a research method that retains some of the precision and control of the laboratory experiment without necessitating the removal from their customary social surroundings of the individuals who are studied" (1960, 273). Gerber and Green (2012) are another good source on the design, analysis, and interpretation of such studies.

Evaluation researchers certainly recognize that the results of efficacy studies may not be replicable under real-world conditions, hence the emphasis on retesting promising interventions initially evaluated under ideal conditions via a progressively more complicated series of effectiveness investigations. If positive efficacy findings are replicated in real-world practice, it is at this point that the advocates of a new treatment can legitimately advocate expanding the therapy into everyday settings outside the context of experimental trials. This should be done *after* suitable evidence has been documented, not before, although the latter is the more common practice. Table 1.1 lists some of the distinctions between efficacy and effectiveness studies. Gartlehner et al. (2006) and Singal, Higgins, and Waljee (2014) are additional useful resources in this regard. Behavioral scientists have always recognized that treatments found effective in tightly controlled investigations should be successfully replicated a number of times in the world of real-life service delivery before a new therapy is routinely offered. From the perspective of professional standards, the enthusiasm of a new treatment's advocates is no basis to recommend applying this therapy to clients. Nor are strong claims made by authority figures, nor what theories suggest, nor practices supported only by clinical anecdotes. Nor are a series of posttreatment-only studies, wherein clients who received the new treatment are assessed some time after completing treatment. Nor, as we shall see, are one or more studies conducted on the new treatment, with pretests and posttests completed for the participants, no matter how favorable the results initially appear. The road to determining whether a new treatment has adequate empirical support to recommend its use in everyday social work practice is a steep and thorny one.

Why Do We Need Experimental Designs to Evaluate Practice Outcomes?

It is clear that we have a professional mandate to evaluate the outcomes of what we do. Evaluation can be done prior to widely implementing a given therapy, program, or policy and is the best course of action. Very often social care programs of some sort get adopted because they appear to make sense or have strong advocates behind them. Sadly, sometimes years later, it turns out that they have not worked as planned and service recipients have not been helped. An illustrative case is the premature promotion of intensive family preservation (FP) programs. These were massively funded in the mid-1980s and into the 1990s by the federal government, well before much had been done in the way of evaluation research. Only after a decade or so of program expansion did it emerge that FP services did not work well and were often harmful to children (Gelles 1996). If we knew what we know now back when legislation regarding these programs was being advocated, it never would have passed. A much better approach would have been to thoroughly pilot test FP programs in a couple

TABLE 1.1 Some distinctions between efficacy and effectiveness studies of psychosocial treatments

	Efficacy studies[a]	Effectiveness studies[b]
Question	Does the treatment work under highly controlled and ideal conditions?	Does the treatment work under everyday conditions?
Clients	Strict criteria used to select clients without complicating issues	Real-world clients are selected, often with comorbid problems or difficult life circumstances and from diverse backgrounds
Therapists	Highly trained, often licensed practitioners if a mental health problem is the focus of the study	Real-world practitioners with varying expertise, which may be of unknown quality
Intervention	Provided by practitioners well trained in the intervention; they may follow a treatment manual, protocol, or algorithm; measures of treatment fidelity often used; efforts made to ensure that only the treatment in question is provided, with nothing else added to the mix	Provided by practitioners who may not have formal training in the intervention; no measures of treatment fidelity or adherence to the treatment model are used; practitioners may apply additional interventions as they judge clinically necessary
Assessment	Formal, using DSM criteria or structured evaluation scales; data usually obtained before and after treatment, sometimes at follow-up and sometimes repeatedly during treatment; evaluators may be blind to treatment condition	Less formal; may be based on DSM criteria or an assessment completed by treatment providers; reliable and valid measures of client functioning rarely used before treatment and even more rarely afterward; systematic follow-up assessments rare
Supervision	Regularly scheduled sessions with well-qualified supervisors; observations (live or recorded) often used	Less formal, more like that provided when delivering treatment as usual; meetings may be sporadic, briefer, and less well documented
Resources for clients	Practitioners have access to effective client resources; e.g., parking passes, money to cover public transportation costs, incentives to remain engaged in the study, workbooks as needed, journals or logs; smartphones or laptops for data collection	Not much, usually! Copies of workbooks may be provided to help clients engage in treatment

[a]Well-controlled, research-based treatment.

[b]Everyday agency-based treatment.

of states and follow the results up for a couple years. Then, and only then, if the results had been satisfactory, should the programs have been rolled out across the country. Similar stories can be told about programs such as Scared Straight and military-style boot camps for young people labeled juvenile delinquents. Such boot camps were initially met with great enthusiasm and widely adopted, only to have them yield disappointing results when systematically evaluated after having been in place for some time. One youth, Martin Lee Anderson, was made to exercise vigorously in the hot sun and was beaten by staff for his inability to run shortly after his admission to a Florida boot camp. He died the next day in the hospital. (A documentary of his case is available on Vimeo: https:// vimeo.com/20647722.) Single instances of a particular outcome are not generally considered to be sufficient scientific evidence of a program's effectiveness or harmfulness, but such anecdotes can dramatically illustrate the findings of well-conducted evaluation studies.

One might think that given the emphasis on evaluation research, such studies would be predominant in our field, but this does not appear to be the case. Rosen, Proctor, and Staudt (1999) undertook a review of every article published from 1993 to mid-1997 across thirteen social work journals. They classified each article as to whether it represented empirical research, and for those that did, they noted the focus of the study. They then classified the research studies as reflecting descriptive research, explanatory research (aimed at understanding the causes of problems), or research intended to "control" clients (a poor choice of word; what they meant were evaluation studies aimed at helping clients). They found that of the 1,849 published articles, 53 percent presented no form of research at all! They categorized the remaining 47 percent (863) and found that 36 percent were descriptive studies, 49 percent were explanatory studies, and only 15 percent were evaluation studies. They further categorized the evaluation studies and found that, of these, relatively few had been conducted rigorously. All told, only 3 percent of the 1,849 publications reflected well-designed outcome evaluations. In other words, a social worker reading our professional journals would have to examine one hundred published papers to find three well-conducted outcome studies. This is a shockingly low proportion, considering the oft-expressed view that such research is the most important type of work social work scholars can undertake.

Throughout my professional career I have read that the most rigorous type of research on the outcomes of social work practice, using the designs with the greatest capacity to control for various biases and to arrive at a valid conclusion regarding the true effects of social work, is what is called a randomized experiment. At the same time, I frequently encountered leading authorities in our field who made disparaging remarks in the professional literature about randomized experiments. How they were impractical in agency settings, unethical, too blunt an instrument to assess the subtle but important benefits in clients' lives that were undoubtedly being brought about through social work intervention, too expensive, lacking in generalizability to real-world practice, and so on. A selection of these anti-experimentalist views is presented in box 1.3. I knew that Segal's (1972) and Fischer's (1973, 1976) reviews of the empirical outcomes literature in social work found that fewer than twenty randomized experiments had been published by that point, but paradoxically, from the late 1970s onward I kept coming across articles published by social work authors who used experimental designs. My subjective impression was that there were quite a few scattered about the professional literature of social work and other human and health care professions, an impression at odds with what I had read.

Box 1.3 Examples of Anti-experimentalist Critiques Within Social Work

"In the laboratory experiments of these days where each factor and all the conditions are controlled, it is not such a difficult matter to analyze and evaluate results; but in experiments with human beings where the factors have not yet been clearly differentiated by science and where the conditions are only partially controlled, an analysis of results may be interpreted in a different way by each observer" (Pratt 1921, 90).

"She (Mrs. Sidney Webb) pointed out that science uses three methods of procedure—observation, the analysis of documents, and experiment. . . . In experimentation the individual investigator in social science is seriously limited" (van Kleeck and Taylor 1922, 167).

"The randomization principle cannot be employed in the community situation" (Chapin 1957, 119).

"Many theories, hypotheses, or generalizations that hold under artificially . . . controlled experimental conditions . . . fall apart . . . when applied to confounding situations which social workers encounter in professional practice" (Brennan 1973, 7).

"Proof in the logical positivist tradition is not possible for interpersonal phenomena, given the limitless variety of variables and the rudimentary nature of the research instruments" (Vigilante 1974, 112).

"Past research efforts . . . have vividly exposed the limitations encountered when attempting to utilize experimental designs when evaluating social programs. . . . The experimental and quasi-experimental design models may be premature for many of the issues related to the evaluation of the effectiveness of psychotherapy" (Kolevzon 1977, 211–12).

(continued on next page)

(*continued from previous page*)

"If the group-comparison experimental model has not proved useful, then other research models must be sought. . . . A number of social work writers have been calling for a 'moratorium' on group comparison evaluative research" (Wood 1978, 455).

"The development of an empirical (as opposed to a theoretical, clinical-intuitive) basis for practice using experimentally derived knowledge will produce a new model of practice based upon the same interactional paradigm that governs experimental research. Practice will become frankly manipulative and practitioners will employ all the devices that experimenters now use to assure the internal validity of experiments—deception, control of idiosyncratic behavior, stifling of dialog, and the repression of two-way synergistic learning" (Saleebey 1979, 267).

"The belief that social work models can and should be reduced to simplified, quantified time-limited, experimentally 'testable' models without any loss of valuable information is an example of the logical empiricist belief in reductionism in social work research" (Heineman 1981, 377).

"Despite the fact that social work does not readily lend itself to empirical, scientific, experimental studies, the strong desire to believe that it does has led us to accept any research that purports to be scientific" (Guzzetta 1980, cited in Karger 1983, 201).

"Saleebey argues that when used in social work, the experimental paradigm elicits an operational perspective that is predisposed toward the dispassionate manipulation of people and their situations" (Karger 1983, 201).

"Raynor next attacks experimental methodology, presenting this as a sort of cruel sport engaged in by academics" (Sheldon 1984, 636).

"Research that distorted practice with the introduction of experimental procedures was unlikely to yield information that would be relevant to their practice. . . . Casework practice models were viewed as unscientific unless they were put on the Procrustean bed of experimental design, a procedure that cut or stretched many casework models so that they were no longer recognizable to the practitioners. . . . So casework models derived from experimental research are inherently no better than casework models derived from other methodologies; social workers have no ethical obligation to adopt them. . . . Heuristic researchers recognize that experimental controls simply introduce different biases" (Tyson 1992, 542, 544, 546).

"The reductionist search for truth, through the use of solely experimental designs, tends to look for exclusively 'black and white' outcomes, resulting in denying all possibility of human complexity, contradiction and ambiguity. . . . It is rare that a fully experimental design can be used in social work situations because of moral, methodological or pragmatic considerations. . . . Although randomization is not impossible in social work, nevertheless there can be both ethical and practical objections to it in many instances" (Triseliotis 1998, 89–91).

"Experimentation does not often serve the purposes of social work evaluation. . . . It is often impractical, unethical and operationally difficult to control and administer treatments of variable strength in the context of human services[;] experimental designs alone cannot totally satisfy the social workers' political and administrative purpose of making judicious decisions on resource allocation . . . the experimental paradigm applied to social work evaluation did not and probably will not add much to the theoretical foundation of this profession" (Yin-Bun 1998, 77, 81–82, 84).

"The use of classic randomized control trials . . . poses continued ethical worries with the potential for service users to be randomly allocated to treatment or non-treatment groups. The practicality of conducting pure experiments on human subjects outside of laboratory conditions is also questioned, given the many potential influences on a person's behaviour" (Gibbs 2001, 696).

"Research, specifically experimental research . . . produces at best, partial analysis, reducing complex situations to elemental components" (Witkin 2001, 200).

"Social work has produced few studies that exemplify randomized clinical trials" (Witkin and Harrison 2001, 294).

"Whilst the RCT [randomized controlled trial] standard might be relevant for more scientific professions such as medicine, it is not relevant in social care" (Webb 2002, 49).

"Random assignment of individuals to an experimental or control group may not be feasible or ethical" (Zlotnik and Galambos 2004, 260).

"One of the major concerns about the RCT is that it is unethical to deliver a service on the basis of chance allocation. . . . The measures of outcome employed in psychosocial trials are too unreliable or too simple to capture the subtle changes that are meaningful to practitioners and the recipients of the service" (Rushton and Monck 2009, 21–22).

"The traditional golden standard RCT per se is an obstacle to finding interventions worth considering in the complexity of routine clinical settings. The design itself obstructs the 'healing context' and . . . the potential

(continued on next page)

(continued from previous page)

effect of studies' interventions may thus be underestimated" (Salander 2011, 334).

"RCTs are too controlled and too disconnected from the interactions of participants and environments, due to the positivistic epistemology which underlies them" (Bonell et al. 2012, 2302).

"RCTs are . . . controversial within social work, seen by some as unethical, positivist, uncritically imported from other disciplines, and unable to yield the certainty they promise" (Dixon et al. 2014, 2).

"Social work researchers and evaluators do not conduct RCTs, as it is unethical in our current environments to do so . . . *RCTs are hardly ever used*" (Holosko, Hamby, and Pettus 2013, emphasis in the original).

"RCTs have a specific relevance problem: at the outset, they have high legitimacy, but their narrow focus tends to reduce their practice relevance in dynamic social work contexts" (Petersen and Olsson 2014, 9).

"RCTs are challenging to undertake in 'real-world' situations . . . particularly with complex social interventions. Many social scientists view them with hostility—in part because of the ethics of randomization, as one group is deprived of access to a potentially effective intervention" (Webber 2015, 12).

Source: Thyer 2015, 753–93.

I began collecting paper copies of randomized experiments published by social workers, and over a number of years my collection greatly expanded and soon surpassed my optimistic expectations! Apparently the naysayers regarding the feasibility of experimental outcome research in social work were simply wrong. I prepared an article describing this journey and accompanied it with a bibliography of such studies published between 1949 (the earliest experimental project I found) and 2013 (Thyer 2015). All told I had located more than 740 experimental papers authored or coauthored by social workers over this sixty-four-year period! To my mind, at least, I had provided an irrefutable demonstration that experimental social work research was common, practical, ethical (for decades now, almost all proposals for experimental studies have had to go through federally monitored institutional review board approval), and contributing greatly to knowledge development in our field. Many studies seemed to show that certain interventions worked pretty well, and others demonstrated that some did not work so well. Moreover, I learned that some programs, policies, and practices were iatrogenic; that is, they harmed clients.

I likened my paper to the use of the philosophical technique called *solvitur ambulando*, meaning "it is solved by walking away." The Greek philosopher Diogenes was said to have responded to a loquacious peer who was arguing that motion was impossible simply by standing up and walking away from the discussion—a very effective demonstration indeed! More broadly, this phrase means that a question is solved by a practical demonstration. In Ayn Rand's novel *Atlas Shrugged*, the industrialist Hank Reardon silenced critics of his innovative new metal (which threatened vested interests) by driving a heavily laden train across a bridge made of his alloy. In real life, Andrew Carnegie led a parade headed by an elephant across the first steel bridge built across the Mississippi River to refute those who said the bridge would collapse. By showing that a large number of social work experiments had been completed and published, my paper effectively silenced those who said that such designs were impractical.

In 2012, I wrote a book titled *Quasi-experimental Research Designs* (Thyer 2012) as a part of a series of books on social work research. In it I described the need for and usefulness of such research methods for evaluating social work practice. I described each design conceptually in its own chapter and illustrated how each had been used in social worker–authored publications to try to answer questions about the effectiveness of social work practices, ranging from individual psychotherapies to group work, educational practices, and welfare policies. It was an enjoyable book to write, and shortly after I published my bibliography on true experiments in 2015 it occurred to me that a similarly structured book about how randomized experiments are designed and have been used across many areas of social work for more than seventy years needed to be written. You are reading the result. The next chapter will describe what an experiment is and what it is not, and this will be followed by descriptions of the various types of experimental research designs. Later in the book these will be illustrated by published examples of research authored by one or more social workers who used these designs.

Summary

In many ways the profession of social work is thriving. At the federal and state levels, ever greater expenditures are provided for social welfare programs, and social workers are now the largest provider of psychotherapy services in the United States. Licensed social workers are entitled to third-party payments from insurance providers, can diagnose people with mental disorders, and in cases of crisis admit people for psychiatric hospitalization. However, as Uncle Ben said to the young Peter Parker (a.k.a. Spider-Man), "With great power comes great responsibility." Among the responsibilities that we are not fulfilling very well is the empirical demonstration that the widespread social work services the public is paying for produce true benefits for our clients and that the welfare policies we advocate are effective. Despite our decades-long endorsement of the need for quality evaluations of social care, such studies remain relatively few in number compared to the efforts expended in services. Experimental studies are among the most powerful research tools we have to see if interventions are effective, yet they remain underused. In part this is because of a long and misguided anti-experimentalist sentiment within our field. The balance of this book will demonstrate the need for and value of experimental research in social work, the philosophy of science underlying experimental analysis, the types of questions experiments can answer, and the varieties of designs that can be used. I will provide examples of published experiments conducted by social workers across the spectrum of practice and describe newer developments to enhance the quality of such studies. In chapter 10, I will discuss some of the unique ethical considerations that need to be taken into account when designing and conducting experiments. The appendix lists more than one thousand published experiments authored by social workers over an eighty-year time span, demonstrating the practical value of such studies to the discipline.

CHAPTER 2

WHAT ARE EXPERIMENTS?

Let us make an experiment.

—William Shakespeare, *All's Well That Ends Well*

There are many uses of the word "experiment" as a noun and of "experimental" as an adjective. The definitions of these terms used in this book reflect the commonly accepted views of mainstream behavioral and social science. Box 2.1 presents selected definitions from the field of experimental design. Not all are perfect, and some include inaccuracies (e.g., Barker's contention that in experimental studies, subjects must be randomly selected). More on this later.

Some features that exemplify a high-quality experimental study include the following:

- You begin with a clear research question, from which are derived one or more specific and directional hypotheses. A hypothesis is a prediction, such as "treated clients will improve statistically significantly more than untreated clients."
- You have a sufficient number of participants per group.
- It is possible to randomly assign participants to the various arms or conditions of the study; for example, real treatment versus no treatment, treatment

as usual (TAU), or a placebo treatment or immediate treatment versus delayed treatment.

- The results within and across groups are statistically analyzed appropriately.
- You use one or more reliable and valid outcome measures.
- Your treatment (the independent variable) is replicable, meaning that the salient features of it can be reliably reproduced by other qualified people.
- The experimental treatment has a plausible theoretical basis. Any theory the intervention invokes should not be based on supernatural or metaphysical explanations. If a treatment were said to readjust invisible energy patterns surrounding clients, there should be compelling evidence for the existence of this energy force prior to investigating any treatments supposedly derived from it. It is possible to test supernatural treatments and their effectiveness, of course. A large amount of literature on the usefulness of intercessory prayer in healing people exists, for example. But there is no well-supported mechanism of action for treatments such as prayer, thought field therapy, Reiki, or acupuncture, which renders their scientific investigation particularly complex.

These features can be seen as ideals to strive for, and sufficient compromise to any one of them can render an experimental study invalid.

Box 2.1 Selected Definitions

Experiment: "A research study in which one or more independent variables is systematically varied by the researcher to determine its effects of dependent variables" (Holosko and Thyer 2011, 39).

Experiment: "The deliberate manipulation of one or more independent variables (treatments) conducted under controlled conditions to test hypotheses, especially for making inferences of a cause and effect nature" (Corcoran and Roberts 2015, 1278).

Experiment: "Controlled arrangement and manipulation of conditions in order to systematically observe particular phenomena with the intention of defining the influences and relationships which affect these phenomena. The variables and conditions of an experiment are the experimental variable which is systematically varied or manipulated by the experimenter; the dependent variable which is the phenomenon to be observed and is assumed to be affected by the manipulation of the experimental variable; all extraneous conditions are held constant as far as possible in that they do not confound results" (Wolman 1973, 132).

Experiment: "The manipulation of one or more independent variables conducted under controlled conditions to test one or more hypotheses, especially for making inferences of a cause-and-effect nature. Involves the measurement of one or more dependent variables" (Corsini 2002, 351).

Experimental design: "A type of research design that uses random assignment of study participants to different treatment groups. Randomization provides some level of assurance that the groups are comparable in every way except for the treatment received. In general, a randomized experiment is regarded as the most rigorous and strongest design to establish a cause-effect (treatment outcomes) relationship. These designs usually collect data before and after the program to assess the net effects of the program" (Roberts and Yeager 2004, 984).

Experimental design: "A research method that tests the relationship between independent (treatment) and dependent (outcome) variables. In nomothetic research, a true experimental study must meet all of the following criteria: (1) randomization, (2) a manipulated treatment condition (X), (3) a comparison or control group that does not receive any treatment condition, and (4) a specification of hypotheses" (Holosko and Thyer 2011, 39).

Experimental study: "Research conducted under carefully controlled conditions, in which the subjects being investigated are randomly selected and systematically compared to control groups; treatment variables are then introduced to the experimental group but not the control group. Statistical analysis is then used to determine if significant differences occur between the groups observed" (Barker 2014, 149).

Experimental study: "One in which the independent variable is manipulated by the researcher in order to see its effect on the dependent variable(s). It is defined as a research study in which people are randomly assigned to different forms of the program or alternative treatments, including a control group and/or a placebo group" (Roberts and Yeager 2004, 984).

How Many Participants Are Enough?

If you do not have enough participants, your study will be underpowered, meaning that it will be statistically incapable of detecting significant changes. Take a simple two-arm randomized trial. If you have ten participants, you can randomly assign them via coin toss to either condition, and you may get two groups of five or possibly groups of four and six or three and seven, for example. The number of participants is closely related to what inferential statistics (used in tests aimed at assessing changes or differences) calls degrees of freedom. In the study of an experimental treatment that produces large effects, you can get by with studying a smaller number of people than when studying an intervention that produces only modest effects. Most social work treatments fall into the latter type. If you used a coin toss to randomly assign one hundred people to a two-arm study, you'd likely end up very close to two groups of fifty, and the resulting degrees of freedom would make it possible to detect smaller changes or differences than a study with only five participants per group. But one must be concerned with economics. If you would be able to detect effects with fifty per group (this number being referred to as N), recruiting four hundred participants would be an unnecessary expenditure of resources.

If you have some idea of the anticipated effects of your treatment (from prior research, for example), you can use any number of online power calculators to get an estimate of the number of participants your study will require. If you anticipate a small effect, the sample size calculator will say that you will need a lot of people to detect an effect. Conversely, if you predict a large effect, it will provide a smaller number. Using the ClinCalc.com sample size calculator (https://clincalc.com/stats/samplesize.aspx), if I propose a two-arm study with a dichotomous outcome measure (yes or no) and expect 50 percent of participants to be cured (yes, cured) in the treatment group and 20 percent to be cured in the no-treatment (or placebo or TAU) group, the calculator tells me I need a sample size of about nineteen per group (N totaling 38). While it would be foolish to greatly exceed recruiting about forty people, having fewer would mean that my statistics are unlikely to find anything. If prior research leads me to believe that only 30 percent of treatment subjects and 10 percent of control subjects are likely to be cured, the sample size calculation increases to a required minimum N of 124 participants, sixty-two per group, a considerably larger recruitment effort. If I predict that 80 percent of treatment subjects and only 10 percent of control subjects will be cured, the sample size calculator estimates that I will need only fourteen people, or seven per group. So you can see how a randomized controlled trial could be credibly undertaken with a small-scale study (e.g., N = 14), *but* very few social work interventions are capable of producing such powerful effects.

The example in the previous paragraph reflects the use of a dichotomous outcome measure (e.g., yes, no; cured, not cured; employed, unemployed; voted, did not vote; pregnant, not pregnant). Similar online power calculators can also be used to estimate the sample size needed for data using an interval or ratio level of measurement, perhaps through the use of mean scores pre- and posttreatment or between two groups. You can enter your anticipated mean values posttreatment for both groups, along with the anticipated standard deviations for each mean, and the calculator will tell you how many participants you will need in each arm of the study at the pretreatment assessment. Some calculators also allow you to factor in estimated attrition (e.g., if you expect 10 or 20 percent of participants to drop out) by increasing the sample size needed at the beginning.

Social workers can use information about sample size calculations in two ways: as a consumer (a reader) of experimental research or as an experimental researcher themselves. In the first role, you can review an experimental paper to see if the authors report having completed an a priori ("before the fact") sample size calculation before beginning their study. If they did, and they recruited the needed number of participants, you can be somewhat assured that this study did indeed have enough subjects to provide a statistically legitimate test of the hypothesis in question. In the second role, as a researcher, you need to do the calculation before beginning your study so that you will have an idea of how many people you need to recruit. If this number is unrealistically high, it might be wise to abandon your project before wasting further time on it. Or you may wish to scale it back, say by changing your plan from a three-arm study comparing active treatment with TAU and no treatment to one comparing active treatment with TAU only (potentially reducing your need for subjects by one-third). As a practical matter, many experimental researchers in social work avail themselves of the services of a skilled statistician, for not only initial sample size calculations but also the subsequent analysis and interpretation of results. This is a common practice in the world of randomized controlled trials, since statisticians are typically much better at this element of experimental design than most social work researchers (and most physicians, psychologists, and other researchers who have not specialized in statistics, for that matter).

You might ask, Why go to the bother of all these contrivances to evaluate the outcomes of social work? Isn't it enough to treat people and see how they do? The short answer is no. It is not enough. Human beings, even highly skilled social workers, are not perfect judges of client improvement. For example, here is a quote from a psychiatrist regarding the effectiveness of a treatment developed to help people with chronic mental illness: "I am a sensitive observer and my conclusion is that a vast majority of my patients get better as opposed to getting worse after my treatment" (cited in Dawes 1994, 48). What treatment was he referring to? Lobotomy: the severing of nerve fibers in the brain. The psychiatrist Walter Freeman, a tireless promoter of lobotomies in the United States, claimed, "The operation brings peace of mind and added zest for life, a good prelude to comfortable old age, with little danger of personality damage" (1962, 15). Over the years, Freeman published many articles in professional journals describing how lobotomies could be performed and the supposedly positive clinical results obtained in hundreds of patients. Lobotomy has since been thoroughly discredited as an ineffective treatment, illustrating that Freeman's "expert clinical observations" had little credibility. His belief was not an anomaly among mental health practitioners. According to Garb and Boyle, "Despite common lore, a large body of research evidence contradicts the popular belief that experience and clinical competence are positively related. In fact, research suggests that it is very difficult for mental health workers to learn from experience. Numerous studies investigating clinical judgement have demonstrated that when clinicians are given identical sets of information, experienced clinicians are no more accurate than less experienced clinicians" (2003, 17).

In earlier years of social work, efforts were made to develop reliable ways to judge client improvement (e.g., Hunt, Blenkner, and Kogan 1950), but even when the measure was simple (e.g., much improved, improved, no change, or worse), it proved impossible to come up with a measure of improvement that had useful clinical applications. Other early efforts were made to develop assessment methods for more subtle phenomena, such as clients' insights (Chapin 1942). More recently, the National Association of Social Workers (NASW) sponsored the development of the person-in-environment assessment system, an effort to code clients' psychosocial problems. A couple descriptive articles on this system were published and a book written, one that continues to be marketed and sold by the NASW Press (Karls and Wandrei 1994), and the system continues to be used in clinical social work. Unfortunately, nothing has been published about the reliability or validity of the person-in-environment coding scheme, so we have no way of knowing whether it is of any value. Fortunately, there *are* ways to assess client function reliably and validly, both in clinical situations and in the context of experimental investigations (Fischer, Corcoran, and Springer 2020; Franklin and Jordan 2021). These will be reviewed later in this book.

Accurate methods to ascertain clients' improvement, and to measure their psychosocial problems and strengths, are crucial to conducting legitimate evaluations of practice outcomes. Mary MacDonald said it well:

> The first essential, then, for evaluative research on practice is to make explicitly, specific, and concrete the objectives towards which practice is directed. . . . The essence of research is that the findings relate to *that which is observed and not to the individual observer*. This is the criterion of objectivity, or liability, and it is one to which until recently such evaluative research as we had in social casework had given little or no attention. In research, the burden of proof is on the investigator, and he is expected to show that his results are not a matter of personal whim. One step in this direction has been taken when success is defined in specific and concrete terms.
>
> (1957, 136, my emphasis)

It is obvious that we must do more than rely on the subjective judgments of clinicians who delivered a social work intervention to validly assess client functioning and changes following treatment. Clinicians have a vested professional interest and personal investment in seeing that their clients improve following their services, hence the temptation to be positively biased is huge when asked to make such judgments. Almost all forms of evaluative research require using more objective measures of potential improvement. This includes using pre-experimental research designs involving one group of clients only; quasi-experimental evaluation research designs involving two or more groups of clients who are treated differently; and true experimental designs wherein there are two or more groups of clients and the composition of each group is determined based on random assignment.

Threats to Internal Validity

Obtaining reliable and valid measures of client functioning is one method of attempting to reduce bias and other confounding factors that may preclude reaching a true conclusion regarding the effects of a treatment. Many potentially biasing and confounding factors can get in the way of accurate evaluation, but efforts can be undertaken to prevent or control them. Collectively, these potential confounds are known as *threats to internal validity*, with "internal validity" meaning the confidence we can have that we have discovered a true causal relationship between treatment and outcome. In an internally valid study, we hope to be able to say something like, "Participants improved, and we are reasonably confident that they got better because of our treatment, not because of other reasons."

In the next section, I list some of the more common threats to internal validity and some ways experimental researchers try to control for them. By doing so, we are able to make more legitimate conclusions about the effects of a given treatment by ruling out alternative explanations.

Selected Threats to Internal Validity

Passage of Time

When people begin participating in an experiment, outside events may transpire that can affect their mood for good or ill; for example, the election of a president; a tumultuous presidential transition; a natural disaster such as a hurricane, flood, tornado, or earthquake; a human-caused disaster such as a terrorist attack; a sudden economic downturn, as when a local factory closes or the country slips into recession; an economic boom; seasonal changes (e.g., people may be gloomier in the winter); and variations in the academic year (final exam weeks may be stressful). Social work researchers can try to control for such influences by assigning not just a single group of clients to active experimental treatment but also another group who will receive no treatment. If both groups are assessed at roughly the same time, extra-therapeutic events will impact both groups equivalently; hence, their impact will have been controlled for. Say, for example, you wish to test a six-week-long job-finding program for unemployed people. Knowing that some people in the no-treatment group may find jobs on their own, you realize that you need to account for this by subtracting those jobs from those found by participants in the treatment group. If you randomly assign your unemployed clients to the job-finding program or to no treatment, you can assess their employment rates after a given time period, say six weeks. If 80 percent of the experimental participants found work through the program and 20 percent of the no-treatment group found work on their own, the real impact of the program is that it helped about 60 percent of participants to find work (80 percent – 20 percent = 60 percent). This is still a good result, but it is more modest (and more accurate) than claiming an 80 percent success rate. Similarly, if at the end of a treatment program for clients with post-traumatic stress disorder (PTSD), 60 percent of treated clients no longer meet the DSM-5 criteria for PTSD whereas only 10 percent of untreated clients no longer meet the criteria, then the benefit of treatment is a 50 percent "cure" rate (60 percent – 10 percent). By making this calculation, we take into account the natural cure rate or remission. Thus, a no-treatment control group helps us come closer to the truth about the effects of our services. By controlling for the *passage of time*, our studies have stronger internal validity. Since we often do not know in advance that a new treatment will be helpful, it is not usually seen as an ethical problem to have a no-treatment control group if the condition being treated is not serious. However, it is good practice to offer the untreated participants the treatment the experimental group received when the formal evaluation is over if it has been found to be helpful.

Maturation

Maturation refers to normal developmental changes that occur over a person's lifetime. These changes tend to occur more conspicuously among the young and the old and usually take time. Still, lengthy studies may reflect changes related to maturation rather than the effects of treatment. For example, if a social worker undertook to treat children with primary nighttime enuresis (bedwetting without having attained continence previously) and offered a program of, say, five months of group therapy, it would not be surprising to find that a number of children improved irrespective of the treatment. To ascertain the true effect of treatment, the children would need to be randomly assigned to receive treatment or no treatment and be assessed pre- and posttreatment. To arrive at the true estimate of treatment effect, the proportion of untreated children who had achieved continence would need to be subtracted from those in the treatment group who had achieved continence.

The problem of wandering sometimes occurs among older people with dementia. A program could be designed to reduce the frequency of wandering among a sample of older people with dementia, with pre- and posttest measures of wandering taken, say, after a six-month program of care. In the context of an experiment, a large group of wandering older people, with appropriate consent provided by caregivers, could be assigned to the wandering-reduction program or to TAU. Wandering could be validly assessed before and after the six-month intervention for both groups. Wandering decreasing in the treatment group and increasing in the TAU group (e.g., owing to maturational changes such as an increase in dementia severity) could be seen as evidence that the treatment had been helpful. Or, if wandering increased in both groups but much more in the TAU group, the intervention could be seen as having some preventive effects, reducing the increase in dangerous wandering that might otherwise be expected.

Although maturation is primarily a confound in studies involving the young or the old, it can occur when dramatic shifts occur at particular ages. For example, in a study involving youth turning twenty-one years old and now able to legally buy alcohol, episodes of drunkenness or receiving citations for driving while being impaired by alcohol might be expected to increase. And when people retire, they experience significant changes in areas such as lifestyle, exercise, socializing, travel, and finances. A lengthy treatment study the duration of which embraces retirement age may show large changes in participant functioning, well-being, life satisfaction, and quality of life, but these may be an effect of retirement, not of the intervention. Again, a control is needed to take this confound into account when attempting to interpret the legitimate effects of treatment.

Regression to the Mean

Many psychosocial problems wax and wane in severity, sometimes in response to endogenous factors (e.g., menstrual cycles, pregnancy, medications, or a diagnosis of bipolar I or II disorder or cyclothymic disorder) and sometimes in response to external variables (e.g., changes in loving relationships, employment, the economy, births, or deaths). These variations in behavior, affect, and cognition may occur rapidly or over longer periods. Many experimental social work studies involve testing therapies for people and rely on people seeking treatment volunteering to participate in a controlled clinical trial. People tend to seek treatment when their problems are at their worst, and if after undergoing assessment and beginning treatment, clients are observed to improve, in the absence of a suitable control group, the social work researcher cannot tell if these improvements are the result of therapy or a reflection of the natural ebb and flow of the clients' disorder or of the severity of their psychosocial problems. An appropriate control group can weed out this *regression-to-the-mean phenomenon*: the tendency of problems to become less severe than observed when the clients were motivated to seek treatment and enroll in a study.

Regression to the mean is a possible confound when recruiting or selecting study participants based on the seriousness of a particular problem. For example, a school social worker might be concerned with excessive absenteeism among students. If she selected those students most absent during the tenth grade and enrolled them in a truancy reduction program during the eleventh grade, she might find that at the end of the year this group had a much lower rate of absenteeism than during the previous year. While it would be tempting to claim credit for successfully reducing truancy, the well-trained, research-informed social worker would be aware of the possibility that what was observed was at least partially due to regression effects. In the tenth grade, absences will have been distributed across all students, with some having a low number of absences and some a high number. In the tenth grade, the students with many absences are likely to have many reasons for being absent, besides just being incorrigibly truant. One could have become seriously ill; another could have had a car accident that required hospitalization; and another might have needed to stay home to care for an ailing parent. These causes of high absenteeism can largely be seen as chance events unlikely to recur among the *same* students. So, in the eleventh grade, their absenteeism is likely to return to more normative levels. If this outcome were to occur, it could appear that the truancy reduction program had "worked," whereas in reality, we are simply seeing the regression-to-the-mean phenomenon in action. To control for this, what would we need? Yes, a control group. We would need to design a study in which the highly truant tenth-grade kids were randomly assigned in the eleventh grade to a truancy reduction program or to no treatment (i.e., just leave them alone). At the end of the eleventh grade, we would assess whether the students in the truancy reduction program had had fewer absences compared with those in the no-treatment group. Only if absences among the treated youth were appreciably lower than those among the untreated youth could we possibly claim that the program had been a success.

Attrition or Mortality

In evaluation research, some participants will drop out during the course of the project, a process known as *attrition*. This is also sometimes referred to as *mortality*, but this is not usually meant in the sense of people dying. Occasionally people do die during the course of an experiment, which can (we hope) be due to natural events unrelated to social work services, but sometimes their deaths can be legitimately attributed to the experimental treatment or even standard care, as we saw in the study by Blenkner, Bloom, and Nielsen (1971). Regardless of the cause, client attrition can pose problems in making causal inferences (did treatment cause improvements?), because the number of participants assessed at the end of the study is not the same number as at the beginning. Why is this a problem? Here are some examples.

You wish to test a psychosocial weight loss program for morbidly obese people. You weigh all participants at the beginning of the study and again at the end and find an average weight loss of fifty pounds per person. This seems like a substantial weight reduction and clinically as well as statistically significant. If one hundred people begin the study, but twenty drop out over the six-month study period, the pretreatment average weight is based on one hundred participants, whereas the posttreatment average weight is based on only eighty of the original subjects. But still, you are looking at average weight per person, so that should be okay, right? Not really. Who would you think would be most likely to drop out of a weight reduction program: those *most* obese and unfit, or those *less* obese? If it turns out that the most overweight folks dropped out (which is likely to be the case), then your final sample of eighty participants will exclude the twenty heaviest people in the original group. This will dramatically skew your average weight posttreatment in the lower direction, not because of genuine weight loss in the remaining participants but because the most obese and unfit people dropped out. One way to partially control for this problem is to undertake what is called an *intent-to-treat analysis*, which in this case would involve contacting the twenty people who dropped out to obtain their weights at the time treatment concluded. Thus, you can compare the initial and final weights of all original one hundred participants, including those who completed the program *and* those who dropped out. Making this effort provides a more realistic, albeit conservative, estimate of the actual effectiveness of the weight loss program for everyone who began it, not just those who completed it. The intent-to-treat analysis approach will be discussed more fully later on in this book.

Another example involves people seeking treatment for depression. Again, let's say we begin with one hundred participants, each diagnosed with clinical depression and assessed pretreatment with the Beck Depression Inventory (BDI). Then treatment begins, say, some sort of cognitive therapy, and continues as per protocol, for three months, and then all participants complete the BDI again.

The analysis of the effectiveness of the program involves a comparison of the participants' pretreatment and posttreatment mean (a.k.a. average) BDI scores. If the mean score were dramatically lower posttreatment as revealed by statistical tests, one would be tempted to conclude that the participants had experienced a reduction in their depression. But wait! You'd need to ask the legitimately critical question, How many of the one hundred original participants dropped out? If, say, twenty had stopped attending therapy and were initially lost to follow-up at the conclusion of treatment, an unsophisticated evaluator might compare the average BDI scores of the original one hundred participants with the average scores of the eighty folks who completed treatment. This could be problematic. Why? Among people with clinical depression, who would be more likely to drop out of treatment, in the context of an evaluation study? Those who were initially *more* depressed or those who were initially *less* depressed? It is plausible to expect that the answer would be the more depressed participants, given the debilitating nature of clinical depression. So, if those with higher BDI scores removed themselves from the study, the average posttreatment score could drop appreciably, irrespective of the effects of treatment (if any), making it appear that the average level of depression for everyone improved. However, the reality would be that subject attrition was responsible for this apparent improvement. How can this be partially controlled for? The intent-to-treat analysis principle is one approach. In this case, that would mean tracking down the twenty participants who had dropped out and persuading them to complete the BDI again, so that you can obtain posttreatment measures for all original participants.

Differential Attrition

In evaluation research, attrition can be expected. When it occurs evenly across groups, for example in both the experimental treatment and no-treatment groups, it is a bit less of a problem than when it occurs more in one group than the other, which is referred to as *differential attrition*. Take, for example, a study in which you start with one hundred participants in the experimental group and one hundred in the TAU group. At the conclusion of the study, say at follow-up, you find that seventy people remained engaged in treatment among the experimental participants and that ninety remained engaged in the TAU condition. Twenty more participants dropped out from the experimental group compared with those getting standard care. So you have the problem of attrition, but because participants dropped out at uneven rates between groups, it is a greater problem in terms of making a causal inference as to whether the experimental treatment was more effective than standard care. Again, the intent-to-treat analysis can come to the rescue, and the more follow-up information you can obtain from participants who dropped out, the better.

Pretest Sensitization

Evaluation studies make use of various outcome measures, often on more than one occasion, such as before and after treatment, and perhaps some time later during a follow-up period. Sometimes the experience of taking a test once impacts one's performance on the test the second time, absent any influence of treatment. This is known as *pretest sensitization* or the *testing effect*. Say a study was conducted to evaluate a social skills training group, and one outcome measure was a standardized role-playing test. Participants know they are going to be asked to undergo a role-playing exam of some sort at the beginning of their treatment and at the end, and they may have some anxiety over doing this. However, by having done the exam once and now knowing what to expect, they may be less nervous and have an idea of how to improve their initial score for the posttreatment exam. Thus, the evaluators might pop the champagne corks to celebrate the apparent effectiveness of their social skills treatment program. "Not so fast," says the skeptical critic. "Maybe the apparent improvements are simply the result of taking the test twice."

Skilled program evaluators can forestall such criticism with a few methods. One is to have a no-treatment comparison group who take the same role-playing test at the same times as the experimental treatment participants. Then, one could subtract improvements on the outcome measure obtained by the no-treatment group from those observed among the treated participants to figure out the real effect of treatment. Another way to control for pretest sensitization is to have two or more equivalent versions of the outcome measure. At pretest, half the participants in the treatment group are randomly assigned to receive version A of the measure, while the other half are randomly assigned to be assessed using version B. Then, at posttreatment, each group is tested with the other version. Another method is to use a type of randomized experiment called the Solomon four-group design (Solomon 1949), which assesses some participants pre- and posttest and others posttest only. This design will be discussed in greater depth later on in this book.

Another testing confound is the use of a commonly encountered assessment tool that participants are likely to have had some experience with already. So, what is said to be the first administration of the outcome measure (as per the study protocol) may actually be the second or third time the participant has completed it. Examples of such assessments include the Myers-Briggs Personality Type Inventory and the Implicit Bias Test, popular scales that most social work students complete at least once across their various classes. And the questions in a mental status exam (e.g., What year is it? Do you know where you are? Count backward from one hundred by seven) will no doubt be familiar to people with chronic mental illness and a history of repeated hospitalizations. Where the possibility is strong that a common measure will have been used on potential participants in the past, you may wish to choose a less common tool.

For example, the BDI is a widely used self-report scale to assess the severity of depression. If you are doing a study of depression treatment and your potential participants are likely to have completed the BDI as a part of their clinical care, you could choose from among a wide variety of equally reliable and valid depression measures in lieu of the BDI.

Instrumentation

In its crudest sense, the threat to internal validity called *instrumentation* refers to malfunctioning instruments of some sort, perhaps an error in analyzing biological samples (e.g., a urine screen during a drug treatment study) or an inaccurate device (e.g., a biofeedback machine). If your assessment methods are not accurate all the time, the validity of your conclusions regarding the effects of treatment will be compromised. Another form of instrumentation error occurs when human beings are used to assess research participants and the fidelity with which they undertake their tasks varies over time or across groups. In an evaluation study, let's say a human observer was asked to keep track of hyperactive behaviors occurring among young students in a classroom throughout the day. A coding scheme is used that has been demonstrated to be reliable and valid. However, the study makes use of just a few observers who are kept busy all day, watching for instances of hyperactive behavior. It can readily be seen that the diligence of the observers may tend to fade as the day passes owing to fatigue, boredom, or distraction. Thus, the data collected at the end of the day may be less reliable and valid than the data gathered earlier. Over a greater period of time, say in the context of a pretest–posttest study, near the end of the project observers may just become bored with the whole thing and their observations distorted owing to fatigue.

Various methods can be employed to help control for this confound. Extensive training in the observational protocol is useful, and periodic fidelity checks by the experimenters can be made during the course of the study to help ensure accuracy. Or, in the example of observing children's behavior, instead of asking observers to spend long periods of time observing behavior, the classroom could be videotaped and the videos reviewed in smaller blocks of time (e.g., thirty minutes) to avoid observer fatigue. If the observational rating task is more onerous when observing one group of participants versus another (e.g., rating noncompliant behavior in a classroom with many hyperactive kids versus another classroom without hyperactive kids), the observers could be rotated between classrooms so that the workload is more evenly distributed among them, helping to control for the effects of fatigue and tedium. Another method is the use of two or more observers (though two is the most common) to rate participants at the same time using a structured observational protocol. At the conclusion of an observation session, the experimenters can compare the two sets of ratings to calculate what is referred to as interrater reliability. The design methodology for conducting structured observations is well established, as are various methods of calculating interrater agreement (see, for example, Bloom, Fischer, and Orme 2006; Grinnell and Unrau 2008; Rosen and Polansky 1975).

If the raters are aware of the experimental condition to which study participants have been assigned, say an experimental treatment versus TAU, bias may come into play. If the raters are favorably disposed to the new therapy, they might, perhaps unconsciously, provide more favorable ratings of participant functioning to those they know have received the experimental therapy as opposed to standard care. This bias could even extend to posttreatment assessments using a diagnostic system such as the DSM-5, in that less (or more) severe diagnoses could be given to one group or the other. One way this can be partially controlled for is obvious, is it not? Keep the observers unaware of the condition (e.g., experimental treatment versus no-treatment) to which participants have been or will be assigned. Doing so will mitigate the effect of any biases the raters have as they conduct their assessments. This is called *blinding* and is characteristic of well-designed evaluation studies using human raters of behavior. Blinding is also used by mental health diagnosticians. Highly sophisticated studies ask each rater, when completing their evaluations of individual participants posttreatment, to guess which treatment condition each had been assigned to. Blinding is considered successful when the accuracy of their guesses for all participants is no better than chance. However, if their guesses are fairly accurate, it is clear that the blinding has not been successful and that rater bias has not been controlled for.

Desire to Please the Therapist

In social work treatment outcome studies in which services are delivered face to face by a human social worker, the relationship variables embedded in all live therapies come into play. Sometimes clients, whether receiving an experimental therapy or TAU, may come to like their therapist, appreciating their efforts to help them, as well as the care and compassion they express. The *desire to please the therapist* is normal and to be expected. What is also to be expected is that clients may rate the effectiveness of therapy more highly than was actually the case and complete standardized measures of their functioning more favorably. They may exaggerate the benefits they received and complete their outcome measures to reflect fewer problems, less distress, and greatly reduced psychopathology. In posttreatment interviews, they may similarly exaggerate the benefits they received, minimize the problems they continue to have, or report fewer difficulties during the course of treatment than really transpired. Evaluation study participants know that at some point, their therapists will learn of the results they reported and, in order not to disappoint their therapists, may rate their outcomes more positively. Given that these tendencies are baked in to most treatment models and practices, how can this confound be controlled for? One approach is to compare the results of the experimental treatment with those of an equivalent (at pretest) group of clients who received TAU; in doing so, similar client–therapist relationship phenomena are likely to be present in both groups. But for this approach to sufficiently control for such influences, the comparison condition should involve roughly equivalent therapist contact and demands upon the client. Comparing highly structured cognitive therapy involving weekly two-hour sessions and extensive homework assignments against a comparison treatment of weekly one-hour supportive psychotherapy sessions with no homework assignments is not a fair comparison, since the comparison condition is unlikely to give rise to the same degree of desire to please the therapist as is the treatment condition. So, for this factor to be controlled for, comparison treatments should involve similar relationship variables, time commitments, and extra-therapeutic workload (if any).

The Placebo Effect

For people in psychosocial distress and those with a mental disorder, a significant relationship struggle, or problems in everyday living, experiencing such conditions can be socially isolating. It is not uncommon for a client to experience a great sense of relief after the first few sessions of treatment to learn that they are not alone with their particular problem. Many therapies include psychoeducation: teaching people about their difficulty, including what is known about its etiology, prevalence, and prognosis. Some problems that can be very socially isolating and disabling are actually rather common, such as obsessive-compulsive disorder, social phobia, and panic disorder. To learn that many others have similar difficulties, that their problem behaviors are not precursors to "going crazy," and that effective psychosocial treatments are available can be of tremendous psychological benefit (e.g., symptoms of anxiety and depression may be reduced), in the absence of any treatment effect. And treatment involving group therapy wherein clients meet with "normal-looking" people experiencing the same difficulty can also be helpful in itself. Such experiences, common in many forms of therapy, can give rise to what is called the *placebo effect*, "placebo" being the Latin for "I shall please." The placebo effect has been known to occur in clinical medical practice for many years, with physicians giving some nostrum (e.g., a fake pill, salve, or other ineffective treatment) to people with nonserious conditions as a means of placating them or to genuinely ill people when there was little in the way of effective therapies to provide. Similarly, a parent's kiss can appear to relieve the pain of a child's minor injury, though it is likely to have resolved quickly on its own. Mother Nature has provided that many distressing conditions are self-limiting or subject to temporary remission. This clinical beneficence is offset by the difficulty such variability presents to experimental researchers.

When a medical treatment is administered, at least two factors are involved in any effects. One is the genuine impact of the intervention, and the second is the ubiquitous influence of placebo factors. To determine the real effects of treatment, medical researchers make use of placebo treatments: interventions that resemble the real treatment but lack any true therapeutic properties. The use of a placebo treatment is easy to undertake in drug trials simply by preparing fake pills that look identical to the real medication and randomly assigning participants in a controlled trial to receive either the real treatment or the placebo. In such trials, participants provide informed consent, meaning that it is explained to them, and they understand, that although they have a 50 percent chance of receiving an actual treatment, they also have a 50 percent chance of receiving a placebo treatment. If at the end of the trial, the experimental treatment proves to have worked better than the placebo, those who initially received the placebo are offered the real treatment. In this approach, apparent improvements experienced by the placebo-assigned participants can be subtracted from the improvements of those who received the real treatment; thus, the true effect of treatment can be ascertained.

Placebos can be tricky things. Bigger pills are usually more powerful placebos than smaller ones. Injections are better placebos than pills. The placebo effect can be influenced by the very color or shape of a pill or by the size of syringes and needles, with larger ones having a greater placebo effect than smaller ones. Some medications have side effects, and if participants receiving active treatment experience these, they may become aware of which arm of the study they have been assigned to, thus breaking the blinding of the study. Medical research tries to control for this by sometimes using an *active placebo*, a medication with no known impact on the condition being assessed but that will produce some benign side effects, such as dry mouth, mild dizziness upon standing up, or constipation. These side effects serve the function of persuading the placebo-assigned participants that they are getting the real medicine and thus strengthen the placebo-control element of the study. When many participants assigned to a placebo control group learn that they are getting the placebo, blinding has been broken, and this group is essentially downgraded in value to a no-treatment control group. Taylor et al. (2003) is an example of a placebo-controlled trial of an herbal medication coauthored by social workers.

The placebo-control approach has even been used to evaluate surgical techniques. In such studies, patients volunteer to take part in a trial comparing real surgery with fake surgery, knowing they have a fifty–fifty chance of having fake surgery, with the understanding that they will subsequently receive the real operation if it turns out to be more effective than the fake one. The placebo surgery involves the same preoperative preparation, sedation, incisions, and suturing as in the real operation but without the actual surgery within the skin. Studies of this nature have been used for knee and shoulder problems, and in about half the studies, real surgery produced no better results than placebo surgery. Such studies can be important in reducing the numbers of unneeded operations (Wartolowska et al. 2014).

Less intrusively, placebo controls have been used extensively to evaluate the effects of acupuncture. In real acupuncture, the acupuncturist inserts needles into precisely prescribed areas under the skin to try to treat a variety of conditions. According to the theory of acupuncture, the positioning of needle placement is crucial to the success of the treatment. For years, clinical researchers in the fields of complementary and alternative medicine have been evaluating "real" acupuncture versus sham acupuncture. In such studies, participants are randomly assigned to receive true acupuncture or sham needle placement, with the needles being inserted randomly on the participant's body. Results have shown that participants receiving the true treatment got better. This is good. But the participants who got fake acupuncture improved to the same extent, suggesting that the acupuncture industry is a house built on the placebo effect. A study coauthored by social workers on the effectiveness of acupuncture to treat cocaine addiction found that true acupuncture and sham acupuncture produced the same results (Margolin et al. 2002). See Lopes-Júnior et al. (2016) and Mu et al. (2020) for systematic reviews of studies comparing real versus sham acupuncture also suggesting that true acupuncture is primarily a placebo treatment.

The power of placebo treatments and their influence on client self-reports of improvement is well illustrated in a study by Wechsler et al. (2011). Asthma patients were assigned to receive each of the following in random order: a real inhaled medicine, a placebo inhaled medicine, sham acupuncture, and no treatment. The outcome measures were patients' self-reports of breathing improvement and objective measures of breathing via spirometry. Patients receiving no treatment reported no improvements in breathing, and the objective measures also showed that their breathing had not improved. No surprise there. But patients receiving the real inhaled medication, the placebo inhaled medication, and sham acupuncture all reported being able to breath better. However, the only treatment that objectively demonstrated improvements in breathing was the real inhalation therapy. The authors note, "Placebo effects can be clinically meaningful and rival the effects of active medication in patients with asthma" (Wechsler et al. 2011, 119). This is a striking example of how a placebo treatment can persuade people they are better when in reality they are not. And social workers, of course, would not be content with such an outcome. With an effective treatment, we want people to really feel better, and act better, and think better, not just *say* they are better. Faith healers can do that.

As in medical research, research into the outcomes of social work treatment is complicated by placebo influences, so it is crucial that we be able to empirically determine if a given treatment yields improvements above and beyond a comparably delivered placebo treatment. As professionals, we need to demonstrate that we are better therapists than needle-wielding acupuncturists. Recall the previously cited study by Strupp and Hadley (1979) wherein it was found that college students with depression improved no more after receiving psychotherapy from highly trained doctoral-level psychologists than those who had received psychotherapy from doctoral-educated college faculty with *no* training in psychotherapy. This finding suggests that years of graduate school education specializing in mental health care are not necessary to be an effective psychotherapist. There is good evidence that many forms of legitimate psychotherapies produce effects that are equivalent to those of placebo psychotherapies (Prioleau, Murdock, and Brody 1983), thus the need for placebo control groups in experimental studies evaluating the outcomes of treatments delivered by social workers. Again, it is important for the legitimacy of the profession that we, ourselves, provide credible evidence that what we do produces better results than therapies provided by untrained professionals or by otherwise bogus or placebo treatments.

The field of medicine is clear about the use of known placebo treatments:

Opinion 8.20—Invalid Medical Treatment

The following general guidelines are offered to serve physicians when they are called upon to decide among treatments:

(1) Treatments which have no medical indication and offer no possible benefit to the patient should not be used.

(2) Treatments which have been determined scientifically to be invalid should not be used.

(AMA Council on Ethical and Judicial Affairs 2013)

Psychiatry goes further, saying that placebo treatments should not be given to uninformed patients (AMA 2022). The use of placebo treatments is ethically justified in randomized experiments when participants are given sufficient information about the purpose of the study and the need for a placebo control condition and provide informed consent to be randomly assigned to any arm of the study (e.g., active treatment, no treatment, TAU, placebo therapy). Informed consent is usually accompanied by the promise of providing participants who end up in a nontreatment group with the real treatment following the conclusion of the study if the findings show that it is effective.

Placebos can also be used clinically, and ethically, in studies assessing the effectiveness of a medication by providing participants with a bottle of real medicine and an identical bottle of similar-looking inert pills, asking participants to toss a coin each day to determine which pill to take, and having participants record their symptoms daily. Participants are not told which bottle contains the real medicine. After a certain amount of time, say two weeks, the researcher discusses the participants' symptoms with them and discloses which pill they took each day. If it is found that the participants experienced a reduction in symptoms on the days they took the real medicine, this is powerful evidence of the value of the drug versus the placebo. If no such relative benefit is found, this is evidence that the medication is not providing the symptom relief it had promised. (This approach works best with rapid-onset medications with effects of relatively short duration.) The television show *Better Call Saul* features a character supposedly extremely and painfully sensitive to electromagnetic radiation from sources such as electricity, radio waves, the internet, and microwaves. His life is a misery, and he is forced to leave his job, isolate himself at home, and disconnect from the power grid. Visitors have to leave all electronic devices (e.g., cell phones, car fobs) outside when they visit. However, at one point, a physician turns on an electronic device near the man without his knowledge, and he fails to react in any way. This was done to demonstrate to the invalid's brother that his so-called hypersensitivity to electromagnetic radiation did not exist. In terms of logical inference, this is similar to the process of distinguishing true treatment effects from placebo effects (in this case, *nocebo*, or harmful, effects).

The role of placebo influences in healing has been known for centuries. In the late eighteenth century, Dr. Elisha Perkins invented a medical device purported to have amazingly curative powers on painful conditions such as arthritis. "Perkins' Tractors" consisted of two rods resembling large chopsticks, each made of a different metal. Perkins would slide the "tractors" downward along the patient's skin (drawing them upward apparently made the problems worse), upon which many patients reported intense sensations, twitching, and pain relief. Some even reported the complete cure of formerly intractable (pun intended) conditions. The sale of Perkins' Tractors went through the roof, and Perkins traveled widely giving demonstrations of their healing powers, making a huge profit along the way. Around this time, the properties of electricity were being discovered and the use of batteries made of alternating disks of copper and zinc to generate a current and sparks was a novelty, one that added to the scientific allure of the tractors and provided plausibility that they were somehow based on the latest "science." There were skeptics, of course, including Dr. John Haygarth ([1800] 2018) who described how Perkins' Tractors were proved to be a placebo treatment in an engaging essay called "Of the Imagination, as a Cause and as a Cure of Disorders of the Body; Exemplified by Fictitious Tractors, and Epidemical Convulsions." Haygarth used fake tractors made of wood, not metal, but they otherwise resembled Perkins's. Working with a medical collaborator, five patients were selected for "tractorization." One had gout, and the others suffered from rheumatism of the ankle, knee, wrist, or hip. All were swollen and had been ill for months, and all were treated with the fake tractors first. Haygarth reports,

> All the five patients, except one, assured us that the pain was relieved, and three much benefited by the first application of this remedy. One felt his knee was warmer, and he could walk much better, as he showed us with great satisfaction. One was easier for nine hours, and till he went to bed, when the pain returned. One had a tingling sensation for two hours. The wooden tractors were drawn over the skin so as to touch it in the slightest manner. Such is the wonderful course of the imagination. Next day, January 8th, the true mettalick tractors of Perkins were applied exactly in like manner and with similar effects. All the patients were in some measure, but not more relieved by the second application. . . . This method of discovering the truth, distinctly proves to what a surprising degree mere fancy deceives the patient himself; and if the experiment has been done with mettalick tractors only, they might and most probably would have deceived even medical observers.
>
> ([1800] 2018, 3–4)

The logic used to uncover this placebo effect had also been employed a few decades earlier by the noted American scientist Benjamin Franklin. In the late 1700s, a German physician named Franz Anton Mesmer took Europe by storm with demonstrations of what he called Mesmerism. As with acupuncture, thought field therapy, Reiki, therapeutic touch, and many other alternative and complementary medicines, Mesmer postulated the existence of an invisible energy field, in this case called animal magnetism, that could be used to heal people. Originally, he held naturally occurring magnetic rocks (called lodestones) in his hands and waved them about ailing people; he sometimes also waved iron rods. Once, after arriving at a session having forgotten his lodestones, Mesmer proceeded with his treatment using empty hands and obtained the same results as with the magnetic rocks (this should have told him something). Soon rocks and rods were dispensed with in favor of waving just his hands or using finger pressure, with no apparent diminution of Mesmerism's efficacy. Under the influence of the animal magnetism (and in the presence of Mesmer's forceful personality), people would report

pain relief and unusual sensations, sometimes convulse, and respond readily to suggestions; many apparent cures were reported among people with
chronic conditions. Arriving in France in 1776, Franklin heard of Mesmer
and his miraculous claims. Like any good scientist, Franklin was skeptical,
writing to a friend in 1784,

> As to the animal magnetism, so much talked about, I am totally unacquainted
> with it, and must doubt its existence till I can see or feel some effect of it. None
> of the cures said to be performed by it have fallen under my observation, and
> there being so many disorders which cure themselves, and such a disposition
> in mankind to deceive themselves and one another on these occasions, and
> living long has given me so frequent opportunities of seeing certain remedies
> cried up as curing every thing, and yet soon after totally laid aside as useless, I
> cannot but fear that the expectation of great advantage from this new method
> of treating diseases will prove a delusion.
>
> (Franklin 1784, cited in McConkey and Perry 2002, 324)

Fortunately, Franklin was given an opportunity to investigate. In 1785, the
French king appointed a scientific commission to test Mesmer's claims with
Franklin at its head. Some simple tests were made, corresponding to what we
would call single-blind conditions today. Subjects were "Mesmerized," and clear
effects were observed. They were then blindfolded, and observers watched for
effects when the Mesmerist did or did not engage in Mesmeric hand-waving.
The so-called effects of Mesmeric treatment bore no relation to the actual
practice of the Mesmerist. Many people blindfolded and led to believe they
were being acted on by the Mesmerist behaved dramatically, reporting pain,
tingling, and sensations of cold and heat, and some experienced convulsions.
None, however, had actually been treated. All effects had been self-induced by
the participants.

In another instance, certain objects such as cups and trees were reported to
have been "infused" with so-called magnetic fluid, and individuals claiming
to be Mesmerists were asked to select the magnetized object from among an
array of nonmagnetized ones. Of course, they could not reliably do so. A more
elaborate test was also performed in which a doorway was covered from top
to bottom with paper and a female research subject sat on one side of the
paper while a Mesmerist stood on the other, alternating between attempting
to Mesmerize the woman and doing nothing. Nothing happened—that is,
not until the Mesmerist was brought into the sight of the woman. After three
minutes, the woman did appear to experience the powerful effects of animal
magnetism, having a complete convulsive crisis. The report of the commission
was clear: "When the woman could see, she placed her sensations precisely
on the magnetized area; whereas when she could not see, she placed them

haphazardly and in areas far from those being magnetized. It was natural to conclude that these sensations, true or false, were being determined by the imagination" (Franklin et al. [1795] 1996, 345). Franklin and his colleagues concluded, "Touching, imagination, imitation, these then are the real causes of the effects attributed to this new agent, known under the name Animal Magnetism, to this fluid said to circulate in the body and to spread from individual to individual. . . . This agent, this fluid, does not exist, but as chimerical as it is, the idea of it is not new. . . . Magnetism is only an old error. This theory is being presented today with a more impressive apparatus, necessary in a more enlightened century; but it is not for that reason less false" (Franklin et al. [1795] 1996, 359).

I quote so extensively of Haygarth's work on Perkins' Tractors and Franklin's investigations of Mesmerism to stress two points. First, placebo effects are ubiquitous and powerful and have been identified as such for centuries. This means that any investigation of the effects of social work should seriously consider the potential role of placebo influences on any observed and apparent effects. Second, appropriate placebo control conditions are sometimes remarkably simple to arrange. Having people blindfolded while being treated or not treated is one way. The more recent fraudulent therapy called facilitated communication (FC) received much attention in the field of autism treatment in the 1990s. Its proponents miraculously claimed that people with severe autism spectrum disorder (ASD), people who did not speak and had never learned the alphabet, could communicate effectively by having a "facilitator" hold their hand over a keyboard or letterboard and typing responses to questions. It was reported that with FC, they could carry on conversations, write stories, compose poetry, and even attend and graduate from college. Tens of thousands of facilitators received training in FC and were placed in schools and residential facilities around the United States and in other countries.

Skeptics thought the reported results too good to be true, believing a more likely explanation was that the facilitators were guiding the hands of people with ASD to the correct letters. This was easy to test—blind the facilitator so that only the person with ASD could see the keyboard. When this happened, no legible typing was produced. Another test involved asking the person with ASD a question that the facilitator could not hear or asking them a different question from the one posed to the facilitator. When this was done, the answers were wrong. Not just once but in hundreds of trials, across many study participants and facilitators. The evidence is overwhelming, accumulated in dozens of published randomized controlled trials and single-subject experiments (see Schlosser et al. 2014), so much so that all the major mental health and speech professional associations have since condemned the treatment. FC is not simply benign and a waste of people's time and money but can be actively harmful, as are many placebo treatments presented as real.

Many parents whose children were being treated with FC were shocked to discover that their children were supposedly typing messages stating that they had been sexually abused by one or both parents. In many instances, parents were arrested and children were taken from their homes and placed in state care, at least until an investigation could be carried out. Thus far, no such cases have been substantiated. When tested in court, facilitators failed to demonstrate that children were authoring the messages, resulting in all cases being dismissed. Still, the damage had been done. (For more information on these horrific allegations, see Wikipedia 2022.)

In one instance, a female professor of philosophy (lacking any mental health credentials) provided FC to a thirty-year-old man with severe intellectual disabilities and cerebral palsy who could not talk. Over time, his "typing" supposedly disclosed his love for her, which she then reciprocated. She eventually arranged several trysts during which she raped this person incapable of providing conventional consent (his parents refused her permission to become their son's lover). Her defense was that he had provided consent via his FC messages to her (which she authored). The judge failed to be convinced. The professor was convicted of rape and sent to prison. The professor's husband and children were devastated, as was the man with ASD and his family. Yet another group of victims of a placebo treatment gone awry (see Sherry 2016). In another instance, a facilitator working with a nine-year-old girl with ASD generated messages that convinced the girl's mother that her daughter was a "spirit guide" sent from beyond, conveying messages from God (see Madrigal 1995). Were the messages true? Was the facilitator a charlatan? Was the mother being deceived? Thanks to Benjamin Franklin, it would be easy to test what was going on in a case like this simply by using a blindfold. Lilienfeld et al. (2014) provides a good explanation for the persistence of FC in the face of overwhelming refutative evidence.

Placebo Treatments in Social Work

What would a placebo treatment look like in a study of social work? Let's assume we have a new therapy that has been evaluated in a single-group study involving a number of participants being assessed, treated, and then reassessed, with improvements reported. This promising result could be used to justify a more complex study that would control for or rule out some threats to internal validity that may have given rise to these early apparently positive results. We could decide to compare the new therapy with no treatment and with a placebo therapy within the context of a randomized controlled trial. We would explain to potential participants that we are assessing a new treatment with promising results, but it is not yet clear if it is better than no treatment or a placebo therapy, hence the present study. If they provide informed consent, participants would be randomly assigned to one of the study arms. If assigned to no treatment, they would be aware that they were not receiving treatment. However, if they were assigned to receive either the new therapy or the placebo therapy, they would not know which treatment they were receiving.

Some forms of treatment seem likely to be effective but are known to have little real clinical benefit, for example structured relaxation training. Such treatments may make viable placebo treatments for serious conditions such as chronic mental illness, obsessive-compulsive disorder, or phobias. Colosetti and Thyer (2002) used relaxation therapy as a placebo control condition in a study of the effects of a therapy called eye movement desensitization and reprocessing (EMDR) on female prisoners with PTSD. Similarly, supportive psychotherapy provided individually or in a group setting has been shown to have little effect upon focal symptoms in people with certain serious conditions (e.g., hallucinations, delusions, anhedonia, severe anxiety, compulsive rituals, obsessions) and thus can be used as a convincing placebo therapy. Hypnosis is of no known clinical benefit above and beyond placebo value for any condition commonly encountered by social workers among their clients, not even for issues such as quitting smoking or anxiety (Coelho, Canter, and Ernst 2008). Audio programs, formerly called subliminal tapes (when they were recorded onto cassette tapes), provide soothing background noise (e.g., rain, waves) and supposedly contain embedded messages aimed at some therapeutic end (e.g., weight loss, smoking cessation, stress relief) that are undetectable to the listener. These messages are said to penetrate the unconscious and produce positive effects. Such programs lend themselves to solid placebo-controlled experiments, as two versions of the audio program can be assessed: one with subliminal messages and one without (but otherwise identical). People listening to the real tapes report improvements, but so do the folks listening to the placebo tapes, convincingly demonstrating that the real tapes are no better than placebo (Greenwald et al. 1991).

Monica Pignotti, a licensed social worker, was engaged for many years in providing a treatment called thought field therapy (TFT). TFT involves clients thinking about traumatic events while the therapist taps on certain parts of the client's body, spots said to be "energy meridians," focal points for invisible energy forces produced by the human body. (These are conceptually similar to acupuncture points, and neither set of "points" has been shown to exist.) As with acupuncture, specific points are meant to be tapped and in a particular sequence for TFT to be effective. Elaborate treatment manuals and theoretical explanations describe this treatment. Pignotti became increasingly concerned about the highly positive claims being made by the founder of TFT and his followers, including that TFT could cure cancer and other physical disorders, not just PTSD. These claims, as well as her own work (and increasing doubts about the technique) led her to conduct her own study. Real clients seeking TFT were randomly assigned to receive real TFT or a placebo procedure in which the tapping points were randomly chosen. She found that the clients who had received the sham procedure reported the same degree of benefit as those who had received real TFT. This finding is pretty convincing evidence that TFT is little more than a placebo (Pignotti 2005).

In the early years of the development and promotion of EMDR, it was believed that having the client move their eyes back and forth while tracking the psychotherapist's finger in a prescribed rhythm was a crucial element of the therapy. And people with PTSD, phobias, anxiety, and other conditions reported improvements after receiving EMDR, often in a remarkably short period of time. Practitioners spent a good deal of time pursuing the specialized proprietary (and expensive) training required to become certified to deliver EMDR, which involved studying the supposed neurobiological underpinnings and brain functioning mechanisms that made the eye movements critical to the success of the treatment. The eye movements were important, because otherwise EMDR was simply a variant of cognitive behavioral therapy (CBT), as claimed by Hyer and Brandsma (1997). After a few years, EMDR expanded in popularity, and several psychologists decided to test the hypothesis that the back-and-forth eye movements were essential to treatment success by conducting an experiment in which participants were randomly assigned to receive real EMDR with back-and-forth eye movements or a therapy identical to EMDR but with up-and-down eye movements. Those who had received sham EMDR reported equivalent benefits to those who had received real EMDR, providing convincing evidence that the original theory behind EMDR was incorrect (see Gunter and Bodner 2009). Over time, the theory of EMDR expanded to include the use of any type of rhythmic stimulation, including eye movements, finger tapping, alternating vibrations, and music. But what is evident is that from its inception, the theoretical rationale for EMDR was based on the equivalent of a placebo premise. The underlying physiology said to be the basis of EMDR's effectiveness was false (hence that aspect of training unnecessary), as was the explanation given by EMDR therapists to their clients. This finding demonstrates the curious phenomenon of an apparently effective therapy deliberately including placebo-like elements in its treatment protocol. To be fair, much the same can be said for many treatments.

Again, for a placebo treatment to be an adequate control, it must mirror the real experimental treatment as much as possible. A real one-to-one psychotherapy should be compared with a placebo psychotherapy (e.g., relaxation training, supportive counseling, hypnotism), not to a placebo treatment in the form of a pill. A real treatment in pill form should be compared with placebo pills, acupuncture with sham acupuncture, TFT with sham TFT, and so on. Therapist characteristics should be also similar—it would be unfair to

compare an experimental psychotherapy provided by highly attractive therapists in plush offices with a placebo psychotherapy delivered by less attractive
therapists in shabby spaces. The time spent in treatment should be the same
in both conditions as well. Having the experimental group get three hours of
therapy a week and the placebo participants only one hour would not be a fair
comparison.

Because social workers are in the business of trying to help people, not just
study human phenomena, it can be uncomfortable to design a study comparing an experimental treatment against a placebo therapy that involves clients
with serious conditions. Using placebo controls for less serious problems
(e.g., fingernail biting, speech anxiety, insomnia) is easier to reconcile with
our mandate to provide real help. Thus, it is common practice to use existing
services, referred to as TAU, as a comparison. More on this later. But before
the value and practicality of placebo control groups is summarily dismissed
in evaluation research, a reading of Blenkner's (1962) paper titled "Control
Groups and the 'Placebo Effect' in Evaluative Research" is worthwhile, as
is recalling Roger Scruton's observation that "the consolation of imaginary
things is not imaginary consolation." Few people today derive a sense of
safety from grasping a medallion of Zeus they wear around their neck and
uttering supplications to him, but at one point in history Zeus seemed to be
a very real and powerful god, capable of providing aid and solace in times of
need. These effects, placebo or not, were real. When I was a small child, I was
taught that I had a guardian angel watching over me at night. This helped me
to sleep better. Placebo belief or real spiritual intercessor? Who can say with
certainty? While we might accept placebo beliefs as acceptable in the daily
lives of individuals, promoting and fostering such views should not be the
primary therapeutic technique of the professional social worker. We can do
better than that.

Margaret Blenkner firmly grasped the painful nettle of placebo influences
in social work intervention, and our need to control for these in our outcome
studies, when she said,

> Are we psychologically capable of entertaining the unpleasant idea that
> workers can be placebos, and that our precious mystique—the worker-client
> relationship—may be only the ubiquitous placebo effect? Are we willing to give
> up our . . . prejudices long enough to find out whether it is possible that regard-
> less of theory, school, diagnosis, client symptoms, or worker conceptualiza-
> tions, if a worker has enthusiasm and conviction about his way of helping, most
> clients will *feel* helped and some will even *be* helped? If we are willing to do this
> we may finally get to the really effective factors in technique and method and
> begin to justify our claims to having a science-based art.
>
> (1962, 58, emphasis in the original)

Experimental research designs incorporating credible placebo control groups are among the best tools we have to sort out placebo influences from genuine treatment effects. Rosenthal and Frank assert this need:

> Improvement under a special form of psychotherapy cannot be taken as evidence for: (a) correctness of the theory on which it was based; or (b) efficacy of the specific technique used, unless improvement can be shown to be greater or qualitatively different from that produced by the patient's faith in the efficacy of the therapist and his technique. . . . To show that a specific form of psychotherapy . . . produces results not attributable to the nonspecific placebo effect it is not sufficient to compare its results in patients receiving no treatment. The only adequate control would be another form of therapy in which the patient had equal faith . . . but which would not be expected by the theory of the therapy being studied to produce the same effect.
>
> (1956, 300)

Regarding point (a), the usefulness of the geocentric theory of the universe (that the earth is at its center) in terms of predicting eclipses does not mean that that theory is correct (it is not). The apparent efficacy of EMDR does not prove that the theory of saccadic eye movements causing neuropsychologically based therapeutic changes is correct (it is not; see Cahill, Carrigan, and Frueh 1999). The effectiveness of traditional systematic desensitization in alleviating phobias did not prove that its underlying theory based on reciprocal inhibition was correct (it is not; see Tryon 2005).

Clinical outcomes are weak proof that the theory upon which a treatment is based is *correct*, but they can demonstrate that a theory is *incorrect*. If a theory predicts that a properly delivered therapy will result in client improvements, it may be that the positive outcomes result from the truthfulness of the underlying theory. *But* they may also be explained by any number of competing theories. Say a positive result was obtained from an outcome study of client-centered therapy. The Rogerian-minded therapists would wave their hands wildly saying something like, "See? Our theory is true!" But at the same time, the Freudian-minded therapists would stroke their chins and say something like, "Perhaps you did get positive results, but I can explain it via psychoanalytic principles, not your client-centered theory." Meanwhile the behaviorists would look up from their graphs and say, "Clearly your positive results can be explained more parsimoniously through learning theory. Perhaps the mechanism of action of client-centered therapy is the counselor subtly reinforcing certain things the client said, slowly shaping their verbal behavior along more healthy lines." These perspectives illustrate that positive results are not convincing evidence of the truthfulness of an underlying theory. Theory testing may require independent evidence of its validity apart from treatment outcome.

While *positive* therapy results are not generally capable of proving a theory is *true*, *negative* results can provide strong evidence that a theory is *false*—as long as the scientific experiment is a credible and fair test. Finding that a study design is legitimate and that the results do reflect reality can go a long way toward demonstrating that the theory underlying a treatment is incorrect. With respect to intervention research outcomes and conclusions about theory, scientific results tend to whisper "yes" but shout "no." A sound outcome study on a therapy based on a legitimate theory that obtains negative results tells us two things: (1) the therapy does not work, and (2) the theory is incorrect. So when proponents of FC claim that people with ASD have normal brains in malfunctioning bodies (a theory) that do not allow them to express themselves verbally or in writing, uncontrolled tests of FC are of little value in demonstrating the effectiveness of the treatment or the validity of the theory. The blind tests of FC in which no effective communication took place demonstrated two things: (1) the treatment does not work, and (2) the theory of normal brains in dysfunctional bodies is incorrect. Similarly, if a theory says that schizophrenia is caused by hidden infections under the teeth, repeated tooth extractions that fail to improve symptoms go a long way to disproving the theory.

Allegiance Bias

Allegiance bias is a threat to internal validity that occurs when a person conducting an investigation has a preexisting allegiance for one or more therapies under investigation (Leykin and DeRubeis 2009). This bias is particularly likely to be at play when the researcher has invented one or more of the treatments under investigation. Fame, prestige, and sometimes financial benefits accrue to someone who invents a novel treatment, and one way for a new treatment to gain credibility is to publish research showing it works. It makes sense for the inventors of a new therapy to want to try to show that it is genuinely helpful. So when Aaron Beck conducted tests of his newly created cognitive therapy, or when Francine Shapiro published outcome studies on her novel treatment called EMDR, these efforts can be seen benignly as professionals trying to advance the research foundations of their discipline and demonstrate the usefulness of new interventions. Just as it is benign, no doubt, for pharmaceutical companies that have invested millions of dollars in developing a new drug to arrange for clinical researchers to be paid to investigate that new drug.

There are ways to reduce the potential impact of an allegiance bias on the outcomes of experimental studies. One of the most effective is for the new therapy to be tested independently by investigators not connected with the development of the treatment (and not by former students of the intervention's originator) and not provided a financial incentive to show that the treatment is effective (such as researchers who provide training in the treatment for a fee). Researchers are usually required to disclose such conflicts of interest when they publish their outcome studies.

Having investigators with a vested interest in a study's outcome can be mitigated as a problem by having them distanced from the actual conduct of the study. Others (e.g., paid assessors) should conduct the pre- and posttest evaluations, not the therapy's inventor. Someone else should provide the therapy. Someone else should tabulate and enter the data, and someone else should analyze the data.

A few years ago I read a study of a randomized trial comparing the effectiveness of CBT versus CBT plus hypnosis for the treatment of pain. The combined treatment obtained better results. It was not clear from the article who provided the treatments in the two conditions, so I emailed the author to ask, and to his credit he replied that he had provided the treatments for both groups, and he recognized this as a problem. His résumé revealed extensive publications in the area of hypnosis to manage pain, so the potential for allegiance bias was strong in such a study. Much of his professional career was focused on promoting hypnosis as an effective treatment. Maybe the omission to mention that he had provided both treatment conditions was an accidental oversight, or perhaps it was a deliberate attempt to conceal this potential allegiance bias (which would reduce the credibility of the study). I do not know, but the proactive disclosure of such potential biases is always indicated when publishing outcome studies. And allegiance bias can work both ways. A study comparing the results of behavioral therapy versus psychoanalysis might turn out quite differently, depending on whether the authors were behavior therapists or psychoanalysts. A study comparing medication versus psychotherapy might turn out differently depending on whether the study had been commissioned by psychiatrists invested in the drug or by psychologists invested in the psychotherapy. Can you see how studies on the preventive effects of home visiting on child abuse, comparing nursing home visits versus social work home visits, could be impacted by who was doing the investigation, nurses or social workers? Controlling for allegiance bias can be hard, but its impact can be minimized.

The Hawthorne Effect

Imagine an intervention study is being conducted in an elementary school classroom, and part of the data collection involves having a research assistant sit at the back of the classroom, recording the children's behavior. It is easy to see how having a stranger in their class might induce the children to behave differently from how they do when only the teacher is there. A change in behavior caused by knowing that one is being observed or studied is called the *Hawthorne effect*, named after Hawthorne Works, a factory in Cicero, Illinois. A study was conducted there in the 1920s to see if changes in lighting to see affected the workers' productivity. It turned out that any changes in lighting were associated with improvements in productivity—but simply because the workers knew they were being studied. Another example of the Hawthorne effect is provided by a study showing that when hospital workers knew their handwashing behavior was being observed, the rate of hand hygiene compliance was much greater than when they did not know it was being observed (Eckmanns et al. 2006). The Hawthorne effect can have a greater impact in a study comparing a real treatment with no treatment and less of an impact when a placebo control group is used as the comparator condition. Another way to reduce this threat to internal validity is to collect data unobtrusively, without participants knowing it, or to use as data information already collected and available in agency records. The Hawthorne effect is believed to be real and needs to be taken into account when conducting experiments (McCambridge, Witton, and Elbourne 2014).

Wrong Sample Size Bias

An experimental study will not provide a legitimate test of its hypotheses unless the sample size is suitable. In studies involving small numbers of participants in each group (e.g., treatment versus no treatment), most statistical tests are underpowered in terms of their being able to detect changes or differences. Even in the case of a treatment that is fairly effective, the results will likely come out as nonsignificant, leading to an unfair rejection of the null hypothesis. For example, if a small-scale randomized controlled trial on solution-focused brief therapy were undertaken with only five people per group, the statistical analysis would indicate $p > .05$, meaning that the posttreatment results of the two groups did not differ significantly. Thus, the research would unfairly conclude that the treatment had not worked. Alternatively, if the sample size were quite large, say one hundred participants per group, small differences in outcome could likely be detected and lead to a statistically significant result (i.e., $p < .05$), leading the author to conclude that the treatment is effective. A potential solution to *wrong sample size bias* includes performing a power analysis prior to collecting your data to determine how many participants you will need in each group to perform a valid statistical analysis. If you cannot recruit a sufficient number, then, frankly, the study is not worth doing.

Treatment Contamination

The threat of *treatment contamination* occurs in experiments that attempt to compare the results of one experimental treatment (let's call it X) with another active treatment (let's say Y). The treatment groups are created using random assignment, and qualified clinicians deliver X to one group and Y to the other. To legitimately compare the outcomes of X versus Y, it is crucial that the participants assigned to receive X receive only X and no elements of Y and that those assigned to receive Y get only Y and no elements of X.

Treatment contamination can occur in at least two circumstances. First, clinicians themselves, inadvertently or deliberately, may provide participants of one group with elements of the other therapy (i.e., X plus some of Y or Y plus some of X). Doing so can compromise the purpose of the study: to see whether there is a true difference in outcome between the two treatments. One way to control for treatment contamination is to have therapists adhere to a treatment protocol or practice guideline. Another is to include supervision so that the therapists' sessions are observed (e.g., via audio or video recording) to ensure treatment fidelity. Ensuring experimental therapists understand the purpose and importance of keeping the two therapeutic practices distinct is also crucial.

An example can be provided by an actual experimental outcome study on a type of therapy called systematic desensitization (SD) (Wolpe 1958). It had been established that office-based SD involving exposing clients to their phobias by imagining fearful situations worked reasonably well. What was not clear was the role of the office-based SD in producing improvements versus that of practicing graduated limited-exposure exercises in the real world between sessions, which clients were instructed to do. An experiment was designed to try to find out. One group of participants with phobias were randomly assigned to get traditional office-based SD involving exposure in imagination only and were strictly enjoined *not* to engage in any real-world exposure exercises between sessions. A second group was also assigned to get office-based SD, but they were also strongly *encouraged* to engage in real-world exposure practice. In this manner, the contributions of real-world exposure could be ascertained. Obviously, then, for this experiment to maintain its internal validity, it was imperative that the therapists providing the office-based SD not encourage participants in the first group to practice exposure between sessions. If they did so, the experimental logic would collapse. When studies such as this were conducted, it was found that traditional SD was much more effective when combined with real-life exposure. Later experimental trials showed that traditional SD itself could be omitted and replaced solely with real-world gradual exposure therapy, since the latter was the true active ingredient (McNeil and Zvolensky 2000). Nowadays traditional SD is limited in practice to clients who initially refuse to engage in any element of real-life exposure and to clients who fear events that are difficult, if not impossible, to recreate in the natural environment, such as being in a plane crash or going to hell.

A second source of treatment contamination occurs when participants assigned to different treatment conditions encounter each other and discuss the treatment they are receiving; for example, a study comparing two therapies in the treatment of recurring nightmares with one group receiving insight-oriented psychotherapy and the other narrative exposure therapy (NET). If two participants meet each other, say in a waiting room, and one receiving NET tells one receiving psychotherapy about how their therapist has them repeatedly write out descriptions of their nightmares, the psychotherapy-assigned participant might choose to try the writing exercises on their own. So this participant is now receiving one treatment and elements of the other. If this type of contamination occurs frequently, it can collapse a study's internal validity. A solution to this problem is asking participants not to discuss their treatment with one another or ensuring that participants receiving one therapy are treated at different times from those receiving the other therapy. Conducting a cluster randomized controlled trial (more on that later), in which clients at one agency get one therapy and clients at another agency get the other can also mitigate the problem of treatment contamination.

Summary

Experiments are one powerful way to try to make discoveries about nature. In social work, experiments have many purposes, and in the design of such studies researchers attempt to reduce bias as much as possible. The more we eliminate or control for bias, the closer we narrow in on nature's reality. The biases addressed in this chapter focused on intervention outcome studies. The more successful the authors of such studies are in reducing threats to internal validity, the more confidence we can have that the treatments evaluated truly resulted in change and that these changes were not the result of factors other than treatment, such as the passage of time, a person's concurrent history, or attrition. Properly controlled experimental investigations are typically better able to permit valid conclusions about treatment effects compared to quasi-experiments and other forms of evaluation designs. Of course science recognizes that almost all findings from a single study should be considered provisional and subject to being revised as new and better data accrue. Indeed, many apparently well conducted experiments come up with incorrect conclusions, called false-positive claims (Ioannidis 2005; Munafo and Flint 2010). Science tries to catch such incorrect findings via the process of replication: reproducing a study, perhaps by the original investigator but better if conducted by independent research teams. Incorrect false-positive conclusions (e.g., "this treatment worked for clients with this problem") are unlikely to be reproduced in an independently con-ducted, high-quality replication study. This principle—that a single study's findings should be considered provisional—must be stressed, as it is basic to science. The results of a single study can rarely be seen to provide a definitive answer to a research question; for example, that a given treatment is truly effective. Any commonly accepted conclusion based on solid research can be overturned via the results of additional studies of higher quality. Does adherence to the scientific method provide iron-clad assurances that erroneous conclusions will not occur? Not at all. But science does provide a surer path to finding truth than most other ways of knowing. Its inherently self-correcting nature is not characteristic of knowledge derived from theory, authorities, divine revela-tions, the use of psychedelics, or mystical insights.

Box 2.2 Examples of Pro-experimentalist Opinions Within Social Work

"The experimental method has contributed in large measure to the striking achievements of modern science. This method allows us to analyze our relations of cause and effect more rapidly and clearly than by any other method. It permits verification by many observers. It has substituted for unreasonable prejudice a definite sort of proof that has attained sufficient certainty to justify prediction" (Chapin 1917, 133).

"The faculty and students of a professional school of social work should together be engaged in using the great method of experimental research which we are just beginning to discover in our professional education pro-gramme, and which should be as closely knit into the work of a good school of social work as research has been embodied into the program of a good medical school" (Abbott 1931, 55).

"Experimentation in a natural setting is well suited to investigate the research problems so frequently encountered in social work" (Thomas 1960, 273).

"As a result of the adoption of the scientific attitude, Conference speakers and programs looked forward toward progress. . . . They believed in the future; that it was possible by patient, careful study and experimentation to create a society much better than the one they lived in" (Bruno 1964, 26–27; "Conference" refers to the 1891 National Conference of Social Work).

"Our clients deserve the best services our profession can provide, and for the determination of social work effectiveness there is no substitute for controlled experimental research" (Thyer 1989, 320).

"We welcome program evaluations so that we can know more about what seems to 'work.' We need outcome studies, which may call upon a range of ways of knowing, through a single case study, experimental designs, or longitudinal reviews that reflect upon the consequences of events or conditions or interventions" (Hartman 1990, 4).

"The preferred method for inferring a causal relationship is the classical experiment, which permits the systematic alteration of a treatment (the independent variable) and the control of extraneous variables" (Witkin 1991, 159).

"Our basic argument is that social work activities, particularly those that can be described as 'interventions,' should be justified, whenever possible, by proofs of effectiveness, including, where possible, RCTs [randomized controlled trials]. . . . The interests of people . . . dependent on public welfare services will be better served if welfare purchasers invest in strategies on proven effectiveness and if researchers focus their efforts on producing information that enable such decisions to be taken" (Newman and Roberts 1997, 294–95).

CHAPTER 3

THE PHILOSOPHY OF THE SCIENCE OF EXPERIMENTAL DESIGNS

The strongest arguments prove nothing so long as the conclusions are not verified by experience. Experimental science is the queen of sciences and the goal of all speculation.

—Roger Bacon

Scientific inquiry is grounded on various philosophical foundations, with different research methods emphasizing some philosophical positions more than others. There is not an extensive literature on the philosophy of social work (apart from ethics and values) and even less on the philosophy of social work research. Some of the few exceptions include Towle (1930), Bisno (1952), and Reamer (1993). Some knowledge of the philosophy of science that forms the basis of social work research can be useful in understanding the approach that experimental methods use to investigate the question of causation.

Philosophy is a broad field, as exemplified by the definition provided by Corsini: "a discipline that attempts to understand the first principles of all knowledge based primarily on reason and logic, and covering such topics as theology, metaphysics, epistemology, ethics, politics, history and aesthetics" (2002, 720). The profession of social work touches on all these topics to some degree. Faith-based social work practitioners are certainly engaged in theology—indeed the profession of social work largely emerged from religious institutions. Considerable attention is given to the topic of ethics, as demonstrated by the codes of ethics of our professional associations in the United States, such as the National Association of Social Workers, the Clinical Social Work Association, and the National Association of Black Social Workers, as well as similar codes endorsed by social work associations in many other countries. The field of political social work is of course closely aligned with the philosophical positions of political parties, with positions such as conservatism, liberalism, progressivism, collectivism, and individualism being grounded in diverse philosophical perspectives. The philosophical field of aesthetics, concerned with the meaning of art and beauty, is not so prominent in contemporary social work, but we as a field have always been concerned with promoting the arts and culture among the underserved and disadvantaged in our populations. Beginning in the early 1890s, Jane Addams's Hull-House regularly offered courses in music, murals, painting, weaving, sculpting and ceramics and gave free concerts to members of the local community. Indeed, Hull-House housed Chicago's first public art gallery. The young Benny Goodman got his musical start playing the clarinet in Hull-House performances (Lyon 1985), and many social workers today integrate the arts into their practices.

The study of the history of social work is very much enmeshed in how various philosophical positions have waxed and waned across the decades. Franklin Roosevelt's New Deal was based on philosophical positions quite different from those of his immediate predecessors, at least as disparate as those separating the policies of Presidents Obama and Trump. Metaphysics deals with the fundamental nature of reality and overlaps slightly with epistemology, the theory of how we know things. The very act of undertaking scientific research involves staking epistemological positions: philosophical assumptions that can be seen as similar to Euclid's first axioms. Euclid asserted certain claims; for example, that a point describes a position in space but has no shape or size, that parallel lines never meet, and that lines are sets of points extending forever in two opposite directions. His axioms could not be proved to be true, but he demonstrated that, if we *assumed* them to be true, we could construct an intricate system called Euclidean geometry, which was useful in practical fields such as surveying, astronomy, navigation, and other areas of applied mathematics. In other words, Euclidean geometry worked very well in our everyday world to solve problems. Similarly, science assumes a variety of philosophical positions that can be considered axiomatic, not capable of being proved to be true but if accepted allowing us to design research studies in social work and other behavioral and social sciences that yield accurate answers. As Ann Hartman (1990), once the editor of the journal *Social Work*, wisely asserts, "It is important for epistemological convictions to be made as explicit as possible. . . . These assumptions must be made explicit, because knowledge and truths can be understood and evaluated only in the context of these framing assumptions" (3–4). A similar point of view is expressed by Robbins, Chatterjee, and Canda (1999): "When theory and knowledge are presented as 'objective' truths that can be empirically demonstrated and objectively verified through supposedly impartial scientific methods, *it becomes all too easy to bypass the philosophical and ideological underpinnings of what we know*" (375, my emphasis).

In "The Basic Philosophy of Experimentation," published in the journal *Smith College Studies in Social Work*, Levitt (1959) notes,

> The tendency among research workers in applied disciplines like social work and psychiatry is to specialize in the pre-scientific study to the neglect of the scientific experiment. While the preliminary spadework provided by the pre-scientific study is continually needed, an imbalance cannot be productive. It is, after all, only the truly scientific study which can furnish facts. It is as if we begin by digging a foundation, and simply continue to dig it, forgetting to erect the building for which the foundation was originally intended. . . . The *fundamental principles* which underlie scientific research are the same for all sciences. These principles compromise what is usually called *the philosophy of science*. It is a guide to the design of experiments in every field.
>
> (63–64, emphasis in the original)

Next I will outline what some of these generally philosophical principles are and provide a brief rationale for each.

Determinism

The principle of *determinism* is the contention that what happens in the world, including individual human activities, is at least partially determined by forces outside our control. We cannot have a genuine science about a subject matter that leaps capriciously about. Some scientists can be seen as relatively strict determinists, including the psychologist B. F. Skinner and the psychiatrist Sigmund Freud. Skinner believed in a largely environmentally based determinism that focused on one's learning history, wherein past behaviors were followed by reinforcing or punishing consequences, and future behaviors were strengthened or weakened accordingly. This is very much a person-in-environment perspective. For Freud it was more a determinism of the mind, a *mental* determinism, not so much an *environmental* one. But both only minimally invoked the idea of free will as a cause of why we behave the way we do. Others, such as the psychologist Carl Rogers, who developed the person-centered approach to psychotherapy, held the view that people behave more as a result of conscious free choice than their mental or environmental learning history. But even the strongest advocates of free will, such as Rogers, acknowledge that there are some deterministic factors in our lives. Rogers believed that people have an innate tendency to grow in the direction of becoming self-actualized, provided that one is exposed to facilitative interpersonal relationships, much in the way that a flower cannot help but grow if placed in nurturing soil and given sufficient water and sunlight. Thus, this self-actualizing tendency can be seen as at least a partially deterministic factor affecting our lives and behavior. Few advocates of free will deny the impact of one's biology on one's behavior. For example, the skin tone one is born with has a strong impact on individuals (see Hall 2010). Our height, weight, physical attractiveness, parents, and country of upbringing are all deterministic factors outside our control. We are impacted by temperature, humidity, pollen in the air, gastric distress, the food we ingest, and the beverages we drink. Thus, a good case can be made that our behavior is at least partially determined. Whether one believes that our behavior is 80 percent determined and 20 percent a function of free will or 80 percent free will and 20 percent determined, to the extent that at least some of our behavior is determined by outside forces, science can focus on those variables to try to discover some of the causes of what we do.

Social work as a profession has long accepted the principle of determinism. The very idea that we can engage in professional intervention to improve people's lives is an implicit acceptance of some degree of determinism. This of course relates to the idea of *causation* mentioned earlier in this book. As Warner put it early on, "Social work interprets human troubles in terms of natural processes, that is '*laws*' *of cause and effect*" (1930, 560–61, my emphasis). Hollis defined social work assessment as the "gathering of facts about the internal and external life of the client, *to understand the causative factors* in the client's difficulty" (1964, 192, my emphasis). And Robbins, Chatterjee, and Canda state that "social work emphasizes practice that is based on scientific theories of human behavior, *causation*, prevention, and intervention" (1999, 376, my emphasis). Were there no laws governing human affairs, efforts to remedy social ailments would be fruitless. The very first book on social work theory states it plainly: "*Human behavior can be understood and is determined by causes which can be explained*. We may not have a mastery of the methods of understanding behavior, but any scientific approach to behavior presupposes that it is not in its nature incomprehensible" (Bruno 1936, 192–93, my emphasis).

Kassan (2021) emphasizes the importance of causality: "Without causality, the very notion of scientific inquiry in meaningless. Science goes beyond mere correlation—noticing that it's all just one damned thing after another—to causal explanation of *why* and *how*" (52, emphasis in the original). Social work, too, is concerned with *why* and *how*: why social problems come about and how we can prevent and treat them. The mere description of social or individual conditions can be a good start at developing such an understanding, as demonstrated by Jane Addams's Hull-House maps and the large-scale social surveys of the late 1800s and early 1900s. However, these descriptions do not directly improve the conditions studied. Similarly, surveys of individuals, focus groups, epidemiological works, correlational studies, ethnographies, and longitudinal investigations, among other forms of scientific methods, only circle around the central issue of developing solutions to social problems. Since social work is an applied discipline, our research should focus primarily on investigations that have a clear application to helping people (see Harrison and Thyer 1988), not simply observing them or using them as guinea pigs to test theories on. We need to do analyses of causes.

There is no assumption of any form of pure billiard ball determinism. Science recognizes that a multiplicity of factors historically and concurrently can give rise to human behavior, but this complexity does not mean that we have to throw up our hands in despair at ever understanding things. Rather, ever more sophisticated research methods evolve or are newly invented to enable us to better grapple with more complex issues. Conceptually, general systems theory and its derivatives, such as the ecological model, and the recently developed idea of *intersectionality*, help us understand events from the perspective of multiple concurrent determinants. Multifactorial research designs and statistical techniques such as multiple regression help us to tease out complex influences on human behavior. Polansky also endorsed determinism in his *Social Work Research* textbook when he said, "Scientists assume that there is, in fact, an underlying orderliness in nature, and that the chaos is more apparent than real" (1975, 19).

To the extent that we attempt to explain the causes of clients' problems as a function of their free will, we diminish the value of planned, directed interventions to promote changes in their lives. As a profession we do not know much about altering a client's free will—indeed the very effort seems oxymoronic, for if you can intentionally change another's free will, how could it be said to be "free"? Guild and Guild (1936) noted this philosophical conundrum when they said, "Many people attempt to simplify, but actually make the problem of delinquency or crime unsolvable by declaring it is all a matter of spontaneous 'free will.' An effort to locate and describe 'free will' is as baffling as an effort to place a finger on the rushing wind . . . for though the conduct of men may be said, in a sense, to depend on something called 'free will,' on what does 'will' depend?" (83). The very act of attempting social work treatment, either in the context of one-to-one practice or a large-scale randomized controlled trial, is in a sense an endorsement of the philosophical principle of determinism. Everyone is to some extent a determinist.

Empiricism

The philosophical assumption of *empiricism* refers to the preference of science for evidence obtained via the bodily senses and for evidence gathered systematically through observation or experimentation. It also means a preference for experiments that can be replicated and produce the same results. Bruno endorsed this position when he said, "Social work holds as its primary axiom that knowledge of human behavior can be acquired and interpreted by the senses and that inferences drawn from such knowledge can be tested by the principles of logic" (1936, 192). Data collected from the world informs scientific conclusions much more than other ways of knowing. It may well be that knowledge obtained from authorities (e.g., holy books, clergy, politicians), theory, tradition ("We have always done it this way"), intuition, meditation, prayer, and other sources is useful. Alfred Wallace independently thought of the theory of evolution via natural selection while in the midst of a malarial fever and later sent a scientific paper on the subject to Charles Darwin. The chemist August Kekulé discovered the ring-like structure of the benzene molecule while daydreaming, thinking of a snake biting its own tail. The notion of relativity came to Einstein in a dream, as did Mendeleev's breakthrough that led to the periodic table of elements (Mowbray 2017).

But the problem with these sources of knowledge is that one cannot decide to "sleep on it" and be sure of awakening in the morning with the solution at hand. In contrast, scientific research methods can be taught to almost any reasonably intelligent human being and used to make discoveries about the world. One cannot be taught how to dream up solutions or achieve scientific breakthroughs via meditation or prayer. Would that we could. Unfortunately, for most of us mortals we must have recourse to scientific research to make discoveries.

Another drawback to these sources of knowledge is that there is no mechanism for self-correction. If you make a mistake in a scientific study that is published, keen-eyed readers will delight in bringing it to your attention, perhaps in an embarrassing letter to the editor published in the journal your article appeared in. If your critics are correct, you can reanalyze your data and make corrections or even retract your study if it is fatally flawed. With empirical research you have data that can be checked, rechecked, and subsequently examined by others. Indeed, the *Publication Manual of the American Psychological Association* (APA 2020) actually "prohibits authors from withholding data from qualified requesters for verification through reanalysis in most circumstances. . . . Authors must make their data available after publication subject to conditions and exceptions, within the period of retention specified by their institution, journal, funder, or other supporting organization" (14). Supposed knowledge obtained through prayer or learned from authorities lacks the potential for independent analysis and verification possessed by empirical research. Another benefit of sharing your data is that your study and related ones published by other authors may be combined by independent researchers to create larger data sets capable of revealing further or more refined truths. Techniques such as meta-analysis are an example of such recycling of data.

Realism

Realism is the point of view that the world has an independent or objective existence apart from the perception of the observer. In the words of the science fiction writer Philip K. Dick (1978), "Reality is that which, when you stop believing in it, doesn't go away." At a particular point in time, for example, a certain number of people are living in the United States. The US census attempts to approximate this number as closely as possible, and flawed though the census may be, it provides us with a better estimate than guessing. There is an objective reality to the question of the number of clients seen in a given agency during a given year. There is an objective reality to the ages of those clients. And there is an objective reality to the question of whether the clients benefited from the agency's services. Science tries to capture these realities using the tools of empirical inquiry. The noted social work educator Bertha Capen Reynolds endorsed the philosophical position that an objective reality exists when she said, "The scientific base for a profession like social work, engaged in helping people live, *cannot make ideas and emotions the primary reality*. Like science in other forms of contact with the real world, a science of human adjustment has to take what it finds by experience to be true, and to *deal with this reality* as experience shows to be necessary" (1942, 130, my emphasis).

More recently, Jeane Anastas explained this perspective in this way: "There are several key tenets in realism. The first premise is that there is a 'mind-independent' reality, which stands in contrast to many forms of social constructionist thinking" (2012, 160).

To assert that there exists an objective reality is not to deny that some portions of our reality are subjectively constructed. When I was a child, I was taught that there were nine planets in our solar system, with the outermost being Pluto. However, in 2006 the International Astronomical Union (IAU) came up with a new definition of "planet," and Pluto no longer fit the bill. While generations past were taught that Pluto was a planet, children today are taught that it is not. This is an example of how subjectivity bears upon the establishment of scientific facts. However, this aspect of subjectivity has no bearing on the objective reality of Pluto, which continues to float along in the far reaches of outer space, undisturbed by the petty humans arguing back and forth about what to call it. Imagine that in 2006 you attended a meeting of the IAU and listened in on sessions during which learned astronomers bitterly argued about whether Pluto was a planet. Eventually a vote was held, and Pluto was demoted. Then you moved to another room where astronomers presented the latest empirical research on Pluto—its speed, composition, color, distance from the earth, and other physical properties, all supported by systematic and replicated empirical observations. Which of these two sessions would have contributed the most to astronomical science? Clearly the latter. Arguing about Pluto's status as a planet in 2006 made as much sense as medieval scholars arguing about categorizing the inhabitants of heaven—seraphim, cherubs, archangels, angels, putti, guardian angels, and so on. The list was extensive and greatly varied among Christian, Muslim, and Jewish theologies. Many books and articles were written on the topic, but the issue is no more resolved today than in the Middle Ages. Perhaps the angels above look down upon these corporeal disputes with amusement. Or perhaps not. Science cannot tell us.

For many decades the *Diagnostic and Statistical Manual of Mental Disorders* (DSM) stated that same-sex attraction (referred to as homosexuality in the DSM) was inherently pathological and was its own category of mental illness (a legacy of psychodynamic theory and religious teachings). This position became increasingly controversial, so much so that in 1973 members attending the annual convention of the American Psychiatric Association held a vote to determine the status of homosexuality as a mental disorder. The majority voted to eliminate it from the DSM, and so the majority ruled. Homosexuality began to be phased out as a mental disorder, initially being replaced by "ego-dystonic homosexuality" (a so-called condition in which you were only mentally ill if you were gay but did not like being gay). It was finally eliminated from the DSM in 1987, only (!) fourteen years after the vote to remove it took place. Sexual orientation is of course very real and exists independently of the votes and opinions of psychiatrists, just as the constellation of symptoms formerly labeled Asperger's syndrome continues to exist even though it has been eliminated from the DSM. But the consequences of removing the diagnosis of homosexuality were very real, and positive, helping to eliminate the stigma and discrimination experienced by members of the gay community. In this case the subjective judgments of the reality of a mental disorder had important consequences. The reality of the world exists independently of the votes of scientists on a particular issue. A vote in favor of the world being flat would change nothing about the structure of Earth.

What science focuses on is not the subjective opinions of individuals about the nature of the world but rather objective features, based on data gathered by reliable and valid methods. Science is concerned with reality independent of subjective impressions. As Daston and Galison state, "To be objective is to aspire to knowledge that bears no trace of the knower-knowledge unmarked by prejudice or skill, fantasy of judgement, wishing or striving" (2007, 17). The radium discovered by Marie Curie, the relativity theory formulated by Albert Einstein, and the agricultural products invented by George Washington Carver themselves bear no imprint of gender, religion, or race. To be sure, the chosen fields of study of these individuals were strongly influenced by their backgrounds, but their *discoveries* are available to all and exist today independent of subjective opinions or beliefs.

Scientific research is conducted by fallible human beings, but this fallibility does not condemn the research enterprise as inherently useless. Gorenstein addressed this point when he stated, "It makes no sense to reject the scientific importance of a construct simply because social values may have played some role in its formulation. The question of whether a construct has any scientific import is an empirical one. It has to do with whether the construct exhibits lawful properties" (1986, 589).

While some social workers choose to investigate what it *feels* like to be homeless or what it *means* to be a victim of domestic violence, studies on the outcomes of interventions designed to prevent or reduce the impact of homelessness or domestic violence are of far greater value to directly helping *improve* the world. And determining the reality of the effectiveness of social work interventions is what true experiments are well positioned to do. As Hardy notes, "For realists, the world in which we co-exist is objectively true, but our ability to know and understand how it works and with what effects is inherently limited and so inevitably dependent on some degree of subjectivity" (2014, 584). Subjectivity can be a form of bias, and conventional science is a good, albeit imperfect, approach to reducing the influence of subjectivity. The early observational claim that Mars was crisscrossed with canals made by intelligent beings was eventually refuted owing to the development of more powerful telescopes. Enhancements in our professional ability to assess human beings, their behavior, and behavioral changes for the purposes of practice and evaluation research are occurring all the time. These refinements bring us into closer contact with the real world through the reduction of bias and error.

Operationalism

This philosophical assumption of *operationalism* bears on social work research in that it requires that we develop acceptable definitions of the factors and variables we are investigating. This view asserts that the concepts or variables used in our theories and scientific research must be definable in terms of identifiable and repeated operations that can be reliably replicated by others. Operationalism was endorsed by none other than the founder of clinical social work, Mary Richmond, who said, "To say that my client is mentally deranged is futile; to state the observations that have created this impression is a possible help" ([1917] 1935, 335). The importance of measurement in social work has long drawn the attention of our field (McMillen 1930; Hunt and Kogan 1950; French 1952; Ormsby 1951; Mullen and Magnabosco 1997). Tripodi explains that "an operational definition specifies all of the procedures required for defining a concept so that it can be measured" (1983, 6). Relatedly, Bisman and Hardcastle state that "operational definitions offer observable data with specifics about how to measure or judge a phenomenon or manipulate its dimensions. Necessary for either quantitative or qualitative research, these propositions link concepts to the real world by stating how to observe or measure them" (1999, 53).

The principle of operationalism is important, as its application in scientific research allows us to arrive at findings that are as accurate as possible. Some examples of operationalism in clinical social work research include the definitions of mental disorders used in the DSM and the World Health Organization's International Statistical Classification of Diseases and Related Health Problems, known as the ICD. Recruiting participants for an outcome study of therapy who meet the inclusion criterion of meeting the DSM criteria for a particular disorder is one way to achieve a more homogeneous group. If we simply recruited people who said they were fearful, we'd have a much more varied sample than if we had recruited people who met the DSM-5 criteria for specific phobia. With a more diverse sample, it would be more difficult to draw conclusions about the effects of a treatment. Outcome measures need to be operationalized in some manner. For example, in a study of a depression treatment, researchers could use Beck Depression Inventory scores as a measure of depression. Doing so would provide more accurate—and more *objective*—results than using clinicians' *subjective* ratings of people as "depressed" or "not depressed." A study of the outcomes of psychoanalysis should use therapists who have graduated from a recognized psychoanalytic training program and hold a valid license as a psychotherapist. And a study of the effects of eye movement desensitization and reprocessing (EMDR) should use licensed EMDR practitioners. An intervention study that uses practitioners lacking proper training in the therapy under investigation is not a fair test of that treatment. If this were the case in the EMDR study, and the treatment showed no effect, this might be because EMDR truly is ineffective. *Or* it might be because the "therapists" were not properly trained. Treatments may be further standardized by being operationally defined as requiring a particular amount of time per week or a particular number of sessions. Efforts to determine what is called *treatment fidelity* are now routinely undertaken in psychotherapy outcome studies. This can be done by having therapists use a treatment protocol and by having sessions observed by supervisors to ensure that the protocol is being implemented correctly. We can't have a Rogerian counselor using contingent reinforcement of client statements they approve of and still retain the integrity of client-centered counseling. We can't have a behavior therapist aid in the discussion and interpretation of a client's dreams if we are testing the efficacy of a behavior therapy. Many treatments have practice guidelines or treatment manuals, and the appropriate use of these contributes to the validity of both clinical practice and experimental studies on psychotherapy and other social work interventions.

Addressing the significance of operationalism, the social worker Walter Hudson correctly notes,

> Among the working tools for conducting evaluative research, the role and function of measurement is most important. Without measurement of the study variables, there can be no science as we know it, nor any way for psychotherapists to obtain and present reliable evidence concerning the quality, value, or effectiveness of their work. . . . The client's problem must be defined in measurable terms; if that is not done, the tools of science cannot be brought to bear on the evaluation of treatment and the therapist cannot produce evidence to show that help has been provided.
>
> (1978, 68)

Hudson goes on to describe two of what he calls "first axioms of treatment." The first is that "if you cannot measure the client's problem, it does not exist," and the second is that "if you cannot measure the client's problem, you cannot treat it" (1978, 68). These are rather strong statements and can be legitimately argued against. Bacteria and viruses existed long before we could measure them, as did protons, electrons, and neutrons. Mental disorders have existed since the dawn of humanity, yet ways to measure them were not established until fairly recently. And, of course, treatments for mental disorders have been provided for centuries, predating effective assessment measures for these conditions. To make Hudson's views more palatable and supportable, I propose a few modifications:

1. If something exists, science can likely find a way to validly measure it.
2. If you validly measure a client's problem, you are in a better position to treat it.
3. If you validly measure clients' problems, you are in a better position to conduct empirical evaluations of outcomes.

These qualified sentiments, I hope, are less objectionable than Hudson's diktats yet still support the principle of operationalism.

The British physicist Lord Kelvin expressed related views of operationalism in the late 1800s (n.d.):

- "If you cannot measure it, you cannot improve it."
- "When you can measure what you are speaking about, and express it in numbers, you know something about it."
- "If you cannot measure it, then it is not science."

When speaking about social casework, Mary Richmond emphasized the importance of counting and measuring client phenomena: "Special efforts should be made to ascertain whether abnormal manifestations are *increasing* or *decreasing* in number and intensity, as this often has a practical bearing on the management of the case" ([1917] 1935, 435, my emphasis). A similar stricture obviously applies to larger-scale outcome evaluations.

Social work researchers are regularly making improvements to our measurement tools and technologies. Just as the measurement precision afforded by optical microscopes was dramatically enhanced by the development of the electron microscope, social work's unreliable movement scales of the 1940s were replaced with rapid assessment instruments with greater reliability and validity (see Fischer, Corcoran, and Springer 2020). Corresponding developments have been made in the reliability and validity of measures of observable human behavior. In some instances, assessments of physiological functioning are being used as outcome measures in social work experiments on the effects of psychotherapy (e.g., Hsiao et al. 2012).

It has been argued, and still is by some misguided souls, that human activities are too complex to be measured objectively. Bertha Capen Reynolds responded to this nihilistic position by saying, "In social work, there is this significant difference that the observer cannot avoid being a part of the social situation he is studying. *Special methods must be worked out* to take this factor into account" (1942, 23, my emphasis). Note that Reynolds did not abandon the idea of measuring people's actions validly; she just cautioned us to be aware of the problem and to address it with research and assessment methods intended to reduce observer bias and other threats to valid measurement.

This issue was also raised—and refuted—by Isidor Chein in his essay "On Some of the Difficulties of Doing Social Welfare Research," in which he notes that "many people still share the illusion that the uniqueness of each individual makes research in matters involving human behavior hopeless and meaningless. For if each person is unique, how can the study of one case yield information that is applicable to another? And how can conclusions arrived at in the study of one group of individuals be transferred to another?" (1959, 121).

If one accepts the philosophical principle of determinism, then at least some aspects of human behavior have potentially identifiable naturalistic causes, which if discovered may yield insights into ways to change human actions in a planned manner. The foundation of socialist and progressive thought is the belief that by creating sufficiently sound social policies, we can bring about improvements in people's lives—that is, we can exert control. The objection that people are unique falls apart pretty readily in some areas. For example, each snowflake is unique, as is each person's fingerprint. But this uniqueness does not mean that science cannot do research on snowflakes or fingerprints. The question of the applicability of scientific findings to others relates to the philosophical problem of *induction*: Just because the sun has risen in the east every day in the past, what assurance do we have it will rise in the east tomorrow? Philosophically we have none, but pragmatically it is a pretty good bet that the sun will rise in the east tomorrow. Science depends on the principle of replication to help address the problem of induction. David Edmonds writes, "If the inductive method helps us to build bridges (that do not collapse), cure diseases, land humans on the moon, then why worry about it? And the idea that it is never rational to use induction seems crazy" (2020, 256). The philosophical nihilist has little doubt that her feet will meet the floor when she gets up in the morning or that the bathroom light will turn on when she toggles the switch.

Similarly, if a scientific finding is reliably replicated, we can (provisionally) accept it as true (unless and until it is overturned by better evidence). If a given treatment has been demonstrated to help clients via credible randomized controlled studies, we can provisionally accept the premise that it is effective. Such studies form an important basis for the choice of treatments provided to clients (but they are not the sole consideration).

As has been asserted, clients have a right to effective treatment when such treatments are known to exist (Myers and Thyer 1997). This is a view held by Jayaratne and Levy: "The clinician would first be interested in using an intervention strategy that has been successful in the past. . . . When established techniques are available, they should be used but they should be based on objective evaluation rather than subjective feelings" (1979, 7). Tutty expresses similar sentiments: "It is important to provide the most effective treatment available. This entails professionals keeping current on the research on treatment effectiveness for their particular client populations" (1990, 13). This principle of the client's right to effective treatment is (loosely) codified in the *Code of Ethics of the National Association of Social Workers*: "Social workers should base practice on recognized knowledge, including empirically based knowledge, relevant to social work and social work ethics" (NASW 1996). This limp endorsement can be unfavorably contrasted with much stronger statements found in related health disciplines, such as that provided by the *Professional and Ethical Compliance Code for Behavior Analysts*: "Clients have a right to effective treatment (i.e., based on the research literature and adapted to the individual client). Behavior analysts always have the obligation to advocate for and educate the client about scientifically supported, most-effective treatment procedures. Effective treatment procedures have been validated as having both long-term and short-term benefits to clients and society" (BACB 2014). And, of course, determining which treatments actually have worked well in the past for people similar to your client is best undertaken by reviewing high-quality outcome studies.

Sometimes I hear students and practitioners objecting to doing research on some construct, let's call it X, because they think it cannot be measured. When I hear that, I ask, "Do you mean that in the entire history of humanity, no one has ever come up with a way to measure X? Or do you mean something like, 'I don't know of any way to measure X'?" Usually, humility causes these individuals to reassess their original view and acknowledge the truth of the latter statement. That gives me an opening to offer to help them find out if there is a way to measure X. We could look in compilations of rapid assessment instruments such as *Measures for Clinical Practice and Research* by Fischer, Corcoran, and Springer (2020) or *Practitioner's Guide to Empirically Based Measures of Depression* by Nezu et al. (2020). There are many such books. We could search the PsycINFO or APA PsycTests databases to locate relevant existing scales. No matter how obscure the concept, I am usually successful in helping my colleagues find one or more preexisting instruments they can use "off the shelf" so to speak. If not, perhaps we could develop some form of observational method to operationalize the subject. After all, how do we know something exists? Because people do it or talk about it, or there are some physical indicators like biological tests. It is certainly possible to measure observable behavior—and what people talk about, for example by conducting a thematic analysis of spoken content or reports of thoughts and feelings. Some areas of study such as critical race theory have been openly antagonistic toward efforts at quantitative measurement and have resisted the tenets of operationalism. However, more recently scholars have described how to conduct critical race theory research using quantitative methods that are completely compatible with the theory (Sablan 2019). The same is happening in other areas that have traditionally taken a solely qualitative approach to research, with a mixed-methods approach involving both qualitative and quantitative methods yielding more insights into analyses. The seventh edition of the *Publication Manual of the American Psychological Association* (APA 2020, 105–8) now contains guidelines on how to comprehensively report the design and conduct of mixed-methods research. Operationalism—it's a beautiful thing.

Scientific Materialism

Scientific materialism is the philosophical theory that physical matter and various forms of energy are fundamental realities and that all worldly and human phenomena can be explained in terms of physical matter and energy. Also known as *physicalism*, scientific materialism examines potential causes of human dysfunction (and well-being) solely in terms of natural phenomena. No attention is given to the idea that natural disasters are sent to destroy cities by an angry god (as suggested by some prominent religious leaders; for example, see NBC News 2005), any more than we lend credence to the idea that lightning strikes are caused by Zeus throwing thunderbolts down to the earth from Mount Olympus. The origins of pandemics like COVID-19 are sought in natural causes such as viruses, and prevention programs involve masking, physical distancing, sanitation, and the development of effective vaccinations—not prayers, supplications to heaven, or human sacrifices to appease angry gods. The field of psychotherapy seeks to account for human dysfunction and mental illness in terms of material conditions, learning history, external conditions, and biology, not demonic possession, although there are a few lamentable exceptions (e.g., Peck 2005).

Bruno states this physicalist position: "Social work is based essentially upon the first hypothesis: that all the person is, or does, or is capable of becoming is derived from his physical equipment, in which the brain is the significant element. . . . But the whole methodology of social work is strictly monistic. It is only thus that it can hold scientific hypotheses of human behavior or of human nature" (1936, 192).

Edmonds describes materialism in the following way: "Most philosophers insist that all facts must ultimately be grounded in physical facts. In that sense, colors and consciousness, though they may not initially seem physical, can nonetheless be accounted for in physicalist terms. There is no difference between brain states and mind states. Beliefs and desires and emotions are all reducible in some way to brain states" (2020, 261). This sense of the term is also found in *The Social Work Dictionary*: "Materialism: . . . in philosophy, the idea that reality is limited to the physical universe" (Barker 2014, 261). I take exception to this latter, somewhat overreaching definition because a philosophically informed scientist would be hesitant to say that *nothing* exists except for the physical universe. Science rarely claims that something does not exist. The scientist may claim that so far, the evidence does not support the existence of, say, ghosts, or that there is no credible evidence for the existence of ghosts, but she must remain open to the possibility, however unlikely, that ghosts may be real. Maybe heaven is indeed populated by angelic hosts. Because the scientist has no evidence either way, she should not venture an opinion on the topic when speaking professionally. (Over cocktails with friends is another matter.)

In social work, "scientific materialism" also refers to the position that the physical realities in which people find themselves are exceedingly import-ant and that improvements to these conditions are a primary focus of many forms of intervention. Hewes articulated this view simply more than ninety years ago: "I believe in materialism. I believe in all the proceeds of a healthy materialism, good cooking, dry houses, dry feet, sewers, drainpipes, hot water . . . long vacations away from the village pumps, new ideas . . . operas, orchestras, bands—I believe in them for everyone" (1930, 83). Jane Addams, one of the founders of social work and of the Hull-House community in Chicago, epitomized this material focus with her neighborhood sanitation campaigns and rodent abatement programs and with her advocacy for child labor laws and workplace safely. In contemporary times our national pol-icies pertaining to providing food assistance, public housing, health care, welfare payments, social security, and so forth are continuing manifesta-tions of the focus of social work on the material conditions of people's lives. Burghardt (1996) provides further views on the links between materialism and social work. The philosophical principle of materialism does not imply that a person's value should be measured by their physical possessions or that the acquisition of wealth should be the driving force in a person's life. This common view of materialism has nothing to do with the use of the term in the philosophy of science.

Many social workers hold nonmaterial views of human beings and of the causal factors in their lives. Indeed, there are professional groups of social workers aligned with various religious traditions, and from the founding of our field such individuals and faith-based groups have performed exemplary services. For example, the first settlement house, Toynbee Hall, was a Christian missionary outreach effort in late-nineteenth-century London. Jane Addams's visits there inspired her to establish the more secular American equivalent, Hull-House, which in turn led to the establishment of dozens more settlement houses in the larger American cities. Religious groups such as the Salvation Army have housed and fed homeless people for almost 150 years, and the Boy Scouts have served youth around the world for almost as long. The Church of Jesus Christ of Latter-day Saints has an extensive social welfare program for members of their church as well as nonmembers and is often the first on the scene to provide material assistance after natural disasters (Rudd 1995). Scien-tifically minded, secular social workers generally welcome and applaud these efforts, and nothing in any scientific philosophy requires hostility toward reli-gion. We are mindful that our positions are axioms that cannot be proved to be true. Perhaps the world in which we believe we live is like the one in the movie The Matrix: an artificial dream created by a computer. Or perhaps we are sleep-ing, and what we believe to be the world around us is present only in a lengthy dream. As René Descartes famously asked, "How can you be certain that your whole life is not a dream?" This is a possibility, one that is exceedingly difficult to prove or disprove (at least until I take the red pill or wake up). In both my professional and personal lives, I have friends who hold spiritual views much different from mine, which I frankly (but privately) think are wrong, but I do not make it my business to try to correct their views and make them believe as I do. Everyone is entitled to the spiritual views that make sense to them or have been inspired solely by faith, not rationality. But when behavioral scientists undertake research into the causes of psychosocial problems or into the mechanisms of action of psychosocial interventions, the conventional philosophy of science disavows any attempt to make use of supernatural or metaphysical explanations.

Parsimony

The principle of *parsimony* refers to a preference to consider the simpler of the available and adequate explanations of a phenomenon prior to accepting a more complex account. This view is exemplified by Occam's razor: "originally a form of the more general principle of parsimony stating that 'entities should not be multiplied beyond necessity.' In this case 'entities' refers to demons, spirits, or anything invoked to explain phenomena" (Corsini 2002, 659). William of Occam also put it another way: "It is vain to do with more what can be done with less." For example, if someone is acting in a bizarre way, it would make more sense to first check to see if they have a high fever, have recently ingested hallucinatory drugs, are dehydrated, or are acting before considering that they are having a psychotic break or have been possessed by an evil spirit. This principle is also expressed by the aphorism, "If you hear hoofbeats, think of horses, not zebras." One should be stingy with assumptions. If something can be adequately explained by factor A alone, there is no need to explain it by invoking factors A and B. Parsimony is the use of the fewest assumptions needed to explain something. More than one hundred years ago, physics postulated the existence of an invisible medium called the ether, through which light traveled (as well as everything else). With time and research, this hypothesis was disproved and is no longer used as an explanation for the transmission of light. Parsimony does not mean a preference for only *simpler* explanations but rather for the *simpler* of the *adequate* explanations.

When building theories in social work, we should make use of as few mechanisms as needed to get the job done well. And when investigating claims relating to treatment, try to rule out unneeded processes. For example, the theory of EMDR originally included the hypothesis that bilateral eye movements were essential to treatment success, and this had been supported by studies showing that EMDR with bilateral eye movements resulted in people improving. Subsequently various experimental studies of EMDR with and without eye movements showed that similar improvements were obtained without them; hence, the mechanism of action of EMDR has had one unnecessary entity (factor) excluded.

As mentioned in chapter 2, an early theory of systematic desensitization said that pairing imaginal exposure to frightening situations with progressive relaxation was crucial to the success of this approach. And early work showed that traditional systematic desensitization did help people. But when it was tested with and without progressive relaxation, people improved just as much without progressive relaxation, demonstrating that this explanatory factor was not needed to explain the positive results of systematic desensitization. Also as discussed in chapter 2, facilitated communication was intended to help people with autism spectrum disorder (ASD) communicate by typing with a "facilitator" holding their hand above a keyboard. However, skeptical scientists conducted blind tests that showed that the facilitators had been guiding the hands of the people they were meant to be helping; none of the communication had come from the individuals with ASD. The evidence was so strong that professional disability and mental health professional associations have since condemned the practice of facilitated communication.

Parsimony can guide our assessments. If a person has a specific phobia, for example, it makes sense to initially explore their learning history. Take a phobia of snakes. Has the client been harmed or severely frightened by an encounter with a live snake? Have they seen a scary movie or read a scary book involving snakes? Did they witness a parent or sibling react with terror when encountering a snake? The answers to such queries may be negative, but these types of questions are worth exploring since research into the etiology of phobias finds that in a large percentage of cases, such an event triggered the onset of the phobia (Merckelbach et al. 1996). Conditioning as an explanation for the etiology of a specific phobia is a more parsimonious theory than those invoking more complex assumptions and is therefore preferred.

Now let's contrast these ideas with those behind psychoanalytic theory. According to Freedman, Kaplan, and Sadock (1976),

Freud viewed the phobic neurosis as resulting from conflicts centered on an unresolved childhood oedipal situation. In the adult the sexual drive continues to have a strong incestuous coloring, and its arousal tends to arouse anxiety. The anxiety then alerts the ego to exert repression to keep the drive away from conscious representation and discharge. When repression fails to be entirely successful in its function, the ego must call on auxiliary defenses. In phobia patients, these defenses involve primarily the use of displacement. The sexual conflict is displaced from the person who evokes the conflict to a seemingly unimportant, irrelevant object or situation, which now has the power to arouse the entire constellation of affects, including signal anxiety. The phobic object or situation selected usually has a direct associative connection with the primary source of the conflict.

(625–26)

The authors further explain that "phobias about infection and touching often express the need to avoid dirt and show that the person has to defend themselves against anal-erotic temptation. Fear of open streets and stage fright may be defenses against exhibitionistic wishes" (Freedman, Kaplan, and Sadock 1976, 259).

The etiological factors involved in a psychodynamic explanation of a phobia are both multiple and complex: neurosis, conflict, oedipal situation, ego, repression, defenses, discharge, displacement, sexual conflict, anal-erotic temptation, exhibitionistic wishes. When such an account is contrasted with the simpler explanation of conditioning, the differences are striking. In this case, empirical research on the etiologies of specific phobias clearly supports the more parsimonious approach to conceptualizing a client's fear.

Parsimonious explanations are not always the correct ones, but science suggests investigating them and ruling them out before investigating more complex accounts. Parsimony has clinical implications, too: a clinician adopting an etiological explanation of learning for their client's phobia may suggest treatment with the well-established method called gradual real-life exposure therapy, which has been shown to provide considerable benefit to most clients in a relatively brief period of time (Thyer 1987). A clinician who makes use of psychoanalytic etiological theory may subject the client to a lengthy and expensive treatment involving psychoanalysis, an approach with little empirical evidence of effectiveness in resolving phobias (Zane 1984).

Parsimony also has research implications, beginning with the initial stages of the research process. If an opportunity is given to investigate the validity of some tenets of an etiological *theory* that is exceedingly implausible, the researcher may simply decline to pursue that study, perhaps justly deeming it a waste of time and resources. Similarly, if an opportunity arises to test an extremely implausible *therapy*, based upon prior research, theory, and ethical considerations, they may opt not to devote energy to work in that area. A wild-eyed inventor with a new idea for a perpetual motion machine will have a hard time finding legitimate researchers to collaborate with them. Likewise, someone who claims to have invented a psychotherapy that will "cure" same-sex attraction would probably not be able to find credible clinical researchers to design a study to test this supposed "therapy" or sponsors to fund it. Such investigations would be seen as extremely unlikely to yield valid findings, since the existing research-based evidence mitigates against the legitimacy of such ideas. Epstein (1984) provides a particularly erudite exposition of the value of parsimony: "A modern principle of parsimony may be stated as follows: When we have no reason to do otherwise and where two theories account for the same facts, we should prefer the one which is briefer, which makes assumptions with which we can easily dispense, which refers to observables, and which has the greatest possible generality" (119).

Parsimony can also guide our choice of research design. To control for the influence of the placebo effect in a study of a particular psychotherapy, some participants should be randomly assigned to receive a sham, or placebo, therapy. If we do not do this, we cannot exclude the possibility that any positive outcomes are a result of placebo influences. Similarly if one wishes to test the comparative effectiveness of two therapies using a randomized experiment and both appear to yield equivalent results, one might conclude that both are equally effective. However, the damned scientific skeptic will come along and say, "Perhaps both treatments are effective because of placebo influences. You should have used a placebo control group." And she would be right. You would need a third group to control for that more parsimonious accounting of your results. Back to the drawing board!

Rationalism

Rationalism is the belief that reason and logic are useful tools for scientific inquiry and that truthful accounts of human behavior are rational or logically understandable. From the perspective of science, both theories and treatment effectiveness should be rationally understandable. Mechanisms and processes should be able to be understood by reasonable people. To continue to support a theory or treatment that considerable sound evidence shows to be false or ineffective is seen as irrational and encourages the proliferation and application of pseudoscientific treatments by social workers. Supporters of the view that the earth is flat are generally seen as irrational, given the preponderance of evidence proving that it is more or less round.

The field of experimental research in social work relies on logic to make inferences regarding causation, the etiologies of disorders, and the effects of interventions. The English philosopher John Stuart Mill provided some early examples of the type of logical reasoning used to help determine causation, and he propounded five types of logical reasoning that form the basis for causal inference via experimental (and some nonexperimental) methods. One is called the *direct method of agreement*, which states that "if two or more instances of the phenomenon under investigation have only one circumstance in common, the circumstance in which alone the instances agree, is the cause (or effect) of the given phenomenon" (Mill 1843, 454).

Imagine a group of people with a particular disorder. If careful histories are taken and one thing is shown to be common to everyone, then that factor is provisionally considered to be a causal agent. Let's say you hosted a party and served hamburgers and cheeseburgers. The next day, a friend calls to tell you she became sick after your party. You ask what she ate, and she says a cheeseburger. If you then call everyone who attended the party and find out that all those who had eaten a cheeseburger got sick, whereas those who had eaten a hamburger were fine, you'd have logical grounds, according to Mill's logic, to infer that it was the cheese that had made people sick.

A less clear-cut example involves investigating the etiology of pedophilia among adults. If your research revealed that a large proportion of adult pedophiles had themselves been victims of childhood sexual abuse, that would be tentative evidence that the experience of childhood sexual abuse leads to the development of pedophilia as an adult. Stronger evidence could be obtained for this provisional hypothesis by also interviewing a large number of adults who are *not* known to be pedophiles. If you found that the experience of childhood sexual abuse was the same among both groups, your hypothesis of an association between childhood sexual abuse and adult pedophilia would be weakened. But if few nonpedophiles reported having been sexually abused while young, the hypothesis would be strengthened. If this finding were then replicated in other localities, countries, and cultures, as well as among both men and women, the hypothesis would be strengthened even further. However, it is important to note that this would be strictly correlational evidence, as would also be the case in the cheeseburger example.

It would not be ethical to deliberately feed a random half of your guests hamburgers with tainted cheese and the other half hamburgers without cheese to see who, if anyone, got sick. It would provide stronger experimental evidence but is not something we'd want to do. Fear not, however, as we do not always require experimental evidence to draw causal inferences. For example, we are confident that smoking causes lung cancer (or at least greatly increases the risk of developing it). But no one has done an experiment in which a large group of young people forced to become smokers and another group forced to abstain from smoking are followed for forty years to assess the prevalence of lung cancer. It would provide good evidence, but it would not be ethical. So we rely on other evidence. We determine the smoking history of people with and without lung cancer and find that many more people with lung cancer are smokers—this is evidence. We identify adolescents who choose to smoke and those who do not and follow them over decades. If we find that the prevalence of lung cancer is higher among the smokers than the nonsmokers, this too is evidence. We look at the prevalence of smoking and lung cancer in other countries. If the prevalence of lung cancer is higher in countries with higher rates of smoking, this is evidence. We look at the prevalence of lung cancer among groups

generally known not to smoke, say Mormons, and compare them with demographically similar groups with a high rate of smoking. If the prevalence of lung
cancer is much lower among the Mormon group, this is evidence. As findings
like these are replicated across decades and countries, a causal link is generally
inferred despite the absence of experimental studies. So, although experiments
are a useful route to making causal inferences, they are not the only way.

Another way to draw causal inferences according to Mill is the *method of difference*: "If an instance in which the phenomenon under investigation occurs,
and an instance in which it does not occur, have every circumstance save one
in common, that one occurring only in the former; the circumstance in which
alone the two instances differ, is the effect, or cause, or an indispensable part of
the cause, of the phenomenon" (1843, 455).

Take a job-finding program. You recruit a number of unemployed people
and randomly assign them to the experimental job-finding program or to
no program. After the intervention concludes, say three months, you assess
employment again. The two groups were identical at the beginning of the study,
in terms of not only employment status but also other relevant variables. If the
treatment group has a much higher rate of employment following the intervention, and the only difference between the groups is participation in the
job-finding program, you can infer that this one difference, the treatment, is the
cause of higher employment.

Another of Mill's principles is the *method of residue*: "Subduct [subtract]
from any phenomenon such part as is known by previous inductions to be the
effect of certain antecedents, and the residue of the phenomenon is the effect of
the remaining antecedents" (1843, 465).

Say you have a group of study participants with depression. You randomly
assign half to a real treatment, say cognitive therapy, and the other half to a treatment not known to positively impact depression but is a credible placebo therapy,
say progressive relaxation training. You look at outcomes after the study has
concluded. You subtract any improvements seen among the placebo-assigned
participants from the improvements demonstrated by those in the active-treatment
group, and the remainder is the presumptive impact of the real treatment.

A fourth principle of Mill's is the *joint method of agreement and difference*:
"If two or more instances in which the phenomenon occurs have only one circumstance in common, while two or more instances in which it does not occur
have nothing in common save the absence of that circumstance; the circumstance in which alone the two sets of instances differ, is the effect, or cause, or a
necessary part of the cause, of the phenomenon" (1843, 463).

Let's look at an example of a study of the effects of exposure to various
factors in childhood associated with certain outcomes in adulthood. If child
abuse, paternal alcoholism, and low socioeconomic status (we'll call these factors A, B, and C, respectively) are associated with aggression (D), poor school

performance (E), and poor social skills (F) later in life, and if child abuse (A), being raised in a single-parent family (G), and shyness (H) are associated with later aggression (D), thumb-sucking (I), and self-cutting (J), we can infer that the cause of aggression (D) is child abuse, since child abuse is common only to the outcome of aggression. Put simply, if $A + B + C = D + E + F$, and if $A + G + H = D + I + J$, then we can infer that A causes D. This line of reasoning does not deal with what are called *intersecting* or *multivariate lines of causation*, but these can be controlled for and investigated using various research designs.

Mill's fifth principle is the *method of concomitant variations*: "Whatever phenomenon varies in any manner whenever another phenomenon varies in some particular manner, is either a cause or an effect of that phenomenon or is connected with it through some fact of causation" (1843, 470).

We can think of a dose–response relationship to understand the reasoning behind this principle. For many years, people smoke along a continuum ranging from never to many times each day. If the likelihood of developing lung cancer is consistently shown to increase as the intensity of smoking increases, there is certainly a correlation. By adding to this correlation other lines of evidence, as discussed earlier, we may be able to arrive at a causal inference.

Research studies using the well-known Adverse Childhood Experiences Scale (Dong et al. 2005) have demonstrated that the more adverse events children experience, and the more intense those experiences, the more stress, dysfunction, and psychopathology they are likely to experience in adulthood. Numerous studies in many countries have demonstrated this correlation, so much so that a causal link has been reasonably inferred: "Clearly, a number of research studies, along with the extensive findings from the ACE [Adverse Childhood Event] Study, indicate that childhood physical, sexual, and emotional abuse, as well as neglect, are risk factors for an array of adverse mental health consequences in childhood and adulthood alike" (Chapman, Dube, and Anda 2007, 364).

This brings us to the often-mentioned admonition that correlation does not equal causation. Causes *are*, to be sure, correlated with many antecedent factors, but most antecedent factors are not themselves causes. To infer causation from among correlated variables, we must exclude or rule out those factors that are only correlated and not causal. By eliminating all rival hypotheses, we gradually narrow in on nature's truth and hopefully emerge with one potential candidate cause that has withstood all attempts to disprove or falsify it. A mental disorder in adulthood cannot plausibly be said to have caused an experience of abuse in childhood, but a case can be made for the reverse. In scientific inferences, any presumed cause must have occurred *before* an event (Hill 1965). Sir Bradford Hill established clear criteria for inferring causality that have been widely adopted in epidemiological work among many disciplines. In addition to temporal order, Hill laid out other forms of evidence that can be used to help us arrive at conclusions regarding cause-and-effect relationships. Some of these include the following:

- *Strength of association*: Stronger associations are greater grounds for inferring causality than are weaker associations. If it were found that only 10 percent of the perpetrators of interpersonal violence had witnessed such violence as children, this association would be less convincing evidence that childhood exposure causes adults to commit interpersonal violence than if it were found that 90 percent of perpetrators had witnessed such violence as children.
- *Consistency*: Inferring a causal link between an apparent etiology and some later problem across many settings (e.g., populations, countries) provides stronger evidence than a link found in only one setting.
- *Plausibility*: A clear and logical mechanism of action exists between a presumed cause and its effect, some theoretical (if not empirical) rationale that makes sense. Proposed explanations that involve pseudoscientific accounts are rarely seriously entertained.
- *Coherence*: Many sources of evidence provide greater support for causation. Numerous studies helped establish the link between smoking and lung cancer, including animal experiments, human epidemiological studies, quasi-experimental case-control and cohort studies, and international studies.
- *Dose–Response Relationship*: The longer a person smokes, the more likely it is that they will develop lung cancer; the more psychotherapy a person receives, the more likely it is that they will experience improvements.
- *Reversibility*: With treatment, a person's problem improves; when treatment is stopped, the problem worsens. And this finding can be replicated. For example, a child given a stimulant medication on school days demonstrates better behavior than on weekends when she does not take the medication. And this pattern is repeated over time. For example, when points are given to students for being present in class, attendance is higher than when points are not given. Such evidence would support the hypothesis that giving points for attendance reduces absenteeism.
- *Experiment*: The strongest evidence for a causal relationship is provided by a well-crafted experiment. Properly designed and conducted experiments can provide the most robust evidence of causality owing to their ability to control for sources of bias. In Hill's words, "Here the strongest support for the causation hypothesis may be revealed" (1965, 298–99).

Hill was clear that these criteria were not definitive or absolute but that they were good benchmarks to help us make decisions about causal hypotheses: "All scientific work is incomplete—whether it be observational or experimental. All scientific work is liable to be upset or modified by advancing knowledge. That does not confer upon us a freedom to ignore the knowledge we already have, or to postpone the action that it appears to demand at a given time" (1965, 12). Hill's criteria remain influential in assessing causal evidence: "We agree that Bradford Hill's criteria remain, half a century after their description, relevant factors that influence our confidence in a causal relation" (Schünemann et al. 2011, 393). Deming (1975) and Sidman (1960) are two sources I particularly value for their cogent explanations of scientific logic.

Positivism

The term *positivism* is often bandied about in the social work literature, incorrectly in many instances and used as a scapegoat by advocates of postmodernist philosophies (see Bolland and Atherton 2002). As always, it is good to consult authoritative resources to clarify terms. For example, Corsini defines positivism as "a philosophical doctrine that knowledge is limited to observed facts and what can be deduced from those facts: an approach that underlies empiricism and behaviorism and rejects metaphysical speculation" (2002, 740). In their influential social work textbook, Rubin and Babbie describe positivism as "a paradigm introduced by Auguste Comte, which held that social behavior could be studied and understood in a rational, scientific manner, in contrast to explanations based on religion or superstition" (2008, 642). It is important to note that this principle applies to knowledge about the natural world only, not other forms of knowledge such as ethical, legal, or theological knowledge. Science does not weigh in on the nature of God. Is she a monotheistic being? A triune being? A polytheistic being? As Ludwig Wittgenstein said in *Tractatus Logico-Philosophicus*, "Whereof one cannot speak one must be silent" (1922, 6.54). Science has no purview over the nature of God or whether certain religious views are correct. It is similarly quiet about the legitimacy of ethical principles and legal reasoning. These are important areas of human life, including the lives of social workers and their clients, and should not be ignored in good practice. But they are not issues amenable to scientific investigation, verification, or refutation. Positivism attempted to elevate the study of human phenomena out of the mists of obscurity by applying the tools of science to investigations of other features of the natural world, such as animals, plants, microorganisms, the earth, other planets, and elements of the solar system.

Positivism was introduced in the early 1800s in France by Auguste Comte, who initially labeled his approach to understanding people "social physics," based on his hope that human science could eventually move closer to the precision of physics. However, the term never caught on, so Comte coined the term "sociology" for what he hoped would become a legitimate discipline. Sociology thrives today, although sometimes in a form far removed from Comte's vision.

Mary Pickering (1993) lays out some of the positions of positivism in her biography of Comte:

> The word *positive* came from *ponere* and had been employed since the fourteenth
> century to mean *laid down*. In the sixteenth century, it began to refer to
> knowledge that was based on facts and was thus reasonably certain. Eighteenth
> century thinkers used the word positive to oppose the *metaphysical*. . . . Unlike
> theological beliefs, scientific truths could be proved if necessary. . . . Scientific
> *truths* were always provisional because they could be proved wrong at any
> time. . . . Scientific laws were only *hypotheses* constructed by man with *exter-*
> *nal materials* and confirmed by observation; they amounted to no more than
> approximations of a reality that could never be rigorously understood. . . .
> Social science was not . . . just an intellectual mixture of history, the phys-
> ical sciences, physiology, and political economy. It has a practical vocation:
> *to regenerate society*. . . . Although Comte admitted that we could never fully
> know external reality, he assumed that scientific theories were getting closer to
> representing it *exactly*.
>
> (65, 294, 296, emphasis in the original)

Comte's positivism had an enormous influence on the establishment of the
American Social Science Association in 1865, especially its emphasis on using
social science knowledge to remedy society's ills and improve the human condition (Haskell 1997). From this association came the Conference on Charities (1879), the National Conference on Charities and Corrections (1884), the
National Conference on Social Work (1917), and the National Conference on
Social Welfare (1957), which later dissolved after the founding of the National
Association of Social Workers in 1955. Glashow provides a succinct summary
of contemporary positivism: "We believe that the world is knowable, that there
are simple rules governing the behavior of matter and the evolution of the
universe. We affirm that there are eternal, objective, extrahistorical, socially
neutral, external and universal truths, and that the assemblage of these truths
is what we call . . . science. Natural laws can be discovered that are universal,
invariable, inviolate, genderless and verifiable. They may be found by men or
women" (1989, 24E).

It has occurred to me that Glashow's words are a scientist's version of the
Nicene Creed, a statement of belief asserted to be true by many Christians.
Can the beliefs stated in the Nicene Creed be proved to be true? No, they are
accepted as valid by an act of belief and cannot be subjected to a scientific
analysis of their legitimacy. Similarly, scientists who adopt positivism as a
principle (not all do, although it is a mainstream position) openly acknowledge that their philosophical beliefs are similarly incapable of ultimate validation. Can we prove the truthfulness of realism or determinism? No. But the

proof of the pudding is in the eating. Are the *products* of scientific inquiry guided by positivism and the other philosophical principles outlined in this chapter capable of replication and of the development of provisionally certain knowledge? Including determining the true effectiveness of social work policies and practices? Yes. And because these building blocks of science, philosophical tools if you will, have proved to be so valuable, social work scientists (notice that "social work" comes first) undergo the lengthy time it takes to become MSW-level practitioners and then obtain further doctoral-level education usually (though not always) needed to become effective behavioral and social science researchers. Why do they take this steep and thorny path? Because they have the same vision as did Auguste Comte: to improve society and the welfare of individuals. Are there competing points of view regarding philosophies of science? There are many, and some are quite strident. However, positivists tend to adopt something analogous to article 11 of the Articles of Faith of the Mormon Church: "We claim the privilege of worshipping Almighty God according to the dictate of our own conscience, and allow all men the same privilege, let them worship how, where, or what they may" (LDS n.d.).

Positivists have their views on a functional set of principles to guide their research. They are pretty sure they are useful, but if others wish to pursue other ideas, they are free to do so without critique from mainstream scientists. Let each tend to her own garden and see the respective harvests. Are you listening, postmodernists?

Scientific Skepticism

The principle of *scientific skepticism* is the idea of learning about new ideas with an attitude of "doubt, not denial." If a new therapy is promoted, the scientific skeptic says something like, "That's an interesting idea. Where are your data?" Scientific skepticism was promoted by the Scottish enlightenment philosopher David Hume, who said,

When anyone tells me that he saw a dead man restored to life, I immediately consider with myself whether it be more probable that this person should either deceive or be deceived or that the fact which he relates should really have happened. I weigh the one miracle against the other and according to the superiority which I discover, I pronounce my decision. Always I reject the greater miracle. If the falsehood of his testimony would be more miraculous than the event which he relates, then and not till then, can he pretend to command my belief or opinion.

(1748, x)

When it is claimed that people with severe ASD are suddenly able to communicate intelligently via typing when their hand is held above a keyboard by a facilitator, several explanations are available. One is that the facilitator is *deliberately* deceiving observers. Another is that the facilitator is *unknowingly* guiding the person's fingers over the keyboard. A third is that an intelligent person who had been trapped in an uncooperative body is now able to express himself owing to treatment with facilitated communication. The third explanation contravenes much of what is known about the nature of ASD and as such would require considerable evidence in support of it before Hume and other scientific skeptics would consider accepting it. As we have learned, evidence does not support this explanation (Heinzen et al. 2015).

In the 1980s, a horrific series of sexual abuse allegations arose from the McMartin preschool in California. Many children were said to have been forced to undergo anal sex and participate in orgies and satanic rituals in tunnels under the school, among other appalling claims. The original allegation was made by the angry divorced spouse of one of the McMartin teachers and spurred an extensive series of interviews of all the children, teachers, and other staff. The allegations, supposedly supported by the children's eyewitness testimony, resulted in an infamous court case. There are several possible explanations for these allegations and testimony. One is that a group of Satanists abused the children. Another is that the allegations were made up and that the children's testimony was strongly guided by interviewers (including social workers) who believed the charges. In the end, the latter explanation was supported (Garven, Wood, and Malpass 2000; Wyatt 2002). More recently, the QAnon conspiracy theories, unsupported allegations of a cult of worshippers of Satan, cannibalistic pedophiles, and sex traffickers plotting against Donald Trump were so absurd as to rise to reasoned skepticism, similar to that engendered by the McMartin preschool case.

When we are told that a woman named Sybil was found to have sixteen personalities (in what is one of the most famous cases of so-called multiple personality disorder) and that this diagnosis and her treatment were based on scientifically discredited theories (Schreiber 1973), two explanations are possible. One is that sixteen discrete personalities did inhabit this person's body. Another is that the whole thing was faked so that the patient and her psychiatrist could earn money and become famous. It turns out that the latter explanation was true, as disclosed by the parties involved (see Nathan 2011). The older diagnosis of multiple personality disorder has been transmogrified in recent years into dissociative identity disorder. However, simply relabeling something the existence of which is in doubt does not resolve those doubts, and serious questions remain about the validity of the condition (Paris 2019). Similar skepticism is warranted regarding a variety of otherworldly claims such as the existence of UFOs, Bigfoot, and ghosts. History suggests an approach of examining the evidence both for and against the phenomenon in question, but initial outright denials are rare in science (and correctly so).

I was raised in south Florida, where for years a creature called the Skunk Ape, akin to Bigfoot, was said to reside in the Everglades. One can stop at a roadside shop in south Florida and purchase a video purporting to show the Skunk Ape walking in a Florida swamp. Such videos and other similar "evidence," including photographs, hair samples, and casts of footprints, have all been shown to be hoaxes. But does this history of falsification prove that the Florida Skunk Ape does not exist? No at all. It is like saying there is no such thing as a black swan. All it takes is one example to prove the reality of black swans. Perhaps one day, the Skunk Ape will be captured and shown to be a real primate of a previously unknown species. Until that happens, the proprietor of the Skunk Ape shop can continue to earn a nice living selling his videos and the pamphlets he wrote describing his encounters with the creature and offering expensive Skunk Ape "hunts" in swamp buggies to gullible tourists. As with the cases of the McMartin preschool and Sybil's many personalities, we await credible evidence that the Skunk Ape exists. The fact that the claims involved in these cases were proved to be untrue does not prove that satanic ritual abuse never occurs or that multiple personality disorder does not exist. Similarly, the absence of evidence to date does not prove the Skunk Ape is a myth. Perhaps, just perhaps, the next sighting will be real!

Keep in mind that a principle of scientific skepticism is that the burden of proof rests on the person making the claim. It is not up to the skeptic to prove the claim wrong. So when someone comes up with a new therapy for social workers to adopt, our attitude should not be, "It does not work" (even though most new therapies do not work), but rather the reasonable question, "What is your evidence?" Until reasonable evidence is provided, any claims of effectiveness should be considered of doubtful validity. Skepticism also takes into account theoretical plausibility. Any new treatment that invokes mysterious energies that have not yet been validly detected gives rise to more doubts than a treatment based on established principles of legitimacy. As Hume said, the more implausible the claim, the greater the amount of evidence needed to support it. Blurry photos or ambiguous radar images of UFOs do not prove the existence of flying saucers. Having one land in front of the White House might be sufficient evidence—if trained scientists can investigate it. Science cannot prove that a new treatment would never work. It might fail in study after study after study, but that does not mean it will not work the next time. It is far more profitable to show that something *does* work by providing the evidence asked for by the skeptical scientist. And if it is good evidence, it will be accepted. Many previously unsupported complementary and alternative medicines have been shown to have value. What do we call a complementary medicine with scientific support? Medicine. But treatments that have been around for a long time with little scientific support, and much evidence that they do not work and are based on scientifically implausible theories, arouse the ire of people genuinely concerned with the well-being of clients seeking help. Examples of treatments that refuse to die despite lack of evidence and implausible mechanisms of action include homeopathy, chiropractic, magnetic healing, the laying on of hands, psychic healing, naturopathy, facilitated communication, holding therapies, therapy using crystals, acupuncture, and so-called energy therapies (see Pignotti and Thyer 2009; Thyer and Pignotti 2015). The attitude of scientific skepticism should be invoked whenever a new therapy is introduced into the field, or a new widespread social policy is proposed. Good evidence should precede practice, not be belatedly sought after huge sums have been expended upon it.

Scientific skepticism is also intimately related to the principle of parsimony. Did Sybil really have sixteen distinct personalities? Or was she a disturbed young person who was making up things as she went along to garner attention and money? Did the entrepreneurial man in the Everglades really see the Skunk Ape and film it, or did he make it up to earn money from tourists?

The magician Harry Houdini investigated dozens of mediums who claimed to communicate with the dead. Time after time he proved fakery was afoot (Houdini 1924). What if a new medium comes forth? What would parsimony suggest? The biggest proponents of facilitated communication built their careers on teaching and delivering the technique, earning money and earning respect and prestige. Thanks to scientific skepticism, Janice Boynton, a practitioner of facilitated communication, became a nonbeliever based on her personal experience and a review of the scientific evidence (Boynton 2012). Similarly, the social worker Monica Pignotti was closely involved at the highest levels with the bogus treatment called thought field therapy (TFT), one of the supposed "energy therapies." As outrageous claims expanded regarding implausibly large numbers of unrelated conditions TFT was said to cure, she designed and conducted her own randomized experiment comparing real TFT with a similar placebo treatment. She clearly showed that TFT was itself essentially a placebo treatment. She brought her results to the attention of the founder of TFT, with whom she had worked closely for more than five years. His refusal to entertain the possibilities that the theory of TFT was incorrect and that the treatment was fraudulent led Pignotti to break with the practice and pursue a PhD in social work focusing on exposing quack treatments (see Pignotti 2007). Both Boynton and Pignotti deserve credit for their courage in exposing pseudoscientific treatments after years of personal belief and involvement in such methods. David Hume advised that "a wise man proportions his belief to the evidence." This was good advice in the 1700s and good advice now. Skepticism is central to the scientific attitude. As Anastas and MacDonald assert, "All activities called scientific are undertaken in a spirit of skepticism" (1994, 7).

Progressivism

Social work researchers are inherently progressive. The perspective of *progressivism* is shared by scientific efforts that aim to improve the human condition. Far more scientists work toward helping humanity than harming it, despite the anomalies of the Nazi doctors who experimented on concentration camp prisoners (Lifton 2017) and the psychologists who collaborated with the Central Intelligence Agency to devise effective forms of torture (Welch 2017). Behavioral scientists and social workers seek to design and conduct research studies to understand the causes of individual and social pathologies, as well as normative human development. The hope is to develop effective preventive programs and policies and treatments that can help humanity. Governments, at least democratic ones (in theory), are meant to promote the general welfare of their citizens and in contemporary times are explicitly supportive of scientific inquiry. For example, in 2016 the US federal government, through bipartisan efforts, established the Commission on Evidence-Based Policy Making (HHS n.d.).

We regularly hear calls for state and federal government initiatives to be based on scientific evidence. The reduction of social injustices such as racism, gender bias, and poverty can be helpfully brought about via empirical data collection (e.g., police killings of Black people, gender disparities in salaries) and then addressed via preventive and interventive initiatives tested and validated using small-scale pilot evaluation studies before being expanded state- or nationwide. Behavioral and social science are ideally positioned to promote such efforts, and this is being done through many state and federal agencies and nongovernmental organizations. Social work science very much has an applied focus, in keeping with the profession's pragmatic orientation. It is aimed at solving problems, not simply discovering knowledge. As Goldstein states, "Progress is the benchmark of science" (1992, 48).

Principles Science Does Not Usually Endorse

The philosophy of science typically disavows some common views. (In the interests of parsimony, this section will be much briefer than the previous one.)

Anecdotalism

Anecdotes are case illustrations of something, as in "This treatment cured me; therefore, I recommend it," or "My baby developed autism right after receiving a vaccine. People should avoid vaccines because they cause autism." Single instances, even when plentiful, cannot usually prove a case. No matter how many people achieve sobriety after joining Alcoholics Anonymous (AA), this evidence alone is a thin reed upon which to base a claim of AA's effectiveness. You also need to know how many members of AA have not become sober, as well as the numbers of people with alcoholism who are not members of AA who have become and who have not become sober. It is only when all four sources of information are available can we make a possibly legitimate causal inference about the effectiveness of AA. This example is a type of controlled comparison. Sometimes anecdotal stories reflect truth, and sometimes they reflect error. The major problem with anecdotes is that there is no way to sift the truthful ones from the false ones. Accumulated cases of infants who supposedly developed autism after receiving vaccinations cannot ever prove that vaccinations cause autism (they do not). Nor do many stories of supposed religious healing experiences prove that a particular faith healer is a true servant of God with divine hands. The first case history of a person with tuberculosis who was cured following treatment with the newly developed antibiotic streptomycin reported a truthful finding. But this could not be confirmed simply by reporting a series of successful outcomes. It was confirmed only through rigorous studies comparing streptomycin with no treatment (because many disorders are self-limiting), with a placebo, and with treatment as usual and then following people for years. Only then could the efficacy of streptomycin be said to be firmly established. Testimonies by themselves are usually incapable of proving anything. They can be true. Or false.

Nihilism

Nihilism is the belief that all values are baseless and that nothing is knowable or can be communicated. At its extreme, nihilism says that nothing can be known with any certainty, a position called Pyrrhonian skepticism, named after its advocate, Pyrrho of Elis (about 370–271 BCE). This suspension of judgment is fine for the professional philosopher, but for the science-minded social worker, we need information to take action, to provide a therapy or promote a policy. We must make choices based on available evidence, even though it may not be perfect evidence. A disguised form of nihilism can be found in social work among those who grandly claim that all therapies are of equal value, that all research methods produce equally credible findings, or that all social work theories have equal merit. The first instance can be labeled *theoretical nihilism*. Francis Turner, the editor of one of social work's most comprehensive textbooks on theory, says that "we argue that *all* the various approaches to strengthening our theoretical base that have been taken over the past six decades are valuable in themselves. *No one is better than another*" (1996, 9, my emphasis). Seriously? Were the racist theories adopted by the Nazified social work profession in the

1930s and early 1940s *valuable* contributions to our knowledge base (Kunstre-ich 2003; Barney and Dalton 2008)? Were Freud's ideas about the development of same-sex attraction useful in any therapeutic sense? Indeed, they were not, and their harmful consequences continue to linger today in the form of the ongoing stigma experienced by gay people. Any contemporary biologist who claimed that the discredited theoretical doctrines of Lamarckism or Lysenko-ism were on a par with Darwin's theory of evolution via natural selection would have a very hard time finding an academic position. Science is about making judgments, trying to determine fact from fiction, and separating the credible from the incredible. Absent a sound foundation of research, judgment on cer-tain issues should be suspended. But once the evidence is obtained, decisions must be made.

Nihilism also takes form in the *equality of therapies*, the contention that all conventional psychotherapies yield equal results, so it makes no difference which techniques we employ because the result will be the same no matter what, and they will usually be positive. As said by the social worker Stanley Witkin, "Virtually any intervention can be justified on the grounds that it has as much support as alternative methods" (1991, 158). A more sophisticated form of this argument is known as the *common factors hypothesis*, the contention that much more treatment improvement is attributable to client–therapist rela-tionship factors than to treatment techniques. One social work advocate of this position, James Drisko, states, "The results of many meta-analyses indicate that there is little difference in the yield of different types of psychotherapy. This result suggests that factors other than theory and technique are the core sources of therapeutic change" (2004, 87). This is the treatment equivalent of the idea that all theories are of equal value. If all are equal, what difference does it make which theory you use or which therapies social workers are taught to apply? The answer is simply to question the assumptions. Reid (1997) does a nice job of disputing the equality-of-therapies hypothesis, and there is considerable evi-dence to dispute it. If the relationship between client and social worker is the most important influence on therapeutic outcome, what is one to make of the impressive body of literature showing that many self-help books based solely on teaching people treatment *techniques* that they can apply to themselves or others can work well? All in the absence of any form of therapeutic rela-tionship? For example, the self-help book *When Once Is Not Enough: Help for Obsessive Compulsives*, coauthored by the eminent clinical social worker and researcher Gail Steketee (Steketee and White 1990), is based on solid research from the field of behavior therapy on effective methods to treat obsessive-compulsive disorder. Research has shown that people who follow this manual on their own improve just as much as those who receive one-to-one behavior therapy from a psychotherapist using the same principles and homework exer-cises as described in the book—and both groups improve more than people who receive no treatment at all. Evidence such as this suggests that technique can be a strong factor in client improvement, as is the growing body of evidence demonstrating the effectiveness of computer-based and smartphone-app-based self-help treatment programs designed to help people with a variety of problems, including depression, anxiety, weight loss, and insomnia. Actually, it is a great thing when treatments that do not require a therapist prove to be effective, as they allow more people to access effective treatment owing to their lower cost and wider availability. Social workers are primarily concerned with promoting effective therapies, regardless of the mode of delivery (e.g., office-based one-to-one psychotherapy, self-help groups, self-help books or smartphone apps), as long as the aim of helping people improve their lives is achieved. We are not a discipline based solely on relationship-based services. We are much more than that. To be sure, therapeutic relationship variables are an important component of the effectiveness of many treatments, but the essence of being a qualified *professional* is that we provide more than the comfort provided by Grandma and her loving hugs. We do not need to pursue several years of graduate training, post-MSW supervision, and national licensure examination to be a good listener who provides sentiments of support and encouragement. Friends can do that. Social workers need to provide much more to be considered worthy of professional designation.

A third form of disguised nihilism is the notion that all research methods are equally valuable, that none is intrinsically superior to another, and that the methods of conventional science are ill suited to the investigation of social work research questions. This idea is called *research nihilism* and has been expressed within social work in an article title "The Obsolete Scientific Imperative in Social Work" (Atherton 1993; Heineman 1981) among many others (Witkin 1991). Blau puts it bluntly: "The latest upsurge of interest in scientific social work is no more likely than any of its predecessors to address the problems of the profession" (2017, 73). It will be difficult to reconcile the dramatically diverse perspectives on the design and conduct of social work research, especially since they are primarily grounded on the philosophical assumptions noted earlier in this chapter. As noted, the philosophical positions of mainstream science cannot be proved or disproved, so continued arguments about their fundamental validity will likely prove similarly unproductive.

Arguments about the virtues of scientific methods can be handled in a number of ways. One was suggested by Hudson: "We shall wait eagerly to see whether and to what extent Heineman Pieper and her colleagues produce the knowledge that she promised will be forthcoming from the adoption of her perspective. In all sincerity, I hope she can do better than those of her colleagues whom she has attacked so pejoratively. The 'proof' will lie in the 'pudding' and I hope the pudding will be served shortly" (1986, 2). Hudson advocated peaceful coexistence. Let the positivist-oriented researchers tend to their own gardens and see what harvest they reap. Let the advocates of "other ways of knowing" grow their own crops in the form of published studies convincingly demonstrating that certain forms of treatment are genuinely effective at helping clients (ultimately the true test of the pragmatic value of social work research). The profession, the public, government officials, and other groups can decide which approach has served social work in the best manner.

Another approach is expressed in Latin as "solvitur ambulando," meaning "it is solved by walking away" (Thyer 2015). This method of argument was said to have been employed by the Greek philosopher Diogenes while listening to an earnest young scholar arguing that motion was impossible. Without saying a word, Diogenes got up and walked out of sight. Similarly, the authors of the more than one thousand studies of randomized experiments that appear in the appendix of this book refute the naysayers who claimed that such studies were inappropriate for use within social work. These positivist-oriented scholars did not *argue* the *merits* of experimentation; they simply *did experiments*, a very powerful refutation of the antiexperimentalist position—much more convincing than arguments without actual demonstrations.

Another reasonable approach is to use whichever research methods are best positioned to answer certain questions. This approach is exemplified by the noted feminist and primarily qualitative researcher Liane Davis's description of what she did when presented with a research opportunity. She was asked by the National Association of Social Workers to examine gender disparities within the social work profession. Recognizing that this was an issue best addressed with quantitative research methods, she convincingly demonstrated that male social workers were paid more than female social workers using a large national database of salary information. No combination of qualitative studies would have sufficed to address the issue. In Davis's own words, "Clearly this was a task that can only be accomplished with quantitative methodology" (1994, 73). Research tools have their proper roles. In-depth interviews, focus groups, ethnographic studies, and other qualitative methodologies, for instance, can be effective in answering certain questions and developing certain hypotheses. Experiments, quasi-experiments, pre-experimental studies and single-subject research designs can be useful in evaluating the outcomes of practice, but these methods are not necessarily the best approach to developing a hypothesis. Other research methods can often do that better (Thyer 2012).

Metaphysics

Since science limits itself to studying the natural or real world to determine causes, not the metaphysical worlds of Dr. Strange depicted in the Marvel

Universe, the various heavens and hells described by many religious traditions, or supernatural beings, it generally eschews metaphysical explanations of phenomena. The positive or negative attributes of a person are not usually explained by entities such as fairies who sprinkle dust over a sleeping baby or the astrological influences of the planets at the time of a person's birth. Santa Claus is not invoked to explain the mysterious appearance of presents under the tree on Christmas morning, and the apparent overnight cure of a person with a mental illness is not explained by departing demons. This is not to say that fairies, Santa, or demons do not exist. Maybe they do. But science generally leaves them alone. Science can certainly investigate the purported physical effects of supposed metaphysical therapies such as intercessory prayer (see, for example, Hodge 2007) or the impact of silent mantra-based meditation (Wolf and Abell 2003) on depression and anxiety, but such research should take no position on the supernatural mechanisms of treatment supposedly involved. As long as the outcomes being claimed occur in the material world, such claims are grist for the unforgiving mills of the behavioral scientist. But when a supernatural claim is made that does not involve anything physical, science should be silent because it has no tools to investigate nonmaterial claims.

An example is the Catholic miracle of transubstantiation. During the Roman Catholic Church service, the priest elevates and blesses bread and wine. When the blessing is uttered by the priest, the adjacent alter server rings a bell to signify that at that moment the bread and wine were supernaturally changed into the body and blood of Jesus. The Church no longer claims that the bread and wine physically change; rather, it is said to be a spiritual or nonmaterial change. The absence of physical alteration renders the claim of a nonmaterial spiritual change a phenomenon that science cannot investigate. There are no microscopes or chemical analyses that can be brought to bear, since no physical change is said to be made. This doctrine of transubstantiation is an untestable claim. Science should be silent as to the validity of transubstantiation—the phenomenon is outside its scope of expertise.

But when a supposed psychic claims to read minds, the scientific skeptic, mindful of parsimony, can investigate simpler explanations than that extrasensory perception is at work. For example, the magician James Randi exposed the fraud of the self-proclaimed psychic healer Peter Popoff by showing that Popoff used a concealed radio receiver to learn from his wife (who collected prayer requests prior to services) what health issues a member of the congregation was concerned about. Randi recorded these secret radio messages and filmed the healing services to show that Popoff was tricking people with his supposed powers of diagnosis and laying on of hands (and incidentally collecting large sums of money). During a live recording of the Tonight Show Starring Johnny Carson with Popoff was a guest, Randi appeared (unexpectedly to Popoff) and played the recordings to devastating effect. Randi's book

The Faith Healers (1989) provides an entertaining look at his exposure of fraudulent faith healers. Does his work prove that faith healing cannot occur? No. But repeated exposure of demonstrably fraudulent practices does promote a significant degree of skepticism.

Dualism

According to *dualism*, human actions are explained by two things: the body and the mind. When Napoleon asked the French polymath Pierre-Simon Laplace why he did not mention God in his landmark book on astronomy, Laplace responded, "I have no need of that hypothesis." Parsimony at its finest. Analogously, readers of contemporary books on neurology and brain function that attempt to explain human behavior, thoughts, and feelings will be looking in vain if searching for explanations invoking the mind. If the word "mind" appears in such a book at all, it will be used in reference to historical usage, not described as a causative agent in human activities. Dualism also is used in the view that the world is made up of natural and supernatural aspects. As mentioned, science does not entertain investigations of supernatural phenomena. When the COVID-19 pandemic struck, we did not seek out shamans, sacrifice virgins, or ritualistically slaughter animals to appease angry gods. We relied on science, particularly vaccine development, and within a year had several effective vaccines—a wonderful achievement for applied science. One might almost call it miraculous. Almost, but not quite. For the nondualist, human cognition arises from the operation of the brain and the body, with some influence from genetics and the environment, not a hypothetical entity called the mind.

Reification

Reification is the error of attributing the status of reality to something that has not been shown to exist. Science deals with unobservable things all the time. Atoms and molecules were postulated long before they could be observed, but observed they eventually were. Even subatomic particles have been shown to exist, many decades after they were established to be part of the structure of our world. Freud's ego, in contrast, has not been proved to exist in the material world. Talking about the ego as a hypothetical construct is acceptable, but talking about it as if it were real, absent convincing evidence of its existence, is a mistake. The energy fields of the acupuncturist, the thought field therapist, the polarity worker, and the Reiki practitioner can be discussed as hypothetical entities the existence of which can be fruitfully investigated (just as one can investigate the existence of ghosts or Bigfoot), but one would be committing the error of reification to speak of these concepts as actual *things* when there is no evidence of their existence. The DSM is full of reified constructs. With only a few exceptions (e.g., genetic disorders such as Down syndrome and Alzheimer's disease), the diagnoses in the DSM (e.g., major depression, panic disorder, schizophrenia) have not been validated (i.e., proven to exist in the material world) through chemical tests or brain scans. The entities listed in the DSM-5 are groupings of behaviors, types of affect, and patterns of thinking that are used as diagnostic criteria to determine whether a person has a particular mental disorder—a label like "bipolar disorder." But a label does not mean that something actually exists. The problem with reifying such concepts is that doing so frequently leads to another philosophical error called circular reasoning.

Circular Reasoning

Circular reasoning occurs when an explanation is provided wherein cause and effect cannot be distinguished. For example, say you see me scream in terror and run away at the sight of a snake, and a passerby asks you, "Why does he scream and run away like that?" If you respond, "Oh, that's easy to explain. He has a specific phobia," you have provided a superficial explanation, which is of little value. To use the label "specific phobia" as an explanation, the explanation will fall apart on further questioning. If the passerby then asks, "How do you know he has a specific phobia?" and you reply, "Because he screams and runs away when he sees a snake," the circularity of the account becomes obvious. Why do I scream and run away? Because I have a phobia. How do you know I have a phobia? Because I scream and run away. *You cannot use behavior to explain behavior.* If a given DSM-5 diagnosis is arrived at based on what a client does and tells you, it is logically untenable to use that diagnosis to explain the client's behavior. A diagnosis is a form of shorthand to aid in communication; it is not in itself an explanation. A better explanation for my phobic behavior would be my telling you that I saw the movie *Anaconda* when I was very young. Before then, I had no fear of snakes. But since seeing the movie, I react with fear whenever I see a snake. This is a noncircular account of my fear and one that could be investigated, say by asking my parents about the genesis of my snake fear.

Similarly, a person with depression does not experience frequent crying, reduced appetite, an inability to experience pleasure, a reduced sex drive, or lethargy (see how it is easy to reify?) because they *have* depression. Labeling these behaviors does not explain them. One must look elsewhere for causal variables. If it is revealed that the person with depression recently experienced the death of a spouse, a job loss, or a diagnosis of a life-threat-ening illness, it is much more likely that such an experience is responsible for the behaviors the DSM-5 groups together and labels "major depression" than a mythical, nonphysical construct termed a psychiatric diagnosis. Inferring that depression is caused by conflicts between the id, ego, and superego or anger turned inward (more reified constructs) are other examples of circular reasoning. One day, perhaps, some DSM-5 conditions will be determined to have biological underpinnings. Schizophrenia, bipolar disorder, and ASD are promising candidates, but the science does not yet support biological explanations of these disorders. Until such biologically based accounts are determined, most DSM-5 conditions should be considered only as labels, not as explanations.

Scientism

The perspective of *scientism* refers to an elevation of science as the most important tool for understanding human affairs and that the investigational methods of natural science are the only legitimate approach to research. Scientism, among its many faults, tends to ignore or dismiss other important factors that pertain to the human condition and its improvement. Social work is a values-based profession, and our values are not scientifically justifiable constructions. Derived from our values are our ethics, personal and profes-sional, religious and secular, many of which are reflected in the formal ethical codes established in our professional disciplines, licensing boards, and legal traditions. Anastas (2012) provides a useful critique of scientism as it pertains to social work practice research. The problem with scientism is that it goes too far. Rather than saying that scientific methods can be useful, it says they are of supreme importance and superior to other perspectives. No credible social work researcher would endorse scientism, as science alone, unmoored from its foundations of philosophy, values, ethics, and legal traditions, would be fright-ening. Cohen expresses this well:

> To emphasize scientific objectivity at the expense of values and goals can make of social work something completely apart from its traditional intent and pur-pose. Scientific objectivity without relation to goals and values can result in a "preoccupation with techniques and gadgets as an end in themselves," in a "directionless and conscienceless scientism." Social work, to live up to its intent of being both scientific and social minded, must meet the challenge of helping to integrate the two. Social work is most honest to its tradition when it views itself as science at work in the furthering of human values.
>
> (1958, 291)

Summary

This chapter has presented a brief overview of the philosophical assumptions adopted by mainstream positivist science that have proved useful in conducting inquiries into the nature of human affairs. Originating as professional social work did, in large part from the behavioral and social sciences, disciplines that emerged from the broader field of philosophy as they embraced conventional methods of scientific analysis, it is natural that social work adopted their principles and practices. Similarly, social work has rejected some philosophical positions that have also been repudiated by the broader sciences. The legitimacy of accepting or rejecting various assumptions cannot be proved to be correct or incorrect, but by adopting the positions we have, we have acquired useful tools called scientific methods. And these methods have been shown to be of immense value in discovering valid knowledge about our clients and the world in which they live, as well as about ourselves, given that we share the world with the people and processes we observe.

These generally accepted philosophical positions can be rightly critiqued and analyzed, and debates about their merits and deficiencies are ongoing. Critics of the mainstream positions of the philosophy of science outlined in this chapter usually take aim at a straw-man portrayal of these positions. They rail against determinism, claiming that the principle holds that *everything* is 100 percent determined, against empiricism by asserting this principle means that *only* evidence available via the senses is useful in science, and against realism by suggesting that this principle implies that human subjectivity has *no effect* on the conduct of true science. The problem with these critiques is that they take aim at false portrayals of these principles through the use of absolute and unqualified statements. Determinism does not claim that *everything* is clearly determined and *not* a function of free will. Rather, determinists say that *much* of human behavior is determined by forces outside our control. "Much" is much less objectionable than "all." A rigid and unqualified depiction of determinism does seem unattractive, whereas an accurate use of the qualifiers "much" and "some" takes a lot of the steam out of objections to determinism. Similarly, empiricism, which values evidence obtained via the senses, does not deny the potential role of other sources of knowledge. Claiming that empiricism completely excludes other sources of data makes for a stronger argument against it, but this is again a false portrayal. Certainly empirical data can be useful. Empiricism is not to claim that nonempirical sources of information have no value. To assert that realism means that science considers there to be only one objective reality is yet another superficial, misguided critique. Realism readily acknowledges the subjective elements of the world and the scientific analyses of it. When I look at a pencil immersed in a glass of water, it looks broken where the pencil enters the water's surface. This is subjective visual evidence.

(And my friends would say the same, providing for interrater agreement.) But the appearance of a broken pencil does not prevent me from knowing that it is not broken. Science can account for such illusions, as well as for the role that human biases and assumptions can play in conducting research.

While these debates are unlikely to be resolved (e.g., there are still members of the Flat Earth Society), the effectiveness of this array of philosophical principles cannot be denied as a means of making valid discoveries. When the COVID-19 virus impacted the world, we did not turn to prayer or meditation or consult with governmental leaders for guidance on how to develop effective vaccines. We used established scientific methods to create vaccines. And they worked. Thank goodness. We strive for similar accomplishments in our social work practices and policies, which we have developed with scientific guidance and evaluation. One important way we have done so is through experimental research, as will be discussed in the following chapters.

CHAPTER 4

THE PURPOSE OF
EXPERIMENTAL DESIGNS

The true method of knowledge is experiment.

—William Blake

To reiterate, the purpose of experimental designs is to test one or more hypotheses predicting a causal relationship between two or more variables. The virtues of true experiments were lauded within social work far before they began to be used. For example, F. Stewart Chapin, the director of the School of Social Work at Smith College in 1919 and at the University of Minnesota School of Social Work from 1922 to 1949, had this to say about experiments as far back as 1917:

The experimental method has contributed in large measure to the striking achievements of modern science. This method allows us to analyze our relations of cause and effect more rapidly and clearly than by any other method. It permits verification by many observers. It has substituted for unreasonable prejudice a definite sort of proof that has attained sufficient validity to justify prediction. . . . Experiment is simply observation under controlled conditions. When observation alone fails to disclose the factors that operate in a given problem, it is necessary for the scientist to resort to experiment. . . . The line between observation and experiment is not a sharp one. Observation tends gradually to take on the character of an experiment. Experiment may be considered to have begun when there is actual human interference with the conditions that determine the phenomenon under prediction.

(133)

Chapin made this statement about twenty-five years before the first true experiment in social work was published, which, as far as I can determine, was authored by Simon, Divine, Cooper, and Chernin (1941), a team consisting of a future Nobel laureate (Simon) and a future dean of the School of Social Welfare at the University of California, Berkeley (Chernin). This gap between aspirational sentiments and the actual implementation of experiments is not uncommon. In his 1925 novel *Arrowsmith*, Upton Sinclair describes a medical experiment in which participants are randomly assigned to receive or not receive a vaccine during a virulent epidemic. This book appeared years before the first true experiment in therapeutic medicine was published in 1946, which evaluated the effect of streptomycin versus bed rest (treatment as usual) among patients with tuberculosis. Since this new antibiotic was in limited supply, comparing it with treatment as usual was seen as ethical. Sir Bradford Hill, who later developed the Bradford Hill criteria for inferring causation (discussed in the previous chapter), was a statistician for this successful trial (Bhatt 2010). Thus, being slow on the uptake of advances in research methodology is not unique to social work. It is also characteristic of the slow dissemination and implementation of research-supported therapies in clinical practice across many disciplines.

Although thus far we have focused on the use of randomized controlled trials (RCTs) to evaluate the effectiveness of psychotherapies delivered by social workers, these designs have a wide range of applications in addition to their use in evaluating psychotherapy treatments. Here are some other useful purposes for which RCTs can be employed.

Studies of Clinical Decision-Making and Judgments Using Vignettes

Social workers make judgments about and decisions regarding their clients that impact these people's lives. Child protective service (CPS) workers visit with caregivers and their children in their homes and are charged with evaluating the risks children may be exposed to. They do so by observing caregivers' behaviors, caregivers' interactions with their children, and the home environment. The decisions they make have important consequences that may be life-changing for the parties involved. If a child is deemed to be at risk, a social worker can arrange for them to be removed from the home and placed in foster care, a temporary home, or a group home. The social worker could even recommend that the child be placed for permanent adoption with another family. Such actions may be traumatizing for all concerned and the consequences of an incorrect decision even more so. A child erroneously allowed to remain in an unsafe home may be injured or even killed. A child erroneously deemed to be at risk may be unnecessarily removed from their home, disrupting child–parent bonds.

Clinical social workers also evaluate people with mental health concerns and are expected to be competent in assessing clients using the diagnostic criteria found in systems such as the DSM-5 and the International Statistical Classification of Diseases and Related Health Problems (ICD). On a simpler level, some of us determine whether clients are eligible for certain forms of social service or public assistance. Incorrect conclusions regarding diagnosis can take two forms. One is deciding that a client meets the DSM-5 criteria for a particular mental disorder when they do not; this is referred to as a *false-positive error*. The second is deciding that a client does not meet the criteria when in fact they do; this is called a *false-negative error*. Both errors can have deleterious consequences for a client.

One would expect that professionals such as social workers conduct their assessments in a reliable and valid manner, and in a way that is free of bias with regard to client characteristics such as race, gender, religion, political affiliation, sexual identity, and cultural identity. Sometimes we have grounds to suspect that bias in assessment exists. Numerous anecdotes support the contention that people in nondominant groups (e.g., certain racial groups, people living in poverty, those who identify as LGBTQ+) are more likely than those in dominant groups to experiencing bias in assessments.

One approach to investigate possible bias is the *experimental vignette study*. In this type of study, the social work researcher begins with a broad question, such as "Does racial bias exist in decisions to remove children from their home for safety reasons?" Based on past research studies, theory, practice experience, or other influences, one or more directional hypotheses can also be formulated, such as "Compared with white mothers, Black mothers are more likely to have a child removed from the home for safety reasons." The feature that distinguishes the research question from the hypothesis is that the latter poses a risky prediction, risky in that it can be falsified. Guided by a broad research question, and with at least one directional hypothesis or prediction in hand, the investigator can devise a vignette—a short story or case illustration—describing a family situation and home environment. Two vignettes are created, identical in all respects except one, for example the mother's race. To continue our example, in one vignette the mother could be described as white and in the other Black. The researcher could then recruit a large sample of CPS workers, people who make decisions on home removal every day as a part of their job, and randomly assign them to read *one* of the two vignettes and recommend whether the child in the vignette should be removed from the home. With random assignment, close to half will end up reading the vignette depicting the Black mother, and half will read the vignette with the white mother. If no racial bias is present, the number of recommendations for removal should be about the same in both groups. If more CPS workers recommend the child of the Black mother be removed, this may be evidence of bias. This difference could then be subjected to a simple statistical test to see whether it is due to chance (i.e., a random variation in the data) or likely indicative of bias. A statistically significant result provides evidence that bias was present in the CPS workers' recommendations. Additional descriptive statistics such as measures of effect size can tell us more about the clinical or practical meaning of the difference. If enough CPS workers are randomly assigned to each group, a simple study like this could yield strong evidence of racial bias or its apparent absence.

Vignette studies can be used to examine many factors that may indicate bias. For example, with a sufficient sample of Black and white CPS workers, you could assess whether differences exist in how white and Black workers make decisions about white and Black clients in terms of recommending the child be removed from the home. For her PhD dissertation, the clinical social worker Anna Yelick used a vignette study to examine the effect of caregiver race (white versus Black) and the number of parents present in the home (one versus two) (see Yelick and Thyer 2020). Because vignettes are identical in all respects except the feature or features manipulated by the researcher, and because participants reviewed only one vignette, any differences in decision-making can be said to have been caused by the manipulated variable or variables. Many years ago, vignettes were mailed to potential respondents or distributed to agencies or at professional conferences. Today vignette studies can be efficiently set up online, for example using low-cost platforms such as Qualtrics (https://www.qualtrics.com) or SurveyMonkey (https://www.surveymonkey.com). Once set up and pilot tested, a researcher can post an invitation describing their study and providing a link to the survey site to potential respondents on social media platforms, targeting the type of people they wish to survey. The study description is usually veiled to disguise the study's true purpose but still truthfully describes it. For example, a study could be said to be investigating the broad subject of clinical decision-making rather than the specific question of whether parental race is a factor in CPS workers' decision-making regarding the removal of a child from the home. Potential respondents who visit the site answer screening questions to see whether they meet the researcher's inclusion criteria (i.e., they have the desired background and characteristics). Those who do not cannot proceed with the study. Those who do are prompted to continue and are provided with one of the vignettes to respond to. Depending on the complexity of the study, respondents may be provided with a small token of appreciation for their participation, such as a gift card. The availability of web-based platforms to host experimental surveys has greatly facilitated the design and conduct of vignette studies on clinical judgment and decision-making.

Case and Lingerfelt (1974) conducted a classic social work experimental vignette study on labeling theory. The authors presented the vignettes of clinical cases via video. The features that varied between vignettes were the supposed client's apparent socioeconomic status and whether they had a mental disorder. The respondents were a mix of professional social workers, graduate social work students, and undergraduates taking a social work course. The aim was to see if cases from lower incomes were more likely to be given a diagnosis of a mental disorder compared to cases from higher incomes. Related vignette studies were conducted by the social worker Stuart Kirk. In one investigation of social rejection, more than eight hundred community college students responded to vignettes in the form of brief case histories (Kirk and Hsieh 2004). A review of the studies included in the appendix will reveal the numerous studies of this nature to be found in the social work literature, particularly in more recent years. Kirk (1974) does warn of one problem with vignette studies: They typically do not reflect real-life situations. Rather, they are artificial simulations of decision-making. Still, such vignettes can help us establish whether bias may be affecting decision-making and set the stage for more sophisticated studies involving greater verisimilitude to everyday life.

One such study, and a troubling one, was conducted by Bertrand and Mullainathan (2003). The researchers responded to help-wanted advertisements in Boston and Chicago newspapers and mailed résumés to potential employers. Half used what were considered "white-sounding" names, and half used what were considered "Black-sounding" names. In all other respects, the résumés were the same. The study's dependent variable (outcome) was the number of callbacks received from employers, and the independent variable (the feature that varied between the two groups) was the apparent race of the fictitious job applicants. The authors found that applicants with "white-sounding" names received 50 percent more callbacks than did those with "Black-sounding" names. This is compelling evidence of the ongoing discrimination Black people in the United States experience in the employment marketplace and goes some distance in explaining the continuing socioeconomic disparities and inequities present in American society. This study is also an excellent example of an experimental vignette methodology used in the service of promoting social justice.

Evaluating Clinical Psychosocial Interventions

An RCT is ideally positioned to test whether a psychosocial intervention works. It does so by asking a series of increasingly complex questions that initially attempt to rule out one or more threats to internal validity. If the experimental treatment "survives" (i.e., it seems to work), then it is justifiable to subject it to more searching evaluations using more complex designs with the larger sample sizes necessary to conduct such studies. If the intervention does not prove effective when tested using a simpler design, then more ambitious studies are not usually needed. If the new treatment proves *not* to be better than no treatment, comparing it to a placebo or to treatment as usual is a waste of time and resources. The following are examples of the types of questions RCTs are used to answer.

1. What is the status of clients after they receive an intervention compared with that of clients who did not receive the intervention?

With random assignment and a sufficient sample size, you do not need a pretest measure to conduct this type of RCT. From this broad question you could pose a testable hypothesis, such as "After treatment, more clients assigned to treatment X will demonstrate statistically significant and clinically important improvements than clients assigned to no treatment." This hypothesis could be tested with the following design, with R meaning that both groups (treatment and no treatment) were created using random assignment, O_1 referring to the first (and perhaps only) assessment for this group, and X referring to the intervention being tested:

R	X	O_1
R		O_1

This is the *posttest-only, no-treatment control-group experimental design*. It is called a *posttest-only* design because participants are assessed only once, after treatment. It is called a *no-treatment control-group* design because the control group does not receive treatment. It is an *experimental* design because at least two groups are created through random assignment. You need a sufficient sample size to warrant doing an RCT consisting of participants who meet your inclusion and exclusion criteria. Eight or ten participants per group are not usually enough. That small a study *could be done*, but it is unlikely that the statistical tests used to examine posttreatment differences would reveal much.

Potential participants, with informed consent, agree to be randomly assigned to either the treatment or no-treatment group. After a predetermined amount of time has passed (e.g., a certain number of treatment sessions) that is considered to provide sufficient time for treatment effects to be observed, participants of both groups are assessed using a valid outcome measure at about the same point in time. If the measures taken at O_1 differ in a way that is both statistically significant and pragmatically important, your hypothesis has been supported: "Treatment was more effective than no treatment." If they do not differ as predicted, the hypothesis is refuted, and it seems unlikely the treatment works. If the hypothesis was derived from a particular theory, that theory is correspondingly supported or weakened. Many interventions are derived from one or more formal social or behavioral science theories, and intervention research can be useful in determining a theory's validity. But many psychosocial interventions are not clearly and explicitly derived from a theory, in which case any *post hoc* (after-the-fact) application of a theory to explain your results may not be useful. Why? Because your choice of *one* theory to explain your results ignores the potential myriad of *other* theories that may also explain your results. To provide a robust test of a theory in an outcome study, the theory should be included in the development of your hypothesis and clearly articulated *before* you conduct an experiment, not after the results are in.

In the example described at the beginning of this section, with one assessment made following the receipt of an intervention, we may legitimately infer that the experimental treatment *caused* posttreatment differences because participants in the no-treatment group did not improve as much or at all. And thanks to the magic of random assignment, we can safely assume group equivalence at the beginning of the data collection, which provides the basis for inferring treatment effects posttreatment. The no-treatment group allows us to control for improvements that may be attributable to threats to internal validity (rival plausible explanations), such as the passage of time or clients' concurrent histories, as discussed in chapter 2. An improvement on this design is discussed next.

2. Did clients improve more compared with what would have been expected had they not received treatment?

Sometimes we wish to determine more than the posttreatment comparative status of two groups of participants: We want to see if there are any *improvements*. To judge improvements, we usually need some sort of pretreatment assessment. While an $O_1 \times O_2$ design could determine if clients improved, it could not be classified as a true experiment because there is no comparison group created using random assignment. So to answer question 2, we need a no-treatment control group to test the hypothesis, "Treated clients will demonstrate more *improvement* posttreatment compared with untreated clients." Having a single point of assessment posttreatment does not usually permit inferences about improvements. So to answer question 2 and its associated hypothesis, we need a design like this:

R	O_1	X	O_2
R	O_1		O_2

Here, participants are assigned to an active treatment, X, or to no treatment, indicated by the absence of X in the bottom group. The pretreatment and posttreatment assessments are labeled O_1 and O_2, respectively. Each group is assessed using one or more valid outcome measures, and then the treatment group receives the intervention and the no-treatment group does not. Ideally, at O_1 there are no significant differences between the two groups, and at O_2 the experimental group has improved both statistically significantly and clinically or pragmatically, whereas the no-treatment group shows no improvement. Clear results like this both answer the research question and provide a test of its hypothesis. And they provide a legitimate test of the theory upon which the hypothesis was based—*if* its use was clearly explained prior to collecting the data; that is, how the theory was chosen and why it was used to create the hypothesis. (Recall that a hypothesis is a directional prediction using terms like "better," "worse," "higher," or "lower.")

Sidebar: I prefer to use the term "pretreatment assessment" when referring to evaluations taken before clients are exposed to the independent variable as opposed to the more commonly used term "baseline." These assessments are not often part of a *line*. In contrast, the multiple pretreatment assessments often undertaken in single-system research studies *do* form part of line. Therefore, I tend to reserve "baseline" for discussions of single-system studies and use "pretreatment assessments" for the analogous assessments in group research studies.

Showing that a treatment is better than nothing is a good thing, and such information can be a useful prerequisite for more advanced investigations of a treatment. However, given the ubiquitous role of placebo influences in psychotherapy research and in studies of the outcomes of psychosocial treatments in general, we need to entertain the possibility that any positive effect could be due to placebo factors. Recognizing this fact, if the treatment we are investigating has survived the two types of experimental testing described thus far, we may wish to conduct a stronger experimental investigation, one that answers question 3.

3. Did clients who received an experimental treatment improve more compared with what would have been expected had they received a credible placebo treatment?

Here, too, we must have a sufficiently large sample for the study to be worth-while scientifically (i.e., by the standards of nomothetic or between-subjects group research designs). To answer this question, participants are randomly allocated to one of two conditions: experimental (or active) treatment or placebo treatment. The hypothesis being tested could be stated as something like, "Clients receiving experimental treatment will demonstrate greater improvements, statistically and pragmatically, than will clients who receive placebo treatment." The design for this type of study can be diagrammed as follows:

R	O_1	$X_{treatment}$	O_2
R	O_1	$X_{placebo}$	O_2

Ideally at O_1 the two groups are almost identical on all relevant demographic and clinical variables, including the outcome measure or measures. Both groups then engage in their respective treatments, therapies that are considered roughly equally plausible and that require about the same amount of time and effort. If at the time of the second assessment, the treatment group is indeed better off than the placebo group, we have good evidence that the therapy under investigation produces improvements above and beyond those brought about by placebo factors. This is important to demonstrate; for social workers to be considered credible, they must deliver therapies and produce results that are superior to those generated by placebo factors.

We can roughly estimate the relative merits of a real treatment over a placebo treatment by subtracting improvements seen in the placebo group from those observed in the experimental group. If the placebo group improves 30 percent and the experimental group improves 80 percent, then the true improvement, those caused by the experimental treatment above and beyond placebo effects, is about 50 percent (80 percent − 30 percent). Our choice of outcome measure determines how we analyze the results. If all participants meet the DSM-5 criteria for a particular disorder at O_1, whereas at O_2 some in the experimental group no longer meet these criteria, expressing outcomes in terms of the percentage of cure rate may be legitimate. If the primary outcome measure is a pencil-and-paper measure scored on an interval or ratio scale, then the pre- and posttests may be expressed as means (arithmetic averages), and statistical tests can be used to assess the changes in mean scores. (These tests are different from those used to analyze changes in numbers, frequencies, or percentages.)

If at pretreatment, participants in both groups scored about 28 points on the Beck Depression Inventory, and at posttreatment participants in the experimental group scored an average of 15 points (a drop of 13 points) and participants in the placebo group scored an average of 22 points (a drop of 6 points), the true effect of therapy can be considered to be about 9 points ($15 - 6 = 9$) on average. These examples show why having an effective placebo control group is invaluable for contextualizing treatment gains observed in an experimental group. In appraising the effects of social work interventions, it is best to err on the side of being conservative. We do not want to exaggerate the effects of our care—to do so would constitute deceiving the public, as well as ourselves.

In well-designed studies of therapy using a placebo control condition, at the conclusion of the study, apart from assessing clinical improvements, participants can be asked to judge the believability or credibility of the treatment they received. Ideally these evaluations will be similar; if so, this result demonstrates the credibility of the placebo treatment. If the active treatment was appraised as more credible than the placebo treatment, the placebo treatment likely did not fulfill its function. Another approach is to ask participants to guess which treatment they received, real or placebo. If they can do so reliably, the placebo control is considered a failure owing to its transparency. If participants guess no better than chance, the placebo treatment is considered effective as a control for that threat to internal validity.

4. Is the experimental treatment better than treatment as usual?

If the experimental treatment is better than nothing and better than placebo treatment, we can then fruitfully investigate whether it is better than what is currently available, or treatment as usual (TAU). If prior research has shown the experimental treatment to be better than placebo, it would be tempting to omit a placebo control condition and compare just the experimental treatment with TAU. Or if the experimental treatment has been shown to be better than nothing, it could be tempting to omit a no-treatment comparison group. Following this logic, you could use one of the following designs:

R	O_1	X_{exp}	O_2
R	O_1	X_{TAU}	O_2

or

R	O_1	X_{exp}	O_2
R	O_1		O_2

If the results demonstrated that the experimental treatment was superior to TAU, you might think that the experimental treatment is not only better than TAU but also no treatment or a placebo treatment (since prior studies had demonstrated these findings). This practice is commonly used, but a more conservative approach is to draw such conclusions only when all these conditions have been tested head-to-head in the *same study*. Not all placebo therapies produce the same effects, and no-treatment control conditions can differ over time, particularly since studies like this are often undertaken years apart. For example, the dismal conditions in the United States and elsewhere during 2020, at the height of the COVID-19 pandemic, were quite different from the euphoric circumstances elevating the public mood following President Obama's election (Goldman and Mutz 2008). Such differences in conditions can impact the comparability of no-treatment control conditions used in studies conducted at different times.

Similarly, the placebo control treatments used in previous studies may not be equally impactful (or nonimpactful, as the case may be). A relaxation treatment used as a placebo control in a previous study is far less likely to be a credible placebo treatment in a current investigation of psychotherapy compared with a type of nondirective supportive group therapy. Therefore, to determine whether an experimental treatment produces superior results to no treatment, a placebo treatment, *and* to TAU, a study needs to be more sophisticated, providing all four conditions separately and concurrently. The design would look like this:

R	O_1	X_{exp}	O_2
R	O_1	X_{TAU}	O_2
R	O_1	$X_{placebo}$	O_2
R	O_1		O_2

It is not legitimate to conclude that if treatment X was better than treatment Y in study 1 and treatment Y was better than placebo in study 2 that treatment X is better than placebo. A head-to-head comparison is the best way to draw such a conclusion, although, as mentioned, clinical researchers do not always take this approach (Washburn, Rubin, and Zhou 2016). The added complexity of conducting such direct comparison studies (e.g., recruiting a larger number of participants, monitoring treatment fidelity across more treatment groups, needing more resources to conduct the many assessments) makes it seductive to cut corners and cite prior findings as if they apply to your investigation. The logic goes something like, "Since a prior study showed that treatment X is clearly better than a placebo treatment, we can dispense with a placebo control group (or a no-treatment control group) and just compare the experimental treatment with TAU." Such studies do accumulate, showing that X is better than placebo or to no treatment. Studies can also come along that show that treatment Y is better than placebo or no treatment. But at some point, the question will arise, "Which is better: treatment X or treatment Y?" You could choose to be guided by the two literatures, studies comparing X alone to placebo or no treatment and studies comparing Y alone to placebo or no treatment. But would it not be better to have evidence from studies that directly compared X to Y, placebo, *and* no treatment? Cross-study differences in factors such as participant sampling, time frame, therapist or assessor bias, consistency in outcome measures, and statistical analyses can be controlled for in a single study. When aggregating the results of a number of studies, the effects of all such differences need to be considered. In a single larger study involving head-to-head comparisons, randomization to the four arms of the study (experimental treatment, TAU, placebo, no treatment) will ensure the groups are equivalent across all relevant (and irrelevant) clinical and demographic factors, equalizing them so to speak. Given their complexity and the sample sizes needed, head-to-head comparative studies are more expensive to run than their simpler counterparts.

As an example, some outcomes research has shown that social skills training can help children with conduct disorders, and another body of outcomes research demonstrates that play group interventions can also help. One could read these separate literatures to try to understand which treatment would be most effective. However, a better approach would be to review head-to-head comparative studies evaluating both treatments. This was done by Katzmann et al. (2019) with about one hundred children between the ages of six and twelve years. The children were randomly assigned to a social skills training treatment or to a play therapy group. Valid assessments were made of their conduct problems before and after treatment, and the results found the social skills training to be superior to play therapy. Such head-to-head comparative studies are among the best ways to demonstrate whether one treatment is more effective than another.

5. Are the effects of an experimental treatment long lasting?

A social work intervention that produces only temporary benefits is not as useful as one that produces long-term benefits or a complete cure. Tranquilizing drugs such as benzodiazepines are effective in reducing generalized anxiety for a few hours and are widely prescribed for this purpose. But the half-life of these agents is usually not long, often just a few hours, meaning that as the drug is metabolized, the effects wear off and the anxiety returns (Davidson 2009). People with anxiety may take these drugs on a long-term basis and experience relief while on the regimen, but they are not usually cured of an anxiety disorder via such medications. The risk of addiction is also present. In such circumstances, cognitive behavioral therapy is an alternative treatment that produces much longer-lasting effects with no risk of pharmacological dependence (Freshour et al. 2016).

In many clinical trials of psychosocial interventions, assessments are made shortly before treatment begins and again shortly after it ends. To assess long-term effects, potential for cure, or the occurrence of relapse, the social work researcher must include one or more follow-up assessments. The timing of these is guided by practicality, theory, and prior research. Practically speaking, conducting a follow-up assessment one year after treatment completion will likely yield greater attrition than a six-month follow-up, given that participants may be harder to locate the more time passes. Some participants will have moved, others may no longer be interested in participating, and phone numbers and emails can change. Some people may die. Shorter-term follow-up assessments increase the likelihood of obtaining data, but sometimes we need to assess how people are doing over a long period of time. An example of this is when a treatment is expensive. The cost of the treatment may be only justifiable if its positive effects are long lasting, and the only way to assess this is over an extended period of time.

Another reason for long-term assessments is to determine whether adverse effects have emerged over time. Sometimes psychosocial treatments can have iatrogenic effects (i.e., unintended negative effects caused by intervention) that emerge only later. As an example, let's say a type of couples' therapy was provided to couples of whom one partner had alcoholism, and it proved highly effective. But then it turns out that these couples ended up having a much higher divorce rate than couples who had received no treatment. Perhaps this outcome could be explained by the couples' therapy having disrupted the homeostasis of the couples' relationships, with newly sober partners becoming less pleasant or deciding to leave now that they are functioning better. Such an impact would not be reasonably expected to be seen shortly after treatment had concluded. It might emerge only after some months or years had passed.

Such circumstances are not hypothetical. The social workers Blenkner, Bloom, and Nielsen (1971) compared the outcomes of intensive social work services provided by experienced MSWs with TAU provided by nonprofessional staff among older people in Cleveland, Ohio. This was an RCT, and assessments were undertaken before treatment, halfway through the one-year treatment, at the end of treatment, and five years after treatment had ended. At the five-year follow-up, it emerged that the clients who had received intensive services had a higher death rate than those who had received TAU. This counterintuitive finding was not only unexpected but also frightening in its implications—and it illustrates the importance of long-term follow-ups. This study also provides a lesson in never assuming that a social work intervention, no matter how benign the intent or plausible the rationale behind it, cannot cause harm to our clients. Retrospective analyses revealed that the excess in mortality primarily occurred among clients who were referred to nursing home care, a type of referral that occurred more often in the experimental group as opposed to the TAU group.

The research design for the study by Blenkner, Bloom, and Nielsen (1971) can be diagrammed as follows:

R	O_1	$X_{intensive\ tx}$	$O_{2(6\ mo)}$	$O_{3(12\ mo)}$	$O_{4(5\ y)}$
R	O_1	Y_{TAU}	$O_{2(6\ mo)}$	$O_{3(12\ mo)}$	$O_{4(5\ y)}$

The length of follow-up is determined by many factors, including practicality and expense. As the number of assessments and the number of groups increases, so does the cost of running the experiment. Attrition is another factor. Clients become unwilling to participate and drop out, or they move without providing updated contact information. Thus, your pool of participants grows smaller with each passing month. This reduces the statistical power of your inferential analysis and makes your sample less representative of the original group. But the benefits of long-term follow-up can be significant. Long-term follow-up allows us to better judge whether improvements endure or whether unexpected negative effects emerge. An early RCT in social work (Powers 1949) followed its participants for eight years after treatment had concluded (McCord and McCord 1959), which was a heroic effort that has been emulated all too rarely in the history of social work experimentation.

6. Did clients who received an experimental treatment improve more than clients who received treatment as usual?

Once you have experimental evidence that a new treatment is better than no treatment and that it produces better results than a credible placebo treatment, it is then worthwhile to test it against TAU. TAU is the usual care provided to clients with a particular problem and might itself be a research-supported intervention (but in many agencies it might not be). Showing that the new treatment is better than nothing would not be a surprising result. Showing that it is better than nothing *and* better than placebo would be a more stringent test of the intervention. Demonstrating that it is better than existing care can really advance the profession. In the late 1960s, systematic desensitization (SD), a research-supported office-based treatment, was being used for people with phobias. As discussed, in its early days, the treatment involved imaginal exposure to feared situations as well as progressive relaxation exercises. It turned out that SD worked pretty well and was better than no treatment and placebo (Fischer 1971). Its use grew, and for a time it was considered a TAU. As mentioned, in the early 1970s, researchers showed that SD was equally effective without the progressive relaxation component. From there, it was decided to assess the relative effectiveness of having clients move from less fearful to more fearful imaginal exposures (the standard form of SD) versus moving from more fearful to less fearful exposures. Clients were randomly assigned to receive either standard SD or the form of SD in which exposures moved from more fearful to less fearful. Surprisingly, the outcomes were similar, suggesting that, like progressive relaxation, a gradual approach was not a crucial ingredient to the effectiveness of SD. The treatment was then evaluated in RCTs in which participants were randomly assigned to receive the original, complete treatment (i.e., imaginary exposure to fearful situations, moving from less to more fearful; progressive relaxation training, and real-life practice between sessions) or the same treatment *minus* the practice of gradually exposing themselves to feared situations in real life. It turns out that this made a big difference. Those who received complete SD made much better gains than those who did not do the real-life homework.

The next step was to compare standard SD with therapist-assisted exposure in the real world *minus* all other elements of SD. The result was that the real-life exposure alone was much better—clinically and in terms of both time and cost—than standard SD (see, for example, Watson, Gaind, and Marks 1971; De Araujo et al. 1995).

Through such research, the field slowly evolved, and few psychotherapists continue to offer traditional SD. It has largely been replaced by the more effective type of SD: real-life exposure therapy alone. Now, real-life exposure therapy can be considered a TAU, and it is being used as a comparison condition to evaluate new experimental treatments. In its way, the field of psychosocial treatments evolves via a process similar to that of natural selection, with more effective therapies slowly replacing less effective ones as more and more research is done, particularly RCTs.

A new experimental treatment need not produce better outcomes when compared against a TAU to be seen as a more useful therapy. If the experimental treatment is less intensive, induces fewer side effects, is less expensive, or requires fewer sessions, for example, it may be preferred to the TAU it was tested against regardless of whether it has proved to be more effective. Sometimes briefer types of a treatment are compared against lengthier types. In such instances, the established, lengthier treatment is considered the TAU and the shorter treatment the experimental treatment. Social work researchers have conducted such studies by comparing the results of brief versus extended casework, often finding similar results or even that briefer treatments have better outcomes (Reid and Shyne 1969). Such studies can be invaluable since briefer treatments can be provided to more clients and possibly at a lower cost compared with therapies of a longer duration. The empirical demonstration of the equivalence of a brief version of a standard treatment can sometimes justify the replacement of the standard treatment.

The study by Blenkner, Bloom, and Nielsen (1971) mentioned in the previous section is an example of the comparison of an experimental treatment with TAU.

7. Did clients experience meaningful improvements in other important areas of their lives (e.g., quality of life, life satisfaction) in addition to those that were the focus of treatment?

Most studies of the effectiveness of social work services focus on a specific problem or condition, often a mental health concern. Sometimes we examine a difficulty typically considered not to be a mental health issue, such as child or partner abuse. Such studies usually include measures that assess these focal problems, such as a valid client-completed pencil-and-paper measure of depression or mania or a measure of parenting skills or physical abuse. (Keep in mind that off-the-shelf measures are available for most clinical and nonclinical problems people bring to social workers.) These measures may be client-completed rapid assessment instruments, scales completed by others such as caregivers, parent reports of their children's behavior, systematic observations of clients, direct measures of behavior, or in some instances physiological indices of stress, substance abuse, alcohol intake, blood sugar, blood pressure, or cortisol levels. More rarely clinical outcomes are measured by the percentage of experimental research participants who are found to have completely recovered from their originally diagnosed disorder (a very robust measure indeed).

Social work tends to take a more holistic and comprehensive view of human beings, seeing them as more than a collection of problematic signs and symptoms. They have full lives, relationships, families, employment, and so forth, and these domains of functioning can also be fruitfully assessed in an outcome study in addition to the focal problems for which clients seek help. A social work colleague of mine works in the field of kidney transplantation and has been involved in a number of studies evaluating patient outcomes following transplantation. Most such studies look only at the focal problem—kidney function—and usually find dramatic improvements once a diseased kidney is transplanted with a healthy one. Following surgery, assessments are made of kidney function via serum creatinine values, for example, and ultrasounds of the kidney and urinalysis tests of other markers of kidney damage are performed. Large-scale studies typically show that these measures are greatly improved months after the transplant. This is a great outcome, but how do patients fare in other areas of their life following a transplant? Assessments of psychosocial variables, such as quality of life, life satisfaction, marital satisfaction, sexual satisfaction, and social life would bring added value to the research base of kidney transplantation. Showing that improvements were made not only in kidney function but also in these areas of patients' lives would provide a more well-rounded appraisal of the effects of kidney transplantation. But these psychosocial variables would not be considered the focal or primary outcome measures; rather, they would be evaluated as indirect outcomes.

8. Did clients experience any negative side effects or consequences of treatment?

Many therapies, whether psychosocial or somatic, may result in negative outcomes. Knowing the prevalence of negative side effects for only one therapy provides little guidance in treatment selection. One must also know the prevalence of negative outcomes for all potential therapies being considered. If one study showed that 20 percent of participants who received treatment X experienced negative side effects, and another showed that 40 percent of clients who received treatment Y experienced negative side effects, it could be tempting to conclude that X would be a better choice than Y, assuming equivalency of focal clinical outcomes. Tempting but wrong. Comparing two studies in this manner does involve a consideration of evidence, but this evidence is nowhere near as conclusive as *one* study that compares X with Y, randomly assigning participants to receive one of the two treatments and evaluating both focal outcomes and side effects. As when comparing treatment outcomes, when appraising adverse side effects, a direct head-to-head comparison of two treatments is a methodologically superior approach to making causal and comparative inferences.

Studies of prostate cancer treatment often evaluate not only posttreatment blood levels of prostate-specific antigen (PSA), a marker for this cancer, but also sexual performance and urinary continence, which can be impaired following treatment (Hoppe et al. 2012). There are multiple ways to treat prostate cancer, including manual surgery, robotic-assisted surgery, chemotherapy, focal ablation therapy, conventional radiation therapy via photons, radioactive metallic seeds implanted in the prostate gland, and a newer form of treatment called proton therapy, which uses beams of protons, not the photons generated in regular radiation treatment. Social workers have long been involved in the care of cancer patients (Boynton and Thyer 1994; Sugerman and Livingston 2014), as it is important to evaluate the potential negative side effects of various treatments on patients' lives. Apart from considerations of clinical efficacy, an appraisal of negative or adverse outcomes in addition to the assessment of a focal measure (e.g., PSA level) can help determine which treatment to provide. Given two treatments that produce similar outcomes in terms of cancer remission, the one that results in fewer impairments in sexual functioning, bowel difficulties, or urinary continence may be preferable, for example. RCTs are the best way to assess for potential negative outcomes or adverse side effects. In a specialty clinic, patients could be randomly assigned to receive one of two treatments, for example radical prostatectomy or proton therapy, and sexual function could be assessed a few years later, in addition to PSA level. If the focal clinical outcome (cancer recurrence) were similar between groups but one treatment resulted in less sexual dysfunction or urinary incontinence, the one with fewer side effects might become a preferred treatment.

Adverse effects are commonly assessed in pharmacological outcome studies but are much less so in experimental assessments of psychosocial treatments social workers provide. This is a lamentable lacuna that should be rectified. The Consolidated Standards of Reporting Trials of Social and Psychological Interventions (CONSORT-SPI) checklist recommends reporting harms among the outcomes assessed in any study. "Harms" are defined as "all important harms or unintended effects in each group." An "interpretation consistent with results, balancing benefits and harms, and considering other relevant evidence" should also be included (Grant et al. 2018, 5). More will be said about the CONSORT-SPI, but it is worth mentioning at this point that social workers were involved in the development and authorship of publications about this cutting-edge development in publishing RCT studies.

9. How does the intervention work?

A more intricate and ambitious form of outcome study consists of taking an existing therapy that has been shown to work and then using an RCT to try to determine exactly how it works. This principle was elucidated by the great physician Claude Bernard in his classic text *An Introduction to the Study of Experimental Medicine* ([1865] 1949) when he stated that it is not sufficient to show that a treatment *works*. A science-based profession, as he believed medicine should be, should also strive to determine the *mechanism of action* of a successful treatment:

> It is not enough for experimenting physicians to know that quinine cures fever; but what is above all significant to them is knowing what fever is and accounting for the mechanism by which quinine cures. . . . Experimental physicians . . . want to know what they are doing; it is not enough for them to observe and act empirically[;] they want to experiment scientifically and to understand the physiological mechanism producing disease and the medicinal mechanism effecting a cure. . . . The experimental scientific spirit is utterly averse to producing effects and studying phenomena without trying to understand them.
>
> (Bernard [1865] 1949, 209–10)

This aspiration is tremendously ambitious, but researchers are taking steps toward figuring out exactly how various treatments work. The story of SD is an example of this process. First it was shown that people who received it improved. Then it was shown that SD worked better than no treatment, placebo, and existing talk therapies (i.e., TAU). Once its effectiveness was provisionally established, the question of *how* it worked could be explored (it would have made no sense to investigate its mechanisms of action until after it was shown to be effective). This was done through a series of dismantling studies (i.e., studies that take bits and pieces of a treatment away), which gradually showing that neither relaxation training, nor imaginal exposure, nor a graduated approach to imaginal exposure scenarios was necessary to the success of the treatment. When some clients were instructed to practice exposure exercises in the real world between sessions and others were not, things became clearer. When clients practiced in real life, they got better. When clients were instructed to avoid real-life exposure practice, they either made no improvements or got worse. Thus, the unnecessary elements of SD were gradually eliminated, and the pared-down approach of real-life exposure therapy emerged by the mid-1970s as a highly effective and efficient treatment. And it remains a well-supported treatment to this day:

> A consensus has developed that the treatment of choice for specific phobias is exposure-based procedures, particularly in vivo exposure. Exposure has been shown to be effective for a wide spectrum of specific phobias. Although imaginal exposure has been shown to produce fear reduction . . . and should be used if situational in vivo exposure treatment is not feasible, in vivo exposure is generally accepted as the most powerful treatment for specific phobias.
> (Barlow, Allen, and Basden 2007, 367)

As dismantling studies and investigations of real-life exposure alone proved to isolate the critical ingredient in SD, like a peeled onion, the field was presented with a new question: How does real-life exposure therapy work? It appeared that complex mentalistic accounts involving concepts like the mind, the id, the ego, the superego, schemas, or social constructs were unlikely to be crucial mechanisms of action, since experimental psychology research had long shown that animals could also be taught to overcome learned fears via a process of graduated real-life exposure. This evidence provided support for the philosophical principle of parsimony, as a less complex mechanism of action appeared to be at work, one involving habituation and extinction, components of learning theory.

The parallels between how animals can learn to become less fearful and how humans respond to real-life exposure therapy for phobias are compelling (see Thyer, Baum, and Reid 1988). This finding suggests that the process involved in learning and unlearning fears can be explained in terms of biological processes, not an abstract concept like the mind (whatever that is!). One potential mechanism of action of exposure therapy that was proposed was that the treatment stimulates the body's production of endogenous opiates, naturally occurring substances produced by the brain when a person is under stress that have both anxiolytic and analgesic properties. A preliminary single-subject study showed for the first time that endogenous opiate production was indeed stimulated during real-life exposure therapy (Thyer and Mathews 1986), which provided some early evidence for this proposed mechanism of action. During real-life exposure therapy, clients experience sustained levels of fear, as a result of which endogenous opiates are produced in an attempt to restore homeostasis in bodily functioning and enable people to calm down. Subsequent well-controlled studies have since supported this proposed mechanism of action (Egan et al. 1988; Arntz, Merckelbach, and de Jong 1993).

The social worker Matthew Smith undertook a study attempting to isolate the mechanism of action responsible for the effectiveness of virtual-reality job interview training. He and his colleagues conducted four RCTs involving participants with one of three mood disorders: post-traumatic stress disorder (PTSD), schizophrenia, or autism spectrum disorder. The intervention was a skills-focused training program involving reinforcement and feedback. Using the aggregated data from all four studies, the authors conducted a mediational analysis of what seemed to distinguish those who successfully obtained jobs subsequent to the intervention from those who were not successful. A powerful predictor turned out to be the number of proxy job interviews completed during the intervention. They found that "the results support our hypothesis that job interviewing skills fully mediated the relationship between completed virtual interviews and obtaining a job offer. Specifically we observed that performing more virtual job interviews enhanced job interviewing skills, which predicted a greater likelihood of obtaining a job offer" (Smith et al. 2017, 749). Other factors including psychiatric diagnosis, measures of neurocognition, and months since previous employment were found not to be significantly predictive. RCTs like this one are a powerful tool that allows us to take our analyses beyond an evaluation of whether an intervention works to understanding *why* it works or does not work. This understanding is a key feature of a comprehensive scientific analysis of social work, and more studies like this are needed.

Studies investigating the potential mechanisms of action of psychosocial treatments can provide evidence that is both theoretically and clinically important. Theoretically, we gain new knowledge. Clinically, this knowledge can be applied in the real world to help people. The knowledge that the stimulation of endogenous opiate production is the (or one) mechanism of action behind how people are able to calm down during a prolonged exposure to a fearful situation is primarily of concern to a basic-science discipline like neuro-psychology. But when applied to clinical social work practice in the real world, this knowledge has practical value: it helps people. For example, with this knowledge, it might be predicted that a person being treated with a narcotic antagonist for an opioid addiction might not respond as rapidly to real-life exposure therapy for a phobia as would a person not concurrently receiving a narcotic antagonist. Narcotic antagonists block the brain's opiate receptors, therefore reducing the ability of these substances to produce a feeling of eupho-ria (in the case of a person with an opioid addiction) or to exert analgesic and anxiolytic effects (in the case of a person who is very frightened). A clinical implication of this knowledge would be to ask clients during assessment if they are taking a narcotic antagonist. If they are, it may be best to consider an alter-native treatment to exposure therapy or to anticipate that treatment may take longer than usual to produce an improvement.

The mechanisms of action of many psychotherapies have been and continue to be investigated; for example, cognitive therapy (e.g., DeRubeis et al. 1990; Floyd and Scogin 1998), mindfulness (e.g., Kuyken et al. 2010), offender rehabil-itation therapy (Yesberg and Polaschek 2019), and sleep restriction therapy for insomnia (Maurer, Espie, and Kyle 2018). Such investigations often make use of RCT methodology. For example, studies have been done on the effectiveness of real-life exposure therapy for people with phobias by randomly assigning par-ticipants to receive either a narcotic antagonist pill before a therapy session or a placebo pill. In these studies, assessments are made of phobic avoidance, sub-jective fear, and physiological arousal before and after treatment sessions. The finding that clinical improvement is impaired in those who receive the narcotic antagonist is suggestive, albeit indirectly, that endogenous opiate production during exposure is one possible explanation of how this treatment works on a biological level. This is fascinating work and an area largely neglected by social work clinical researchers.

10. How cost-effective is the experimental treatment?

In this line of research, investigators are interested in a couple issues. One is how much it costs to provide a given therapy. Another is how much it costs to pro-duce a certain outcome. Both questions can be answered by a cost-effectiveness study. Once answers to these questions have been determined, it is often useful to determine whether one treatment is more cost-effective than another.

Cost-effectiveness can be determined simply by dividing the cost of a treat-ment by the number of clients treated. If a child welfare agency has an annual budget of $500,000 to conduct CPS investigations and completes five hundred investigations in a year, the cost is $500,000 ÷ 500 = $1,000 per investigation.

To be accurate, such assessments need to include all pertinent costs. And this example also ignores the issue of successes and failures in outcomes. We want to determine more than the number of clients we served; we want to know how many clients we have actually helped. Take, for example, an employment counseling program that costs $1 million a year and serves one thousand clients. Roughly, this means the service costs about $1,000 per client. A more valuable metric would be the number of clients who had a favorable outcome, not only completing the program but also finding a job. If we use finding a job as our more pertinent benchmark and learn that of the one thousand clients who took part in the program, only five hundred obtained employment, the service would be considered to cost about $2,000 per successful outcome ($1 million ÷ 500 = $2,000). Thus, we find that it costs twice as much to help people obtain work than it does to simply have them complete the program. This type of study is called a cost-benefit analysis (see Royse, Thyer, and Padgett 2016).

Another example of a cost-effectiveness study is an evaluation of a treatment program for people who meet the DSM-5 criteria for PTSD and receive a social security or Veterans Affairs (VA) disability pension. If it costs $500,000 to treat one hundred people and fifty achieve complete remission, the cost per successful outcome is about $10,000 ($500,000 ÷ 50 = $10,000). That may be a lot of money, but if people with PTSD are able to return to work and stop receiving their social security or VA pension, the cost of those pensions could be recovered in less than a year.

RCT methods can be used for both cost-effectiveness and cost-benefit analyses of treatments. While they are not common in the social work literature, Rizzo and Rowe (2006) provide a review of about forty such studies. Cost-effectiveness and cost-benefit studies should not be done until an intervention has been shown to be effective. It makes little sense to know how much it costs to provide a treatment or produce some unit of improvement if we do not already know, through high-quality RCTs, that the treatment is genuinely beneficial.

Evaluating Clinical Pharmacological Interventions

As with the effectiveness of clinical psychosocial interventions, the effectiveness of pharmacological (drug) treatments is best investigated using RCT methodology. Again, it is important to remember that to say something is the *best* method of evaluation does not mean it is the *only* method or the only useful method. Clinical researchers have many tools to ascertain the effects of a given treatment, whether psychotherapeutic or pharmacological. Apart from RCTs we have quasi-experimental designs, studies involving two or more groups that are formed naturalistically or in any other manner except random assignment (Thyer 2012). We have case-control and cohort studies, epidemiological investigations, correlational studies, and single-subject evaluations. All can be valuable under the right circumstances. But when the question is causal in nature (e.g., "Does the treatment cause an improvement?"), the RCT approach is usually the best, as it can control for bias and eliminate threats to internal validity.

I will now review in the abstract the various designs that can be used to investigate pharmacological agents. Structurally, the bare bones of the designs consist of the same patterns of Xs and Os depicted earlier in this chapter and in table 4.1. Similar outcome questions of increasing complexity are investigated using the same designs used to test psychotherapies. Ideally, a new therapy is initially compared against nothing (e.g., in one arm of the study participants receive no treatment). If there is no difference in outcome, then you likely have a dead end and can conclude the experimental treatment does not work. If it is better than nothing, then it can be tested against one or more placebo treatments. Placebo medications are usually easier to implement than placebo psychotherapies. Placebo pills can typically be made identical to the experimental ones, allowing for neither the participant nor the provider to know which medication a participant is receiving. If the experimental treatment produces some side effects, a placebo medication that causes similar side effects should be used. For example, if an experimental medication causes slight sedation, a suitable placebo medication might contain diphenhydramine, a common allergy medication with a slight sedative effect. Such drugs are called *active placebos* (as opposed to *inert placebos*, which have no effects). When an active placebo is used, it is easier to maintain a single-blind or double-blind condition. In single-blinding, the participant does not know which therapy or medication they are receiving, but the researcher does. In double-blinding, neither the participant nor the researcher knows. Obviously the more similar the placebo medication is to the experimental medication, the greater the ability to control for placebo effects.

Placebo effects themselves can be manipulated. For example, bigger pills are usually more effective than smaller ones at inducing a placebo effect. Red pills have a different impact from blue ones. Pills that are described to participants as expensive produce a greater effect than pills described as inexpensive. And injected placebos are more powerful than pill placebos.

One does not usually think of social workers as undertaking trials of medications, psychopharmacological or otherwise. Such studies are more often considered the purview of physicians. However, social workers have an extensive history of conducting studies of medications. Nowadays this commonly occurs when a social worker is a part of an interdisciplinary treatment team, including physicians and perhaps other health care professionals. (See the appendix for numerous pharmacological outcome studies authored or coauthored by social workers.) Many medications have been evaluated for the treatment of many diseases and clinical disorders over the years. Social work involvement

TABLE 4.1 Selected types of RCTs and the threats to internal validity they are designed to control for

Design[a]				Threats potentially controlled for
Posttest-only				
No-treatment control				
R	X	O_1		Passage of time
R		O_1		Maturation
				Concurrent history
No-treatment and placebo control				
R	X	O_1		Passage of time
R	$X_{placebo}$	O_1		Maturation
R		O_1		Placebo factors
				Concurrent history
Comparison treatment				
R	X	O_1		Passage of time
R	X_{TAU}	O_1		Maturation
R		O_1		Concurrent history
Comparison treatment and placebo control				
R	X	O_1		Passage of time
R	X_{TAU}	O_1		Maturation
R	$X_{placebo}$	O_1		Placebo factors
R		O_1		Concurrent history
Pretest–posttest				
No-treatment control				
R	O_1	X	O_2	Passage of time
R	O_1		O_2	Maturation
				Pretest differences
				Regression to the mean
				Concurrent history
Placebo control				
R	O_1	X	O_2	Placebo factors
R	O_1	$X_{placebo}$	O_2	Pretest differences
No-treatment and placebo control				
R	O_1	X	O_2	Placebo factors
R	O_1	$X_{placebo}$	O_2	Pretest differences
R	O_1	X_{TAU}	O_2	

Comparison treatment

R	O_1	X	O_2				Placebo factors
R	O_1	X_{TAU}	O_2				Pretest differences
R	O_1	$X_{placebo}$	O_2				Maturation
R	O_1		O_2				Regression to the mean
							Concurrent history

Switching replication

R	O_1	X	O_2		O_3	Pretest differences
R	O_1		O_2	X	O_3	Maturation
						Concurrent history
						Regression to the mean
						Maintenance of gains

Solomon four-group

R	O_1	X	O_2				Concurrent history
R	O_1	X	O_2				Pretest differences
R	O_1		O_2				Maturation
R		X	O_1				Effects of repeated testing
							Passage of time

Stepped-wedge

		Month[b]					Concurrent history
		1	2	3	4	5	Pretest differences
R	Group 1[c]	O_1	XO_2	XO_3	XO_4	XO_5	Maturation
R	Group 2	O_1	O_2	XO_3	XO_4	XO_5	Passage of time
R	Group 3	O_1	O_2	O_3	XO_4	XO_5	
R	Group 4	O_1	O_2	O_3	O_4	XO_5	

[a]Each of these RCT designs can be strengthened by adding additional posttests (to assess the durability of any changes) or pretests (to control for possible preexisting trends in the data, whether upward or downward).

[b]The time period need not be one month. It can also be days, weeks, or years, for example.

[c]The groups can consist of individuals assigned to each group or some sort of "clustered" group, as in a school, dormitory, village, town, or county. If clustered groups, the design would be called a stepped-wedge cluster randomized design.

in pharmacotherapy outcome studies is by no means limited to the treatment of mental illnesses such as depression or schizophrenia; a good many somatic disorders have also been assessed.

In some instances, social workers have been leaders in medication outcome studies. For example, Gerard Hogarty, MSW, was the first author of an interdisciplinary study looking at the effects of family psychoeducation, social skills training, and maintenance drug therapy for people with schizophrenia published in the *Archives of General Psychiatry* (now *JAMA Psychiatry*), one of the world's premier psychiatric journals (Hogarty et al. 1986). This article is just one of the dozens evaluating medication use that Hogarty has published. This paper has been cited more than 1,100 times according to Google Scholar, an astonishing measure of influence. Hogarty reached the rank of full professor with the Department of Psychiatry at the University of Pittsburgh School of Medicine even though he lacked a doctoral degree in any field (Eack 2010).

Another world-class social work clinical researcher in the area of psychotropic medications alone, in combination with psychosocial treatments, and compared with psychosocial therapies is Myrna Weissman. She received her MSW from the University of Pennsylvania, and her PhD in epidemiology from the Yale School of Medicine. Weissman quite literally wrote the book on a new and effective treatment called interpersonal psychotherapy for depression (Klerman et al. 1984). Interpersonal psychotherapy has been extensively evaluated for almost four decades, and Weissman's book has been translated into many languages and cited more than 3,300 times. Weissman has also published many high-quality RCTs in leading journals in the areas of depression, panic disorder, and other conditions, as well as basic science investigations of the underlying neurobiology of psychiatric conditions. Weissman's efforts are proof that social workers, with their person-in-environment, life-span, and biopsychosocial perspectives, are well positioned to make contributions in treatment outcome studies in areas not normally considered within the scope of social work practice. Few of us conduct trials of medications, but the potential is there for any of us to do so. Doing so does not mean abandoning our identity as social workers. Nurses, psychologists, statisticians, and indeed professionals of many disciplines all provide valuable contributions to RCTs evaluating medications and other somatic treatments without being seen to abandon their home discipline.

Evaluating Other Somatic Clinical Therapies

In the broad field of health care, social workers are involved as therapists and clinical researchers not only in evaluating the effects of psychosocial treatments such as psychotherapy and behavior analysis but also in the design and conduct of RCTs of psychopharmacological agents. Less recognized are our professional contributions in the evaluation of other forms of somatic therapies. Examples of these treatments include massage, electroconvulsive shock therapy, yoga, biofeedback, weightlifting, hip protectors to prevent hip fracture, exercise programs, nicotine transdermal patches to reduce smoking, methadone maintenance, sex therapy, and the bell-and-pad device for nocturnal enuresis. All have been evaluated using RCT designs in articles published by social workers. (See the appendix for many of these.)

Evaluating Complementary and Alternative Treatments

RCTs are also used by social workers to evaluate the ever-more-popular complementary and alternative treatments. A review of the appendix will show that among the independent variables (i.e., treatments) that have been evaluated are prayer, so-called energy therapies, hypnosis, music therapy, tai chi, dance therapy, clay art therapy, meditation, hip-hop therapy, and craniosacral therapy. In some instances, social workers have provided these treatments, whereas in others they did not provide treatment but were involved in the design of the study and developed sufficient elements of the project to warrant authorship. Herbal products, such as echinacea and lecithin, have also been evaluated in experimental outcome studies authored by social workers.

Evaluating Community-Based Interventions

In addition to providing clinical services to individuals, small groups, couples, and families, social workers also provide community-based interventions. Unlike most clinical services, which are delivered in social workers' offices, community-based interventions tend to be delivered in community environments, such as local neighborhood sites like the premises of nongovernmental organizations, community centers, schools, libraries, parks, and governmental offices. Selected examples of the types of community-based interventions that have been investigated by social workers using RCTs include programs such as individual development accounts (matched savings programs targeting goals such as building a home or funding a college education; see Richards and Thyer 2011), child development accounts (externally funded saving accounts opened in the name of a child used to fund selected goals), home visitation programs designed to prevent child abuse, home visitation programs to provide support for older people, supported employment and job-finding services, housing programs for people who are homeless, welfare rights advice, community-integrated home-based depression treatment, wraparound services for adolescents, counseling provided in hospital emergency departments, in-home family-focused family reunification services, cancer screening, child care services, programs to promote voting among Black people living on a low income, and foster care services. Designing RCTs to evaluate community-based social work services presents a unique set of challenges. Books are available that describe these types of studies, broadly labeled field experiments (as opposed to office-based services). Solomon, Cavanaugh, and Draine (2009) and Gerber and Green (2012) are valuable in this regard.

Evaluating Large-Scale Social Programs

Large-scale social programs are social welfare interventions, broadly conceived, that are implemented on a scale larger than that of community-based treatments. These may be undertaken within the context of a city, state, or nation or may be undertaken internationally. As might be imagined, the challenge of participant recruitment and carrying out a truly randomized assignment, one that does not break down, is formidable. However, an impressive number of large-scale RCTs of social welfare and other policy innovations have been published. Examples of such evaluations undertaken by social workers have involved the Aid to Families with Dependent Children program (now called Temporary Assistance for Needy Families), negative-income tax policies, and Medicaid (looking at the health and psychosocial effects of Medicaid on people living on a low income). The social worker Heidi Allen has been extensively involved in the Oregon Health Insurance Experiment and has authored a number of studies on this impressive RCT (e.g., Allen et al. 2010; Allen, Wright, and Broffman 2018), some of which will be described in a later chapter.

There is a substantial literature describing the application of experimental methods to the assessment of large-scale social programs, such as the Head Start initiative, the evaluation of which has been going on for decades. Some of this literature can be found in works by Stoesz (2020); Crane (1998); Campbell and Russo (1999); and Rossi and Williams (1972). RCTs of large-scale social programs are often very complex and illustrate the numerous obstacles to maintaining the integrity of random assignment, treatment fidelity, and other essential elements of experimentation, but there are enough successes to illustrate that the endeavors are worthwhile.

Evaluating Educational Interventions

Social workers practice in a wide array of settings, including hospitals; community clinics; private, state, and federal agencies; the military; VA facilities;

schools; and private practices. One practice niche is occupied by social work faculty, typically individuals with an MSW or doctoral degree in social work or another field who engage in teaching, service, and scholarly research. Faculty are always seeking effective methods of teaching and field instruction to provide a high-quality educational experience for their students. One of the best sources of credible information about effective pedagogical practice is the findings of empirical outcome studies of teaching methods. Reviews of such studies (e.g., Sowers-Hoag and Thyer 1985; Wodarski et al. 1991) have found that most made use of pre-experimental or quasi-experimental research designs. Very few true experimental studies have been used for this purpose. The difficulties of conducting educational experiments mitigate against the widespread use of these designs. For example, students self-select the section of a class they enroll in, so they usually cannot be randomly assigned to an experimental educational technique or TAU (in this case, teaching as usual), and it would not be feasible or ethical to provide a placebo education to tuition-paying students. But with a little thought, experiments are possible.

For example, if two required classes were taught in back-to-back school terms, half the students could be randomly assigned to one class (say a human behavior course) first and the second class (say a research methods class) the next term, and vice versa. This study design could be diagrammed as follows:

| R | O_1 | $X_{behavior}$ | $O_2 O_3$ | $Y_{research}$ | O_4 |
| R | O_1 | $X_{research}$ | $O_2 O_3$ | $Y_{behavior}$ | O_4 |

Assume we have separate valid pencil-and-paper tests of students' knowledge of human behavior and research methods. At the first assessment, O_1, the beginning of the first term, both classes take both tests. Because of the magic of random assignment, they should score similarly. At the second assessment, at the end of the first term, they take both tests again. If we hypothesized that the course teaching was specific and effective, the top group, taught human behavior, would have improved scores on the measure of human behavior knowledge at O_2 but would improve little, if at all, on the measure of research methods knowledge. The second group would have improved scores on research methods but not on human behavior on at O_2. At O_3 (the beginning of the second term), both groups retake both tests and likely score similarly to O_2. In this term, the top group of students is taught research methods, and the bottom group is taught human behavior. At the end of the term, O_4, both classes are again assessed with both tests. We would now hypothesize that if teaching had been specific and effective, the research methods students would improve on their research methods assessments but not on human behavior (which they had taken the previous term), and the human behavior students would improve their scores on the test of human behavior but not research methods (which they had taken the previous term). To illustrate further, let us say the tests have a maximum score of 100 points and that we obtained the following results:

Mean scores at each assessment

			O_1	O_2	O_3	O_4
	R	Research	50	52	52	94
Group 1 (behavior first)	R	Behavior	50	80	78	76
	R	Research	50	80	77	75
Group 2 (research first)	R	Behavior	50	53	52	92

See if you can follow the logic of concluding that teaching was specific and effective, as demonstrated by the experimental data. At O_1, all groups scored about the same, which is what one would expect owing to random assignment. At O_2, the group taught human behavior improved their human behavior knowledge but not their research knowledge, whereas the group taught research methods improved their knowledge in that domain but not in human behavior. At O_3, both groups' scores of knowledge of both subjects remained about the same at as at O_2. At O_4, each group showed improvement in their knowledge of the course they were taught that term and little change in their knowledge of the other subject. This design could be used to test the following hypotheses:

1. At the beginning of term 1, each group will earn similar scores on both tests and at the end of the term will have improved scores only on the test of the subject they were taught that term.
2. At the beginning of term 2, both groups' scores on both subjects will remain similar to those from the end of term 1.
3. At the end of term 2, each group will improve their scores only on the test for the subject they were taught that term.
4. At the end of term 2, the scores on the test of the subject each group was *not* taught will remain similar to their scores on that subject at the beginning of term 2.

If we had posed these hypotheses in advance and the data we collected looked like what has been described, we could say that each hypothesis was corroborated or supported. (Recall that we rarely claim that hypotheses are proved to be true, or confirmed, in the social and behavioral sciences.) This finding would indicate that the education provided had been specific and effective. Score improvements only on the test of the subject taught each term provide evidence of subject-specific knowledge gains that are a result of the content taught, not some general increase in overall social work knowledge over time. This type of design, in which two groups of participants undergo two treatment conditions sequentially and which demonstrates that improvements were consistent but limited to receiving a specific treatment, is a powerful form of RCT design called the *switching replication design* or *crossover design*. Both descriptions convey the logic of the design. A variation is to compare an experimental treatment with no treatment and then to provide the experimental treatment to those initially denied it, again assessing both groups at three points in time.

Although true experimental outcome studies on social work teaching methods are rare, they are not unknown. Two solid ones were published by Tennille et al. (2016) and Pecukonis et al. (2016). More use of this valuable method is needed given the relatively sparse empirical foundations of social work pedagogy.

Evaluating Preferences

Experimental designs can be used to test people's preferences. This is usually done under blind conditions involving multiple presentations of stimuli. Think of blind taste-testing in wine-tasting competitions. The expert judges do not know the brand or vintage of what they sip, and they are presented small amounts of different wines in unmarked glasses and in a random order. This is done to try to minimize subjective biases related to various vintners as disclosed by bottle shape and label.

De Wit et al. (1986) is an example of this type of study coauthored by a social worker. In this study, the researchers wished to test whether a tranquilizer drug (diazepam) was preferred over a placebo or an amphetamine. Forty-two participants with anxiety were recruited, and the initial sample consisted of twelve control participants (people without anxiety), thirteen participants who met the DSM-III criteria for generalized anxiety disorder, and eleven participants who experienced subclinical anxiousness. Participants were administered one of three consistently different-colored capsules containing diazepam, placebo, or amphetamine. They returned for multiple administrations of these drugs and completed ratings of their mood one, three, and six hours after drug ingestion. At hour six, they also indicated their liking for the drug on a scale ranging from "disliked a lot" to "liked a lot." They were asked to note the color of the capsule they had ingested and to guess which drug it contained. Each trial consisted of three sessions a week over three weeks, and the drugs were administered in a random order under blind conditions. During the last five sessions, the participants could choose the colored capsule they wished to ingest (thinking that based on their past experience, it was either diazepam or amphetamine). According to the authors, "the experimental hypothesis was that diazepam would be preferred over placebo by the anxious subjects but not by the controls" (de Wit et al. 1986, 534). They reported,

> The main findings from these experiments were as follows: (1) Anxious subjects were no more likely to either choose or to like diazepam than normal subjects. All groups chose diazepam less often than placebo. . . . (2) Diazepam did not affect the anxious and normal subjects' mood differently, nor was it labeled as a tranquilizer more or less accurately across the groups. Anxiety scores in all three groups were decreased by the drug. . . . (3) Amphetamine was preferred to placebo by the majority of the subjects in all experimental groups. . . . Amphetamine and diazepam produced typical stimulant-like and tranquilizer-like mood changes that did not differ among the groups.
>
> (de Wit et al. 1986, 539)

One conclusion arrived at by the authors was that none of the groups preferred the tranquilizer over the placebo and that a person's level of anxiousness may not impact their likelihood to develop drug dependence. This finding was unexpected. However, six people had dropped out from the original forty-two recruited, and the findings from this small sample size begged for replication.

In an experimental study, Hargreaves et al. (1974) used a posttest-only design to evaluate clients' preferences for individual therapy, formal group therapy, or a daily nonappointment contact group. The contact group was a control condition in which clients could attend or not as they wished and was run as a form of peer support, rather than formal treatment provided by a mental health professional. The study was conducted over a nine-week period at an outpatient mental health clinic in San Francisco, which randomly assigned all new clients seeking treatment to one of the conditions. The outcome measure consisted of whether clients appeared for their first appointment and, if they did, how satisfied they were with their experience of that session. New clients were offered participation in the study, and it was explained to them they would be randomly assigned to get individual therapy, group therapy, or the peer-support group. This study design can be diagrammed as follows:

Treatment assigned

Individual therapy	R	X	O_1
Group therapy	R	Y	O_1
Informal support	R	Z	O_1

The primary dependent variable consisted of whether clients attended their first session. There were a number of other secondary measures, and these were correlated with attendance. A number of client demographic and clinical factors were also recorded at intake and used to assess their possible interactive effects with the major outcome measure of first-appointment attendance. The authors found that 85 percent of clients randomly assigned to individual therapy attended their first appointment, 59 percent of those assigned to group therapy attended their first session, and 71 percent assigned to the peer-support group attended their first meeting. These results were statistically significant and showed a preference for individual therapy over group therapy and peer support and for peer support over group therapy.

This study was seen as an exploratory investigation and rightly so. Few like it have been undertaken. And rate of attendance at a first appointment is not necessarily an indicator of subsequent appointment-keeping, much less of the potential effectiveness of the assigned treatment. However, the study was worth doing because peer-support groups are less expensive to offer than group treatment provided by a trained therapist, which is in turn less expensive than individual psychotherapy. If there had been no differences in client preference, agencies might have decided to assign clients to less expensive treatments. But clients had demonstrated their preference for treatment type by attending more of the individual therapy sessions than the other treatment modalities. Regardless of the clinical practicality of the results of this study, it does illustrate the use of experimental methodology to assess preferences.

Inappropriate Use of the Term "Experiment"

Having reviewed the useful purposes to which experimental research can be put, let us take a look at what experiments are *not*. In 1932, a long-term field study was begun in Macon County, Alabama. The study's intent was to examine the natural course of syphilis, a sexually transmitted infection that was greatly stigmatized. At the time, treatments for syphilis were little more than unpleasant placebos. Macon County was chosen because large-scale blood-testing studies being conducted across the southern United States revealed that a large proportion of its residents had syphilis. Roughly four hundred men with syphilis were recruited and promised free treatment for "bad blood," and about two hundred men without syphilis served as a comparison group. All participants were Black. Under the guise of "treatment," spinal taps were used to collect specimens of spinal fluid. No participants were told they had syphilis. Perhaps this was understandable given the stigma associated with the disease at the time. If word had gotten out that the men were participating in a "syphilis study," recruitment would likely have been very difficult, and the dropout rate would likely have been very high. However, being truthful with research participants is of paramount importance, and the failure to properly inform them of the nature of their disease was clearly an unethical practice. A similar epidemiological study had been conducted several decades earlier in Norway, exclusively using white participants, and a second goal of the study was to compare disease progression and symptom development between Black and white populations using the data from the Norwegian study.

Well into the study, an effective syphilis medication became available—penicillin—and the researchers held meetings to decide what to do with this information. Tragically, they decided to continue the study, withhold treatment, and refrain from telling participants in the treatment condition the name of their disease for fear they might seek treatment elsewhere. This unconscionable state of affairs persisted until 1972, when the study was discontinued and the surviving men with syphilis were provided effective treatment. More than two dozen had died from the disease. This study was named after the county seat of Macon County, Tuskegee, and what became known as the Tuskegee Syphilis Experiment is a textbook case of research ethics gone awry. In 1997, President Clinton offered a formal apology on behalf of the United States government for the injuries and deceptions experienced by the surviving participants and their families. Confusion remains regarding what this study truly was. It was *not* an experiment. No independent variable was introduced (participants were not deliberately infected with syphilis), participants were not randomly assigned, and no real treatment was provided. Yet the literature, even fairly recent literature, continues to refer to this infamous study as an experiment (McGrath 2021). Even medical journals have called it an experiment (Carmack, Bates, and Harter 2008), including one study coauthored by a social worker (Wallace et al. 2007). Publications from other disciplines have followed suit, such as Harter, Stephens, and Japp (2000).

From the beginnings of professional social work, social workers, too, have incorrectly described various formal projects and research studies as experiments when what was being described in no way possessed the prerequisites of true experimental analyses. Although the creation of Frankenstein's monster has been described as an experiment in medicine and the moon landing as an experiment in engineering, these instances are slipshod uses of the term. Innovative educational programs for social workers have also incorrectly been referred to as experiments (e.g., Caddick 1994; Neilson 1919; Hyde and Murphy 1955; Moss and Davidson 1982), as have new research and service programs (e.g., Flynn, Brekke, and Soydan 2008; Webb et al. 1991) and new social policies (Young, Johnson, and Bryant 2002). But none of these examples describes the design and conduct of a true randomized experiment. From these examples, it is little wonder that the general public, social work students, and even seasoned social work professionals are often confused by the research social workers do. Research psychologists who are more conservative in their use of the terms "experiment" and "experimental" smile and shake their heads at these silly social workers who cannot even use the simplest terminology correctly. As a profession, social work needs to curtail the incorrect use of crucial terms like "experimental study" and stop describing every little hiccup of something new in our services and training as an "experiment." These nonexperiments may well convey important information, but incorrectly labeling them detracts from their value. In a later chapter, I will describe a tool called the Consolidated Standards of Reporting Trials of Social and Psychological Interventions (CONSORT-SPI), a checklist to help authors report RCTs of social and psychological interventions. One of its recommendations is to include the term "randomized trial" in the title of any such study. It would be useful for social workers to include this term in all reports of true experimental investigations.

In the meantime, we can scan studies said to be an experiment to see if they provide a clear description of how participants were *randomly assigned* to two or more conditions. If there is no such description, it is *not* a true experimental study. Of course, much more than random assignment goes into the design of an experiment. A research question is essential, from which are derived one or more specific and directional hypotheses. Good hypotheses do more than predict changes or differences—they also state the *direction* and ideally the *magnitude* of the effect expected to be found posttreatment. To say that after treatment, the two groups will *differ* on the mean score of the primary outcome measure is a simplistic start in hypothesis development. To hypothesize that the treatment group will experience greater *improvements* than the no-treatment group adds the valuable element of directionality to the prediction. To further refine the hypothesis by predicting not just the direction of change but also the magnitude is better still, as in "The treatment group will improve by more than 10 points posttreatment compared to the no-treatment group." Each additional element clarifies the hypothesis more but also makes it riskier, more susceptible to refutation. Saying the groups will differ posttreatment is easier to corroborate than predicting which group will do better than the other. Saying the difference will be of a particular magnitude is much easier to refute; thus, if the hypothesis is corroborated, we can have greater confidence that a genuine effect was found. If the hypothesis predicts at least a 10-point difference between groups posttreatment, and an 11-point difference was found, the hypothesis *was supported*. If it was a 9-point difference, the hypothesis *was not supported*. Finding a difference is easy. Finding a difference in a *direction* predicted in advance is harder. Finding a difference in a *predicted direction* with a *predicted magnitude* is harder still. By establishing a clear, directional hypothesis predicting a certain magnitude of difference, we make the hypothesis easier to falsify. Thus, if the hypothesis survives (i.e., is corroborated), we can be more confident that we really did find something representing a true effect.

An experiment must also have an *independent variable*, a factor that is deliberately manipulated in some way. An experimental treatment can be applied or withheld, for example, to see whether treatment is followed by more improvements than receiving no treatment. A vignette study can describe an older or younger person to see whether age impacts clinical judgments of social workers. In treatment studies, the independent variable is ideally something that is fairly structured, such as a therapy that follows a treatment manual, practice guideline, or algorithm. This structure makes for a "cleaner" experiment than an unstructured treatment provided without the use of guidelines of some sort, as the structured treatment will be provided in a more consistent way. An effective experiment also has one or more *dependent variables*, outcome measures that are anticipated to be affected by the independent variable. Dependent variables should have acceptable *reliability* and *validity*; otherwise, it is less likely that you will find effects from the independent variable. The sample size of each group must also be large enough to power inferential statistical tests. If the groups are too small, your tests will not reveal any potential effects of the independent variable. These are just a few of the features of true experiments. If you are reading about a supposed experiment and these elements are absent, then the project is something else. Researchers must preserve the integrity of true experiments by describing their research projects appropriately.

Many so-called experiments are well known because they reflect severely unethical research practices and, in many cases, hurt people. The medical atrocities committed by Nazi doctors on concentration camp prisoners are but one example. Others include the "experiments" conducted by Japanese physicians on Russian and Chinese prisoners of war during World War II, the "Tuskegee Experiment," Milgram's shock "experiments," Zimbardo's Stanford prison "experiment," and the "experiments" conducted by the CIA on nonconsenting people involving the administration of psychedelic drugs. All these projects have two things in common. They were extremely unethical, and they were *not* experiments. Yet these studies continue to be referred to as experiments, which undoubtedly contributes to the aversion the term "experiment" can evoke. Pairing an originally benign word like "experiment" with horrific acts that harmed people can produce unpleasant conditioned responses to that word (see Thyer 2012). This phenomenon may contribute to some of the distain for experiments expressed by otherwise well-informed and intelligent people, including social work scholars.

Summary

Experimental designs have many uses in social work research and are particularly valuable when a research question involves causal inference. We have seen how experiments can be used to study how various features of clients and social workers can bias clinical judgment and decision-making. Via the powerful tool of the vignette study, we can empirically determine whether certain client or social worker features that should be immaterial to an impartial assessment actually affect people's judgments. Conversely, we can determine how social worker characteristics impact clients' appraisals of us. Do white clients prefer to see white social workers? Do Black clients see therapist race as a reflection of a clinician's competence? Is an unmarried, childless social worker seen as less capable of treating children than a social worker who is a parent? Vignette studies can help answer many questions like this.

We have seen the wide array of true experimental designs that can be used to assess the outcomes of a new or existing treatment compared with no treatment, placebo, or treatment as usual. With experiments we can evaluate the durability of improvements and the occurrence of both positive and negative side effects. We can examine the true effect of large-scale social programs and educational methods. Indeed, almost the entirety of social work practice can be fruitfully evaluated using randomized experiments. The term "experiment" has been widely misused and in some cases inappropriately associated with truly awful (and usually low-quality) research studies. This misuse may hinder the profession's embrace of genuine experimental methods.

CHAPTER 5

POSTTEST-ONLY EXPERIMENTAL DESIGNS

Development of Western science is based on two great achievements: the invention of the formal logical system ... and the discovery of the possibility to find out causal relationships by systematic experiment.

—Albert Einstein

This chapter is largely devoted to describing previously published posttest-only randomized experiments, with most examples having been authored by one or more professional social workers. Professional social workers are defined by having earned at least one degree in social work: a bachelor's, master's, or doctorate. To facilitate understanding, the following elements will be described for each study: the citation, the research question(s), the research hypotheses, the intervention(s), the outcome measure(s), and the results. Only summaries of the studies will be presented; for full details, review the primary articles themselves.

As stated, the defining characteristic of a true experimental design is the random assignment of participants to two or more conditions, with at least one being the experimental intervention and the other condition or conditions acting as comparisons for the experimental treatment, such as no treatment, treatment as usual (TAU), a placebo, or an alternative therapy. Random assignment virtually ensures that the assigned groups are essentially equivalent on all relevant dimensions before the study begins. Random assignment requires enough people, of course. If you begin with only ten participants, you may end up with two groups of five, but you could also easily have unequal groups, such as one group of seven and one of three. Too small a number can also result in a lack of distribution of demographic variables (e.g., age, race, or gender) across groups. For example, you could easily end up with more men in one arm of the study and more women in the other, or too many people of Hispanic descent in one group and too few in the other. Or you could end up with groups that are unequal in terms of the severity of a disorder—differences that may emerge only when participants are assessed posttreatment.

In an RCT of a treatment for depression with a small sample size, if there are differences at posttreatment, is that because the treatment was effective or because of (unmeasured) preexisting differences between the groups before treatment began? Absent pretreatment assessments, there is no way to know. However, the potential for an unequal distribution of clinical signs and symptoms is less of a problem with larger sample sizes. While you would not be surprised to obtain a group of six participants and one of four in a small study (from an initial sample of ten), it would be quite surprising to find that after tossing a coin one hundred times to randomly assign one hundred participants to end up with one group of sixty and one of forty. Assuming that you have a normal coin and toss it the same way each time, you would very likely end up with two groups of close to fifty people each. If you do not believe me, take out a coin and toss it one hundred times. Toss a coin in an unbiased way 1,000 times, and you are likely to end up with two groups of very close to 500 each, certainly not 600 and 400 or even 550 and 450. Thus, with a large enough sample size, we can be sure to end up with groups of not only approximately equal size but also similar in terms of demographic and clinical features. This even distribution means that we do not need to measure demographic features and outcome variables pretreatment and that we can conduct experiments lacking pretreatment assessments with some confidence regarding the groups' equivalence on all relevant features. And we can then attribute any posttreatment differences between groups to the interventions they were (or were not) exposed to.

The classic reference work on the topic of experimental designs (Campbell and Stanley 1963) has this to say on the need for pretests: "While the pretest is a concept deeply embedded in the thinking of research workers in education and psychology, *it is not actually essential* to true experimental designs. For psychological reasons it is difficult to give up 'knowing for sure' that the experimental and control groups were 'equal' before the differential experimental treatment. Nonetheless, the most adequate all-purpose assurance of lack of initial biases between groups is randomization. Within the limits of confidence stated by the tests of significance, randomization can suffice without the pretest" (25, my emphasis).

It is worth noting that random assignment works its magic *regardless* of whether you obtained your sample randomly. You *do not need* a *randomly selected* group of people to conduct a true experiment—you need only be able to *randomly assign* them to the various experimental conditions. If you can do this, you can make causal inferences about your sample if an effect is observed posttreatment.

Lacking a sample of participants selected from the population of interest (e.g., people with a particular disorder), you cannot legitimately generalize the findings of your experiment to that larger population of interest. This is a limitation of *external* validity, but most experiments typically do not involve randomly selected participants and hence do not produce generalizable findings, *no matter how large the sample size*. But all experiments must involve the *random assignment* of participants within the context of the study itself.

It should be noted that randomized experiments are not limited to two arms or conditions. It is not uncommon to have three, four, or many more conditions, as long as they are created using random assignment. For a two-arm study, you could use a coin toss to randomly assign participants. For a three-arm study (e.g., experimental treatment, no treatment, and TAU), you could toss a die, with a roll of 1 or 2 assigning a participant to condition 1, a roll of 3 or 4 assigning a participant to condition 2, and a roll of 5 or 6 assigning a participant to condition 3. You could use a single die to assign participants to up to six conditions. However, most researchers use the random-number generator feature of various statistical software packages to assign participants to conditions. Regardless of method, it is good practice to have a second party observe the random assignment process as a control to ensure it was conducted appropriately.

The Influence of Race on Diagnosis

Blake, W. 1973. "The Influence of Race on Diagnosis." *Smith College Studies in Social Work* 43, no. 3: 184–92.

We will begin our review of posttest-only randomized experiments with a relatively simple example. This study was originally submitted as an MSW thesis at the Smith College School for Social Work and subsequently published in the peer-reviewed journal supported by that program. The project built on prior studies indicating that a client's race could have an influence on the severity of the diagnosis arrived at by clinicians. The research question was, "Does a presumptive client's race influence the diagnostic judgments of psychiatric residents?"

The author prepared a four-page case vignette describing a presumptive patient: a twenty-seven-year-old twice-married woman who complained of recurrent nightmares. Two second-year psychiatric residents agreed that the vignette was realistic. Two paper case reports were prepared, each with the same description of the patient but one with a photograph of a Black woman as the presumptive patient attached and the other with a photograph of a white woman attached.

Seventeen first-year psychiatric residents from three metropolitan hospitals in New York City were recruited to participate in the study. All but one were male. The materials were distributed to the residents by the chief resident at each hospital. Each resident was provided one of the two case reports on a random basis and asked to read the vignette and provide a presumptive diagnosis, as well as to rate variables such as favorableness of prognosis, adequacy of ego functions, the resident's interest in potentially treating the "patient," and anticipated treatment success. The hypothesis was along the lines of "The case report depicting a Black patient will be less favorably evaluated than the case report depicting a white patient."

According to the author, "It was evident that the analog in which the patient was identified as Black was classified among the schizophrenia or borderline categories by almost all respondents. . . . The analog in which the patient was identified as white was predominantly diagnosed as obsessive-compulsive. . . . It was found that except for the rating of the respondent's interest in offering treatment, in each of these comparisons the white form of the case material elicited more favorable responses. . . . This research lends support for the hypothesis that the variable of race may systematically influence the process of arriving at a clinical formulation" (Blake 1973, 190–91). The experimental design for this study can be diagrammed as follows:

| R | $X_{\text{Black patient}}$ | O_1 |
| R | $X_{\text{white patient}}$ | O_1 |

The lesson from this investigation by Wilmatine Blake, who was herself Black, is illustrated in a quotation from Curry (1968): "Inter-racial group tensions permeate every aspect of our contemporary society and there is no reason to believe client-workers relationship is immune to them" (551). Blake's article could be a citation from contemporary critical race theory, though critical race theory did not exist when this study was undertaken. As the French say, *plus ça change, plus c'est la même chose* (the more things change, the more they stay the same).

This is an example of a type of randomized experiment called a vignette study, further examples of which we will encounter elsewhere in this book. These are not studies of the effects of social work treatment but are used to help study decision-making and the clinical diagnostic process. Reasonable variations in the independent variable in studies of this type could look at features like gender, sexual orientation, socioeconomic status, religion, or political affiliation.

Virtually any factor can be experimentally manipulated in the narrative reports provided in the vignettes. One can also look at the intersectionality of such variables by creating multiple versions; for example, (male or female) × (white or Black) or (male or female) × (white or Black) × (middle-class or poor) and using suitable inferential statistics to isolate the relative effects of only one factor, one factor combined with another, or all three combined. With only seventeen subjects (psychiatric residents) randomly assigned to evaluate one of two vignettes, Blake's study was statistically underpowered. More subjects would have allowed for a more effective use of statistical tests. She rather cleverly, in my opinion, arranged for the vignettes to be distributed to the residents by their chief resident rather than giving them to the residents directly. She did this to diffuse any potential effect that her race might have had on the residents. In her words, she did this "to avoid the contamination of the study by the presence of the Black investigator" (Blake 1973, 189). It is unfortunate that this factor had to be taken into account, but methodologically it was probably a wise decision on her part.

The Oregon Health Insurance Experiment

Finkelstein, A., et al. 2012. "The Oregon Health Insurance Experiment: Evidence from the First Year." *Quarterly Journal of Economics* 127, no. 3: 1057–1106.

Baicker, K., et al. 2013. "The Oregon Experiment—Effects of Medicaid on Clinical Outcomes." *New England Journal of Medicine* 368, no. 18: 1713–22.

Taubman, S. L., et al. 2014. "Medicaid Increased Emergency Department Use: Evidence from Oregon's Health Insurance Experiment." *Science* 343, no. 6168: 263–68.

Wright, B. J., et al. 2016. "What Does Medicaid Expansion Mean for Cancer Screening and Prevention? Results from a Randomized Trial on the Impacts of Acquiring Medicaid Coverage." *Cancer* 122: 791–97.

Baicker, K., et al. 2017. "The Effect of Medicaid on Medication Use Among Poor Adults: Evidence from Oregon." *Health Affairs* 36, no. 12: 2110–14.

Allen, H., B. Wright, and L. Broffman. 2018. "The Impacts of Medicaid Expansion on Rural Low-Income Adults: Lessons from the Oregon Health Insurance Experiment." *Medical Care Research and Review* 75, no. 3: 354–83.

Baicker, K., et al. 2018a. "The Effect of Medicaid on Dental Care of Poor Adults: Evidence from the Oregon Health Insurance Experiment." *Health Services Research* 53, no. 4: 2147–64.

Baicker, K., et al. 2018b. "The Effect of Medicaid on Management of Depression: Evidence from the Oregon Health Insurance Experiment." *Milbank Quarterly* 96, no. 1: 29–56.

These articles report the results of one single but very large experiment that posed an array of research questions that can be summarized as follows: What are the effects of having access to health insurance on physical health, mental health, dental health, and financial health? While the answers might seem obvious, the number of high-quality studies with actual data to answer these questions were limited, and the presumptively beneficial effects of health insurance coverage were not clear, according to existing studies. An opportunity for a more rigorous study arose in 2008 in Portland, Oregon.

The United States has a public health insurance program for people living on a low income called Medicaid, but not all people living on a low income have access to Medicaid owing to various states' programs having limited funding to enroll everyone otherwise financially qualified. Portland was awarded additional federal money to expand its Medicaid enrollments. This placed the city leaders in something of a dilemma in that there were many more people (about 90,000) on the waiting list eligible to be enrolled in Medicaid than the new funding allowed. Thus, they had to come up with a fair way to determine which families would be enrolled. The solution they came up with was one to gladden the hearts of any experimentalist: They *randomly selected* about 30,000 names from the waiting list and invited them to apply. Those who were deemed eligible were randomly assigned to either receive Medicaid (n = 6,387 adults) or remain on the waiting list (n = 5,842 adults).

Two years later, information was obtained from these participants via self-reports obtained through interviews and various questionnaires and scales in an attempt to answer the research question: "What were the effects of Medicaid enrollment on health-care use and health outcomes?" This is a broad question. Note that health-care *use* and health *outcomes* were investigated separately. Use alone is not sufficient to demonstrate benefit. For health insurance to be of value, it should result in demonstrable health improvements among the people receiving insured services, not simply expand access to services. In the series of studies that followed these patients, "health" was defined broadly, including not only physical and mental health but also financial health. The design used was a basic posttest-only, no-treatment RCT and can be diagrammed like this:

	Group	Assessment at two years
R	$X_{Medicaid}$	O_1
R	$X_{no\ Medicaid}$	O_1

It is worth noting that the use of a no-treatment control group in this situation is ethical. Everyone initially deemed eligible for Medicaid had an equal chance to be selected to receive it. Male or female; white, Black, Asian, or Hispanic; younger or older; gay, straight, bi, or trans; with or without preexisting medical conditions—no one was more or less likely to receive

Medicaid. This random assignment process serves the principle of balance or fairness deemed essential in randomized experiments. As an example, at the two-year follow-up, the uncovered group was 56.9 percent women, while the covered group was 56.5 percent women. White people composed 68.8 percent of the uncovered group and 69.2 percent of the covered group. Black people made up 10.5 percent of the uncovered group and 10.6 percent of the covered group; the corresponding figures for Hispanic people were 17.2 percent and 17.0 percent. These figures are a striking example of how the magic of randomly assigning a large number of people to experimental conditions ensures equivalency across groups at the beginning of a study. Although not measured (remember, this was a posttest-only experiment), health variables such as blood pressure, blood sugar, weight, height, and the presence of preexisting conditions can safely be assumed to have been virtually identical between the two groups upon enrollment in the study.

Because the two groups must have been roughly equivalent on all relevant factors at the beginning of the study, any differences two years later *must* result from the effect of receiving Medicaid. It is difficult to conceive of any plausible rival explanations that could account for any such posttreatment differences. Any potential threats to internal validity such as the passage of time, concurrent history, regression to the mean, and placebo factors were satisfactorily excluded by this strong design. The authors also appropriately noted the limited external validity of their findings, illustrating that sample size has little bearing on the generalizability of a study's results if participants are not originally randomly selected from the larger population of interest. In this instance, it was unknown how representative people living on a low income in Portland were of all people in the United States eligible for Medicaid.

Because there were many outcome measures (dependent variables) to be assessed in this project, and a correspondingly large number of hypotheses, various articles have been published on its results, as well as some serving basic descriptive purposes and discussing methodological issues. It makes sense to do this, given the page limits many journals impose on submitting authors. One key player in this project, known as the Oregon Health Insurance Experiment, is Heidi Allen, PhD, an associate professor of social work at Columbia University. Allen received her MSW and PhD from the Portland State University School of Social Work and is a coauthor on the published studies cited at the beginning of this section. The following are some of the results published across these studies.

Physical Health

Medicaid coverage was found to make no difference on the diagnosis or prevalence of hypertension or high cholesterol levels or the use of drugs to treat these conditions. It also made no difference on the ten-year risk for a cardiovascular event (i.e., heart attack). Receiving a diagnosis for diabetes and obtaining medication for diabetes increased slightly. Self-reported physical health-related quality of life and the experience of pain were not affected by health insurance coverage. The number of visits to a doctor's office and prescriptions increased. Overall, Medicaid recipients' medical expenditures increased over the previous year's by about $1,172 compared with the uncovered group, and recipients obtained greater access to preventive care. Medicaid coverage had no effect on obesity or smoking but slightly increased the number of cancer screenings, especially among women. Medicaid coverage was found to increase the use of medications to treat serious medical conditions and reduced the unauthorized use of prescription medications originally prescribed for someone else. It was also found that unmet dental care needs were substantially reduced, whereas emergency department visits for dental care significantly increased.

Mental Health

Medicaid coverage was associated with a reduction in depression among recipients, based on their responses to a pencil-and-paper survey, but their degree of happiness was not impacted.

Financial Health

Medicaid coverage dramatically improved the financial health of recipients, as they did not have to pay for catastrophic expenditures.

Study Summary

The picture is decidedly mixed in terms of two-year outcomes. In terms of its strengths, the authors note some of the limitations of their study. And they published a study protocol before the data were collected and specified a number of hypothesized outcomes in advance, which helped protect against p-hacking and possibly finding some results statistically significant that may have actually been based on random errors in the data. p-hacking is when an author runs a large number of statistical tests, with no preplanned hypotheses, in the hope of finding significant difference or associations.

The Oregon Health Insurance Experiment is an excellent example of the value of the posttest-only, no-treatment RCT. It was a large-scale investigation involving thousands of participants; it was planned in advance, it was conducted ethically, the random assignment process and statistical analysis possessed integrity; and many threats to internal validity were controlled for. These attributes thus permitted some degree of causal inference to be made regarding the effects (and lack of effect) of Medicaid coverage. It improved upon prior quasi-experimental studies on the effects of health insurance by permitting stronger, more justifiable conclusions, and the results have appeared in some of the world's leading scientific journals. Social work involvement via the skills and talents of Heidi Allen was intimately interwoven into all published studies of this project, which continues to this day. I hope that an entire book will be written about this project, as has happened with other large-scale social work experimental projects.

Like most studies, the Oregon Health Insurance Experiment is not without its limitations. The use of a convenience sample from only one American city limits the generalizability of its findings. The use of patient self-reports is another limitation. *Saying* in an interview that one obtained more services, got better dental care, or became less depressed is not the same as *documenting* access to services or dental treatments or using a validated clinical interview to ascertain if a person meets criteria for depression. Depression, for example, was assessed by the Patient Health Questionnaire, version 8 (PHQ-8; Kroenke et al. 2009), a self-report measure. This scale (codeveloped by the social worker Janet B. W. Williams, DSW) is widely used in studies of this nature, but its scores do not equate to a DSM diagnosis arrived at via clinical interview. The DSM makes no use of patient-report or caregiver-report scales to arrive at a diagnosis; its diagnoses can be arrived at only clinically. However, the logistics of using more *direct measures* of the outcome variables of interest (e.g., appointments made and kept, DSM-based clinical interviews, documentations of medications obtained and used) rendered assessments of greater verisimilitude impractical. So, when we read that at the two-year follow-up, clinical depression was found in 14 percent of the control group and 6.8 percent of the Medicaid-covered group, it looks like having health insurance was associated with a reduction in the prevalence of depression by 50 percent. Although this difference is statistically significant, keep in mind that the outcome measure was a patient-report scale of depressive symptoms, not a clinician-derived formal diagnosis. Actual emergency department visits were not tabulated, only patient *reports* of such visits, which are of unknown accuracy. The security of protected health information makes obtaining more accurate data on things like emergency department visits, medications taken, and diagnoses problematic. The outcome measures used in the Oregon Health Insurance Experiment were the best that could feasibly be used, but the limitations of these data need to be considered when interpreting the results of this study.

Combining Abuse and Neglect Investigations with Intensive Family Preservation Services

Walton, E. 2001. "Combining Abuse and Neglect Investigations with Intensive Family Preservation Services: An Innovative Approach to Protecting Children." *Research on Social Work Practice* 11: 627–44.

This experiment examined services for abused and neglected children, comparing the results of combining child protective service (CPS) investigations with family preservation services (FPS) with TAU. Of 331 high-priority cases of alleged child abuse referred to a state child welfare agency, 97 were randomly assigned to receive both CPS and FPS, and 111 were randomly selected to receive TAU. The research question was, "Did families receiving combined services have different outcomes compared with the families receiving TAU?" The study included several outcome measures, such as scores on the Index of Parental Attitudes scale (completed by caregivers), the in-home status of the children, the numbers of cases that were substantiated, access to available services, and the family's satisfaction with services. Services were provided to both groups for about six months, and then assessments were made. By using each outcome measure to create a specific directional hypothesis, this study tested the following predictions:

1. Parenting satisfaction scores will be higher after treatment among the caregivers who received combined services (CPS plus FPS) compared with those who received TAU.
2. More children whose families received combined services will remain in the home compared with children of families who received TAU.
3. Families receiving combined services will access more ancillary and supportive social services than families receiving TAU.
4. Satisfaction with the services received will be higher among families who received combined services compared with families who received TAU.

This study used a posttreatment-only randomized design comparing an experimental treatment with TAU and can be diagrammed as follows:

	Group	
R	$X_{CPS + FPS}$	O_1
R	X_{TAU}	O_1

The families were assessed after six months of treatment. Some attrition occurred. Of the 97 families receiving combined services, only 65 families agreed to the posttreatment assessment. Of the 111 families who received TAU, only 60 participated in the posttreatment assessment. Attrition can compromise estimates of the true effects of a treatment, so it is important to note that this study experienced a relatively high degree of attrition.

Hypothesis 1 was refuted. In fact, parents in the combined-treatment condition reported *more* problematic parent–child relationships than did parents who received TAU. The author speculated that this may have been because of differential attrition at posttest. Fewer parents who received TAU agreed to participate in the follow-up.

Hypothesis 2 was partially supported. There was no difference in the number of children removed from the home between the two groups, but children receiving combined services were more likely to return to the home and to remain in the home for longer periods.

Hypothesis 3 was not supported. Families in the two conditions did not differ in their engagement with ancillary services.

Hypothesis 4 was largely supported, with the parents who received combined services reporting statistically significantly more positive attitudes about being a parent compared with the parents who received TAU. This effect occurred across multiple domains of satisfaction, including the social worker and services provided, the helpfulness of counseling provided, seeing the social worker as competent and organized, and evaluating the social worker highly.

These mixed results could be used by the agency to make a choice about the types of services to provide in order to do a better job of preserving families. Should it continue with TAU or carry on with combining the CPS and FPS interventions? Having actual data on clinical outcomes places the agency administrators in a better position to make such choices as opposed to relying solely on impressions, being guided only by theory, or relying on what some managerial higher-up dictates should be provided.

Effectiveness of a School-Based Life Skills Program on Emotional Regulation and Depression Among Elementary School Students

Lee, M.-J., et al. 2020. "Effectiveness of a School-Based Life Skills Program on Emotional Regulation and Depression Among Elementary School Students: A Randomized Study." *Children and Youth Services Review* 118: 105464.

This ambitious project was completed at thirty-nine elementary schools in the city of Keelung, Taiwan, in 2017 and 2018. The aim was to evaluate a Chinese adaptation of a validated and widely used life skills training (LST) curriculum codeveloped in the United States by the social worker Steven Schinke (see Schinke et al. 1988). The purpose of LST is to foster communication skills, social skills, media literacy, decision-making, self-esteem, stress coping, and assertiveness. The US curriculum was adapted by Chinese social workers and other scholars using local and culturally specific examples and translated into Mandarin. The training was delivered through twenty-seven sessions over three semesters and administered by local teachers who received training in the curriculum. The participating schools were randomly assigned to provide the adapted LST curriculum or education as usual (the school-based equivalent of TAU), which was delivered in a traditional format of lectures and readings focused on stress, social relationships and communication, and substance abuse.

Twenty-one schools (1,307 students) were randomly assigned to receive LST and eighteen schools (1,355 students) were randomly assigned to receive TAU. No pretest assessments were done. The posttest was completed using a convenient web-based survey platform. The general research question can be framed as, "What are the impacts of LST compared with TAU on children's life skills?" From this broad question, the authors derived the following hypotheses:

1. The adapted LST curriculum will produce more improvements in children's emotional regulation compared with TAU.
2. The adapted LST curriculum will produce greater reductions in depression compared with TAU.
3. The effects of the LST curriculum will be moderated by the child's gender.

This study used a cluster RCT design and can be diagrammed as follows:

	Group	
R	X_{LST}	O_1
R	X_{TAU}	O_1

Posttreatment, responses were received from 1,234 children who received LST and 1,288 children who received TAU. These responses reflected return rates of 94 percent and 95 percent, respectively, which means the study had a very low rate of attrition (which is good). Hypotheses 1 and 2 were supported, with the students who received LST scoring statistically significantly better overall on measures of cognitive reappraisal and depression compared with students who received TAU. These effects were moderated by depression in that boys demonstrated statistically significant improvements in depression whereas girls did not, which supported hypothesis 3. This study is a good example of how a research-supported treatment developed in North America can be successfully adapted via culturally competent modification and language translation. It was a fairly large-scale randomized experiment. This study's design, a cluster RCT, means that instead of randomly assigning *individuals* to

LST or TAU, larger *units* of individuals (in this case, schools) were randomly assigned to one of the two conditions. Many types of units can be used in this type of study, such as hospitals, dormitories, colleges or universities, neighborhoods, cities, states, or countries. By assigning entire schools to deliver *one* intervention, the researcher reduced the likelihood of the interventions being cross-contaminated. For example, if both LST and TAU were provided at the same school, children in one group could pick up on skills learned by children in the other. This possibility is mitigated by having the interventions provided at different locations to different samples of participants.

Promoting Voting Behavior Among Low-Income Black Voters

Canady, K., and B. A. Thyer. 1990. "Promoting Voting Behavior Among Low-Income Black Voters: An Experimental Investigation." *Journal of Sociology & Social Welfare* 17, no. 4: 109–16.

This study was undertaken immediately before the 1988 presidential election, with the Republican candidate George H. W. Bush contending against the Democratic candidate Michael Dukakis. At the time, voter turnout was low, especially among Black and Hispanic people. Social work has long had an interest in encouraging voting among people living on a low income as well as other historically oppressed groups, so the MSW student Kelly Canady undertook an experimental investigation to answer the following question: "What would be the effect of mailing eligible Black voters living on a low income a bipartisan reminder letter encouraging them to vote just prior to the presidential election?" The single hypothesis was that receiving a bipartisan reminder letter would result in more Black people living on a low income voting. (Note the difference between the neutrally worded research question and the predictively worded research hypothesis.)

We chose voting precinct 1 in the town of Dublin, Georgia, as our experimental site because it contained a large number of government-subsidized housing projects and the population was approximately 90 percent Black. We drafted a bipartisan letter reminding voters of the importance of the forthcoming election and obtained the authentic signatures of the chairs of the local Republican and Democratic Parties for this letter.

The voting precinct had about 2,500 registered voters, and Canady legally obtained a mailing list of all these voters from the office of the Registrar of Voters. He randomly selected about four hundred voters and randomly assigned each to one of four conditions. Those in the first group, the no-treatment control condition, did not receive a letter. Those in the second group received *one* letter a couple days before the election. The third group received *two* letters, one arriving about one week and a second arriving a few days before the election. The fourth group received *three* letters, arriving about two weeks, one week, and a few days before election day. We hoped (notice our bias; we are, after all, social workers!) that the receipt of one letter would increase voting and that receiving two or three letters would produce greater increases. So, the independent variable (the intervention) was the letter urging people to vote, administered in three gradations. The dependent variable (the outcome measure) was whether participants voted. Canady obtained a record of who voted (but not how they voted) after the election. This was publicly available information. Since we conducted no voting "pretests," our design and results looked like this:

	Group		**Percent who voted**
R	No treatment	O_1	55 percent
R	$X_{1\,letter}$	O_1	57 percent
R	$X_{2\,letters}$	O_1	68 percent
R	$X_{3\,letters}$	O_1	54 percent

After excluding the letters that were returned to us as undeliverable, we calculated the numbers and percentages of people in each group who voted (shown in the table). A statistical test found no differences in voting across the four groups, meaning our research hypotheses were *not* supported. This was disappointing, as we were hopeful that if the letters were effective, we would have demonstrated a low-cost way to enhance voting. A positive result would have produced a more exciting paper publishable in a more prestigious journal. We did believe that we had demonstrated the potential for a low-cost initiative to enhance voting; perhaps if the letters were more focused and partisan and had addressed issues of concern to voters, they would have been more effective.

Effects of a Randomized Tax-Time Savings Intervention on Savings Account Ownership Among Low- and Moderate-Income Households

Despard, M., et al. 2018. "Effects of a Randomized Tax-Time Savings Intervention on Savings Account Ownership Among Low- and Moderate-Income Households." *Journal of Financial Counseling and Planning* 29, no. 2: 219–32.

This project originated from social workers and other behavioral scientists at the Center for Social Development at the George Warren Brown School of Social Work at Washington University in St. Louis, Missouri, long considered one the finest social work programs in the United States. The researchers undertook a posttest-only, no-treatment control-group design to evaluate the effect of simple messages provided to people living on low and moderate incomes who were anticipating receiving an income tax refund. The general research question was, "Do simple online messages encouraging people to save all or a part of their income tax refund result in more people opening up a savings account compared with similar people who do not receive such messages?" The overall hypothesis was that "receiving savings messages and prompts results in subsequent savings account openings" (Despard et al. 2018, 222).

The participants were people living on low and moderate incomes who were participating in a program called the Refund to Savings initiative and who were using the TurboTax Free Edition software to file their tax returns. Of about 4,682 participants, 4,017 were randomly assigned to receive the intervention (messages encouraging saving all or part of one's refund delivered via the tax return software), and 665 were randomly assigned not to receive the intervention. As expected with such large numbers of people *randomly allocated* to treatment or no treatment, demographically they were virtually identical at the posttreatment assessment. Note the unequal sample sizes. There is no requirement to have treatment and control groups of equal sizes in experiments. What is essential is to have enough participants in the smallest group to ensure adequate statistical power to permit the legitimate application of the type and number of inferential tests the researchers plan to use to test their hypotheses. In this instance, the treatment group was more than six times the size of the control group. Because a larger no-treatment group was not required statistically and because the intervention was low cost (it made no difference if the message were sent to one thousand or four thousand, since it was generated by the software), the study potentially benefited more people because many more people received the intervention than did not.

Multiple variations of the message (the independent variable) were used, with those in the experimental group receiving just one version. Some suggested saving a fixed amount of money (e.g., $100, $250) or a percentage (e.g., 25 percent, 50 percent, 75 percent). Others encouraged saving for an emergency, for a family, or for peace of mind, and another encouraged saving but without a designated purpose. The messages were delivered at different times during tax-filing season: early, middle, or late. The dependent variable was participants' self-report of whether they had opened a savings account. Although the intervention had many variations, the basic design can be construed simply as a posttest-only, no-treatment control-group design and diagrammed as follows:

	Group	
R	$X_{\text{savings messages}}$	O_1
R		O_1

Although there were technically eighteen variations in the independent variable, for the purposes of simplicity and clarity, I will present only the percentages of people in the treatment and no-treatment groups who said they had opened savings accounts. According to the authors, "Results confirmed our hypothesis, as 7.4 percent and 5.1 percent of the treatment and control-group participants added a savings account in the six months after filing taxes. . . . Participants who received an intervention had 60 percent greater odds of opening a savings account in the six months after filing taxes compared to control group participants" (Despard et al. 2018, 225). The researchers also evaluated the effects of the message variations and found that some were slightly more effective than others but not by much. They were quite confident in their conclusions: "We find support for our hypothesis that receiving an online tax-time savings message *induces* a positive change in savings account ownership in the six months after filing taxes. Because tax filers were randomly assigned, we can *conclude* that the Refund to Savings interventions, *and no other factors*, explain the change in account ownership" (Despard et al. 2018, 226, my emphasis). Again we see the magic of random assignment. Given enough people and true random assignment, we can be confident that the groups differed at posttest only because of the treatment group's exposure to the intervention. Therefore, the authors effectively demonstrated a causal relationship.

Importantly, the authors note their study's limitations. They relied upon client self-reports of opening a savings account six months after filing their taxes; they did not independently verify that such accounts actually existed. Can you see how the effort to validate the outcome measure would have resulted in a stronger study? However, the effort to verify the existence and date of opening of more than 4,500 savings accounts would be an immense task. One way around this difficulty would be to verify the self-reports of just a random sample of several hundred participants posttreatment. Doing so would give us greater confidence in the integrity of the outcome measure if it were found that the self-reports were accurate. But if we found that a significant percentage of the self-reports of savings account openings were false, either through deliberate deception or simple errors in recall, the study's findings would be called into question. The authors also noted that their sample was not necessarily representative of all people living on low and moderate incomes in the United States; thus, the external validity of the study's results is unknown. This is a limitation for all intervention studies involving convenience samples (no matter how large), but there is no practical alternative. Obtaining a truly random sample of all low- and middle-income tax filers in the United States and inducing them to use a particular piece of software to file their taxes would be impossible. So, like most social work intervention research studies, this fine study represents a compromise between the ideals of scientific experimental design and the practicalities of field research. Another limitation is that there was no appraisal of the *amount* of money saved from participants' tax refunds or whether savings resulted in meaningful improvements in the family's *financial health*. And although it was clear that the online messages were effective, the overall increase in absolute, not just relative, terms in the increase in savings accounts is small. Given that 5.1 percent of the no-treatment group opened savings accounts posttreatment and 7.4 percent of the treatment group opened such accounts, the absolute difference is an increase of only 2.3 percent (7.4 percent – 5.1 percent). Thus, there was clearly an effect, just not a very powerful one.

Determining Staff Work Loads for Professional Staff in a Public Welfare Agency

Simon, H. A., et al. 1941. *Determining Staff Work Loads for Professional Staff in a Public Welfare Agency*. Berkeley: Bureau of Public Administration, University of California, Berkeley.

When I published an article and bibliography of published randomized experiments produced by social workers (Thyer 2015), I made much of the fact that the earliest such citation I could find was published in 1949. I pointed out that this was about the same time randomized experiments began to be undertaken on medical therapeutics by physicians and on verbal psychotherapies by clinical psychologists. Imagine my delight while preparing the current book in locating a social work experiment published in 1941.

This citation represents my current best finding for a randomized experimental social work outcome study. Interestingly, the first author is Herbert Simon, a psychologist and future Nobel laureate. One of the coauthors was Milton Chernin. Chernin was appointed an assistant professor in the newly formed Department of Social Welfare at the University of California, Berkely, in 1940, and he remained there throughout his career except for an absence of several years of military service during World War II. In 1946, he was appointed acting dean of what had become the School of Social Welfare and then dean in 1947. He served that program for more than thirty years, steering the development of its exemplary MSW and DSW (later PhD) programs before retiring in 1977. Chernin's PhD dissertation ("Convict Road Work in California") was in political science, and he did not have an MSW degree, but surely by osmosis and his years of singular contributions to the profession, he can be considered one of "us," much like we consider Mary Richmond and Jane Addams to have been social workers despite their lack of academic credentials.

The research question for the cited study can be formulated as, "How do changing workloads impact the efficiency of welfare workers?" (The workers referred to in the report were called social workers, so I feel justified including this study in my disciplinary lineage of experimental studies.) The agencies included in the study employed three types of workers: the *qualifiers* who initially approved or denied applications for welfare, the *field intake workers* who conducted home visits to confirm or disconfirm applications, and the *carriers* who periodically visited welfare recipients to ensure that they were still eligible to receive payments. The caseloads of each group of workers were systematically varied. Qualifiers were randomly assigned 50, 75, 100, or 125 cases a week; the field workers 8, 12, or 16 cases per week; and the carriers 60, 100, or 150 cases. The study recruited nine qualifiers, twenty-one field intake workers, and forty-two carriers. The clients initially evaluated by the qualifiers were randomly selected from among all applicants. The differing caseloads are this study's independent variable, and the outcome measure was the accurate determination of eligibility for welfare. Ineligible people were sometimes incorrectly deemed eligible, and eligible individuals were sometimes incorrectly judged to be ineligible. Errors of the first type cost the agency (and taxpayers) an unnecessary expense. Errors of the second type unfairly denied people deserved benefits.

This complex posttreatment-only randomized experiment can be diagrammed as follows:

Staff position	Randomly assigned workload group		Posttreatment assessment
Qualifiers	R	$X_{50\ cases}$	O_1
(n = 9)	R	$X_{75\ cases}$	O_1
	R	$X_{100\ cases}$	O_1
	R	$X_{125\ cases}$	O_1
Field intake workers	R	$X_{8\ cases}$	O_1
(n = 21)	R	$X_{12\ cases}$	O_1
	R	$X_{16\ cases}$	O_1
Carriers	R	$X_{60\ cases}$	O_1
(n = 42)	R	$X_{100\ cases}$	O_1
	R	$X_{150\ cases}$	O_1

Data were collected between January and April 1940. A large number of hypotheses were embedded in this complex project, but among the conclusions reached were the following:

- "The improved performance which accompanied the lowest caseloads was sufficient to justify the increased operating cost. In the case of field intake workers there was no marked improvement in performance with lower loads and the findings did not justify a quota of less than 16 applications per week."

- "The percentage of applicants accepted for relief was substantially smaller with a long than a short office interview. The long interview, although it required a larger staff, resulted in smaller total agency expenditures."
- "In the handling of cases already receiving aid, it was found that if case loads were reduced to 60 per worker, considerably prompter closing of cases could be expected than if case loads of 100 or 150 were established" (Simon et al. 1941, 4–6).

For the first attempt (as far as I can tell) at publishing an experimental investigation of social work services, this was a remarkably ambitious and complex study of a fundamental type of social work: welfare eligibility determinations. It received positive reviews from prominent journals of the day (e.g., Hastings 1943; Palmer 1942; Scarlett 1942), but the groundbreaking nature of this study does not otherwise appear to have been sufficiently recognized at the time. Perhaps the events of World War II overshadowed its significance. It was not listed by Segal (1972) or Fischer (1973) in their reviews of social work outcome studies, which is an unfortunate oversight. Nonetheless, its rediscovery extends the published history of true social work experimentation back by eight years.

The Stepped-Wedge Randomized Controlled Trial

The stepped-wedge design is a newer form of experimental investigation that is likely unfamiliar to most social work readers, so hold on to your hats as you read this section.

A simple stepped-wedge design can be diagrammed as follows:

		Month[a]				
		1	2	3	4	5
Group 1	R	O_1	XO_2	XO_3	XO_4	XO_5
Group 2	R	O_1	O_2	XO_3	XO_4	XO_5
Group 3	R	O_1	O_2	O_3	XO_4	XO_5
Group 4	R	O_1	O_2	O_3	O_4	XO_5

[a]This is just an example of a time period; others could be used (e.g., days, weeks, years).

The inferential logic of the stepped-wedge design can be illustrated with hypothetical data. Say you are doing an RCT on a treatment for depression. Your primary dependent variable is individuals' scores on the twenty-one-item Beck Depression Inventory (BDI) in which each question is scored from 1 to 3 (thus, the maximum score, meaning most severely depressed, is 63).

Treatment effects, if any, are presumed to begin as soon as treatment is completed. There are two types of stepped-wedge RCT: one based on the randomization of individuals, the other based on the randomization of clusters. One example is as follows.

You recruit one hundred participants who meet your inclusion criteria for severe depression according to their pretreatment BDI score (O_1 in the diagram presented earlier; month 1 in the diagram that follows). You explain to them that you can treat only twenty-five people at a time and that to be fair, you will randomly assign each participant to one of four conditions: to get treatment right away or to begin treatment in one, two, or three months. The diagram that follows provides the average BDI score for each group (standard deviations are omitted to simplify things, and numbers are rounded and approximate).

		Month				
		1	2	3	4	5
Group 1	R	60	**40**	**30**	**30**	**24**
Group 2	R	58	56	**43**	**32**	**22**
Group 3	R	61	54	57	**41**	**27**
Group 4	R	57	55	56	54	**26**

Look at these numbers carefully. At O_1 (pretest assessment, month 1), all four groups scored high on the BDI and roughly the same (which is what we would expect thanks to randomization). Group 1 begins treatment right away, and after one month (month 2), their mean score has dropped by 20 points, which is a large decrease. Also at month 2, the mean scores for participants in groups 2, 3 and 4, who have not yet received treatment, remain high. After the month 2 assessment, group 2 begins treatment, and groups 3 and 4 remain untreated. At the month 3 assessment, group 1 has improved even more, and group 2 has improved, whereas the scores of groups 3 and 4 remain high. After the month 3 assessment, group 3 begins treatment, and group 4 remains untreated. At the month 4 assessment, group 1 continues to do well, group 2 has improved more, and group 3 has improved. Group 4 remains the same. After the month 4 assessment, group 4 begins treatment, and groups 1, 2, and 3 continue in therapy. At the month 5 assessment, group 4 shows improvement, and groups 1, 2, and 3 continue to improve. In the previous diagram, the bold numbers represent mean BDI scores after getting treatment, and the nonbold numbers indicate BDI scores before treatment began.

The inferential logic is that if improvements are observed only after treatment begins, and this effect is replicated several times (the more the better) with different groups after the initial demonstration, the internal validity is fairly high as there are few threats to internal validity that could plausibly explain these results. This example does not control for placebo influences, but one could introduce a month of placebo therapy prior to active treatment for each group to help control for that factor, if deemed necessary. The inferential statistics needed to analyze these stepped-wedge design results are a bit complicated (Thompson et al. 2016) but can be addressed via common statistical packages such as R (https://www.r-project.org).

In addition to an RCT on individuals randomly assigned to groups, the stepped-wedge design can also be used in a cluster randomized experiment. Here, random assignment involves assigning not individual participants but *clusters*, such as schools, dormitories, hospitals, or cities. In this case, you would recruit a number of clusters (let's say schools) and complete pretreatment assessments for each, measuring one or more dependent variables (e.g., in the case of schools, you could measure absenteeism if the intervention involved an absenteeism reduction program). One school (cluster 1) receives the intervention immediately, and the remaining ones each receive the intervention after certain amounts of time in a stepped manner. In this instance, we'd hope to see that absenteeism declines right away following the intervention in cluster 1 but not in the untreated clusters. We would hope that with sequential implementations of the intervention, we would see sequential improvements; that is, only after each cluster had received the intervention. Such a data pattern would suggest that the internal validity is strong. The stepped-wedge design appears infrequently in published studies by social work authors. I was able to locate only one when preparing this book, and it is described next.

Stepped Collaborative Care Targeting Posttraumatic Stress Disorder Symptoms and Comorbidity for US Trauma Care Systems

Zatzick, D., et al. 2021. "Stepped Collaborative Care Targeting Posttraumatic Stress Disorder Symptoms and Comorbidity for US Trauma Care Systems: A Randomized Clinical Trial." *JAMA Surgery* 156, no. 5: 430–42.

The focus of this study was an experimental intervention to reduce the symptoms of post-traumatic stress disorder (PTSD) among survivors of traumatic injury. A total of 635 survivors of physical trauma were recruited from twenty-five US trauma centers, including survivors of auto accidents and firearms injuries. Trauma centers are formally designated surgical hospitals that specialize in treating trauma. All patients at each participating site were assessed for trauma and initially received usual care (TAU) for their post-traumatic stress symptoms.

Then, in a randomized sequence, the centers began implementing the experimental intervention, with some offering it immediately after assessment and others at three later time points. The experimental treatment was an evidence-based brief collaborative care intervention that included both pharmacological and psychosocial treatments (primarily cognitive behavioral therapy), as well as proactive case management.

The first author traveled to the various hospitals assigned to one of the four clusters and provided intensive training in the collaborative care model (CCM). The hospitals assigned to cluster 1 then began offering CCM to new patients who had just recently been injured and were recovering from surgery. The hospitals in the remaining three clusters continued to provide TAU. Then, a few months later, the hospitals randomly assigned to cluster 2 received training in CCM and switched from TAU to CCM, while hospitals in clusters 3 and 4 continued to provide TAU. Subsequently, cluster 3 hospitals and then cluster 4 hospitals received training and switched to CCM. They were *not* randomly assigned *within* each cluster to receive *either* TAU *or* CCM. By staggering the introduction of CCM following TAU within each cluster of hospitals, some threats to internal validity were controlled for, such as passage of time and concurrent history.

The general research question was, "What are the effects of CCM versus TAU in reducing the post-traumatic stress symptoms of physical trauma survivors?" A number of primary outcome measures were used to assess post-traumatic stress, alcohol abuse, depression, and physical functioning. Each could be associated with its own hypothesis, such as "After receiving CCM, patients will experience a statistically significant reduction in post-traumatic stress symptoms compared with TAU."

The authors reported that "a brief stepped collaborative care intervention was associated with significant six-month but not twelve-month PTSD symptom reduction. Greater baseline PTSD risk and good or excellent trauma care center protocol implementation were associated with larger PTSD effects. Orchestrated efforts for targeting policy and funding should systematically incorporate the study findings into national trauma center requirements and verification criteria" (Zatzick et al. 2021, 430).

This study had a number of strengths. PTSD is a serious problem, yet one for which a number of research-supported treatments exist. The sample size was considerable, the per-patient cost to provide CCM was not excessive, and CCM reduced patients' PTSD symptoms at six months. The differences between the outcomes associated with TAU and CCM were reduced at twelve months post-treatment because symptoms continued to improve over time, after six months among the patients who had received TAU. The statistical analysis was conservative and sophisticated, the outcome measures were legitimate, and the independent variables were well proceduralized and delivered with fidelity. The study also had a reasonable rate of attrition: 75 percent of the initially treated patients were assessed at the twelve-month follow-up.

Another feature of the stepped-wedge design is that once implemented, the experimental treatment is not removed. A stepped-wedge study can also be conducted with a closed-cohort design in which the participants recruited at the beginning of the study are considered one cohort (called an open cohort) and new participants are recruited over time and become new cohorts. This design can be diagrammed as follows:

		Month				
		1	2	3	4	5
Group 1	R	O_1	XO_2	XO_3	XO_4	XO_5
Group 2	R	O_1	O_2	XO_3	XO_4	XO_5
Group 3	R	–	O_1	O_2	XO_3	XO_4
Group 4	R	–	O_1	O_2	XO_3	

Owing to the vagaries of statistics, the stepped-wedge design generally requires fewer participants than an individual RCT because comparisons are made both *between* and *within* clusters. Determining the degrees of freedom involves taking into account the number of participants overall, the number within each cluster or cohort, and the number of clusters or cohorts. Hussey and Hughes (2007) and Hemming and Taljaard (2016) provide some guidance in this regard, but statistical consultation with an expert is recommended.

The stepped-wedge design is best used at the community level on interventions for which credible evidence of their effectiveness already exists. Given the potential cost of conducting stepped-wedge studies with large clusters, it is best to know that the treatment works. The intervals between sequential implementations of treatment should be of sufficient duration to allow the intervention exert its effect. In a study of vaccine efficacy, for example, a one- or two-year time frame would be more appropriate than one or two months.

The stepped-wedge design is also a good choice when you cannot provide treatment to everyone who is eligible at once. The random assignment of clusters is a fair way to make decisions about treatment allocation. Assessor blinding is important to maintain the integrity of the design, especially since participants will know when they switch from the control condition (usually TAU) to the experimental condition. Assessor blinding is also needed when the outcomes are subjective, such as clinical judgments. Because the clusters or cohorts receive treatment in a random but sequential order, stepped-wedge studies take longer to conduct than RCTs with parallel arms in which all conditions are provided to participants at the same time.

Some Thought Experiments Using the Posttest-Only Experimental Design

I've been adjunct teaching for about six years in the DSW program at the Tulane University School of Social Work. Students are required to complete a capstone research project to earn their degree, and I like to encourage them to consider conducting an experimental study. Almost all the students are licensed social workers with many years of practice experience. During a research design class, one student expressed an inability to come up with an idea for any research project, much less an experimental one. The dialog that follows is a fairly accurate description of how I walked her through the process of arriving at an idea for an experimental study. I will use the pseudonym of Apollonia (the patron saint of dentists) in place of my student's actual name.

Bruce: Where do you work?

Apollonia: I am the office manager of my husband's dental practice.

Bruce: Does your husband treat Medicaid patients?

Apollonia: Yes.

Bruce: Aren't Medicaid patients entitled to two no-cost dental examinations and cleanings a year?

Apollonia: Yes.

Bruce: Are many of your Medicaid patients children?

Apollonia: Yes.

Bruce: Does your practice have many child patients who have not received their free examinations within the past six months?

Apollonia: Yes.

Bruce: How about this? Pull the files of all your child patients on Medicaid, and extract those who are eligible for a free treatment. Using a coin toss, randomly divide them into two groups. In the experimental group, the children's parents receive a standardized prompt in the form of a letter, email, or text. The prompt reminds them that their child is eligible for a free exam and cleaning and explains how important dental care is to their child's overall health. Encourage them to make an appointment. In the control group, the no-treatment group, the parents do not receive the prompt. Three months later, count the numbers of children in each group who had an exam and cleaning. Your research question could be, "Do children whose parents received a prompt to schedule a free exam and cleaning for their children have more appointments than children whose parents did not receive the prompt?" You could analyze the results using simple statistics. There is an existing literature of the role of social workers in promoting dental care, and this could be one of the few true experiments done in this field. Does this sound feasible?

Apollonia: Yes, I could do that. That sounds very doable!

My student left class encouraged, with a clear idea for a useful project, and I was able to use this dialog, conducted in front of my class, as a "teaching moment" illustrating how one can apply experimentalist thinking to one's own practice.

Another example involves a DSW student I will refer to as Midas:

Midas: I don't know what to do for my capstone project.

Bruce: Where do you work?

Midas: I am a development officer at the university here in town.

Bruce: So you help design and manage fundraising campaigns for the university?

Midas: Yes.

Bruce: Do any of your campaigns involve sending letters to past or prospective donors?

Midas: Yes.

Bruce: How does this sound? Following your usual practice, draft a letter for one of your campaigns asking for donations. Make two versions of the same letter, one signed by the university president that includes a professional photo of her and the other signed by a female student of a similar age that also includes a photo. A couple of months after the letters are mailed, tabulate the number of donors and the total amount raised according to which donors received which letter. Your hypothesis could be something like, "Is a donor letter from the university president more effective in raising money than the same letter from a student?" (The opposite hypothesis could also be crafted.)

Midas: Yes, that sounds very doable! I like it!

Disappointingly, neither Apollonia nor Midas carried out these suggested RCTs. But again, I was able to use this spontaneous dialog to illustrate to the other students in the class how opportunities for conducting true experiments can be found all around us, almost lying at our feet begging to be picked up. Both of these hypothetical experiments involved the students evaluating their own practices, the projects were practical exercises that would have furthered their professional activities and potentially contributed to the empirical knowledge base of social work, and they would not have required a research grant to carry out.

In teaching my MSW research classes, I usually provide instruction on critical thinking and scientific skepticism. As context, I provide a presentation on the claims made for and theory underlying homeopathic medicines. I tell my students that homeopathic drugs have been extensively tested and have fairly conclusively been shown not to work above and beyond the placebo effect. I tell them that homeopathic products contain no active ingredients and cannot hurt you, but they do harm people by diverting them from obtaining effective medical treatments and by wasting their money. I explain how the theory and principles of homeopathy (e.g., the law of similars, succussion, molecular memory) are pseudoscientific jargon with no empirical or logical legitimacy. In a course I taught to social work students in Germany a few years ago, I capped things off by producing two new, sealed bottles of homeopathic medicine I had purchased at a local pharmacy: one bottle of homeopathic sleeping pills, the other a bottle of energy pills designed to help one maintain alertness. I invited my students to volunteer (no course credit, no coercion) to be randomly assigned to receive one of the pills in class and provide a rating of their tiredness on a 10-point scale near the end of class. Most readily agreed, out of curiosity perhaps, and I gave the participants one of the two pills under single-blind conditions (they did not know which one they got, but I did). I continued with class and an hour later had them rate their tiredness on a simple data collection sheet. I turned the ratings over to two students who independently calculated the mean tiredness ratings of the two groups, testing the hypothesis that "the students who took the homeopathic sleeping pill would be more tired than the students who took the energy pill." This study design can be diagrammed as follows:

	Group	
R	$X_{sleeping\ pill}$	O_1
R	$X_{energy\ pill}$	O_1

This classroom exercise served several purposes. One is that it was an effective demonstration of the value of a simple experimental design to test a causal hypothesis, namely that homeopathic sleeping pills help people fall sleep. The answer that emerged at the end of class was clear to everyone. I pointed out that many claims regarding social work interventions can be similarly tested, often without great expense, simply requiring the bravery to empirically test one's belief in the effectiveness of a treatment. Doing so exemplifies the value of the attitude of *scientific skepticism*, of doubting claims to effectiveness while not denying them, absent credible evidence either way, and of being willing to test such claims. It also demonstrates the value of empirical research over personal testimony or clinical anecdotes as an elevated evidentiary standard.

Most of my students either know someone who swears by homeopathic remedies (not to be confused with herbal products or dietary supplements), or they have used them themselves. The exercise is eye-opening. I ended the class by making a show of swallowing the remaining homeopathic sleeping pills, usually about twenty, in one gulp, putting my money where my mouth is, so to speak. (You would not want to do this with any medicine containing real ingredients.) But it is impossible to overdose on real homeopathic products.

To check, I called the consumer hotline for the company that makes the homeopathic sleeping pills and asked, "What would happen if I took twenty of these pills?" The representative paused a moment and carefully said, "They would have no more effect than taking two." So I knew I was safe.

Another hypothetical project occurred to me while standing in line at my local airport. I heard two people talking behind me, and social work was mentioned. I turned around and introduced myself as the (then) dean of the Florida State University School of Social Work, and I inquired about their interest in social work. It turned out that one of them was a licensed clinical social worker. Ever on the alert to recruit new PhD students to FSU's program, I exchanged business cards with her. Later I called her and gave her my pitch, explaining the generous stipend and complete tuition waiver (and health insurance) our doctoral students received and how she could do research in pretty much any area of practice she wished. I asked her what approach to treatment she used, and I was a little taken aback when she said shamanism. Open-minded soul that I am, I asked her to explain, and she told me about shamanistic theory and how she performed shamanistic rituals to help her clients. I asked, "You mean shamanistic rituals can help people with mental disorders as well as physical ones?" And she assured me that they can and do. Pressing a bit, I asked if shamanism could help people with high blood pressure and she said absolutely. Pressing further, I asked if performing a shamanistic ritual for a person with high blood pressure would cause the person's blood pressure to drop immediately and was told yes. I suggested that this would make an excellent doctoral dissertation research project. She asked how this could be done. I suggested recruiting people with high blood pressure to come to her office and, with their informed consent, to perform either a real shamanistic ritual to reduce blood pressure, or a placebo one, a similar but made-up ritual of no shamanistic significance. At the end of the session, she would measure their blood pressure and perhaps provide them with a small gratuity like a gift card in appreciation for their participation. The choice of ritual (real or placebo) would be made based on a coin toss.

When this hypothetical experiment was proposed to her, she expressed confidence that her shamanistic ritual would produce real reductions in blood pressure readings and that the placebo ritual would not. So, with my encouragement she applied to the FSU PhD program and was accepted, intending to conduct empirical research on shamanism. Sadly, when she discussed her practice orientation in class with other faculty, they offered no encouragement or support; indeed they were quite dismissive, and she dropped out of the program. My own attitude was (and is) that any intervention hypothesized to change people's behavior can be empirically evaluated. There is some literature on the use of shamanism in social work (e.g., Carpenter-Aeby, Xiong, and Aeby 2014; Laird 1984; Lee and Yuen 2003; Lee et al. 2018; Meuche 2015), and some

LCSWs use shamanism as an intervention. You can Google LCSW and shamanism to locate social workers using shamanism in their practice.

A previous social work PhD student at my university conducted an experimental evaluation comparing the therapeutic effects of "real" mantra-based meditation versus a placebo meditation (Wolf and Abell 2003), so there was nothing inherently unfeasible about the type of experimental study I had proposed. In fact, there is a large empirical literature evaluating the outcomes of prayer, for example (Hays and Aranda 2015; Hodge 2007). Many social workers use unconventional treatments in their practices (see Pignotti and Thyer 2009, 2012), and far too many use dubious, pseudoscientific, and even supernatural therapies (Thyer and Pignotti 2015, 2016; Holden and Barker 2018; Lee et al. 2018). I have devoted a large portion of my lengthy career to discouraging the *use* of treatments that are not well supported by credible research studies, but I have never discouraged *research* into the efficacy and potential mechanisms of actions of interventions used by members of our profession, no matter how dubious in appearance.

To reiterate: The design and conduct of RCTs of treatments need not be unduly burdensome, expensive, or complicated. For example, a research team conducted a study of a treatment called therapeutic touch (TT), the practitioners of which claim that by placing their hands over a client's body, they can detect disturbances in an invisible energy field unknown to science. These disturbances are said to cause a variety of mental and physical disorders. In Rosa et al. (1998), twenty-two TT practitioners were recruited to see whether they could sense if their hand was under a researcher's hand. They individually sat behind a screen and extended their hands through a draped opening to a researcher sitting on the other side. The researcher then placed her hand over one of the TT practitioner's hands, right or left as determined randomly by a coin toss. The practitioner was then asked whether the researcher's hand hovered over the practitioner's right or left hand. This was done hundreds of times, in two separate experiments. When asked beforehand, the practitioners were all confident they could reliably detect the location of the unseen hand. The sessions were videotaped, and the practitioners' answers were recorded as correct or incorrect.

One would expect that on the basis of chance alone, the practitioners would be correct about 50 percent of the time. And if they *could* detect the presence of an unseen hand, they would guess correctly far more than 50 percent of the time. This was a simple yet robust examination of a clear claim, the claim that is the foundation of the notion that TT can cure people. After all, if the purported energy emanating from living tissue cannot be correctly sensed, then the possibility of any genuine therapeutic effects above and beyond placebo value is a moot point. The results of the studies showed that the practitioners accurately guessed the presence of the researcher's hand about 50 percent of the time, and simple statistical tests showed no significant variation in the data beyond chance. This study falsified the foundational claim of TT theory. There is no detectable energy field that can be sensed, as claimed. Lacking the ability to detect the "energy field," treatment effects involving detecting and adjusting this energy cannot exist.

This study was published in the *Journal of the American Medical Association*, one of the world's most well-respected scientific journals. But it started out as the eleven-year-old lead author's school science fair project! If, with a little help, a child can undertake a true experiment and publish it in a prestigious journal, what does that say about those voices in our profession who claim that experiments are too difficult for social workers to undertake? Try Googling the terms "LCSW" and "therapeutic touch" and see how many instances you can find of clinical social workers using TT in their practices (see also Greene 2009). Why do we permit this to continue?

Summary

The theory and logic of the posttest-only randomized experiment have been explained in this chapter and illustrated by published studies undertaken by social workers. The major features of each published study were presented, including the research question, hypotheses, intervention, and outcome measures. Several hypothetical thought experiments were also described illustrating how our everyday practice can serve as opportunities to conduct experimental evaluations of what we do. These designs can be undertaken as small-scale studies involving relatively few participants and costing little, and they can also be used to undertake sophisticated, large-scale evaluations answering research questions of great importance.

CHAPTER 6

PRETEST–POSTTEST EXPERIMENTAL DESIGNS

There are many things we Buddhists should learn from the latest scientific findings. And scientists can learn from Buddhist explanations. We must conduct research and then accept the results. If they don't stand up to experimentation, Buddha's own words must be rejected.

—The Dalai Lama (cited in Iyer 1988, 60)

As noted in the previous chapter, given a sufficient number of participants appropriately randomly assigned to each arm of an experiment, it is not necessary to know the salient features, demographic or in terms of outcome measures, of the participants at the beginning of a study. We can safely assume that the groups are equivalent on *all* relevant and even irrelevant dimensions. The larger the original sample size and the number of participants assigned to each condition, the more confident we can be in this pretreatment equivalence. However, there are some circumstances in which obtaining pretreatment measures of participants' demographic features and dependent (outcome) variables can be useful.

In many instances, especially in research on real-world practice with actual clients, what is called *field research*, the number of potential participants can be limited. If an agency is serving as the host of a research study on, say, people meeting the DSM criteria for bipolar disorder (BPD), the researcher has little control over the number of people who come to the agency seeking help for their BPD. Those who do may be approached for recruitment to a treatment study comparing, say, a novel therapy versus treatment as usual (TAU) as provided by the agency. Not everyone approached will agree to participate. Of those who do, a number will not meet the study's inclusion and exclusion criteria. And of those who do meet the criteria and enroll in the study, some will not complete the study (e.g., some may drop out, some may die, some may move out of town). This process of attrition can result in a less than optimal sample size for the study to have adequate power to justify the use of particular statistical tests.

That field studies are often more difficult to conduct than studies conducted in carefully controlled settings, such as university or hospital clinics, has long been recognized as an obstacle for social work research (e.g., Thomas 1960). Thomas defined field research as follows:

> The field experiment is a research method that retains some of the precision and control of the laboratory experiment without necessitating the removal from their customary social surroundings of the individuals who are studied. . . . The field experiment is a design of research involving *control by the researcher* of the persons who are and who are not to be exposed to the experimental variable. . . . The researcher may exercise control in two ways. Most commonly, he directly manipulates a variable in a social setting. . . . A second defining characteristic of the field experiment is its setting which is a genuine social situation in which the phenomena being studied are commonly found.
>
> (1960, 273–75, emphasis in the original)

At my home university, for example, we have a psychology clinic run by the psychology department's clinical psychology doctoral program. The building is attractive and comfortably furnished, parking is free, and the therapists are PhD students in clinical psychology who are well trained in the use of various research-supported treatments. The student therapists are closely supervised by doctoral-level clinical psychology faculty licensed by the state of Florida, many of whom possess advanced clinical credentials such as the diplomat in clinical psychology offered by the American Board of Professional Psychology. Fees are means-tested and affordable. The clinic often hosts intervention research projects devised by PhD students and their supervising faculty members. While some clients walk through the door unprompted, many are proactively recruited using paper flyers and newspaper and online advertisements with headings like "Are you depressed?," "Do you suffer from panic attacks?," or "Are you afraid of public speaking?" These appear all over the campus and surrounding community for the purpose of enrolling people with particular problems into experimental studies often evaluating a new psychotherapy or a variation of an existing one.

College students often form a large proportion of participants, students who are usually young, well educated, relatively affluent, and intelligent. If an insufficient number of participants are enrolled, recruitment efforts can be redoubled, perhaps with added incentives offered for participation. Once participants are enrolled, it is routine for them to get reminders about upcoming appointments and follow-up calls to reschedule missed sessions. The student therapists usually adhere to an experimental treatment manual or protocol and often receive live supervision from their supervisor (an advanced PhD student or a faculty member) who observes the treatment sessions they provide. If supervision is not provided in real time, sessions are recorded, and videos are subsequently reviewed. It is rare for supervision to be conducted solely on the basis of the graduate student's therapy notes and session recordings or through questioning by the supervisor regarding client progress.

The student therapists often incorporate rapid-assessment inventories or scales into treatment. Clients complete measures of their focal problem (e.g., depression, panic attacks) on a weekly basis, and results are shared and discussed with the therapist. Pretreatment and posttreatment measures of global functioning are routinely gathered. All graduate student therapists earning their PhD in clinical psychology have their tuition paid for and receive an annual assistantship paid for by the psychology program, which constitute incentives for them to perform well. The therapists' caseloads are manageable. Not surprisingly, providing psychotherapy services in these ideal circumstances has been shown to benefit clients (e.g., Cukrowicz et al. 2005, 2011).

Such valuable studies, however, are *not* field experiments. These studies can provide important information about the potential for a new or modified therapy to benefit clients, but their findings must be replicated under real-world conditions. Real-world studies should involve real-world clients. This means people with multiple concurrent and severe problems, who are more diverse demographically (e.g., with regard to race, gender, and socioeconomic status). They may not have stable living conditions or close relationships. They may see therapists who are unlicensed, have diverse educational backgrounds, or who receive less than optimal supervision or opportunities for continuing education in research-supported treatments and assessment methods. Applying promising therapies in these less-controlled (i.e., messier) service settings and replicating positive results from studies conducted in more ideal settings is essential to advance knowledge about the practical effectiveness of social work services.

In this chapter, I will present examples of published experimental research conducted by social workers involving both pretest and posttest assessments. Pretest measures may include one or more primary measures of the presenting problem that is the focus of the study, as well as some assessments of secondary issues that are also a source of concern. Pretest measures can also be taken of strengths or positive features of client functioning, important variables that are ancillary to the focus of the therapy. For example, in a study of an intervention for couples wherein one person has a drinking problem, a reduction in drinking and improvements in marital satisfaction would be major focuses. A secondary measure might involve positive communication skills. Is this important? Yes, but unless the partner with the drinking problem reduces their drinking or stops drinking and marital satisfaction improves, any improvements in positive communication skills will not be central to the goals of the intervention.

Pretreatment assessments also typically include descriptive information of the clients' demographic features, variables not seen as likely to change as a result of treatment (e.g., age, race, gender, religion, sexual orientation) but necessary to adequately describe the sample of participants. Select demographic and clinical features may also be useful in examining potential moderators and mediators of treatment outcome. For example, a person's age or a history of unsuccessful treatment outcomes may influence the success of the current treatment. As in chapter 5, I will begin with the simpler of the pretest–posttest designs and move on to the more complex ones.

The Pretest–Posttest, No-Treatment Control-Group Design

Schinke, S. P., and B. J. Blythe. 1981. "Cognitive-Behavioral Prevention of Children's Smoking." *Child Behavior Therapy* 3, no. 4: 25–42.

This study undertook to evaluate the potential preventive impact of a cognitive behavioral program focused on smoking. The evaluation consisted of randomly assigning children to either the prevention program or no treatment. Both groups were similarly assessed on three occasions: pretreatment, immediately posttreatment, and six months after the posttreatment evaluation. The authors included a literature review on the health effects of smoking cigarettes and of some prevention programs that had previously been evaluated. Prior preventive studies in the areas of smoking cessation, pregnancy prevention, and skills training led the authors to devise a school-based protocol to try to prevent children from ever taking up smoking. The study was conducted in a suburban neighborhood and involved twenty-eight children in the sixth grade who were on average a little older than ten years of age. Both the children and parents provided consent to participate in the study.

Following pretest assessments, the children were randomly assigned to the prevention program (n = 14) or to no treatment (n = 14). The prevention program involved eight semiweekly one-hour group sessions conducted by

MSW interns. The content involved psychoeducation about smoking and its effects, small group discussions, Socratic questioning, films, modeling, role-plays, rehearsal, social reinforcement, feedback, and homework assignments (e.g., asking people not to smoke, proselytizing to classmates). The outcome measures included a knowledge-of-smoking measure, a perspective-taking measure, a measure of means–ends thinking, and standardized role-playing tasks (e.g., refusing a proffered cigarette). The role-playing task performances were videotaped and reliably scored by assistants not involved in program delivery.

The general research question can be phrased as, "What are the outcomes of sixth-grade children who participated in a smoking prevention program compared with those of students who did not participate in the program?" Each outcome measure can be linked to a discrete and singular hypothesis:

1. Children who receive the smoking prevention program will demonstrate greater knowledge of smoking and its ill effects compared with children who do not receive the program.

2. Children who receive the smoking prevention program will demonstrate a greater ability at perspective-taking compared with children who do not receive the program.

3. Children who receive the smoking prevention program will demonstrate greater means–ends thinking compared with children who do not receive the program.

4. Children who receive the smoking prevention program will demonstrate more effective refusal behaviors compared with children who do not receive the program.

Each hypothesis could be predicted for the immediately-after-treatment time point and for the six-month follow-up. The authors could have justified their use of a no-treatment control group for several reasons. One could be that they did not have resources to treat all of the sixth-graders. Another might have been that they wanted to conduct a true experimental and causal analysis of the effects of the program, which treating all sixth-grade students would not permit. Further, the incidence of smoking among sixth-graders at the time was likely low, and the children were not being put in any immediate risk by not receiving the prevention program. And, because the value of the program was not yet certain, a no-treatment control group would be a reasonable comparison.

The hypotheses were largely corroborated. In the authors' words,

Results from this study strengthen cognitive and behavioral training as a strategy for preventing children's cigarette smoking. Sixth grade women and men given cognitive-behavioral prevention training in small groups, more than classmates randomly assigned to a measurement-only condition, improved their knowledge of tobacco and its consequences, their ability to solve problems and make decisions about cigarettes, and their interpersonal communication when implementing nonsmoking decisions. Six months after groups terminated, prevention training condition young people reported more felicitous attitudes and intentions about smoking, had refused cigarettes with greater frequency, and were smoking less than youths in the control condition.

(Schinke and Blythe 1981, 36)

The authors discussed this study's limitations but also note the promise of an effective smoking prevention program offered via small groups in school settings as a potentially important way to reduce the uptake of cigarette smoking among young people.

West, S., et al. 2021. *Preliminary Analysis: SEED's First Year.* Stockton, CA: SEED. https:// socialprotection.org/discover/publications/preliminary-analysis-seed%E2%80%99s -first-year.

Another example of the pretest–posttest, no-treatment control-group design can be found in a study evaluating the Stockton Economic Empowerment Demonstration (SEED) guaranteed income initiative in Stockton, California. The authors conducted an experimental investigation of the impact of this universal basic income program on the financial and psychosocial well-being of poor people living in Stockton. SEED was conceived by Michael Tubbs, then the mayor of Stockton, who recruited two social work faculty members, Stacia West and Amy Castro Baker, to oversee the design, development, implementation, data analysis, and reporting of the project. Financed by outside funding, SEED provided its participants an unconditional cash transfer of $500 a month in the form of a debit card. No strings attached. Stockton is a diverse city, and a random sample of relatively poor residents were contacted (one per household). Of those who qualified (participants had to be at least eighteen years old and living in a Stockton neighborhood with a median income at or below $46,033), 125 were randomly assigned to the experimental condition, and 200 were assigned to the no-treatment control group. The program was projected to last about twenty-four months.

Assessments involved quantitative measures, and a subset of participants also participated in qualitative interviews. Cleverly, SEED's organizers arranged with the state's welfare programs so that those receiving the $500 monthly payment would not be penalized if they were also receiving state-provided welfare services.

Among the study's hypotheses were the following:

1. SEED participation will promote greater income sufficiency compared with no treatment.
2. SEED participation will reduce psychological stress compared with no treatment.
3. SEED participation will lead to enhanced physical functioning compared with no treatment.

Data were collected from all participants three months (in December 2018) before random assignment to one of the conditions. Three follow-ups were conducted postrandomization up to two years out. Monthly surveys were completed electronically to assess any mental health or income changes using standardized, validated measures of physical health and psychological distress. One year into the program, the experimental participants were experiencing less income volatility and were in a better position to cover an unexpected expense of $400 relative to the control group. In the authors' words, "These findings suggest that the treatment group experienced clinically and statistically significant improvements in their mental health that the control group did not. . . . One year after receiving the guaranteed income, the treatment group showed statistically significant differences in emotional health . . . (including) . . . energy, emotional well-being, and pain . . . when compared to the control group" (West et al. 2021, 17).

While the full results of the SEED project have not yet been released, the execution of this well-designed mixed-methods study points to the usefulness of a randomized experiment to evaluate the effects of a universal basic income on people's lives. That two social work faculty are spearheading this project points to the growing contributions that members of our profession can make to informing public welfare policy.

The Pretest–Posttest, Alternative-Treatment Control-Group Design

Heidenreich, T., et al. 2021. "Improving Social Functioning in Depressed Mothers: Results from a Randomized Controlled Trial." *European Journal of Social Work* 24, no. 1: 109–22.

This study was conducted in Germany to determine the effects of clinical social work services delivered to mothers with depression. The major hypothesis can be stated as, "Mothers with depression who receive clinical social work services in addition to TAU will experience greater improvements in depression than those treated with TAU only." The independent variable of clinical social work (CSW) was based on a treatment manual developed by the authors that incorporated relevant German standards for social work with psychiatric patients. CSW services were conducted over four months through ten sessions and included two telephone counseling sessions and two home visits. The CSW services were provided by two qualified clinical social workers with master's degrees. The social workers held sessions with participants so the therapists and clients could get to know each other, conducted an environmental analysis, and provided services related to psychoeducation, motivation training, coping skills for everyday life, family support and social networking, and handling crises. TAU involved psychotherapy delivered by psychotherapists and medication management provided by psychiatrists. In Germany, CSW services are not usually arranged for outpatients unless they are experiencing severe dysfunction.

Sixty-one mothers with depression were randomly assigned to receive CSW plus TAU or to TAU alone, as depicted in the following diagram:

			Group	
N = 31	R	O_1	$X_{CSW + TAU}$	O_2
N = 30	R	O_1	$X_{TAU\ alone}$	O_2

The dependent variables included the Global Assessment of Functioning (GAF) Scale, the Symptom Checklist-90 (SCL-90; an overall measure of psychopathology), the Satisfaction with Life Scale (SWLS), the depression symptom scale of the Patient Health Questionnaire (PHQ), and the General Self-Efficacy (GSE) Scale. You can see how each of these outcome measures serves as the centerpiece for a unique hypothesis, as follows:

1. Clients receiving CSW and TAU will improve more on the GAF Scale than clients receiving TAU alone.
2. Clients receiving CSW and TAU will improve more on the SCL-90 than clients receiving TAU alone.
3. Clients receiving CSW and TAU will improve more on the SWLS than clients receiving TAU alone.
4. Clients receiving CSW and TAU will improve more on the GSE Scale than clients receiving TAU alone.
5. Clients receiving CSW and TAU will improve more on the PHQ depression symptom scale than clients receiving TAU alone.

A hypothesis that makes a prediction about just one dependent variable is more capable of being falsified than a hypothesis that makes predictions about two or more variables at the same time. For example, consider the following "double-barreled" hypothesis: "Clients receiving CSW and TAU will improve more on the GAF Scale *and* on the SCL-90 than clients receiving TAU alone." Would you judge the hypothesis to be falsified or supported if clients showed improvement on the GAF Scale but *not* the SCL-90? If clients who received CSW and TAU showed more improvement on both measures compared with clients who received TAU alone, you could legitimately say that the hypothesis was supported. Or, if clients who received CSW and TAU had similar outcomes to those who received TAU alone, you could legitimately say the hypothesis was falsified. By posing hypotheses making only a *single* prediction, it is usually easier to draw conclusions. The exception is when a researcher has grounds to predict an interaction effect among several variables in advance of conducting a study. (Note that making the prediction in advance of data collection is crucial for the scientific integrity of the study.) Such a hypothesis could be, "Women with depression who have attained at least a high school education will improve more with CSW and TAU than with TAU alone compared with women with depression who have not completed high school."

The results of the study were clear. Although both groups improved, those who received CSW and TAU improved more that those who received TAU alone, according to scores on the GAF Scale. Similar outcomes were observed in clients' scores on the SCL-90 and the GSE Scale. Both groups improved equally in their scores on the depression symptom scale of the PHQ and the SWLS.

Hong, P. Y. P., S. Choi, and R. Hong. 2020. "A Randomized Controlled Trial Study of Transforming Impossible Into Possible (TIP) Policy Experiment in South Korea." *Research on Social Work Practice* 30, no. 6: 587–96.

Professor Philip Hong is the dean of the School of Social Work at the University of Georgia. For a number of years, he has been researching psychological self-sufficiency theory and its potential applications to helping people living on a low income obtain jobs. Drawing on this theory, he has developed an intervention called Transforming Impossible Into Possible (TIP), aimed at strengthening the internal locus of control of job-seekers so that they can be more effective at negotiating barriers to employment. TIP is a participant-driven, group-based approach. It had been evaluated in pilot studies and found to be helpful, with completion of the program being followed by increases in hope about being able to find work, increases in employment, and decreases in perceived employment barriers. But notice the phrasing "followed by," not "caused by." I knew better than to write "caused by" because you, the astute and attentive reader, know that simple pretest–posttest studies ($O_1 - X - O_2$) do not usually permit causal inference because of all those pesky alternative explanations collectively called threats to internal validity. Also knowing this, Hong pursued the next logical approach to further evaluate TIP: conducting a randomized experiment.

Hong conducted his experiment in one province in South Korea, where he recruited 169 low-skilled poor job-seekers already participating in the South Korean equivalent of the national workforce development program for welfare recipients. Such participation is a requirement to receive welfare benefits in South Korea. With informed consent, the participants were randomly assigned to one of two groups: 104 were assigned to receive the TIP program plus the workforce development program (TAU), and 65 were assigned to a wait-list control group, which received only the workforce development program. Pre-treatment assessments were completed before the experimental group received TIP, and posttests were completed after completion of the last TIP session. Pretreatment, both groups were equivalent on demographic and pretreatment measures, which consisted of validated scales of employment hope, perceived employment barriers, economic self-sufficiency, self-efficacy, and self-esteem. The design of this study can be diagrammed as follows:

		Group		
N = 104	R	O_1	$X_{TIP + TAU}$	O_2
N = 65	R	O_1	$X_{TAU\ alone}$	O_2

The TIP program involved ten structured sessions, each focusing on a specific topic (e.g., self-compassion, self-motivation, stress and anger triggers), and was provided to groups of five to ten participants. Participants took part in two brief sessions a day over five to seven days, and all TIP groups received the program within a three-month time period. The relative brevity during which TIP was delivered had the benefit of reducing the likelihood that concurrent history would impact the results. Hypotheses were linked to each outcome measure and can be phrased as follows:

1. Participants who received TIP and TAU will show greater improvement in employment hope compared with those who received TAU alone.
2. Participants who received TIP and TAU will show a greater reduction in perceived employment barriers compared with those who received TAU alone.

The same sort of hypothesis was also made for the outcomes of self-efficacy, self-esteem, and economic self-sufficiency, for a total of five hypotheses.

The results were promising. Four of the five hypotheses favoring TIP over TAU were supported. The authors concluded that "the results . . . showing the significant differences in the intervention group and no significant differences in the control group, indicate that participation in the TIP program may contribute to the psychological empowerment of participants in terms of self-esteem, self-efficacy, employment hope, and [economic self-sufficiency]"

(Hong, Choi, and Hong 2020, 593). The authors acknowledged that issues of treatment fidelity and the brief follow-up period were limitations of their study. Replications are underway.

The Switching-Replications Design

Larkin, R., and B. A. Thyer. 1999. "Evaluating Cognitive-Behavioral Group Counseling to Improve Elementary School Students' Self-Esteem, Self-Control, and Classroom Behavior." *Behavioral Interventions* 14: 147–61.

The switching-replications design has two major strengths. First, it can compare the effects of an experimental treatment to the passage of time alone. Second, it can replicate a demonstration of an effect. Demonstrating an effect of treatment twice, as opposed to only once, increases our confidence in both the study's internal validity (i.e., did treatment *cause* any observed improvements) and external validity (i.e., the positive effects of treatment were demonstrated in two different groups of people, thus strengthening the *generalizability* of the findings, albeit modestly).

The design is implemented by randomly assigning participants to two groups. Both groups are assessed and then the treatment is begun for group 1 but not for group 2 (the no-treatment control condition). After sufficient time has elapsed, both groups are assessed a second time. Assuming that group 1 has improved and group 2 has not, group 2 then receives the experimental treatment. (Note that if group 1 did not improve, you'd likely want to discontinue the experiment.) After group 2 receives treatment under the same conditions and for the same duration as group 1, both groups are assessed a third time. This permits an empirical examination of two possibilities. The first is to see whether the improvements initially seen in group 1 were maintained over time, and the second is to see whether group 2 improved, as group 1 had earlier. This design can be diagrammed as follows:

			Group			
Immediate treatment	R	O_1	X	O_2		O_3
Delayed treatment	R	O_1		O_2	X	O_3

Logically, if group 1 improved at O_2 and group 2 did not, the improvements seen in group 1 can reasonably be attributed to the experimental treatment, not the passage of time, concurrent history, regression to the mean, or any other plausible factor. If group 2 improves after treatment, at O_3, you have *replicated* the effects observed in group 1. Because science gives greater credence to replicated findings than to those supported by only a single experimental demonstration, the switching-replications design is a strong one in terms of internal validity. External validity is enhanced somewhat because of the replicated findings, but because the results were obtained from the same initial sample of participants, which is likely a convenience sample, a more solid demonstration of external validity is needed via further experiments with a more diverse sample of participants.

A switching-replications design was used by the school social worker Rufus Larkin to evaluate the effectiveness of the group therapy sessions he held for elementary school students. Larkin was a licensed clinical social worker (LCSW) in Georgia enrolled in the University of Georgia PhD program in social work. I was his major professor (chair), and when it came time for us to discuss dissertation topics, I asked him the usual questions:

Bruce: Where do you work?

Rufus: At two elementary schools in a modest-sized town in northeast Georgia.

Bruce: What do you do for the kids?

Rufus: Mostly individual and group counseling for kids referred to me by their teachers because of mental health concerns or behavior management issues in the classroom. I do some liaison work with parents, and occasionally I work with Child Protective Services in instances of suspected abuse or neglect.

Bruce: Sounds like very worthwhile work, Rufus. Do you do any good?

Rufus: Oh, yeah, I see great changes in most of the kids I counsel!

Bruce: Great, that must be very rewarding. But do you have any empirical data showing that the kids get better following your services?

Rufus: Well. . . . no.

I replied that that was great. With no data, perhaps we could design an outcome study of Larkin's practice to see if children really were improving following his counseling and use that for his dissertation. He could possibly finish his PhD *and* demonstrate the value of his services to his school. We decided to focus on his group therapy sessions. As Larkin received referrals, he waited until he had a sufficient number (ten to eleven) to compose a small therapy group of children whom he would treat in a cohort-style format. It was not an open-ended group. He was already following a cognitive behavioral group therapy program previously developed by O'Rourke and Worzbyt (1996), and each group met for eight sessions. What we needed to do was select some appropriate outcome measures, choose a suitable experimental design, and obtain institutional review board approval from both the University of Georgia and the local school board where Larkin was employed.

Drawing upon his clinical expertise with children, Larkin decided that the Rosenberg Self-Esteem Scale (RSES) and the Children's Perceived Self-Control Scale (CPSCS) would be relevant rapid-assessment measures and that behavior ratings submitted by the children's teachers would also be an important outcome variable. Behavior ratings were scored from 1 (excellent) to 4 (poor) and were completed for the previous month. The rapid-assessment measures were supported by previously published reliability and validity studies, indicating their psychometric suitability.

Because Larkin received more referrals of students needing counseling than he could see, he routinely had a waiting list of children to begin the next cohort of group therapy. With minimal improvisation, Larkin randomly assigned each newly referred child (n = 51) to the next group therapy cohort or to a wait-list control condition. Upon referral, each child completed the RSES and the CPSCS, and their teacher submitted a behavior rating for the previous month. Children randomly assigned to immediate treatment began the eight-session group therapy program, while the others waited their turn for treatment. Institutional review board approval was obtained before data collection began. After ten weeks, both groups were assessed again (O_2), and the children in the wait-list group were enrolled in the group therapy program. When it was completed, both groups were assessed a third time (O_3).

The overall research question was, "Do children receiving group therapy from the school social worker improve more than children on the waiting list?" The specific hypotheses were as follows:

1. Children who received group therapy will show more improvement in self-esteem than children assigned to the waiting list.
2. Children who received group therapy will show more improvement in self-control than children assigned to the waiting list.
3. Children who received group therapy will show more improvement in classroom behavior than children assigned to the waiting list.
4. Any improvements observed among the children who received group therapy immediately will be maintained at follow-up.
5. Children assigned to the waiting list will not show improvement during the wait-list period but once treated will demonstrate similar improvements to the children who received treatment immediately.

Happily, each hypothesis was supported. Students who received group therapy right away improved on all outcome measures, whereas students on the waiting list did not. But when the wait-list students completed group therapy, they showed a similar improvement to those who had received treatment immediately. And students' gains were maintained two months posttreatment.

There are several takeaway messages from this project. One is that Larkin was able to incorporate a research project into his everyday practice. Our code of ethics suggests that social workers need to evaluate the outcomes of their own work, and Larkin's dissertation project represents one approach to fulfilling this ethical mandate. Another is that he was able to complete a relatively complex experimental evaluation *without* any external research funding or any significant costs. A third is that this work allowed him to have his study published in a high-quality peer-reviewed journal, thus contributing to the knowledge base of the social work profession, which is another mandate of our code of ethics.

Larkin's study does have some limitations, which may have occurred to you, the critical reader. You may have noted that it was Larkin himself who conducted the evaluations and provided the therapy, which introduces the potential for bias in this study. And while the children's teachers provided the behavior ratings, they were also the ones who had made the referrals and thus were not blind to experimental conditions. This fact, too, could introduce a form of bias. While using student self-reports to try to capture changes in self-esteem and perceived self-control can be an effective way to evaluate the outcomes of group therapy, it might have been useful to add blind parental ratings of some sort to the mix of outcome measures, as another useful source of data. Many such measures are available (see Fischer, Corcoran, and Springer 2020). Larkin also conducted the statistical analysis for his study. A better practice would be to have an independent third party perform the analysis.

The Solomon Four-Group Design

Schinke, S. P., B. J. Blythe, and L. D. Gilchrist. 1981. "Cognitive-Behavioral Prevention of Adolescent Pregnancy." *Journal of Counseling Psychology* 28, no. 5: 451–54.

The Solomon four-group design was introduced in 1949 by Richard Solomon. In this important paper (Solomon 1949), he traced the origins of the pretest–posttest, no-treatment control-group experimental design involving two groups and randomized experiments using three groups. He pointed out some of the threats to internal validity which these two- and three-group designs do not adequately control for and suggested a novel design extension to randomized experiments to address this issue. What he called the four-group design randomly assigns participants to four conditions. Group 1 is pretested, receives the experimental intervention and is then tested again. Group 2 receives the pretest and posttest but no intervention. Group 3 receives the intervention and posttest but no pretest. Group 4 receives the posttest only. The Solomon four-group design is helpful in controlling for the passage of time, maturation, and the influence of the pretest on posttest assessments. A participant's experience with a pretest can influence how they perform at posttest. For example, the first iteration of a role-playing test may cause some anxiety because of the evaluative nature of the situation and the unfamiliarity of the experience. But when faced with the same or a similar assessment at posttest, participants may have less anxiety because they are now familiar with what is expected and they may perform better, *not* because of the intervention but because of their familiarity with the assessment. Further, both the pretest experience and the intervention may have an effect on posttest scores, making it difficult to determine the exact cause of any changes between pre- and posttest. The Solomon four-group design attempts to control for pretest influence by having group 3 receive the intervention and posttest but no pretest and by having group 4 receive only the posttest, with no pretest or intervention.

You will not be surprised to learn that this complex design is rarely used in social work intervention research. Concerns about the influence of pretesting on posttest scores or of possible interaction effects of the pretest and intervention on posttest scores are usually not high on the list of threats to internal validity that need to be controlled for. The study by Steven Schinke, Betty Blythe, and Lewayne Gilchrist (1981) is an exception.

This study addressed the prevention of adolescent pregnancy. The paper begins with a review of the negative health and social effects of early and unwanted pregnancy and describes an efficient way to devise an effective prevention program. The study was hosted at a large public high school, and thirty-six students (nineteen female, seventeen male) aged just under sixteen years on average were recruited. Drawing on cognitive behavioral prevention interventions used in earlier research on smoking and substance abuse, the authors developed an adaptation for pregnancy prevention. MSW students provided the intervention, which consisted of fourteen sessions of about an hour each. The outcome measures included previously published measures of sexual knowledge, problem-solving skills, and a behavioral performance role-playing test involving each participant engaging with a research assistant reviewing a series of increasingly stressful dating scenarios. These interactions were videotaped and scored by raters using a reliable scoring system. Post-treatment assessments were made six months following program completion. Students were randomly assigned to one of the four conditions constituting the Solomon four-group design, which can be diagrammed as follows:

Group 1	R	O_1	X	O_2
Group 2	R	O_1		O_2
Group 3	R		X	O_2
Group 4	R			O_2

It was hoped that group 2 would control for the passage of time, maturation, and regression to the mean; that group 3 would control for pretest effects, particularly the effect of the role-playing exercise; and that group 4 would control for any possible interaction or additive effects of the pretest and the intervention.

The overall research question was, "What are the effects of a cognitive behavioral adolescent pregnancy prevention program?" The hypotheses were the following:

1. Youth who received the prevention program will improve more on a measure of sexual knowledge than youth who did not receive the program.
2. Youth who received the prevention program will improve more on a measure of problem-solving than youth who did not receive the program.
3. Youth who received the prevention program will improve more on a role-play measure of refusing to engage in unprotected sex and discussing birth control than youth who did not receive the program.

The results supported these hypotheses and supported the effectiveness of the program: "Group cognitive and behavioral training let young women and young men acquire skills to prevent unplanned pregnancy. High-school sophomores who participated in cognitive behavioral training compared to classmates assigned to assessment-only conditions, gained sexual knowledge, problem-solving abilities, and persuasive patterns of interpersonal communication. Six months after group training, cognitive behavioral condition adolescents were more favorably disposed toward family planning and were practicing more effective contraception than were control-condition adolescents" (Schinke, Blythe, and Gilchrist 1981, 453).

Suitable statistical analyses allowed the authors to control for the effects of pretesting and possible interaction effects of the pretest and intervention. The fact that they followed up on their participants at six months is an example of including a long-term assessment into an intervention study. Of course, any study attempting to evaluate a pregnancy prevention program would be improved by including a measure of pregnancy. Logistics and practical considerations precluded the authors from doing so, and such an investigation would likely need to recruit many hundreds of participants, given the relatively small numbers of unplanned pregnancies that could be anticipated. Any investigation involving rare events needs a sizable sample so that the inferential statistics are adequately powered. In the study by Schinke, Blythe, and Gilchrist (1981), which had only thirty-six participants, and just nineteen female, the number of unplanned pregnancies, if any, would be nowhere near sufficient to permit statistical analysis.

The Placebo Control-Group Design

The use of a placebo control group in social work experimental research is perhaps the most controversial methodological practice in evaluation studies. The mandate to provide services that help people seemingly conflicts with the need to help control for, if not eliminate, the role of placebo influences in intervention studies. Chapter 2 reviewed the influence of placebo factors as among the more ubiquitous threats to internal validity. When an intervention, particularly a psychotherapeutic one, is provided in the context of a respectable agency setting, with fine furnishings and other amenities, delivered by an LCSW who is professionally dressed, charges a significant fee, does something called "therapy" (which is described with a lot of scientific-sounding words), and speaks in a confident manner, conveying the expectation that the client will get better, this cannot but help engender a sense of hope in the client. There are also important nonspecific factors of therapy, such as being listened to by an empathetic person, the sense of relief at being able to unburden one's concerns, no longer feeling alone, being encouraged, and being treated respectfully—these factors can combine to create very powerful placebo effects.

But keep in mind that social work workers need to deliver services the benefits of which accrue above and beyond those accounted for by placebo factors. The so-called dodo bird hypothesis claims that all psychotherapies are similarly effective because of their common relationship factors and that the specific type of treatment is largely unimportant. This view is not only incorrect but destructive, as it questions the purpose of graduate training in the discrete methods of psychotherapy and whether social work merits professional status. As the social worker William Reid (1997, 5) says, "There proved to be little basis for extending the dodo's verdict to the range of problems and interventions of concern to social workers. Moreover, several patterns of differential effectiveness occurred that could help guide the practitioner's choice of interventions." This conclusion continues to be well supported (e.g., de Felice et al. 2019; Lilienfeld 2014; Tolin 2014). First postulated in 1936 by Rosenzweig in a paper titled "Some Implicit Common Factors in Diverse Methods of Psychotherapy," the dodo bird hypothesis may well have been true at the time, when almost all psychotherapies were limited to office-based insight-oriented treatments based on psychodynamic theory. But with the rise of hundreds of research-supported treatments regularly being evaluated against each other and against credible placebos, it is now clear that some psychotherapies do work better than others. And some work better than placebo treatments. But to arrive at this latter conclusion, a psychotherapy must be evaluated against a credible placebo treatment.

Thus, the use of a placebo control condition in a randomized experiment is needed to evaluate the specific effects of the therapy by statistically subtracting any benefits seen among the placebo group from the benefits observed in the active-treatment group. This analysis is required to see whether the therapy under investigation yields better results than nonspecific influences. Some treatments lend themselves more readily to placebo-control comparisons than others. Medications are one example, as it is much easier to create a placebo pill, even one with side effects, than it is to find or create a credible placebo psychotherapy. Therapies like acupuncture (discussed in chapter 2) and so-called tapping therapies also lend themselves to placebo-controlled experimental investigations, as it is fairly easy to create a plausible placebo treatment to compare them with. For example, to evaluate the effectiveness of a tapping therapy, half the participants could be assigned to receive "real" tapping (tapping on specific areas of the body) and the other half to random tapping.

Note that a placebo control condition should be used only with clients whose problems are not too serious. In such instances it would be more ethically appropriate to test the active treatment against TAU, so that nobody is denied necessary care. With milder problems, once the experiment is over, it is good practice to offer the active treatment to participants who received a placebo or no treatment if the active treatment has proved to be more effective than placebo or no treatment. In recruiting participants for a placebo-control study, the researcher may or may not truthfully disclose the use of a placebo treatment. Potential participants may be told something like, "We are testing two different types of therapies for your problem. To participate in our study, you must agree to accept whichever treatment we randomly assign you to. When the study is over, if it turns out that the treatment you received was not as effective as the other treatment, we will then provide you the better treatment at no cost to you." If the participants agree to such conditions by providing informed consent in writing and if the study protocol has been approved by an appropriate institutional review board, then most authorities would consider the study ethical. But because the use of placebo control groups is sometimes seen as controversial, I will now describe several examples of such studies.

Novoa, M. P., and D. S. Cain. 2014. "The Effects of Reiki Treatment on Mental Health Professionals at Risk for Secondary Traumatic Stress: A Placebo Control Study." *Best Practices in Mental Health* **10, no. 1: 29–46.**

Reiki is said to be a form of energy therapy and is based on the premise that the body is imbued with an invisible energy field (as yet undetectable by scientific methods) and that the proper balance and flow of Reiki energy are necessary to sustain health. Ill health, physical and psychological, is said to be caused by imbalances or blockages in the natural flow of Reiki. It is claimed that certain people can be trained to detect Reiki energy in themselves and others. By holding their hands near a client's body, they can feel Reiki imbalances and correct them by moving their hands over the client and visualizing a freer flow of Reiki energy. When they sense that one blockage or disturbance is corrected, they move on to the next. Many social workers use Reiki in their social work practice (simply Google "Reiki" and "LCSW" to locate such practitioners). Novoa and Cain (2014) wished to examine the potential of Reiki therapy as delivered by the first author, an LCSW and "Reiki master practitioner," to alleviate secondary traumatic stress (STS) symptoms. They decided to use not only a placebo control group but also a no-treatment control group to help tease out the possible effects of Reiki versus placebo influences, the passage of time, and other threats to validity addressed by a no-treatment condition.

The overall research question was, "Does Reiki produce more benefits than a placebo Reiki treatment or no treatment?" The hypotheses can be framed as follows:

1. Clients who received real Reiki will benefit more than clients who received placebo Reiki.
2. Clients who received real Reiki will benefit more than clients who received no treatment.

The participants were a convenience sample of licensed mental health practitioners, including LCSWs. Various inclusion and exclusion criteria were used to determine eligibility for participation in the study, including being at moderate to high risk of secondary trauma symptoms based on scores on the compassion, burnout, and compassion fatigue/secondary trauma subscales of the Professional Quality of Life scale. The sixty-seven included participants were then randomly assigned to receive real Reiki (four sessions once a week), placebo Reiki (in which treatment was similar to real Reiki but participants had their eyes covered, and the practitioner did not move their hands over the client's body), or no treatment (in which participants were told they were receiving "distance Reiki"). Note that the no-treatment condition could also be considered another form of placebo treatment. Groups 1 and 2 were treated in the same location (a quiet room free of distractions) by the same practitioner. Standardized measures of secondary trauma, stress, anxiety, hopelessness, depression, and anger were obtained pre- and posttreatment. All measures were based on client self-report scales completed one week before and one week after treatment.

In some ways, this was a very well-designed study. The measures had good psychometric properties, and the therapist was qualified to provide the treatment and followed an established Reiki treatment protocol. If Reiki were effective, the study was well positioned to detect it. However, the authors stated that "the results reported do not provide support for the research hypothesis and no significant differences in risk level for STS and its associated symptoms were found. Thus, Reiki treatment was found to be ineffective for this sample of mental health professionals with moderate STS and associated symptoms. . . . This null hypothesis is supported by other research that found Reiki to be ineffective. . . . Reiki treatment . . . should not be considered among the best practice intervention options for mental health professionals with moderate STS and its associated symptoms" (Novoa and Cain 2014, 39–40).

It is not surprising to find that the true Reiki results did not differ from those of the false Reiki or "distance Reiki." This is because the energy field that Reiki therapy is predicated on has never been shown to exist. Absent the energy field, there can be no way to sense it (beside self-delusion), and with no way to sense it there can be no way to manipulate or fix it. Reiki shares this failing with all other so-called energy therapies (Pignotti and Thyer 2009; Thyer and Pignotti 2015). Hence, it is a shame for LCSWs to be able to obtain the continuing education (CE) hours needed to renew their license by attending CE sessions on Reiki (Thyer and Pignotti 2016).

In 2020, the highly regarded School of Social Work at the University of Southern California (USC) offered Reiki workshops to social workers. The advertisement said, "Highly trained Reiki practitioners and Reiki masters will be present throughout the conference to bathe you with life-force energy known as "Reiki" in Japanese and "Chi" in Chinese and "Prana" in Sanskrit" (USC 2020). And even though Novoa and Cain (2014) had clearly shown that Reiki has no effect on compassion fatigue, the USC School of Social Work also offered a workshop on preventing compassion fatigue to social workers that included Reiki. Its advertisement read, "Self-awareness allows you to better identify personal needs with necessary interventions, like self-care tactics. Relaxation techniques, *like yoga and reiki*, as well as cognitive behavioral therapy and cognitive reframing and boundary-setting are practices we use with our clients, but rarely use for ourselves. . . . If leveraged appropriately, these practices can help boost a social worker's wellbeing and overall resilience" (USC 2019, my emphasis).

Reiki classes are offered by and for social workers in many places. But perhaps most discouraging of all is to find that the first author of the study described here (Novoa) continues (as of the time of this writing) to offer Reiki sessions in her practice. So much for expecting scientific findings to impact research if the authors of studies with negative findings themselves ignore credible evidence that the therapies they provide are of no value.

Safford, F., and B. Baumel. 1994. "Testing the Effects of Dietary Lecithin on Memory in the Elderly: An Example of Social Work/Medical Research Collaboration." *Research on Social Work Practice* 4, no. 3: 349–58.

Contemporary television advertisements tout the advantages of various medicines and herbal products said to restore cognitive functioning or reverse cognitive decline. Before the latest round of products, such as those involving substances found in jellyfish, more prosaic compounds were said to help memory. One is lecithin, long said to benefit memory function. One social worker, with a medical collaborator, designed a placebo-controlled study of lecithin to try to answer the question, "What are the effects of dietary lecithin on memory in the elderly?" The hypotheses derived from this question were as follows:

1. The ingestion of dietary lecithin granules will improve scores on the Brief Memory Test statistically significantly more than the ingestion of placebo granules.
2. The ingestion of dietary lecithin granules will reduce memory lapses statistically significantly more than the ingestion of placebo granules.

Eighty-nine older volunteers were recruited in south Florida for "a study on the effect of a granulated food substance on memory" (Safford and Baumel 1994, 351). Half were randomly assigned to receive lecithin, and half were randomly assigned to receive a placebo. If lecithin proved beneficial, it would be offered to participants in the placebo group at the end of the study. Those in the lecithin group received two tablespoons a day, and those in the placebo group received two tablespoons of placebo granules. Both groups were blind as to whether they were receiving lecithin or placebo. The outcome measures consisted of the Brief Memory Test and recordings of memory lapses, both administered pretreatment and posttreatment. Both groups improved similarly on the Brief Memory Test, but the lecithin group experienced greater improvements in the reduction of memory lapses. The authors report some of their study's limitations, including that the sample size was relatively small and not representative of the larger city's population and that the participants were reasonably healthy whose ages ranged from fifty to eighty years. Considering fifty years old to be "elderly" seems questionable to this sixty-nine-year-old writer! A further limitation of the study was that there was a high rate of attrition. The records of eighteen placebo-group participants were lost, reducing the final sample size to only sixty-one participants.

Another experimental study coauthored by a social worker that examined the effect of lecithin on memory using a placebo control group was conducted by Weintraub et al. (1983). This study examined the effects of lecithin on people with Alzheimer's disease. Thirteen patients were enrolled in a study with a double-blind crossover design. Half received a nine-week trial of lecithin, followed by a washout period, and then nine weeks of a placebo. The other half received this treatment in reverse (starting with placebo and ending with lecithin). This was a powerful design despite the relatively small sample size, using randomization as well as the features of a switching replication study (Weintraub et al. 1983).

Wolf, D. B., and N. Abell. 2003. "Estimating the Effects of Meditation Techniques on Psychosocial Functioning." *Research on Social Work Practice* 13, no. 1: 27–42.

This placebo-controlled study was undertaken by Wolf as his doctoral dissertation project in social work. He was an LCSW and experienced in training people in the form of chanting meditation used by members of Hare Krishna, a branch of Hinduism. He wanted to empirically test whether daily chanting as prescribed by the Hare Krishnas reduced stress and depression more than daily chanting of a placebo mantra. Newspaper advertisements in the university town were used to recruit people wanting to explore an Eastern-style meditation and its effects on depression and stress. Ninety-three participants were randomly assigned (thirty-one per group) to receive training in meditative chanting using a real mantra, to receive training in meditative chanting using a placebo mantra, or to receive no meditation training (i.e., no treatment). The study design can be diagrammed as follows:

	Group			
Real mantra	R	O_1	$X_{real\ mantra}$	O_2
Placebo mantra	R	O_1	$X_{placebo\ mantra}$	O_2
No treatment	R	O_1		O_2

The outcome measures were standardized scales: the Vedic Personality Inventory, a measure of depression, and a measure of clinical stress. The hypotheses can be framed along these lines:

1. Participants who meditated with a real mantra will show greater improvement on the personality inventory than those who meditated with a placebo mantra.
2. Participants who meditated with a real mantra will show greater improvement in depression than those who meditated with a placebo mantra.
3. Participants who meditated with a real mantra will show greater improvement in stress than those who meditated with a placebo mantra.

These hypotheses can be repeated for the comparison of meditation with the real mantra versus no meditation. The real-mantra and placebo-mantra meditation groups chanted three times a day for a total of about 25 minutes. The real mantra consisted of the phrase "hare krishna hare krishna hare, hare rama hare rama hare," and the placebo mantra was "sarva dasa sarva dasa sarva, sarva jana sarva jana sarva," which was said to be "a theoretically meaningless combination of Sanskrit syllables concocted by the researcher" (Wolf and Abell 2003, 34). The third group did no meditation.

All hypotheses were confirmed. The authors concluded that "the results of this controlled trial provide some evidence that the maha mantra can significantly affect stress and depression change scores and can do so greater than an alternate (placebo) mantra. Similar results were found for the . . . modes of personality" (Wolf and Abell 2003, 37).

One must admire Wolf for being willing to put his long-held belief in the value of Hare Krishna meditation to the test—and a strong one at that: comparing the Hare Krishna mantra to a placebo mantra *and* to no treatment. However, before rushing out to begin a daily program of daily chanting, keep in mind that Wolf himself provided the meditation training and collected and analyzed the data. Thus, the role of therapist allegiance cannot be ruled out as a threat to internal validity. Attrition was also high across the groups. Out of the ninety-three participants who began the study, only sixty-one were retained at follow-up: twenty-three in the real-mantra meditation group and nineteen each in the placebo-mantra and no-meditation groups. These limitations indicate the need for caution in accepting the study's findings, as do studies indicating that meditation can have adverse effects (e.g., Goldberg et al. 2022).

Taylor, J. A., et al. 2003. "Efficacy and Safety of Echinacea in Treating Upper Respiratory Tract Infections in Children: A Randomized Trial." *Journal of the American Medical Association* 290, no. 21: 2824–30.

Echinacea is an herbal product that has been used for more than one hundred years. Many claims have been made regarding its effectiveness in preventing and treating a wide array of medical illnesses. One such claim is that it can be used to reduce the duration and severity of upper respiratory tract infections. Taylor et al. (2003) evaluated the use of echinacea for this purpose in a placebo-controlled RCT. The team of authors included an MSW. Over a four-month period, 407 children aged two to eleven years were treated with either echinacea or an identical placebo pill, with the product being given at the onset of symptoms until the infection was resolved (up to ten days). The major dependent variables were the severity and duration of the infection. A total of 707 infections occurred during the four months. Upon enrollment, parents were randomly assigned to be given echinacea or the placebo pills and were given an adequate supply. They were also given a symptom logbook and dosing spoons. The children and their parents were recruited from seven private practices and one inner-city clinic in Seattle, Washington. Since the children were randomized *within* each practice setting, this study is more properly considered a multisite RCT than a cluster RCT (wherein *all* children at each practice would have received either echinacea or placebo). The research question was, "What are the effects of echinacea on the duration and severity of upper respiratory infections?" The hypotheses were as follows:

1. Echinacea treatment will reduce the duration of upper respiratory infections in children to a greater extent than will placebo treatment.
2. Echinacea treatment will reduce the severity of upper respiratory infections in children to a greater extent than will placebo treatment.

A total of 524 children were enrolled and randomized to receive echinacea (n = 263) or placebo (n = 261). After some attrition, 407 children were available at follow-up: 200 who had received echinacea, and 207 who had received the placebo. Measures of treatment compliance were in place to ensure the fidelity of the independent variables. The authors reported that "there were no statistically significant differences between the two groups for duration of symptoms . . . severity of symptoms" (Taylor et al. 2003, 2827). Nor were differences found for any secondary measures, except that the children who had received echinacea experienced more rashes than the children treated with placebo. Thus, another herbal product bites the dust! Well, not really. This study needs to be evaluated in light of the totality of all available high-quality evidence on the subject. In 2014, this was done by Karsch-Völk et al., who conducted a systematic review on the topic. The authors found twenty-four RCTs comparing echinacea against placebo in the treatment of the common cold. They found that "echinacea products have not been shown to provide benefits for treating colds" (Karsch-Völk 2014, 1). That was the evidence as of 2014. Perhaps more current studies could show otherwise, but given the high-quality designs used to evaluate this product so far, that is unlikely. One notable feature of the Taylor et al. (2003) study is that it was conducted in collaboration with faculty of the School of Naturopathic Medicine (a pseudoscientific discipline) at Bastyr University, an alternative medicine university.

This section has described social worker–designed placebo-controlled studies that have been used to evaluate the effects of Reiki, lecithin, mantra-based meditation, and echinacea. Pignotti (2005) conducted another example of this type of study by evaluating a form of energy therapy called thought field therapy (TFT), which involves healing through tapping on specific areas of the body called meridian points. She compared the results of real TFT with a similar placebo treatment that involved random tapping. She found that participants in both groups showed about the same amount of improvement, which suggests that the theoretical basis of TFT, that tapping on specific meridian points is crucial to the success of TFT, is incorrect.

Prisco et al. (2013) tested a form of acupuncture called auricular acupuncture, which involves inserting needles in client's ears. Keep in mind that all forms of acupuncture and other energy therapies are predicated upon a premise that appears to be false: the presence of an invisible, undetectable bodily energy field, variously known as chi, ki, and qi among other terms. This energy field is said to permeate the body and have points of intersection called meridians. It is proposed that stimulating the meridians can improve energy flow and restore physical and mental health. In traditional acupuncture, this stimulation is done by inserting thin needles in precise locations of the body as dictated by acupuncture theory.

Prisco et al. (2013) evaluated the effectiveness of auricular acupuncture versus placebo acupuncture, wherein the needles were placed randomly, not according to acupuncture theory. The authors recruited thirty-five U.S. military veterans who had been diagnosed with post-traumatic stress disorder (PTSD) following combat and were experiencing insomnia. The participants were randomly assigned to the following groups: auricular acupuncture (n = 12), placebo acupuncture (n = 12), or wait-list control (n = 11). Multiple measures of insomnia were used, and participants were assessed pretreatment, midtreatment, and one month posttreatment. The authors clearly stated their major research question: "How does group auricular acupuncture influence the maladaptive perpetuating factors associated with PTSD-related insomnia, compared to sham acupuncture and wait-list controls?" (Prisco et al. 2013, 408).

Participants in all groups received usual care (TAU) provided by Veterans Affairs. Those in the real and placebo acupuncture groups received twice-weekly acupuncture sessions for two months. The wait-list control group received only TAU. At follow-up, no statistically significant differences were observed across the groups on the major outcomes for sleep, suggesting that auricular acupuncture was not an effective treatment for insomnia. This study was limited by its small sample size and considerable attrition over time. Despite the disappointing findings, this study illustrates another example of social workers using a placebo control condition in the context of a randomized experiment.

Properly conducted placebo control trials occupy an exceedingly important position in the armamentarium of evaluation methods used to test the effectiveness of social work and other psychosocial interventions. Unless an experimental treatment yields improvements *superior* to those obtained via a credible placebo treatment, one can have no confidence that the experimental treatment's effects amount to more than the effects of suggestion or expectation alone. For social workers to be considered true professionals, the services we provide must produce effects more powerful than placebo therapies.

Additive Studies

Additive studies attempt to examine the therapeutic value of providing an additional element to an existing treatment. This is done to try to enhance the effectiveness of an existing therapy by combining it with something else that might provide additional therapeutic benefit. Sometimes an added element yields an enhanced benefit, and sometimes it does not. Here is one social work example of an additive design.

Wong, D. F. K., et al. 2020. "Cognitive-Behavior Therapy with and Without Parental Involvement for Anxious Chinese Adolescents: A Randomized Controlled Trial." *Journal of Family Psychology* 34, no. 3: 353–63.

In this study, the authors wished to examine the potential benefits of an existing research-supported treatment, cognitive behavioral therapy (CBT), with anxious youth in China. The treatment had previously been culturally adapted for use in China, and adolescents were recruited in Hong Kong via Lutheran Social Services, a nongovernmental organization providing social work assistance to local secondary schools. The authors wished to compare CBT alone versus CBT with parental involvement to see whether the latter would result in better outcomes than CBT alone. CBT alone involved eight two-hour sessions. CBT with parental involvement required at least one parent to attend five two-hour sessions with other parents, which consisted of similar content to what was provided to the CBT-alone group, as well as training to help their children engage in exposure-based homework exercises.

A total of 136 adolescents were recruited and randomly assigned to three conditions: CBT alone (n = 45), CBT plus parental involvement (n = 46), or a social activity control condition (n = 45). The control condition consisted of eight two-hour sessions involving hiking and playing board games and card games. There was no reason to anticipate that participating in social activities alone would reduce anxiety, so the authors saw this as an appropriate control condition. The outcome measures included two anxiety scales, a self-esteem scale, and a measure of cognitive emotion regulation strategies. The broad research question was, "What are the effects of adding parental involvement to a CBT program intended to reduce anxiety in adolescents?" The hypotheses can be formulated along the following lines:

1. CBT plus parental involvement will yield a greater reduction in anxiety than CBT alone.
2. CBT plus parental involvement will yield a greater improvement in self-esteem than CBT alone.
3. CBT plus parental involvement will yield a greater improvement in emotion regulation than CBT alone.

4. CBT alone and CBT plus parental involvement will yield greater improvements than social activities alone.

The design of this study can be diagrammed as follows:

	Group				
CBT alone	R	O_1	$X_{CBT\ alone}$	O_2	O_3
CBT plus parental involvement	R	O_1	$X_{CBT\ +\ parents}$	O_2	O_3
Social activities	R	O_1	$X_{social\ activities}$	O_2	O_3

Assessments were made pretreatment, immediately posttreatment, and six months after treatment concluded. All treatment sessions were provided by social workers, and appropriate measures of treatment fidelity were used.

The results were not what had been expected. At the six-month follow-up, significant decreases in anxiety and decreased use of negative emotion regulation strategies were found across all three groups. This was unexpected, as the social activity condition was not expected to impact the outcome measures. CBT plus parent involvement produced some small benefits above and beyond CBT alone. In the authors' words, "The present findings suggest that involving parents in CBT for anxious Chinese adolescents may provide a small benefit in treatment efficacy . . . the advantage of CBT-PI [parental involvement] over child-focused CBT for anxious Chinese adolescents may be small" (Wong et al. 2020, 359). The authors provide some retrospective speculations involving cultural expectations and norms as to why the anticipated benefits of added parental involvement were less than expected.

This study has many positive features. The sample sizes possessed sufficient statistical power; the authors used a conservative approach to the statistical analysis (they conducted an intention-to-treat analysis, which will be discussed in a later chapter); the social work therapists were well trained and supervised and followed a clear treatment protocol. The amount of time required of each treatment condition was similar. The lack of difference in most outcomes suggests that either the social activities were more therapeutically effective than the authors had anticipated or that all three conditions were essentially placebo treatments.

Hsiao, F.-H., et al. 2011. "The Long-Term Effects of Psychotherapy Added to Pharmacotherapy on Morning to Evening Diurnal Cortisol Patterns in Outpatients with Major Depression." *Psychotherapy and Psychosomatics* 80: 166–72.

When powerful psychopharmacological therapies were initially developed in the 1950s, the major methods of treatment at the time were office-based, insight-oriented verbal psychotherapy and hospitalization. Pharmacotherapy represented a serious threat to the existing order of psychiatric care and was initially met with considerable resistance by most practitioners and psychiatric organizations. It was feared that drugs, if effective, would merely mask symptoms, leaving the underlying psychodynamic conflicts said to cause neuroses and psychoses unresolved. The pharmaceutical companies sought a way around this resistance by initially billing their new psychopharmacological treatments as *adjuncts to* (not replacements for) psychotherapy. They said that by using these new agents in combination with psychotherapy, patients would prove more amenable to talking treatments. With time, massive advertising campaigns, the patina of scientific jargon, and the publication of controlled experiments, medications infiltrated psychiatric treatments. One advertisement from 1956 for a medication called Serpanray (no longer used) claims that it "opens the door to more successful psychotherapy." Others read, "Psychotherapy and Thorazine . . . a 'combined therapy' most effective in the treatment of hyperkinetic emotionally disturbed children," and "Because Thorazine calms without clouding consciousness, the patient on Thorazine usually becomes more sociable and receptive to psychotherapy." Medications would eventually become the dominant form of treatment for so-called mental illnesses used by psychiatrists, to the extent that there are now more clinical social workers engaged in the practice of psychotherapy than psychiatrists and psychologists combined. After all, it is considerably easier to write a prescription than it is to see a client for fifty minutes of therapy, and one can charge many more patients during the day by prescribing medications than by doing psychotherapy.

However, the question of whether medication combined with psychotherapy yields better results remains an empirical and intriguing one, and a group of social workers conducted a randomized experiment to investigate this question. The study involved the treatment of people with major depressive disorder (MDD) and was conducted in Hong Kong. Sixty-three patients were recruited and randomly assigned to receive either pharmacotherapy alone (referred to as monotherapy; n = 34) or pharmacotherapy combined with a form of treatment involving eight weekly sessions of body-mind-spirit (BMS) psychotherapy (n = 29), a culturally based intervention developed in China. The BMS treatment was manualized and had previously been evaluated and shown to be effective. All patients met the criteria for MDD. The outcome measures were the Beck Depression Inventory, the State-Trait Anxiety Inventory, and what is called the Stagnation Scale (a Chinese concept). Measures were taken pretreatment and after two, five, and eight months of treatment. The authors also collected measures of salivary cortisol, an indicator of stress, as an outcome measure. The general research question was, "Does the combination of BMS plus medication produce greater improvements than medication alone?" The research hypotheses can be framed as follows:

1. Patients receiving combined therapy will show greater improvements on the Beck Depression Inventory than patients receiving monotherapy.
2. Patients receiving combined therapy will show greater improvements on the State-Trait Anxiety Inventory than patients receiving monotherapy.
3. Patients receiving combined therapy will show greater improvements on the Stagnation Inventory than patients receiving monotherapy.

The study design can be diagrammed as follows:

		Assessment time			
Group	Pretreatment		2 months	5 months	8 months
Monotherapy R	O_1	$X_{monotherapy}$	O_2	O_3	O_4
Combined therapy R	O_1	$X_{combined\ therapy}$	O_2	O_3	O_4

The authors reported the following findings:

> The study indicated that during the eight-month follow-up, there were similar effects on reducing symptoms of depression between the COMB [combination therapy] and MT [monotherapy]. . . . The greater reductions in anxiety states and the steeper diurnal cortisol patterns more likely occurred in COMB than in MT. We might attribute the similar effects in reducing symptoms of depression between COMB and MT to the pharmacotherapy provided to both groups of treatments. . . . Psychotherapy produced a long-term protective effect in improving [the] HPA [hypothalamus-pituitary-adrenal] axis psychobiological stress response. Therefore, psychotherapy added to pharmacotherapy could be regarded as a comprehensive treatment for major depression.
>
> (Hsiao et al. 2011, 171)

Perhaps there is something to the notion that combined therapy produces greater improvements than treatments provided alone.

Some strengths of this study include an adequate initial sample size, robust outcome measures (including salivary cortisol, a measure of physiological stress response), relatively long-term follow-up assessments, and a sophisticated statistical analysis. However, attrition was substantial, with eighteen of the initial thirty-four participants in the monotherapy group and nine of the initial twenty-nine participants in the combination therapy group dropping out by the month 8 assessment; this is a significant limitation.

Multisite Randomized Clinical Trials

The name of this type of study accurately conveys what they do and how they are conducted. Imagine you have a protocol for a randomized pretest–posttest, no-treatment control-group design, comparing the effects of a given treatment against no treatment. The design can be diagrammed as follows:

R	O_1	X	O_2
R	O_1		O_2

This can be a strong design for making a causal inference along the lines of the following: "Treatment X was followed by outcomes substantially better than no treatment, and we can conclude that X caused those differences." This design can control for some important threats to internal validity, such as concurrent history, passage of time, maturation, and regression to the mean. But it does not control for testing effects (the effect of a pretest on posttest outcomes), the possible interaction of the pretest and the treatment, or placebo factors. Still, it is a useful design.

Science holds in higher esteem findings that have been replicated, meaning they have been reproduced, ideally by independent researchers at different sites. Thus the logic of the multisite RCT is to conduct an experiment at one site (site 1), and then have another research team at a different site (site 2) conduct the same experiment. If site 2 gets results similar to those obtained at site 1, we can have greater confidence in the study's findings. This is because the study has shown strong internal validity (results were similar across two sites) and external validity (the findings can be generalized to other settings). We can have confidence in the external validity of the study because the findings were reproduced in a different setting with a different group of participants (who were diagnostically similar to those at site 1), different clinicians provided the therapy, and different people did the data collection.

The multisite RCT also presents advantages in terms of statistical inference. Let's look at an example. Say that site 1 treats people with bipolar disorder using a protocol-based psychotherapy at a psychiatric hospital in Miami. The site 1 researchers recruit sixty patients using strict inclusion and exclusion criteria and then randomly assign them to treatment or no treatment. Therapists are properly trained and supervised, and at the end of the study, the posttreatment assessments are carried out by evaluators blind to which group the patients had been assigned to. A properly conducted conservative statistical analysis shows that treatment was much better than no treatment.

At the same time, the study is conducted at a different site, site 2, a psychiatric hospital in Atlanta. (It could also be conducted after the study at site

1 had been completed.) All crucial elements of the study (i.e., the study protocol, patient characteristics and diagnosis, number of patients, treatment, therapist qualifications, supervision, assessments, outcome measures, and statistical analysis) are faithfully replicated, and site 2 obtains the same positive results as site 1. The researchers at each site could publish independent reports of their individual findings, but it is scientifically more powerful to describe each experiment *separately* in *one* article, *as well as* the results of *both* studies *combined* in the same article.

In our example, each site could individually publish a study reporting on results for sixty patients. But together, they could publish findings for 120 patients, which would be considered a more powerful investigation, in terms of both internal and external validity. The combined study would also have the greater strengths of a larger sample size, which permits greater statistical power, meaning a greater ability to make accurate estimates of treatment effects (Flora 2020; Tackett et al. 2019).

Of course, including more sites would result in an even more powerful study. Large-scale multisite randomized controlled trials are considered among the strongest methods to evaluate a given intervention. This design is used primarily to test clinical interventions like medications and psychotherapies, hence the use of the term "clinical trial" in the name of the design. However, methodologically similar designs can be used in more basic research. The following is an example of a multisite RCT conducted in three locations with social work involvement.

McDonell, M. G., et al. 2021. "Effect of Incentives for Alcohol Abstinence in Partnership with Three American Indian and Alaska Native Communities: A Randomized Clinical Trial." *JAMA Psychiatry* 78, no. 6: 599–606.

The authors of this study examined the problem of alcohol dependence among Indigenous peoples in North America. The intervention is a research-supported approach called contingency management, wherein clients earn "reinforcers" when they submit alcohol-free urine tests, which are irregularly scheduled. The study involved three U.S. sites, one in Alaska, one in the Pacific Northwest, and one in the northern Plains. Participants were American Indian and Alaska Native adults who met the DSM criteria for alcohol dependence. Across the sites, 1,003 people were screened, and 158 met the study's eligibility criteria. Of these, 75 were randomized to receive active treatment, a treatment called Helping Our Native Ongoing Recovery (HONOR). HONOR participants submitted urine samples twice a week for 12 weeks and received incentives if their samples were negative for alcohol. Incentives included modest monetary rewards, gift cards, camping and fishing equipment, clothing, shampoo, and arts and crafts supplies. The 83 clients assigned to the control group similarly submitted urine samples but received no incentives for being alcohol free. Both groups also received TAU, a culturally appropriate individual and group counseling program that offered sessions several times a week. Participants were randomized *within* each site. The study's major hypotheses were as follows:

1. Participants assigned to the HONOR program plus TAU will have fewer urine tests positive for alcohol compared with those assigned to TAU alone.
2. Participants assigned to the HONOR program plus TAU will score lower on the Native American version of the Addiction Severity Index (ASI) posttreatment compared with participants assigned to TAU alone.

The study design involved repeated measures: four urine tests over one month, followed by twelve tests over twelve weeks. It can be diagrammed as follows:

Group	
TAU only	HONOR plus TAU
$R\,O_1\,X\,O_2\,X\,O_3\,X\,O_4$	$X\,O_5\,X\,O_6\,X\,O_7\,X\,O_8\,X\,O_9\,X\,O_{10}\,X\,O_{11}\,X\,O_{12}$ $X\,O_{13}\,X\,O_{14}\,X\,O_{15}\,X\,O_{16}$
TAU only	TAU only
$R\,O_1\,X\,O_2\,X\,O_3\,X\,O_4\,X$	$O_5\,X\,O_6\,X\,O_7\,X\,O_8\,X\,O_9\,X\,O_{10}\,X\,O_{11}\,X\,O_{12}$ $X\,O_{13}\,X\,O_{14}\,X\,O_{15}\,X\,O_{16}$

"X" indicates the weekly treatment each group received. The top group, the experimental group, received TAU only for four weeks, then the HONOR program in addition to TAU for the next twelve weeks. The bottom group, the control group, received only TAU over the entire four months. "O" represents a urine test. Both groups received urine tests, but only the experimental group received incentives for providing negative tests. Thus, by Mill's principles of logical inference, any differences posttreatment must be attributable to the single factor that distinguished the two groups: the incentives provided to those in the HONOR program.

The results were positive, and hypothesis 1 was supported: "In this multisite clinical trial conducted in partnership with three geographically and culturally diverse American Indian and Alaska Native communities, adults who received incentives for alcohol abstinence had a 1.70-fold higher likelihood of submitting alcohol-abstinence urine samples relative to adults in the control group. These intervention effects were observed even though the median cost of incentives was only $50 per patient for twelve weeks of contingency management" (McDonell et al. 2021, 603). Hypothesis 2, however, was not supported. There were no differences between groups on the ASI posttreatment. In this study, the results were reported *in the aggregate* across the three sites, not by each site individually. Recruitment was less successful than anticipated, and it is likely that the results within each site would have shown no effect for the experimental intervention. But by combining the data from all participants across all sites, the analysis proved sufficiently powerful to reveal the genuine impact of treatment.

There are many other positive features of this multisite RCT. The intervention targeted an important social problem. Local tribal leaders were heavily involved in the design and other aspects of the project. The independent variable, the HONOR program, was culturally appropriate. The sites were culturally and geographically diverse. Multiple measures were obtained over time, which permitted a more precise analysis of the results than just one pretest and one posttest measure. The self-report measure, the ASI, was supplemented by the use of urine screens, an outcome variable less amenable to deception by participants. The incentives provided to the HONOR program participants did not cost very much. Using multiple assessments prior to implementing the experimental intervention helped screen out people likely not to be compliant with providing the required urine screens (if potential participants missed appointments for pretest urine screens, they were not eligible to complete the study).

On the downside, while genuine, the improvements experienced by the experimental group were modest. The study's use of strict screening criteria means that those who participated may not have been representative of all American Indian and Alaska Native peoples with alcohol dependence.

Towfighi, A., et al. 2021. "Effect of a Coordinated Community and Chronic Care Model Team Intervention vs Usual Care on Systolic Blood Pressure in Patients with Stroke or Transient Ischemic Attack: The SUCCEED Randomized Clinical Trial." *JAMA Network Open* 4, no. 2: e20366227.

High blood pressure is a medical risk factor for a number of conditions, including stroke and transient ischemic attack (TIA, a "mini-stroke"). People of color are disproportionately impacted by high blood pressure and its sequelae. There are many approaches to reducing high blood pressure. Some are medical (e.g., antihypertensive drugs, diuretics); some are structural (e.g., prohibiting the use of certain fats in cooking, prohibiting the sale of large-sized sugary drinks, banning the placement of vending machines dispensing candy in schools); and others are behavioral (e.g., weight loss, exercise, reducing salt intake, sleeping better, switching to a plant-based diet). The study by Towfighi et al. (2021) was a multisite RCT conducted in five hospitals serving people living on a low income the Los Angeles area. It evaluated an intervention package called the Chronic Care Model (CCM) created for patients with high blood pressure, and its effects were compared against TAU by randomly assigning qualified patients *within* each hospital to receive either CCM or TAU. The research question was, "What are the effects of CCM compared to TAU?" There were a number of primary hypotheses, such as the following:

1. Patients who received CCM will have lower blood pressure posttreatment compared to patients who received TAU.
2. Patients who received CCM will have lower cholesterol levels posttreatment compared to patients who received TAU.

There were a number of other secondary outcome measures as well, such as body mass index, diet, and physical activity level. However, the primary dependent measure was blood pressure.

TAU consisted of free blood pressure monitoring, self-management tools, and linguistically appropriate information handouts. CCM included three or more home visits from an advanced practice clinician, three or more home visits from a community health worker, free blood pressure monitors, telephone consultations, free workshops on chronic disease self-management, and some other services. Effective inclusion and exclusion criteria were used to recruit a total of 487 individuals who were randomized to receive CCM (n = 241) or TAU (n = 246). Of these, 58 percent spoke Spanish as their first language, 70 percent were white, 18 percent were Black, and 6 percent were Asian. The participants' mean age was fifty-seven years, and 65 percent were male.

At pretest, both groups were similar in terms of demographic and medical variables, except for salt intake (however, this was statistically controlled for in the analysis of the results). Measures were taken again about twelve months after enrollment. While a large number of predictor variables were assessed and subgroup analyses conducted, the overall results were modest: "At [the twelve-month] follow-up, there were no differences in the mean systolic BP [blood pressure] improvement nor in the proportion achieving systolic BP control across arms, though systolic BP improved within each arm. . . . The intervention participants had a larger improvement in self-reported reduction of salt intake than usual care. . . . Intervention and usual care groups did not differ on changes in the other secondary outcomes" (Towfighi et al. 2021, 8).

Regrettably, most hypotheses predicting superior outcomes for CCM versus TAU were not supported. Despite its largely negative results, this study has a number of strengths. It targeted high-risk individuals with high blood pressure. The involvement of concerned community members was incorporated into the design and conduct of the study. The study used appropriate measures of treatment fidelity and included supervision. The disappointing results are partly the result of a lack of complete uptake of the program by the CCM participants, who did not take advantage of all possible in-home visits. Obviously, evaluating a treatment in which participants do not fully engage reduces the possibility of detecting meaningful impacts.

While preparing this book, I came across a large number of recently published multisite (and in many cases multicountry) RCTs authored by the social worker Samta P. Pandya, a faculty member with the Tata Institute of Social Sciences in Mumbai, India. Her studies are listed in the appendix and reflect a remarkably strong oeuvre of sophisticated research that deserves greater recognition within the North American and European social work communities.

Cluster Randomized Control-Group Designs

In most of the randomized experiments conducted by social workers and others engaged in outcome studies, random assignment is conducted on *individuals*. The usual practice is to recruit individuals who meet a planned study's inclusion and exclusion criteria and then use a random assignment mechanism to assign each qualified person to one arm of the study. In a cluster randomized trial, *groups* (e.g., schools, hospitals, cities) are randomly assigned to different experimental conditions, and the treatment each group is assigned to is provided in that group's setting.

A key reason for doing this is to *control for treatment contamination*. If one wishes to compare two sex education programs for adolescents (say a comprehensive sex education curriculum versus an abstinence-based program), providing both programs at the same location could result in information-sharing between the groups, meaning that at least some participants are receiving elements of the other group's treatment. However, if the programs are randomly assigned to *schools* across a given county, treatment contamination is much less likely.

Another reason to undertake a cluster randomized experiment is to investigate interventions that *cannot plausibly be delivered to individuals*. An example is evaluating the effects of adding fluoride treatment to a village water system. Given that each village has a single water system, it is impossible to provide only some of the residents fluoridated water and others unfluoridated water. But it is feasible to provide fluoridated water in one village and not in a similar village. The dependent variables, the outcome measures, would be things like dental health over the ensuing years, number of cavities, and number of tooth extractions. Another example is for a government with limited funding to randomly select villages to have new health clinics built and then evaluate health-related variables over the next several years.

There are some complications involved in cluster RCTs related to statistical power, and something called the intraclass correlation of data, but discussion of these can be reserved for another time. In a multisite RCT, participants *within each site* are randomized to one of the treatment conditions, and the results are combined to produce a more powerful analysis. In a cluster RCT, entire sites are randomized to a treatment condition such that all participants at a site receive the same treatment. The results are then compared *across sites*.

The following is an example of a cluster RCT authored by social workers that was published in the eminent *New England Journal of Medicine*.

Bass, J. K., et al. 2013. "Controlled Trial of Psychotherapy for Congolese Survivors of Sexual Violence." *New England Journal of Medicine* 368, no. 23: 2182–91.

Sexual violence against women is a worldwide problem and is especially prevalent in low-income, high-conflict countries. Exposure to sexual violence often leads to the development of PTSD. Although a number of psychosocial treatments have been developed to alleviate PTSD in victims of rape and other forms of sexual violence, these have primarily been evaluated in higher-income nations. However, Bass et al. (2013) evaluated a culturally adapted psychotherapy called cognitive processing therapy (CPT) in the Democratic Republic of the Congo, a high-conflict country with a sample of women, most of whom were very poor and illiterate. The authors compared the results of CPT against those obtained from individual counseling (IC), which included psychosocial support and legal, economic, and medical referrals. Participants were recruited from fifteen rural villages, and the participants in each village were randomized to receive either CPT or IC. That is, all participants in the same village received the same treatment, either CPT or IC. In all, seven villages including 157 women received CPT and eight villages including 248 women received IC. Villages randomly assigned to receive CPT were limited to recruiting only twenty-four participants per village, as CPT was delivered in a small group setting. The villages providing IC had no limit on numbers of participants, and treatment was provided in one-to-one sessions.

The outcome measures included previously published, reliable, and valid measures of depression, anxiety, PTSD, and functional impairment, with assessments obtained pretreatment, one month posttreatment, and six months posttreatment. Both interventions were provided by local women with at least four years of postsecondary education and experience providing supportive counseling to women exposed to sexual violence. Those providing CPT received five to six days of intensive training in the treatment protocol and were supervised to ensure treatment fidelity. The design of this cluster RCT can be diagrammed as follows:

Group				Assessment time	
		Pretreatment		1 month	6 months
$CPT_{7\ villages}$	R	O_1	X_{CPT}	O_2	O_3
$IC_{8\ villages}$	R	O_1	X_{IC}	O_2	O_3

This study's hypotheses can be framed as follows:

1. Women who received CPT will experience greater reductions in depression compared with women who received IC.
2. Women who received CPT will experience greater reductions in anxiety compared with women who received IC.
3. Women who received CPT will experience greater reductions in PTSD symptoms compared with women who received IC.
4. Women who received CPT will experience greater reductions in functional impairments compared with women who received IC.

Note that each hypothesis addresses *only one* outcome measure and is *directional*, predicting a change in one direction. You can see how such a parsimonious hypothesis is easier to test, falsify, or corroborate than more ambiguously worded ones, such as "Women who received CPT will change more on measures of anxiety and depression than women who received IC." This hypothesis includes two outcome measures and does not predict the direction of change, whether toward improvement or deterioration. It is certainly *possible* to make complicated predictive hypotheses, but these should be clearly stated in advance of data collection and be based on prior research findings or a credible theory. For example, if data were collected on the recency of exposure to sexual violence, one might hypothesize that "women exposed to sexual violence within three months of beginning treatment will experience less of an improvement in PTSD symptoms compared with women exposed to sexual violence more than three months before beginning treatment" (if one had a legitimate reason to make such a prediction).

The authors reported that each hypothesis was supported. Six months after the end of treatment, the women who had received CPT experienced greater improvements on each of the outcome measures compared with the women who had received IC, and these results were statistically significant. The authors state, "In our study, cognitive processing therapy, as compared to individual support alone, was effective in reducing PTSD symptoms and combined depression and anxiety symptoms and improving functioning in female survivors of sexual violence in eastern Democratic Republic of Congo. The benefits were large and were maintained six months after treatment ended. Participants who received therapy were significantly less likely to meet the criteria for probable depression or anxiety or probable PTSD. Our results are consistent with the results of trials conducted in high-income countries" (Bass et al. 2013, 2187–88).

This was good news. The CPT program, shown to have strong research support in some developed nations, proved to be amenable to cultural adaptation, effective when delivered by nonprofessionals, and capable of generating positive effects above and beyond those of nonspecific IC. It is worth noting that the women who received IC alone also improved on all measures at the six-month follow-up, but the CPT group experienced much greater benefits. It is also important to note that it is possible that some form of naturally occurring trauma resolution or remission was occurring among the women in all the villages.

This fine study, coauthored by a social worker, possesses several admirable features. The design was strong, and the sample sizes were adequate. The independent variable of interest, CPT, was delivered following a protocol, and supervision was used to ensure treatment fidelity. The statistical analysis was sophisticated, and the study focused on a group that is all too often ignored in intervention research. The study's findings demonstrated not only good internal validity but also external validity, as they built on previous evidence of the effectiveness of CPT by showing that CPT was also effective in another population in another country. A limitation is that attrition was moderately high: 35 percent dropped out of the CPT group, and 48 percent dropped out from the IC group. This rate of attrition may have confounded the results.

Suomi, A., et al. 2020. "Cluster Randomized Controlled Trial (RCT) to Support Parental Contact for Children in Out-of-Home Care." *Child Abuse & Neglect* 109: 104708.

In the American child welfare system, children are sometimes removed from the home for their safety, and while the parents try to resolve their difficulties, they may be offered supervised contact visits to remain in touch with their children. Sadly, some parents with children in out-of-home care make less than optimal efforts in attending contact visits, and child welfare workers often go to great lengths to support and encourage visits. The study by Suomi et al. (2020) was a cluster RCT intended to promote contact visits. The study was conducted with families in three jurisdictions in Australia. The experimental intervention, a program called kContact, involved the provision of additional support to parents before and after their supervised visits using a strengths-based approach to "[increase] their parenting skills and [improve] their ability to relate to their children at contact visits" (Suomi et al. 2020, 4). The program involved clarifying expectations before each visit, identifying the parents' challenges and concerns, and meetings subsequent to each visit to reflect on what went well, validate the parents' feelings, and provide support for the next visit. The comparison condition was TAU: checking in with parents prior to each visit, dealing with practical issues, and ensuring compliance with any conditions bearing on each visit. On average, the children were about eight years old, and about 20 percent were Indigenous Australians. They had been in long-term placements, for about four years on average, and most lived in long-term foster care. Most of the caseworkers (n = 182) were in their midthirties, about half had a bachelor's degree, and 77 percent were female, with four to five years' experience in the field.

The host agencies were fifteen out-of-home care agencies, randomized to provide either kContact or TAU to all their families, with eight clusters (i.e., agencies) assigned to deliver kContact only (for one hundred children) and seven assigned to deliver TAU only (for eighty-three children). Following a pretest, treatment began, and data were collected for nine months. The authors outlined four hypotheses: "It was hypothesized that the kContact intervention could, within the nine-month follow-up period in comparison to a control group: (1) decrease children's externalizing and internalizing behaviours (primary outcome); (2) improve relationships between children and their parents; (3) improve the ability of carers and caseworkers to support birth family contact; [and] (4) reduce the proportion of contact visits canceled by parents" (Suomi et al. 2020, 2).

The study design can be diagrammed as follows:

Group		Assessment time		
		Pretest		Posttest
kContact	R	O_1	$X_{kContact}$	O_2
(8 agencies, 100 children)				
TAU	R	O_1	X_{TAU}	O_2
(7 agencies, 83 children)				

At nine months, there was no significant difference in the number of contact visits made between families assigned to kContact and families assigned to TAU. However, significantly fewer contact visits were canceled among the kContact group (about 5 percent) compared with the TAU group (about 15 percent). There were no differences between the parents assigned to kContact and parents assigned to TAU in their scores on the Strengths and Difficulties Questionnaire, which assesses children's behavior (the main outcome measure), or on the Child-Parent Relationship Scale. Further, no between-groups differences were reported for parents on measures of depression or anxiety. Caseworkers' ability to support family contact and parent satisfaction with contact visits were positively improved through kContact. As summarized by the authors, "the kContact intervention significantly reduced the proportion of contact visits canceled by parents . . . significantly improved caseworker receptivity to family contact, and significantly improved parents' satisfaction with contact. . . . These findings demonstrate the value of the kContact intervention in providing support to parents to attend contact visits" (Suomi et al. 2020, 12).

The strengths of this study include that the authors published a research protocol before the study was conducted and explaining in the subsequently published report why there were some deviations from what was planned when the study was actually carried out. The statistical analysis was robust, and the structured intervention's fidelity was monitored via the use of checklists. This was a true field experiment, conducted in real agencies with real clients and caseworkers, subject to all the vagaries and hurly-burly of real-world practice settings.

Kane, J. M. 2016. "Comprehensive Versus Usual Community Care for First-Episode Psychosis: 2-Year Outcomes from the NIMH RAISE Early Treatment Program." *American Journal of Psychiatry* 173, no. 4: 362–72.

The first episode of psychosis is a crucial point in a person's experience of schizophrenia. When a first episode of psychosis is treated rapidly and effectively, normal functioning is more likely to be restored, and future episodes are likely to be less severe. Inadequate treatment can exacerbate symptom severity. This project reports the results of a multisite evaluation conducted in thirty-four mental health clinics across twenty-one states. The experimental intervention was a program called NAVIGATE that embraces four interventions: personalized medication management, family psychoeducation (an intervention pioneered by the social work clinical researcher Gerard Hogarty), resilience-focused individual psychotherapy, and supported employment and education. NAVIGATE is a manualized intervention, and more than one hundred mental health care providers were trained in its use. The control condition was TAU as provided by the selected clinics. Seventeen clinics were randomly assigned to provide NAVIGATE only and seventeen to provide TAU only. A total of 404 individuals were enrolled in the study, with 223 randomly assigned to receive NAVIGATE and 181 to receive TAU. The participants were twenty-three years of age on average, and about 90 percent met the DSM-IV criteria for schizophrenia. Most lived with their families. Treatment outcomes were reported for two years of treatment. Many dependent (outcome) variables were assessed, including access to services, quality of life, positive and negative symptoms, depression, and structured global clinical impressions. Each could be incorporated into a single hypothesis predicting that the patients receiving NAVIGATE over two years would improve more than patients receiving TAU. Measures of the major outcome variables were taken at six-month intervals after the pretest. However, here we will look at the two-year outcomes only.

The study design can be diagrammed as follows:

Group			Assessment time				
		Pretest	6 months	1 year	18 months	2 years
NAVIGATE	R	O_1	$X_{NAVIGATE}$ O_2	O_3	O_4	O_5
(17 clinics, 223 participants)						
TAU	R	O_1	X_{TAU} O_2	O_3	O_4	O_5
(17 clinics, 181 participants)						

At the two-year assessment, participants in the NAVIGATE program had received more key services, remained in treatment longer, and were more likely to have received outpatient mental health care than TAU participants. The participants who received NAVIGATE reported a quality of life that was statistically significantly and clinically meaningfully better than that reported by those who received TAU, and more NAVIGATE participants attended school or were employed. The NAVIGATE group also reported fewer positive and negative symptoms of schizophrenia and less depression; these results were statistically significant. This was a strong study, described by the authors as follows:

> [This study] is the first multisite, randomized controlled trial of coordinated specialty care conducted in the United States, and the first anywhere to simultaneously include all of the following elements: randomized concurrent control; masked assessment of primary and secondary outcomes; and manual-driven intervention with ongoing training and fidelity metrics. Most importantly, NAVIGATE improved outcomes for patients over twenty-four months, with effects seen in length of time in treatment, quality of life, participation in work and school, and symptoms. These are outcomes of importance to service users, family members and clinicians. Our results are likely to generalize to many U.S. community care settings that wish to implement specialty care teams for young persons with first episode psychosis.
>
> (Kane 2016, 367–68)

Hilliard, R. E. 2007. "The Effects of Orff-Based Music Therapy and Social Work Groups on Childhood Grief Symptoms and Behaviors." *Journal of Music Therapy* 44, no. 2: 123–38.

Cluster RCTs are among the most sophisticated forms of intervention research. They are not commonly found among the examples of social work research found in the appendix, but they are not exceedingly rare. The study by the social worker Russell Hilliard (2007) is one example. Hilliard worked with bereaved school-aged children attending three public elementary schools. He randomly assigned the children at one school to receive eight weekly social work group counseling sessions, another school's children to receive eight weekly music therapy sessions, and the third school's children to receive no treatment (at the end of eight weeks, they received music therapy). The outcome measures included a bereavement questionnaire and a behavior rating scale, each completed by the children's parents or guardians. The hypotheses pertained to seeing whether children who received music therapy had better outcomes than those who received group counseling and whether children who received music therapy and group counseling had better outcomes than children who received no treatment.

The study design can be diagrammed as follows:

Group		Assessment time		
		Pretest		**8 weeks**
Music therapy (School 1, 8 children)	R	O_1	$X_{\text{music therapy}}$	O_2
Social work group counseling (School 2, 9 children)	R	O_1	$X_{\text{group counseling}}$	O_2
No treatment (School 3, 9 children)	R	O_1	O_2	$X_{\text{music therapy}}$

The results were varied and will not be delved into here, but I mention this study because it is an example of a practicing social worker, not an academic, using a small-scale cluster RCT to evaluate the outcomes of his own practice. Hilliard is both an LCSW and a board-certified music therapist and also has a PhD in music education. His publication of this study exemplifies the ideal of the practitioner-scientist that many espouse but few embody. He also published an earlier pilot outcome study on music therapy for grieving children (Hilliard 2001) and has authored a number of scholarly papers on social work, music therapy, bereavement, and palliative care. By building on the idea of experimental evaluation, Hilliard has contributed to the knowledge base of our profession.

Many examples of cluster RCTs have been authored by social workers, including those by Robertson et al. (2013), Wechsberg et al. (2016), and El-Bassel et al. (2021).

Summary

This chapter has presented examples of experimental studies authored by social workers that made use of the pretest–posttest RCT and its variants. Each can control for various threats to internal validity and help us make causal inferences about the effectiveness of treatments. The internal validity of each type of RCT is a function of many elements, not just the various Os and Xs composing the skeletons of each design. A study with weak dependent variables cannot have internal validity, no matter how strong the other elements of the study may be. A study with poor treatment fidelity and a finding of no difference may indicate that the treatment did not work *or* that the treatment was not conscientiously implemented and thus was a poor test of the intervention.

Lacking strong evidence of treatment fidelity leaves the study authors (and hapless readers later on) with no way to assert whether the treatment evaluated really works. A strong design with a small sample size may not detect treatment effects using conventional methods of statistical analysis, meaning an effective treatment may be dismissed as valueless. Sample size matters.

Authors must understand which threats to internal validity various study designs can control for. A pretest–posttest, no-treatment RCT can control for passage of time, regression to the mean, and concurrent history, but it is not effective at ruling out placebo effects, testing effects, or interactions between assessments and treatment. The complex Solomon four-group design can control for regression to the mean, concurrent history, testing effects, and interactions between assessments and treatment but does not control for placebo influences. Thus, it is not legitimate to judge any particular study as having low or high internal validity. Such a judgment requires a comprehensive appraisal of *all* salient features of the study, not just its essential structure or the bare bones of its design.

As we shall see in the next chapter, there are ways that researchers designing an experiment can maximize the likelihood that their study will be of high quality and methods through which readers of published RCTs can independently appraise their legitimacy. It is not appropriate to assume that just because a study was published in a peer-reviewed journal that it is of high quality. There are many peer-reviewed journals with very low standards (Xia 2022).

CHAPTER 7

REFINEMENTS IN EXPERIMENTAL DESIGNS

Where do correct ideas come from? Do they drop from the skies? No. They come from social practice, and from it alone; they come from three kinds of social practice, the struggle for production, the class struggle and scientific experiment.

—Mao Tse-Tung

This chapter will present refinements to consider in planning, conducting, and publishing a randomized experiment in social work. This material can also be helpful to those who simply read experimental studies and wish for a structured way to evaluate their credibility. The previous chapters considered some reasons experiments are important to the field of social work, the philosophy of the science undergirding much social work research, the types of causal questions experiments may be able to answer, diagrams outlining the essential features of experimental designs, and examples of published social work–authored articles illustrating the use of each type of design. Now we will look at refinements to experiments that build on the features already discussed.

Use the Journal Article Reporting Standards

Most social work journals require their submissions to be formatted according to the guidelines found in the seventh edition of the *Publication Manual of the American Psychological Association* (APA 2020b). Any social work researcher planning to conduct and publish a randomized experimental study is advised to have a copy of the current APA manual and to become familiar with it. Secondary sources of information on how to format in APA style are not generally recommended. Apart from the APA manual, the APA provides a number of credible resources on its website (https://apastyle.apa.org) to help people learn to use APA style accurately, including a free academic writing tutorial and webinars on topics like style, grammar, and references. One can also register for a free emailed newsletter that provides updates and helpful information on APA writing style.

An important section in the APA manual (APA 2020b, 71–108) describes the Journal Article Reporting Standards (JARS), which are a set of guidelines detailing the essential information that must be included in manuscripts being submitted for publication. Many websites and blogs provide information about using JARS, and a glossary of the terms used in JARS (see https://apastyle.apa .org/jars/glossary).

JARS is divided into several sections. The first provides guidance on elements common to most research reports, such as how to write an abstract, frame the research problem, and articulate the goals of a study. Another section addresses reporting standards specific to quantitative research, the most common type of research done with experimental designs. A comprehensive table describes how to craft a title for a study, prepare author notes, what information to include in the introduction (i.e., a statement of the problem, research questions, hypotheses, aims, and objectives), and what to include in the methods section (i.e., participant characteristics, sample methods, sample size and power analysis, a description of the data collection, the assessments used and their psychometric properties, and the research design). The results section must include a participant flow chart if applicable (more on this to come) and information about participant recruitment, the descriptive statistics of the sample, and the results of hypothesis testing. The outcomes should include not only p values but also suitable measures of effect sizes, their confidence intervals if appropriate, any problems encountered (e.g., missing data), and how problems were addressed. The results section should also state whether the hypotheses were supported or disconfirmed. The discussion should summarize the results and discuss links with prior empirical work, relevant theories, and issues such as external validity and study limitations. Finally, implications or applications for future research, practice, or policy should be included as appropriate.

The JARS website provides helpful tables that summarize the essential elements of reporting experimental studies, including the following:

> Reporting Standards for Studies with an Experimental Manipulation: General Principles (https://apastyle.apa.org/jars/quant-table-2.pdf)
> Module A: Reporting Standards for Studies Using Random Assignment (https://apastyle.apa.org/jars/quant-table-2a.pdf)
> Module C: Reporting Standards for Studies Involving Clinical Trials (https://apastyle.apa.org/jars/quant-table-2c.pdf)

To give you a sense of the level of detail contained in these guidelines, two sections of JARS on reporting clinical trials are listed next.

Experimental Interventions

JARS–Quant table 2 provides the reporting standards for studies involving clinical trials. It requires the following to be included in the description of experimental interventions in an article's methods section (APA 2020a):

- Report whether the study protocol was publicly available (e.g., published) prior to enrolling participants; if so, where and when.
- Describe how intervention in this study differed from the "standard" approach in order to tailor it to a new population (e.g., differing age, ethnicity, comorbidity).
- Describe any materials (e.g., clinical handouts, data recorders) provided to participants and how information about them can be obtained (e.g., URL).
- Describe any changes to the protocol during the course of the study, including all changes to the intervention, outcomes, and methods of analysis.
- Describe the Data and Safety Monitoring Board.
- Describe any stopping rules.

Treatment Fidelity

JARS–Quant table 2 also provides the description of treatment fidelity that must be included in an article's methods section (APA 2020a):

- Describe method and results regarding treatment deliverers' (e.g., therapists) adherence to the planned intervention protocol (e.g., therapy manual).
- Describe method and results of treatment deliverers' (e.g., therapists) competence in implementing the planned intervention protocol (e.g., therapy manual).

- Describe (if relevant) method and results regarding whether participants (i.e., treatment recipients) understood and/or followed treatment recommendations (e.g., did they comprehend what the treatment was intended to do, complete homework assignments if given, and/or perform practice activities assigned outside of the treatment setting?).
- Describe any additional methods used to enhance treatment fidelity.

JARS–Quant table 4 provides the reporting standards for longitudinal studies (studies involving the assessment of participants over lengthy follow-up periods) (see https://apastyle.apa.org/jars/quant-table-4.pdf). JARS–Quant table 6 provides the reporting standards for replication studies (studies that attempt to replicate the findings of a previously published investigation) (see https://apastyle.apa.org/jars/quant-table-6.pdf). JARS–Mixed table 1 provides the reporting standards for mixed-methods studies (studies that involve both quantitative and qualitative methods) (see https://apastyle.apa.org/jars/mixed-table-1.pdf).

An example of the fruitful integration of mixed methods in a social work–authored RCT might involve a quantitative assessment of the effectiveness of an intervention and a qualitative assessment of participants' experiences of the intervention via in-depth interviews posttreatment. There is a great potential for synergism in the combination of quantitative and qualitative methods (Thyer 2012). A number of examples of such mixed-methods studies authored by social workers can be found in the appendix.

Forewarned Is Forearmed

The JARS guidelines are intended to be used *prospectively*, as a guide from the beginning of designing and conducting a study. It would make little sense for a novice social work researcher to design a study, conduct it, and consult JARS only before sitting down to write up their investigation. Some elements of an experiment, if omitted or conducted in a sloppy manner, can be impossible to fix after the fact. By keeping JARS in mind from the onset of conceptualizing an experiment, one can guard against making irremediable mistakes.

Use of JARS by submitting authors is now a recommended practice among a number of U.S.-based social work journals, such as *Research on Social Work Practice*, the *Child and Adolescent Social Work Journal*, the *Journal of the Society for Social Work and Research*, and the *Journal of Evidence-Based Social Work*, as well as those based in other countries (e.g., *Canadian Social Work Review*). Even if not required by a given journal, an author can be assured that their report is more likely to be favorably received by reviewers if it adheres to the JARS guidelines.

Including training in APA style and the use of JARS should be a recommended practice in social work doctoral programs, both PhD and DSW. Most of the journals doctoral students are likely to submit their research to will have adopted the APA manual as their style guide, and JARS is baked into the APA style of preparing manuscripts. JARS also guides readers of published experimental studies, including social workers, in the qualitative evaluation of the rigor of reporting. Checklists can also be used to facilitate the evaluation studies, and we will look at these next.

Use the EQUATOR Network

Professionals who perform important and complex tasks often use some type of checklist to guide them in performing their activities. Surgeons and nurses use them for surgery to ensure that no element of the procedure is missed before, during, or after surgery. (For an example of a surgical checklist, see https://www.ahrq.gov/hai/tools/ambulatory-surgery/sections/implementation /implementation-guide/app-d.html.)

Similarly, aircraft pilots use preflight checklists before taking off to ensure nothing has been overlooked, things like ensuring the plane has enough gas, the tires have enough air, and windows and doors are closed and locked. These appear to be simple tasks, but a number of aircraft accidents have occurred owing to simple things being overlooked. (For an example of an aircraft preflight checklist, see https://calaero.edu/airplane-preflight-checklist.)

Like members of other disciplines, social workers have at various times proposed checklists for use in undertaking or evaluating research. As with surgical and preflight checklists, these are intended to make sure no key element of a study gets overlooked, and, in the case of reviewing an article, that all important elements of the study are accurately described and can be used to screen competent research from incompetent research. Examples of checklists and guidelines that can be used to guide research design and evaluation can be found in Tripodi, Fellin, and Meyer (1969); Thyer (1989, 1991, 2002, 2014a, 2014b, 2017); Shera (2001); Holden et al. (2008); Holosko (2006a, 2006b); Rubin (2000); and Drisko (2012); among other sources.

However, these early checklists have been superseded by a much more universal approach. In 2006, a research group based in the United Kingdom founded the EQUATOR Network, with "EQUATOR" being an acronym for "Enhancing the Quality and Transparency of Health Research." Drawing upon the methodological, theoretical, practice, and research expertise of health, social, and behavioral scientists from around the world, the goals of the network are as follows (Simera and Altman 2009, 132):

1. Develop and maintain a comprehensive internet-based resource centre providing up-to-date information, tools, and other materials related to health research reporting.

2. Assist in the development, dissemination, and implementation of robust reporting guidelines.
3. Actively promote the use of reporting guidelines and good research reporting practices through an education and training programme.
4. Conduct regular assessments of how journals implement reporting guidelines.
5. Conduct regular audits of reporting quality across the health research literature.

The EQUATOR Network's key products are reporting guidelines (see https://www.equator-network.org). The network accurately claims that their website is "your one-stop-shop for writing and publishing high-impact health research." The network describes a reporting guideline as follows (UK EQUATOR Centre n.d.):

A reporting guideline is a simple, structured tool for health researchers to use while writing manuscripts. A reporting guideline provides a minimum list of information needed to ensure a manuscript can be, for example:

- Understood by a reader,
- Replicated by a researcher,
- Used by a doctor to make a clinical decision, and
- Included in a systematic review.

Reporting guidelines are more than just some thoughts about what needs to be in an academic paper. We define a reporting guideline as "a checklist, flow diagram, or structured text to guide authors in reporting a specific type of research, developed using explicit methodology."

Whether presented as structured text or a checklist, a reporting guideline:

- Presents a clear list of reporting items that should appear in a paper and
- Explains how the list was developed.

Use the CONSORT-SPI

The EQUATOR Network website provides a number of reporting guidelines for a wide array of research methodologies, including randomized trials, quasi-experimental studies, systematic reviews, case reports, qualitative research studies, quality improvement studies, and economic evaluations. Randomized trials are supported by the guideline called the *Consolidated Standards of Reporting Trials,* or CONSORT. Within the CONSORT guidelines, one can find information on the wide variety of RCTs that researchers use, information on study design as well as the unique characteristics of studying certain interventions. Individual guidelines are available for randomized crossover designs, N-of-one trials (yes, one can do a randomized experiment with a single participant, as will be discussed in chapter 9), and stepped-wedge cluster designs, among others. Guidelines tailored to the unique elements of evaluating specific interventions are available for studies of traditional Chinese medicine, acupuncture, the alternative medical treatment called cupping, and therapies involving artificial intelligence. Perhaps to the dismay of traditionalists, artificial intelligence is beginning to impact social work practice, and RCTs evaluating such interventions need to be adapted to the unique features of this new practice model (see Rice et al. 2018; Schoech et al. 1985).

For the purposes of this book, we will focus on the *Consolidated Standards of Reporting Trials of Social and Psychological Interventions* (CONSORT-SPI; see https://www.equator-network.org/reporting-guidelines/consort-spi). This valuable reporting guideline was developed and published by an interdisciplinary group of authors, including several professional social workers (Grant et al. 2018; Montgomery et al. 2018), based on the original CONSORT guidelines. In the words of the authors, "We define social and psychological interventions as actions intended to modify processes and systems that are social and psychological in nature (such as cognitions, emotions, behaviours, norms, relationships, and environments) and are hypothesized to influence outcomes of interest. Social and psychological interventions may be offered to individuals who request them or as a result of policy, may operate at different levels (e.g., individual, group, place), and are usually 'complex'" (Grant et al. 2018, 2). With this encompassing definition, it is clear that this checklist is ideally positioned to help social work intervention researchers.

As with JARS, the intent of the CONSORT-SPI is to provide researchers a comprehensive checklist of the elements of an RCT that should be included in a manuscript to be submitted for publication. This checklist is also useful for nonintervention studies, such as vignette-based investigations of clinical decision-making. The CONSORT-SPI is also a valuable tool when planning an RCT to ensure that important design features are not overlooked. Some issues cannot be retrospectively corrected, such as ensuring an appropriate sample size. If you budget for one hundred participants and later find via a post hoc power analysis that you needed two hundred to find a meaningful effect, there is little you can do once the study is over.

The CONSORT-SPI was developed with input from almost four hundred international researchers and from consensus meetings attended by thirty-one funders, journal editors, and scientists. Both quantitative (e.g., surveys) and qualitative (e.g., Delphi studies) methods of data collection and analysis were used before arriving at the current iteration. The EQUATOR Network is committed to learning from past experience, and no doubt future revisions of the CONSORT-SPI will appear.

Table 7.1 presents the CONSORT-SPI checklist. The left-hand column lists the items from the general CONSORT checklist, and the right-hand column

TABLE 7.1 The CONSORT-SPI 2018 checklist

Section	Item #	CONSORT 2010	CONSORT-SPI 2018
Title and abstract			
	1a	Identification as a randomised trial in the title[a]	
	1b	Structured summary of trial design, methods, results, and conclusions (for specific guidance see CONSORT for Abstracts)[a]	Refer to CONSORT extension for social and psychological intervention trial abstracts
Introduction			
Background and objectives	2a	Scientific background and explanation of rationale[a]	
	2b	Specific objectives or hypotheses[a]	If pre-specified, how the intervention was hypothesised to work
Methods			
Trial design	3a	Description of trial design (such as parallel, factorial), including allocation ratio[a]	If the unit of random assignment is not the individual, please refer to CONSORT for Cluster Randomised Trials
	3b	Important changes to methods after trial commencement (such as eligibility criteria), with reasons	
Participants	4a	Eligibility criteria for participants[a]	When applicable, eligibility criteria for settings and those delivering the interventions
	4b	Settings and locations where the data were collected	
Interventions	5	The interventions for each group with sufficient details to allow replication, including how and when they were actually administered[a]	

(continued)

TABLE 7.1 (*Continued*)

Section	Item #	CONSORT 2010	CONSORT-SPI 2018
	5a		Extent to which interventions were actually delivered by providers and taken up by participants as planned
	5b		Where other informational materials about delivering the intervention can be accessed
	5c		When applicable, how intervention providers were assigned to each group
Outcomes	6a	Completely defined pre-specified outcomes, including how and when they were assessed[a]	
	6b	Any changes to trial outcomes after the trial commenced, with reasons	
Sample size	7a	How sample size was determined[a]	
	7b	When applicable, explanation of any interim analyses and stopping guidelines	
Randomisation			
Sequence generation	8a	Method used to generate the random allocation sequence	
	8b	Type of randomisation; details of any restriction (such as blocking and block size)[a]	
Allocation concealment mechanism	9	Mechanism used to implement the random allocation sequence, describing any steps taken to conceal the sequence until interventions were assigned[a]	

Section	Item #	CONSORT 2010	CONSORT-SPI 2018
Implementation	10	Who generated the random allocation sequence, who enrolled participants, and who assigned participants to interventions[a]	
Awareness of assignment	11a	Who was aware of intervention assignment after allocation (for example, participants, providers, those assessing outcomes), and how any masking was done	
	11b	If relevant, description of the similarity of interventions	
Analytical methods	12a	Statistical methods used to compare group outcomes[a]	How missing data were handled, with details of any imputation method
	12b	Methods for additional analyses, such as subgroup analyses, adjusted analyses, and process evaluations	
Results			
Participant flow (a diagram is strongly recommended)	13a	For each group, the numbers randomly assigned, receiving the intended intervention, and analysed for the outcomes[a]	Where possible, the number approached, screened, and eligible prior to random assignment, with reasons for non-enrolment
	13b	For each group, losses and exclusions after randomisation, together with reasons[a]	
Recruitment	14a	Dates defining the periods of recruitment and follow-up	
	14b	Why the trial ended or was stopped	
Baseline data	15	A table showing baseline characteristics for each group[a]	Include socioeconomic variables where applicable

(continued)

TABLE 7.1 (*Continued*)

Section	Item #	CONSORT 2010	CONSORT-SPI 2018
Numbers analysed	16	For each group, number included in each analysis and whether the analysis was by original assigned groups[a]	
Outcomes and estimation	17a	For each outcome, results for each group, and the estimated effect size and its precision (such as 95 percent confidence interval)[a]	Indicate availability of trial data
	17b	For binary outcomes, the presentation of both absolute and relative effect sizes is recommended	
Ancillary analyses	18	Results of any other analyses performed, including subgroup analyses, adjusted analyses, and process evaluations, distinguishing pre-specified from exploratory	
Harms	19	All important harms or unintended effects in each group (for specific guidance see CONSORT for Harms)	
Discussion			
Limitations	20	Trial limitations, addressing sources of potential bias, imprecision, and, if relevant, multiplicity of analyses	
Generalisability	21	Generalisability (external validity, applicability) of the trial findings[a]	
Interpretation	22	Interpretation consistent with results, balancing benefits and harms, and considering other relevant evidence	

Section	Item #	CONSORT 2010	CONSORT-SPI 2018
Important information			
Registration	23	Registration number and name of trial registry	
Protocol	24	Where the full trial protocol can be accessed, if available	
Declaration of interests	25	Sources of funding and other support; role of funders	Declaration of any other potential interests
Stakeholder involvement[b]	26a		Any involvement of the intervention developer in the design, conduct, analysis, or reporting of the trial
	26b		Other stakeholder involvement in trial design, conduct, or analyses
	26c		Incentives offered as part of the trial

Source: Montgomery, P., S. Grant, E. Mayo-Wilson, G. Macdonald, S. Michie, S. Hopewell, and D. Moher, on behalf of the CONSORT-SPI Group. 2018. "Reporting Randomised Trials of Social and Psychological Interventions: The CONSORT-SPI 2018 Extension." *Trials* 19: 407.

© The authors. 2018 Open Access. This article is distributed under the terms of the Creative Commons Attribution 4.0 International License (http://creativecommons.org/licenses/by/4.0/), which permits unrestricted use, distribution, and reproduction in any medium, provided you give appropriate credit to the original author(s) and the source, provide a link to the Creative Commons license, and indicate if changes were made.

[a]An extension item for cluster trials exists for this CONSORT 2010 item.

[b]We strongly recommend that the CONSORT-SPI 2018 Explanation and Elaboration (E&E) document be reviewed when using the CONSORT-SPI 2018 checklist for important clarifications on each item.

lists the SPI-related modifications. The CONSORT-SPI contains fourteen items and sub-items added to or modified from CONSORT. For example, items were added to explain how stakeholders (e.g., intended service recipients, practitioners, administrators, caregivers) should be involved in the design and conduct of an RCT, how incentives should be used to induce participation and retention, the importance of declaring potential conflicts of interest (e.g., if a study reports on an intervention that one of the authors provides training in for a fee or if an author has published a book on the intervention and is receiving royalties on sales). Potential conflicts of interest need not be problematic, but they do need to be disclosed. The checklist also describes how qualified researchers may obtain trial data. This practice of sharing and transparency encourages replication and error detection. With regard to participant demographic characteristics, the CONSORT-SPI recommends including socioeconomic variables, an important aspect of social work research involving poor, underrepresented, or traditionally underserved clients.

In addition to describing clear eligibility criteria for the *recipients* of social work services, it is also suggested that criteria be used to determine the eligibility criteria of the *service providers*. For some clinical interventions, this usually involves stipulating that the providers be licensed mental health professionals. If specialized training is considered a requirement, then clinicians should be recruited who possess the requisite background. For example, a treatment study involving evaluating the effectiveness of psychoanalysis should use as therapists licensed mental health professionals who are graduates of a recognized postgraduate psychoanalytic training institute. If the intervention is described as applied behavior analysis, the service providers should be board-certified behavior analysts with credentials from the Behavior Analyst Certification Board. In addition to having the appropriate credentials, individuals offering a service for which specialized training is needed should have experience providing the service and ideally should be supervised when delivering experimental treatment. You can see the rationale for this. An evaluation of a treatment that does not employ properly trained and credentialled therapists is inherently an unfair assessment and may lead to the conclusion that the treatment does not work if the results show no improvement. However, such negative results could be because the treatment truly is ineffective or because the treatment was delivered ineptly. By employing only properly licensed, credentialled, and well-trained clinicians whose implementation of the treatment is subject to fidelity checks (e.g., through supervision), one increases the likelihood that the treatment was delivered appropriately and that the study's results can be trusted.

The CONSORT-SPI recommends including in the results section a diagram depicting participant flow throughout the study. Figure 7.1 provides an example of such a diagram. The participant flow diagram should state how many potential participants were approached for enrollment in the study, how many were screened, how many were excluded, and the reasons for exclusion. The diagram should also include how many participants were randomized to each arm of the study. The diagram in figure 7.1 depicts a simple RCT with two arms: the experimental treatment and a comparator, which could be TAU, delayed treatment (i.e., if the results show the experimental treatment is effective, it will be offered to participants in this arm of the study upon study completion), a placebo treatment, or no treatment. As has been discussed, offering no treatment in a study is not inherently unethical; such a judgment can be made only in the context of the entire study. If a planned study is unethical, social work involvement would be precluded by our professional codes of ethics.

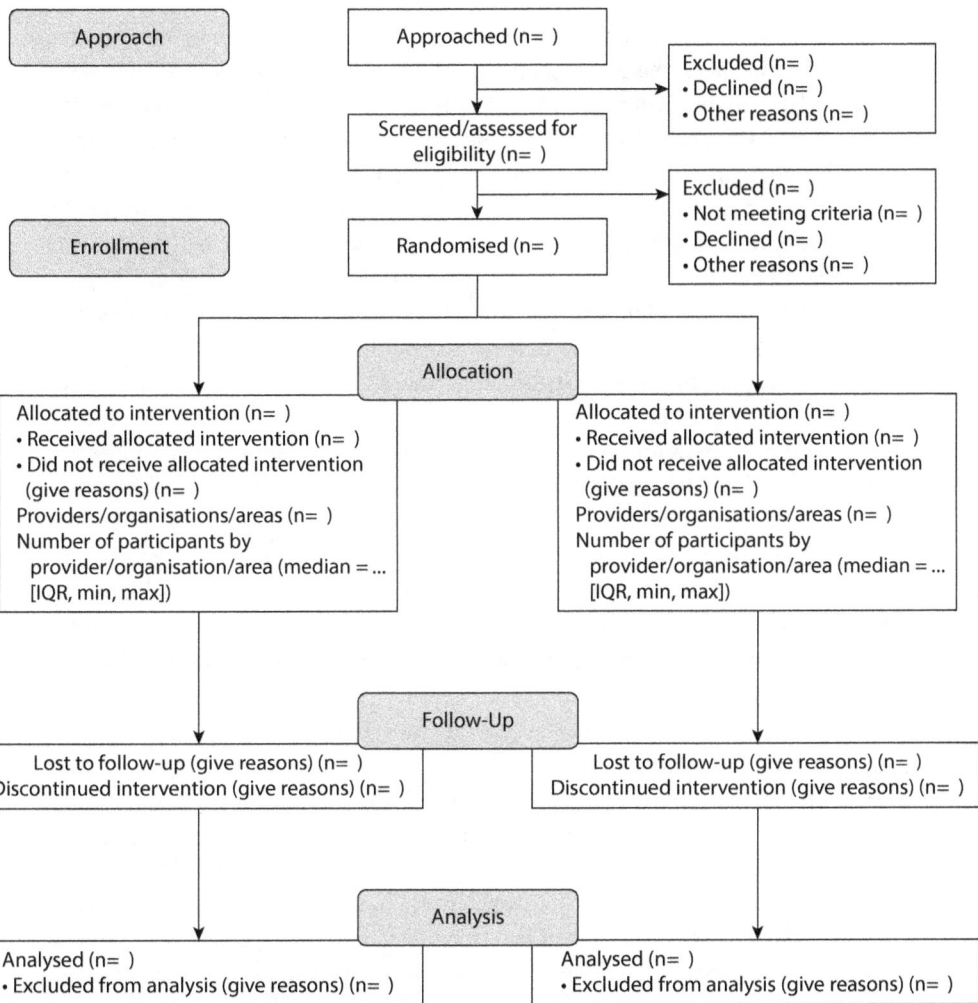

```
Approach          Approached (n= )
                                            ┌──────────────────────────────┐
                                            │ Excluded (n= )               │
                                            │ • Declined (n= )             │
                  Screened/assessed for     │ • Other reasons (n= )        │
                  eligibility (n= )         └──────────────────────────────┘

                                            ┌──────────────────────────────┐
                                            │ Excluded (n= )               │
                                            │ • Not meeting criteria (n= )  │
Enrollment        Randomised (n= )          │ • Declined (n= )             │
                                            │ • Other reasons (n= )        │
                                            └──────────────────────────────┘
```

Allocation

Allocated to intervention (n=)
• Received allocated intervention (n=)
• Did not receive allocated intervention
  (give reasons) (n=)
Providers/organisations/areas (n=)
Number of participants by
  provider/organisation/area (median = ...
  [IQR, min, max])

Allocated to intervention (n=)
• Received allocated intervention (n=)
• Did not receive allocated intervention
  (give reasons) (n=)
Providers/organisations/areas (n=)
Number of participants by
  provider/organisation/area (median = ...
  [IQR, min, max])

Follow-Up

Lost to follow-up (give reasons) (n=)
Discontinued intervention (give reasons) (n=)

Lost to follow-up (give reasons) (n=)
Discontinued intervention (give reasons) (n=)

Analysis

Analysed (n=)
• Excluded from analysis (give reasons) (n=)

Analysed (n=)
• Excluded from analysis (give reasons) (n=)

7.1 The CONSORT-SPI 2018 flow diagram.

Source: Montgomery, P., S. Grant, E. Mayo-Wilson, G. Macdonald, S. Michie, S. Hopewell, and D. Moher, on behalf of the CONSORT-SPI Group. 2018. "Reporting Randomised Trials of Social and Psychological Interventions: The CONSORT-SPI 2018 Extension." *Trials* 19: 407.

Participant flow diagrams become more complex as the experimental design becomes more complex. For example, an RCT may have three or more arms, and within each arm, the participants may be divided into subgroups (based on characteristics like gender, race, or symptom severity) if the researcher plans to test a priori hypotheses. For example, within the active treatment group, it might be postulated that participants with higher socioeconomic status will respond better to therapy than those with a lower socioeconomic status. In the participant flow diagram, such subdivisions would be shown by separate branches. Lengthy follow-up periods can further complicate the participant flow diagram. Data collection that occurs only twice is simpler to illustrate than data collection that occurs at three or more time points. Regardless of its complexity, a participant flow diagram greatly increases the reader's ability to understand an experimental design.

Once clients are randomly assigned, it is essential to report the sample sizes and attrition rates for each arm. Attrition is to be expected in intervention research, but its impact can be mitigated in various ways. Recruiting more participants than your a priori power analysis indicates will be needed is one way. Using sufficiently motivational incentives is another way. Concerted follow-up efforts help as well. For example, meeting participants for follow-up assessments in their local communities may result in greater retention at follow-up than asking them to travel to the researcher's lab or office.

The analysis section of the participant flow diagram states why any participants were excluded. For example, did someone "Christmas tree" their follow-up questionnaire by responding randomly, answering every question with the first multiple-choice option, or with a consistent yes or no, making it obvious that they did not respond seriously? Did someone appear for their follow-up evaluation obviously intoxicated? These are legitimate reasons to exclude a participant's data. But it is not legitimate to exclude data because you do not like the results. Positive results in the no-treatment group or negative results in the active-treatment group are not grounds for tossing data away, no matter how disappointing they may seem.

Outliers (those whose scores are extreme) may reflect meaningful data. This is an argument for separating the various research tasks of an intervention research study. Hire disinterested, competent people unfamiliar with the study protocol and hypotheses to analyze and report your results. A doctoral student who designs and conducts an experimental investigation is obviously going to be invested in seeing favorable outcomes from their project. Hopefully, they adhere to the notion that an experiment is a dispassionate effort to determine the effects of a treatment, whether good, bad, or neutral, and *not* to *prove* that a treatment works (or does not work). However, it is still best that an invested researcher assign the task of analyzing results to an objective outsider. The goal of an experiment is to arrive at truthful findings and to *test* hypotheses, *not* prove they are correct.

Negative results can be immensely valuable to scientific progress (see Greenwald 1975). As Slayter notes, "Sometimes the lack of statistical significance is a good thing, such as when a new treatment is compared to an existing, well-performing treatment" (2021, 1). Without negative results, we would not know when a treatment does not work (e.g., conversion therapy, facilitated communication, lobotomy) or that some theories are wrong (e.g., the "refrigerator mother" theory of the etiology of schizophrenia, the theory that homosexuality is a mental illness). Nevertheless, the temptation to fudge your results by discarding unwanted data from some of your participants can be great. To protect against this, greater transparency can be obtained by using a preregistered study protocol, providing a participant flow diagram, dividing crucial research tasks (especially data analysis) among people uninvested in the results, and sharing your data when asked or, even better, proactively using a data depository.

Similarities exist between the JARS guidelines for randomized experiments and the CONSORT-SPI because the JARS guidelines were modeled on CONSORT. (The APA manual also includes a CONSORT flow diagram [APA 2020b, 237]). While both are excellent resources, the APA manual contains much more than reporting guidelines, whereas the tools provided by the EQUATOR Network are more narrowly focused on how to write up the technical aspects of various research approaches. Social work researchers undertaking experimental investigations should be familiar with both resources. Social work journal editors should require a completed CONSORT-SPI checklist for all submissions of RCTs on social or psychological therapies, and a similar requirement should be made for revisions of initially reviewed papers. If the intervention is pharmacological, the original CONSORT should be used as a guide.

Both JARS and the CONSORT checklists make excellent instructional tools for use by doctoral students. Each item can be reviewed in class and be the focus of a discussion of the rationale for including this information. Then, using JARS and the CONSORT-SPI as a measuring stick, published experimental studies can be critically evaluated in class; by doing so, it will become obvious how omitted information detracts from the scientific integrity of published studies. In late 2021, the EQUATOR Network began listing JARS among its reporting standards, which was a laudable move.

As of 2015, more than six hundred journals and prominent editorial groups had officially endorsed CONSORT (Shamseer et al. 2016), and that number is likely much larger by now. However, few social work journals endorse JARS, and only two (to my knowledge)—*Research on Social Work Practice* and the *Journal of the Society for Social Work and Research*—require a CONSORT checklist to be submitted with manuscripts describing RCTs (Thyer 2020; see also https://www.journals.uchicago.edu/journals/jsswr/instruct). More of our journals need to follow these examples, as the use of CONSORT has resulted in more complete and improved reporting of RCTs in health journals (Turner et al. 2012). One simple example is the CONSORT guideline to identify a study as a randomized trial in the article's title. Doing so immeasurably facilitates searches for such studies. Surveys of the quality of the reporting of RCTs have shown that a considerable amount of misinformation and large gaps in essential information exist among published experimental clinical trials (Adetugbo and Williams 2000; Chan and Altman 2005). The CONSORT guidelines are intended to ameliorate this problem.

One key contributor to the reporting guidelines found in the EQUATOR Network is David Moher, PhD, who received a diploma in social work in Ireland, bachelor's and master's degrees in Canada, and a doctorate in the Netherlands. Moher is the first author on an early version of CONSORT, from which the CONSORT-SPI was modified (Moher 1998; Moher et al. 2010). Paul Montgomery, the first author of one of the CONSORT-SPI articles, is also a social worker, along with one of his coauthors, Geraldine Macdonald. Social work involvement has been considerable in the development and dissemination of these valuable reporting guidelines.

Use the TIDieR Checklist

The EQUATOR Network's reporting guidelines are not limited to describing standards for reporting research designs; they also describe how to report certain aspects within each design. For example, it is important that the independent variables of an RCT are reported in sufficient detail to permit study replication by others. One study examined articles evaluating nonpharmacological interventions published in six leading general medical journals, assessing how well they described the treatments. The study reviewed 133 trial reports evaluating 137 interventions. It was found that,

> More than half (61 percent) of the interventions assessed in this study were not described in sufficient detail in the published primary report to enable replication of the intervention in practice. This problem is partly remediable: a third of the incompletely described interventions could be completed by contacting study authors for further information. Obtaining this additional information took some effort: compilation of omissions, up to three emails, and subsequent piecing together of information from disparate sources. Clinicians wishing to use an intervention in practice are unlikely to invest this amount of time in obtaining the necessary details and materials.
>
> (Hoffman, Erueti, and Glasziou 2008, 3)

A similar analysis of social work RCTs appears not to have been undertaken, but it is hard to imagine that the results would be much better than those reported for medical journals. It will be impossible to develop a scientific foundation for social work interventions if we cannot describe what we do in a manner than facilitates replication and if we do not share such information readily. Social work is no place for "secret remedies" or proprietary "recipes." Unlike the recipes for Coca-Cola or Kentucky Fried Chicken, the crucial elements of social work services must be transparent and accessible to others. To facilitate this, members of the EQUATOR Network have developed TIDieR, the Template for Intervention Description and Replication Checklist (Hoffman et al. 2014). A comprehensive array of quantitative and qualitative research approaches went into the development of the TIDieR, which resulted in a simple twelve-item checklist. Authors are recommended to include the following when describing experimental interventions in their manuscripts:

1. Provide the name or a brief phrase that describes the intervention.
2. Provide any rationale, goal, or theoretical foundation of the treatment.
3. Describe what materials are used to deliver the treatment, such as a treatment protocol, manual or algorithm, and specialized training required.
4. Describe the procedures used in the intervention. Sometimes these take the form of describing the foci of sequential group work sessions or the topics of individual counseling.
5. Describe who provided the treatment, their discipline, specialized training if any, and expertise.
6. Describe how treatment was delivered; for example, face to face, once a week in a small group setting, via telemedicine, by text, or by smartphone app.
7. Describe where the treatment was provided, the name of the agency (if not blinded), and any relevant features (e.g., client's home, community setting).
8. Describe the intensity, frequency, and duration of treatment.
9. Describe any adaptations to the standardized intervention; for example, more or less frequently than recommended.
10. Describe whether the intervention was otherwise modified during the course of the study.
11. Describe any use of fidelity checks: how supervision was provided (i.e., live, via video- or audiotape recordings, or solely by therapist retrospective self-report). Describe any steps taken to maintain fidelity if deviations were detected.
12. Report the extent to which fidelity or adherence to the intervention protocol was maintained; for example, numbers of missed sessions, incomplete homework assignments, shortened meetings.

All this information should be included in the manuscript, and a TIDieR checklist (which can be found on the EQUATOR Network's website) should be provided with the manuscript submission letter indicating the page numbers where each piece of information can be found in the manuscript. TIDieR does not dictate *which* interventions should be used but does suggest *how* they should be reported. If a treatment manual was used, state where it can be obtained. See van Hasselt and Hersen (1996) for a compilation of older treatment manuals, such as the one coauthored by the social worker Stephen Wong describing the rehabilitation and treatment of people with schizophrenia (Wong and Liberman 1996). The social worker Craig LeCroy (1994, 2008) has compiled a list of treatment manuals for use with young people, many of which are available in books or online.

The social worker Gail Steketee has coauthored empirically supported treatment manuals for obsessive-compulsive disorder (Wilhelm and Steketee 2006; Steketee and White 1990) and compulsive hoarding (Tolin, Frost, and Steketee 2014), and the social worker Joseph Himle coauthored a research-based treatment manual on shy bladder syndrome, a form of social phobia (Soifer, Zgouridges, and Himle, 2020). The American Psychiatric Association offers a number of treatment manuals for sale or published in its journals, as does the American Psychological Association (e.g., see Sloan and Marx 2019 for a description of written exposure therapy to treat PTSD).

If a treatment is not delivered using a publicly available protocol, treatment manual, or algorithm, it is incumbent upon the author to provide enough information in their manuscript to allow readers to replicate the essential features of the treatment, and the TIDieR checklist is a great help with this task. As with the CONSORT-SPI (and the EQUATOR Network for that matter), awareness and use of the TIDieR checklist has largely escaped the notice of most social work researchers. One exception is the article describing TIDieR and its benefits for intervention research by Gadaire and Kilmer (2020). The need for a checklist like TIDieR was documented by Bhatt et al. (2018), who conducted a systematic review of how well behavioral interventions are reported in clinical trials. The authors examined a random sample of one hundred clinical trials published between 2012 and 2016 that used the CONSORT checklist for pilot clinical trials. A substantial number of these articles failed to adequately describe the behavioral interventions employed. (Note that "behavioral" is used here in its generic sense. It does not specifically refer to studies of behavior therapy, cognitive behavioral therapy, or behavior analysis.) With these studies lacking adequate procedural specificity, it is difficult for other researchers or practitioners to replicate them. Regular use of the TIDieR checklist can help fill this lacuna. Barbee et al. (2021) is a good example of a cluster RCT on a social work intervention that successfully undertook appropriate steps to ensure treatment fidelity in a complex study.

Prepare Your Study Protocol

In social work research, a *trial* is an evaluation of an intervention. If a trial involves randomly assigning participants to one or more conditions, it is called a randomized *controlled* trial or RCT. If the focus of the experimental intervention is on a disorder, condition, disease, or other aspect of human functioning and behavior, the study is labeled a randomized *clinical* trial (also called RCT). As we have seen, not all RCTs involve treating a clinical condition. For example, many involve evaluating educational interventions, factors influencing decision-making, or enhancing clients' economic well-being. But for the purposes of this book, I will refer to all social work experimental intervention studies as clinical trials, regardless of whether they are "clinically" focused, since the research methodology is essentially the same.

For clinical trials, researchers should develop a comprehensive *protocol*. A protocol is a detailed plan or template describing the planned study. It should include enough information to allow other qualified researchers to replicate the study. It should also include a brief literature review identifying the knowledge gap being addressed and describe the intervention in sufficient detail to allow others to implement it in the same way. A practice guideline, treatment manual, or algorithm may be of help in this regard, and an entire book has been authored on the development of practice guidelines for social work (Rosen and Proctor 2003). The development of practice guidelines has been the source of some controversy within social work (see Thyer 2003). The May 1999 issue of *Research on Social Work Practice* includes eight articles on the topic, using Howard and Jenson's (2003) article advocating the development of practice guidelines as the basis for discussion. As we shall see, the issue has been largely resolved in favor of reporting sufficient information to allow the replication of an intervention tested in outcome studies.

In addition to the independent variable (i.e., the intervention), the dependent variables (i.e., the outcome measures) also need to be fully reported. This is relatively easy to do if the researcher is using an "off-the-shelf" self-report measure to be completed by participants, caregivers, or observers, such as those found in Fischer, Corcoran, and Springer (2020) and in the appendixes to the DSM-5 (American Psychiatric Association 2013). One simply provides a primary citation in which the measure can be found and that describes how it is to be administered, scored, and interpreted (e.g., Westhuis and Thyer 1989). A newly developed measure or observational rating system needs to be described in sufficient detail to assure readers that the measure has adequate reliability and validity. The development of a new scale is typically such an ambitious undertaking (see Abell, Springer, and Kamata 2009) that it should be described in a manuscript that is published prior to and independently of any outcome study using the measure.

A study protocol should also include one or more directional hypotheses and descriptions of how these will be tested. The practice of preparing and publishing an experimental protocol listing each outcome measure, each hypothesis, and how each hypothesis will be statistically tested, *in advance* of data collection, keeps the researcher honest. If three outcome measures were used in a study, each linked to a hypothesis that predicted client improvements, and only one hypothesis was supported, an unscrupulous investigator might be tempted to include in their report only the outcome measure associated with that hypothesis and not mention the other two dependent variables. However, this is much less likely to occur when a study protocol is published in advance of the study.

The attitude of the social worker conducting research should involve a determination to find out what *actually is*, whether the outcome agrees with their preferred findings or not. Remaining neutral can be difficult for an investigator who is heavily invested, psychologically if not financially, in obtaining a particular finding. Doing so may enhance one's reputation as a clinical researcher or social work theorist, but falsely reporting a negative finding as positive, deleting data that do not align with your desired outcome, or making up data will be harmful in the long run. A falsely reported finding will be unable to be replicated by others or will otherwise emerge in the fullness of time. To courageously report legitimate findings at odds with your preferred outcome or theory is the proper course of action. In fact, observers may view such a researcher with greater respect as a person of scientific integrity. Keep in mind the admonition to "let truth be thy aim, not victory" (Himle 2015, 183). Wider use of clinical research protocols can help in this regard. Examples of experimental protocols of social work interventions published in advance of data collection include Fung et al. (2019) and Bobo et al. (2018).

Al-Jundi and Sakka (2016) describe the essential elements of a clinical trial protocol:

- The title of the study, including the words "randomized experiment"
- The study's administrative details, such as contact information for the authors and their affiliations
- A summary of the project
- A succinct literature review
- A description of any preliminary studies or pilot work
- A clear statement of the problem being investigated, including one or more research questions and their derivative specific and directional hypotheses
- The methods used in the study, including the study design, the participants and how they will be recruited, the outcome measures (i.e., the dependent variables) and intervention or interventions (i.e., the independent variable or variables), how the data will be collected, how each hypothesis will be statistically tested, and the project timeline

- The strengths and limitations of the proposed study
- Statements regarding the authors' potential conflicts of interests and how appropriate ethical approvals will be obtained

The authors state,

> The most difficult stage of conducting a research project is the preparation of a protocol that results in a short yet comprehensive document that clearly summarizes the project. Such a proposal is considered successful when it is clear, free of typographical errors, accurate and easy to read. It is important to understand the steps in developing a research protocol in order to perform an appropriate study and obtain reliable results. Extra time spent to write a good protocol will save failures at a later stage besides helping analysis. If the protocol is poorly prepared and not adhered to, it is unlikely that the project will yield the information that you hope for and in all probability the chances of selling your idea to the reviewers of a granting agency would be less.
>
> (Al-Jundi and Sakka 2016, 13)

This outline can be readily modified to prepare protocols for nonclinical social work investigations, such as those involving practitioner decision-making; other forms of vignette studies; diagnostic evaluations; racial, gender, or other forms of potential bias; educational interventions; or conditions without a formal diagnosis, such as child abuse and neglect and domestic violence. A clear experimental protocol serves the scientific value of *transparency*. Unlike the magic tricks of Houdini, scientific investigations are not wrapped in bags or hidden behind screens, preventing observers from seeing what is going on. Like a manuscript describing study results, an experimental protocol should also provide enough information that a study could be replicated following its description.

The National Institutes of Health (NIH) provide resources to assist investigators writing a clinical trial protocol. Protocol modifications for evaluating drug therapies, diagnostic tests, or medical devices are also available. The NIH definition of a clinical trial involves answering yes to the following four questions (NIH 2017):

1. Does the study involve human participants?
2. Are the participants prospectively assigned to an intervention?
3. Is the study designed to evaluate the effect of the intervention on the participants?
4. Is the effect being evaluated a health-related biomedical or behavioral outcome?

You can see that there is some ambiguity here with respect to whether social work research involves a health-related biomedical or behavioral outcome.

Investigations for which the answers to these four answers are clearly yes are classified by the U.S. federal government (and by universities, hospitals, and other entities that receive federal funding) as a clinical trial and as such are subject to extensive approval processes by an institutional review board or funding source. Would an experimental study evaluating an intervention intended to promote keeping medical appointments (many of which exist) be considered a clinical trial? It does not involve a biomedical outcome, but it clearly relates to an effort to modify human behavior. In fact, most (if not all) psychosocial interventions used by social workers are designed to change human behavior if we accept the expansive definition of "behavior" found in *The Social Work Dictionary* published by the National Association of Social Workers: "any action or response by an individual, including observable activity, measurable physiological changes, cognitive images, fantasies, and emotions" (Barker 2014, 38). Thus, even a study of office-based psychotherapy using outcome measures of affect such as depression or anxiety would, in the context of an experimental study, be considered by federal regulatory agencies as a clinical trial and would be subject to the more rigorous standards imposed on the design of clinical trials. For example, clinical trials being proposed to the NIH for funding must be submitted only in response to a funding opportunity announcement or a request for proposals that specifically states the NIH is soliciting clinical trials. To learn more, visit the NIH website.

The most conservative advice is that if there is the slightest chance a proposed experiment could be considered a clinical trial, it is important to check with your local institutional review board to get its determination in writing. If the study is determined to be a clinical trial, then the pertinent regulations governing such studies must be followed.

Preregister Your Study Protocol

A clinical trial should have a clearly developed *protocol* prepared to guide its conduct and reporting, but for maximum value a clinical trial study protocol should be registered in a clinical trials registry. Clinical trial registries have been established by various governmental and private organizations to serve as repositories of study protocols of intervention research. The authors of RCTs are encouraged (and in some circumstances mandated) to register their study protocols on a publicly accessible online platform that serves as an enduring record of research plans. Once a study is completed and its results published, others can compare the published report about what was done in the study against what was *said* was going to be done a few years earlier. Discrepancies, omissions, additions, and other deviations from the previously published protocol will be readily apparent. Ideally a published study will align in all crucial aspects with its published protocol. If fewer outcome measures were reported than were planned to be used or a less conservative method of statistical analysis was used than was planned, questions may arise. Where are the data for the missing outcome measures? Why was a less rigorous method of hypothesis testing used? In the worst-case scenario, a careful reader challenges the results or even the authors' research integrity in a follow-up article or letter to the editor. This is not good for a researcher's reputation.

It is also the case that researchers whose results are not what was expected or hoped for can simply choose not to publish their findings. This is called the file-drawer problem (because the final report ends up languishing in a file drawer), and it biases the published literature such that the majority of published studies report positive results for interventions. The textbook example of this is found in the pharmaceutical industry's evaluations of various antidepressants. The published reports seemed positive, and certain medications were said to work well for people with mild, moderate, and severe depression. These results of course enhance the apparent utility of the medication in question and reinforce the pharmaceutical company's return on their considerable investment in clinical trials. Independent investigators found that the companies had conducted many more studies than were published and that the results of the unpublished experiments could not readily be found. In the case of research funded by the federal government, it was possible to use the Freedom of Information Act to request copies of the unpublished but completed studies. When these unpublished reports were obtained and the data were combined with the information reported in the published studies, it was found that certain antidepressants were *not* effective among people with mild or moderate depression compared with placebo and that these medications were only of value beyond placebo influences for severe depression. Given that most people who are depressed have mild or moderate depression, this more complete picture of the data diminished the clinical and financial value of the medications. The selective reporting of results—to the financial benefit of drug manufacturers—is a widespread problem and is well reviewed by Fisher and Greenberg (1989) and Whitaker (2019). It has also been addressed in the social work literature (e.g., Littrell and Lacasse 2012) and has been found to occur with other classes of medication, such as antipsychotics and anxiolytics. Also, the funders of expensive pharmaceutical trials were displeased that the projects they had supported sometimes never led to the promised publications in high-quality peer-reviewed journals. Since many of these funders are institutes of the federal government, federal contracts for the conduct of clinical trials have begun to require that companies seeking funding agree to preregister their study protocols with acceptable clinical trial registries and publish their findings regardless of outcome.

The NIH now requires that study protocols be registered with a clinical trial registry ahead of data collection for all clinical studies it funds, as does the

European Commission for studies conducted in countries of the European Union, which uses the EU Clinical Trials Register. More journals also now require authors to have registered study protocols or to clearly state whether or not a protocol has been registered. In the United States, the most widely used clinical trial registry is ClinicalTrials.gov. This website has a number of uses. The first is for researchers to publish their clinical trial protocols, as required by some publishers and journals, before collecting data. Once submitted, a protocol can be modified if needed. Although based in the United States, at the time of this writing, a majority of the registered studies were based outside the United States. While many involved drug or other biological therapies, more than one hundred thousand involved behavioral interventions.

ClinicalTrials.gov also allows students and researchers to search the registry. In February 2022, using "social work" as a search term, I found more than 690 registered studies. Each is listed by its title, the condition being investigated (e.g., depression, traumatic brain injury), the intervention or interventions being evaluated (e.g., case management, psychotherapy), and the study location (often a hospital or university). Each entry indicates the status of the project (active or completed) and whether results have been posted. Further study details are also provided. Via ClinicalTrials.gov, one can track down published studies using a particular protocol and in many instances access the results of completed investigations. A researcher planning a clinical trial would be wise to review the registry to see what work in their area is already underway or to find information about completed studies that have not yet been published and are thus not yet registered with databases like PsycINFO. It would be foolish to submit a protocol that describes a study similar to one already in progress or completed—unless it is intended to serve as a replication investigation.

A number of countries have their own clinical trial registries, including the following:

Australia: https://www.australianclinicaltrials.gov.au/clinical-trial-registries
Canada: https://health-products.canada.ca/ctdb-bdec/index-eng.jsp
China: https://www.chictr.org.cn/index.aspx
European Union: https://www.clinicaltrialsregister.eu/
Hong Kong: http://www.hkuctr.com/
India: https://www.india.gov.in/clinical-trials-registry-india
Iran: https://www.irct.ir/
South Africa: https://sanctr.samrc.ac.za/

ClinicalTrials.gov is also a register of the results of clinical trials, making them publicly available prior to publication. By posting complete data, certain forms of publication bias can be mitigated, such as cherry-picking only the most favorable results. And some funders require that data be deposited in a clinical trial registry.

A number of publications discuss the merits of registering clinical trials (e.g., Zarin and Kesselman 2007), and one social work journal is now recommending this practice for all submissions that take the form of a randomized outcome study (Thyer 2020). This follows in the footsteps of the International Committee of Medical Journal Editors (ICMJE):

> Briefly, the ICMJE requires, and recommends that all medical journal editors require, registration of clinical trials in a public trials' registry at or before the time of first patient enrollment as a condition of consideration for publication. Editors requesting inclusion of their journal on the ICMJE website list of publications that follow ICMJE guidance should recognize that the listing implies enforcement by the journal of ICMJE's trial registration policy. . . . The ICMJE defines a clinical trial as any research project that prospectively assigns people or a group of people to an intervention, with or without concurrent comparison or control groups, to study the relationship between a health-related intervention and a health outcome. Health-related interventions are those used to modify a biomedical or health-related outcome; examples include drugs, surgical procedures, devices, behavioural treatments, educational programs, dietary interventions, quality improvement interventions, and process-of-care changes. Health outcomes are any biomedical or health-related measures obtained in patients or participants, including pharmacokinetic measures and adverse events.
>
> (ICMJE 2022)

One should not be troubled by the use of examples of publication and research practices from our allied discipline of medicine. The ICMJE definition of a clinical trial clearly subsumes the majority of randomized experimental social work intervention studies, and these standards simply reflect good scientific practice, not the oft-maligned medicalization of the social work profession.

Prepare a study protocol, register it with a suitable clinical trial registry, refer to relevant published protocols when describing your study outcomes, and submit your outcome data as an amendment to the original protocol when your study is published. Harrison and Mayo-Wilson (2014) provide an excellent overview of the merits of using a clinical registry to prevent reporting bias in social work research.

Consider Using a Data Repository

For many years the APA manual (APA 2020b) has recommended that authors of published research papers retain their original data. Doing so allows the authors to conduct further analysis and respond to requests to view the data, perhaps from researchers interested in conducting new analyses with the data or checking the data for errors. When I was a new assistant professor at Florida State University, one of our social work doctoral students, William R. Nugent, made such a request of me, involving my doctoral dissertation data, as reported in Thyer and Curtis (1984). I was happy to provide the data to him, which he used to test a new form of statistical analysis for his own PhD dissertation and subsequent publication (Nugent 1987). Nugent was fortunate that I had retained my data on computer disks and that I was willing to share them with him.

Nowadays, journals and some funders require that data not only be retained by authors but also shared in a publicly available data repository where other scholars can access them independent of the whims of the original authors. Importantly, data shared in this way must be deidentified; that is, all information that could identify participants must be removed. The requirement to make one's data publicly available helps in situations in which the authors of important research die or their data are otherwise lost. The NIH, a major funder of social and behavioral science research in the United States, maintains a number of domain-specific data repositories for studies of specific clinical problems or domains, such as demographic studies, addictions, and disability. For example, clinical researchers of sleep disorders use the National Sleep Research Resource to access data from completed studies and to archive their own data.

Since there appears to be no data repository established for social work clinical trials, researchers may use a generalist repository such as the Open Science Framework, a free open-source platform that also functions as a clinical trial registry. A large number of social work studies can be found on this platform. I have reservations about using the term "best practice" when referring to psychosocial treatments, but I think that using the Open Science Framework as a data repository for social work experiments would constitute an evolving best practice for the profession to adopt.

The NIH is moving in the direction of requiring its funded researchers to make use of an accepted data repository. Thus, as with JARS and the EQUATOR Network, the Open Science Framework is an aspect of experimental research that clinical social work researchers should familiarize themselves with. Social work journal editors should also encourage, if not require, authors to register their data with a suitable data repository before considering their manuscripts for publication.

Summary

There is more to conducting a social work experiment than simply choosing an appropriate research design to test one's hypotheses. In particular, randomized experiments evaluating an intervention intended to improve people's health, behavior, or other aspects of human functioning are subject to a number of standards. To produce high-quality research studies, researchers should do the following:

- Become familiar with and adhere to the publication guidelines of the *Publication Manual of the American Psychological Association*, seventh edition (APA 2020b). Preparing a manuscript for publication involves much more than spelling correctly and formatting citations properly.
- Become familiar with and adhere to the JARS guidelines found in the APA manual (2020b). Make use of the reporting standards for quantitative research and the additional guidelines for experimental investigations. If an experiment involves a mixed-methods approach, one should comply with reporting standards for both quantitative and qualitative research, paying particular attention to methods of data collection, recording, and transformation. Methodological reporting should provide sufficient information to convey to the reader that the extracted themes and conclusions are both credible and trustworthy, ideally with an audit trail so well described that others could successfully replicate the original methods of analysis.
- Become familiar with the checklists available via the EQUATOR Network, and make use of them in both the design and reporting of an experiment. If the study involves a social or psychological intervention, use the CONSORT-SPI checklist. If you are evaluating another form of health-related intervention, use the updated CONSORT. Also use the TIDieR checklist to ensure you describe all essential features of your independent variables (treatments). When submitting a manuscript to a professional journal, include with your letter of submission completed checklists (CONSORT and TIDieR) with page numbers identifying where in the manuscript particular information can be found.
- Prepare an accurate and detailed study protocol and preregister it with a suitable clinical trial registry. Consider also publishing the protocol in a professional journal that welcomes such submissions (e.g., *Trials*, the *Journal of Evidence-Based Social Work*). Preregistering study protocols is most important for clinical outcome studies, but all forms of experimental investigations can benefit from having their protocols preregistered.
- When your study is complete, register your data with a suitable data repository. This can often be done on the same platform as the clinical trial registry.

Many of the design refinements discussed in this chapter have been developed to promote the design and conduct of high-quality experiments but remain relatively unfamiliar to contemporary social work academics, researchers, and practitioners. However, social workers have been involved in this work from the beginning, including David Moher and Paul Montgomery who contributed to the interdisciplinary development of the CONSORT reporting guidelines. Groups such as the American Academy of Social Work and Social Welfare, the Council on Social Work Education, the National Association of Social Workers, the Society for Social Work and Research, and the European Social Work Research Association could contribute immeasurably to future social work involvement in the development of high-quality experimental research standards were they to undertake systematic and sustained outreach efforts to groups like the EQUATOR Network, the Cochrane Collaboration, and the Campbell Collaboration.

CHAPTER 8

RECRUITING PARTICIPANTS FROM DIVERSE AND UNDERREPRESENTED GROUPS

The proper method for inquiring after the properties of things is to deduce them from experiments.

—Isaac Newton

The primary purpose of experimental designs is to create a series of conditions that permit causal inferences: to determine the effects of a treatment. The treatment under investigation can be compared to no treatment, treatment as usual (TAU), a credible placebo treatment, or another accepted treatment to compare outcomes and, depending on the purposes of the study, demonstrate the *internal* validity of the conclusions. This can be done by effectively ruling out alternative explanations for any observed effects, such as spontaneous improvement, maturation, concurrent history, placebo factors, a desire to please the researcher, or social desirability.

If an experiment recruits a sufficiently large number of participants, *and* these people can be randomly selected from a larger population of interest, the *external* validity of the findings may also be assumed. However, doing so is rarely possible in experimental research. Often the number of participants that can be recruited is insufficient to generalize to the larger population from which they were drawn. For example, the RCT conducted by Young et al. (2020) recruited sixty-two participants with clinical depression to evaluate the effects of an intervention intended to reduce self-stigma among people with depression compared with TAU. The participants, all Chinese residents of Hong Kong, were randomly assigned to receive ten sessions of group therapy using cognitive behavioral methods to reduce self-stigma or ten sessions of TAU (thirty-one participants per group). As hypothesized in advance, the results showed that the experimental treatment produced greater reductions in self-stigma and depression than did TAU. This was a *good* study with strong internal validity and not atypical of RCTs completed in the last decade or so by social work researchers. But to whom can these truthful and valid results be generalized? Did every depressed person in Hong Kong who met the study's inclusion criteria have an equal chance of participating in the study? No. The sample was drawn from volunteers enrolled at community mental health wellness centers whose services barely penetrate the total population in Hong Kong who are clinically depressed. Can the results be generalized to all Chinese people (who compose almost 20 percent of the world's population)? No. Hong Kong is a unique segment of Chinese culture (about seven million people), quite different from the twenty-six million who live in Shanghai and those who live in the Uighur region, in Beijing, in Singapore, and elsewhere around the world. Can the results be credibly generalized to people in North America, Africa, Europe, or Australia? Unlikely.

The most common way that internally valid research findings can be generalized is through the laborious process of replication. This means testing and retesting the intervention in different contexts, countries, and groups of people. If the original study's positive results hold up when retested in this manner, external validity can gradually be demonstrated. This process may take years of work, unless the intervention is an extremely powerful one the effects of which are little influenced by the personal characteristics of the recipient. The first study testing the effect of the antibiotic streptomycin found that it was effective in treating tuberculosis (Medical Research Council 1948), although it was not a panacea. Of fifty-five patients receiving streptomycin, four died, whereas of fifty-two patients allocated to bed rest alone (TAU at the time), fifteen died. All patients were white. This was an RCT with good *internal* validity, but as single study with a circumscribed sample of convenience, its *external* validity with respect to its ability to cure tuberculosis among all people with the disease was unknown. It might work with other patients, or it might not. It might work with non-white patients, or it might not. But, in the eyes of God, or objective reality if you prefer, streptomycin *was* extremely effective across all groups of people around the world. Although this had not been empirically demonstrated through the first study, it was a fact from the day this drug was created. Because its effects were so powerful, its external validity was rapidly established via replication studies around the world. Almost everywhere it was tested, streptomycin reduced deaths. Statistically it could be said that the studies' effect sizes were very large indeed. In social work research, however, and in the social and behavioral sciences in general, interventions tend to have much more modest results (i.e., smaller average changes and wider standard deviations).

Treatments with a modest impact require many more participants to be recruited in order to detect a statistically significant difference. This is one reason that progress in social work intervention research moves more slowly. Another reason is that psychosocial interventions are usually complex, more difficult to administer and evaluate than a standardized dosage pill administered according to a planned schedule. The psychosocial problems social workers attempt to remedy usually have many complex, intersecting causes, whereas tuberculosis has a largely singular cause, infection by a certain type of bacteria, although exposure to certain environmental factors can make one more susceptible. It is unlikely that a single causal agent will be isolated to explain poverty, racism, bipolar disorder, or child abuse. Hence, a singular intervention is unlikely to prove effective. Complex interventions addressing complex disorders are exceedingly difficult to standardize and deliver with fidelity to clients who often have multiple problems, some of which are discrete and relatively isolated and others of which are interactive (e.g., substance abuse and intimate partner violence).

Intervention researchers face something of a dilemma. Their pursuit of finding an effect for an intervention encourages the use of as homogeneous a sample of participants as possible (e.g., only male participants or participants with only one DSM-5 diagnosis). Such a sample often reduces the variance or distribution of the data, resulting in improved p values and stronger effect sizes. If a hypothetical outcome measure has a posttest mean and standard deviation of 20 (2.00) for the treatment group and 15 (1.5) for the TAU group, fewer participants will be needed to obtain a significant p value and a strong effect size than if the values were 20 (7.00) and 15 (9.00). Homogeneous samples enhance internal validity but reduce external validity, the ability to generalize a study's findings. Historically, the focus on demonstrating internal validity led to the widespread phenomenon of many groups being underrepresented in clinical trials and other forms of intervention research. Decades ago, RCTs evaluating a behavioral treatment called exposure therapy and response prevention (ETRP) for people with obsessive-compulsive disorder (OCD) included very few people of color. And underrepresentation remains common today (Hill et al. 2015), leading the social work experimentalist Joseph Himle and his colleagues to conclude that "it is also likely that very few Blacks in the United States with OCD are receiving evidence-based treatment and thus considerable effort is needed to bring treatment to these groups" (Himle et al. 2008, 993).

One approach to deal with the issue of underrepresentation is to conduct large RCTs that recruit a sufficient number of participants from underrepresented groups to permit a legitimate subgroup analysis. An example is a two-arm RCT comparing a new treatment versus TAU that recruits a large and diverse sample of people who meet the study's inclusion criteria. If 1,000 people, 700 white, 150 Black, and 150 Latino, are recruited and randomly assigned to the two conditions, there will likely be enough participants to conduct legitimate subgroup analyses. The researchers could compare the results for *everyone* in each condition, and then repeat this analysis for white people only, Black people only, and Latino people only. In this way, they can evaluate whether there were similar improvements or changes *within* each group and whether there were any differences in outcomes *between* groups. The researchers could also look for differences between groups in terms of side effects and adverse effects. If each group improved or changed similarly, the study could potentially be said to have both internal and external validity with respect to the three larger populations each group represents. However, if a study like this recruited a convenience sample, external validity would be compromised.

Generalizability depends largely on the *random selection* of participants from a larger population of interest, not on the *number* of participants. This is a problem since most experiments use convenience samples, not random selections of people from larger populations. A sample of convenience, no matter how large, does not permit generalizing to a larger population. If I am trying to learn the political views of all registered voters in my city, and I recruit my participants only from among those attending a rally for a candidate of one party, it makes no difference if I sample one hundred, five hundred, or one thousand people—the results will not be generalizable to *all* registered voters. If a large psychiatric hospital provides care for one thousand patients with schizophrenia, and I am doing an outcome study using those patients, whether I randomly sample fifty, one hundred, or two hundred patients makes no difference in my ability to generalize to *all* people meeting the DSM-5 criteria for schizophrenia. I *can* generalize my findings to all one thousand patients in *that* hospital, but they are not a random selection of people with schizophrenia in the United States, much less the world.

An alternative approach to try to demonstrate the external validity of a study that used a homogeneous sample of participants is to replicate the study with a sample of participants from underrepresented groups. Friedman et al. (2003) did just that. As mentioned, several decades of clinical research had found that ETRP was a reasonably effective treatment for people with OCD, but most of this research was done with white participants. Friedman and his colleagues then conducted an RCT of ETRP recruiting exclusively Black and Hispanic people. They found similarly positive outcomes to those of the earlier studies, which enhanced the external validity of the conclusion that ETRP is an effective treatment for OCD. Further positive replications with other populations, such as Chinese people, have also supported the conclusion that ETRP is effective among diverse groups of people (see Tang and Yang 2012).

Positive replications among different groups of people are a common way to ascertain external validity, and it is often a more practical approach than trying to undertake a mammoth RCT and conducting subgroup analyses, particularly when types of participants are hard to reach or recruit. For example, the social workers Kara and Duyan (2022) conducted a delayed-treatment control group RCT in Turkey to evaluate the effects of an eight-session emotion-based group therapy on the emotional regulation and psychosocial functioning of people who identified as LGBT. They recruited twenty participants from Istanbul. This small number was to be expected, given that discrimination against this group of people is common in Turkey. The participants were randomly assigned to the two arms of the study (ten per group). Measures were taken pre- and posttreatment, and when the study was over, those originally assigned to the no-treatment control group were offered the experimental treatment. At the posttest assessment, it was found that the treated participants had improved and that those in the control group had not. The difference between groups was statistically significant, favoring treatment. This small-scale pilot study was the first of its type and was the basis of the first author's doctoral dissertation. As such, it was a worthwhile investigation. However, the sample size was low. Among the diverse sexual orientations reported by the participants, only three in each group identified as bisexual. Therefore, any potentially meaningful subgroup analysis in this study would have been statistically precluded because of the low number of people who represented each of the identities included in the LGBT community. You cannot legitimately use inferential statistics with just three people per group (e.g., to see whether those who identified as bisexual responded differently to the intervention). Hence, subgroup analysis should be avoided in RCTs involving such small numbers. The merits of this study lie not in the generalizability of its findings but in its value as a pilot project demonstrating the merits of the therapy it evaluated and its promotion of social work research involving people who identify as LGBT. Its positive results also justified replication studies with larger numbers of participants, and it provided valuable training for the social work doctoral student who designed and conducted the study. (But do you notice any potential for bias there?)

Replication studies could be conducted using at least three approaches. One is to repeat the original investigation using a larger number of participants but from the same community (i.e., people who identify as LGBT). If a sufficiently large sample could be recruited, subgroup analyses could be possible and useful. Another, perhaps more practical, way to replicate the study is to repeat it with a larger number of participants who report just one sexual orientation (e.g., lesbian, gay, bisexual, or transgender). Keep this distinction in mind as you read further—recruiting sufficiently large numbers of participants to permit subgroup analyses *or* to replicate the original study with a single subgroup. Both serve the same valid purpose: to ensure that intervention research is conducted with underrepresented groups and to enable such groups to benefit from the advances in interventions observed in research largely involving majority groups. A third approach to replication is to conduct the study in another location, for example elsewhere in Turkey or in another country.

The NIH Mandate

Recognizing than a number of groups have been historically underrepresented in RCTs and other forms of research (e.g., epidemiological surveys), the U.S. Public Health Service has mandated that clinical research programs funded by the National Institutes of Health (NIH) take proactive steps to address this problem:

> The NIH is mandated . . . to ensure the inclusion of women and minority groups in all NIH-funded clinical research in a manner that is appropriate to the scientific question under study. The primary goal of this law is to ensure that research findings can be generalizable to the entire population. Additionally, the statute requires clinical trials to be designed to provide information about differences by sex/gender, race and/or ethnicity. . . . All NIH-funded studies that meet the NIH definition for clinical research must address plans for the inclusion of women and minorities within the application or proposal. Using the PHS [Public Health Service] Human Subjects and Clinical Trial Information Form, applications and proposals should describe the composition of the proposed study population in terms of sex/gender and racial/ethnic groups, and provide a rationale for selection of such subjects. Any exclusions based on sex/gender or race/ethnicity must include a rationale and justification based on a scientific or ethical basis. Investigators should also plan for appropriate outreach programs and activities to recruit and retain the proposed study population consistent with the purposes of the research project. . . . Scientific Review Groups will assess each application/proposal as being "acceptable" or "unacceptable" with regard to the inclusion of minorities and both genders in the research project.
>
> (NIH 2022)

Note that outcomes for participant groups based on race, sex/gender, and/or ethnicity are to be reported separately. The intent here is not mere tokenism or to allow the principal investigator of an NIH-funded project to simply tick off a box on the research application but to ensure that clinical trials, particularly RCTs, recruit and retain sufficient numbers of historically underrepresented groups to permit legitimate subgroup analyses. Doing so requires large numbers of participants from such groups; thus, larger-scale studies tend to be favored by the NIH for funding over smaller ones. However, this preference can discourage junior researchers and those who engage in qualitative research from pursuing clinical outcome studies.

Some Reasons Recruiting Participants from Underrepresented Groups May Be Difficult

The historical record shows that underrepresented groups have not been treated well by clinical researchers. The researchers conducting the infamous Tuskegee Syphilis Study lied to poor Black men about the nature of their condition and did not provide adequate treatment once it became available. This study lasted four decades and was funded by the U.S. government, leaving a lasting legacy of mistrust of participating in medical research among Black people (Reverby 2001).

Partly overlapping with the Tuskegee Study timeline was a research study conducted by the U.S. government involving more than one thousand people in Guatemala, including Guatemalan Indians, women, children, child and adult prostitutes, people with leprosy, prisoners, and psychiatric patients, some of whom were deliberately infected with sexually transmitted diseases. The people involved did not provide informed consent. The consequences of this unethical study in terms of the willingness of Latino people and Native Americans to participate in medical research is difficult to underestimate. More recently, about four hundred members of the Havasupai Tribe, a small group of poor Native Americans who live near the Grand Canyon, agreed to participate in a genetic study of diabetes (a common condition among this group of people) by donating samples of their DNA. However, unbeknownst to the participants, their DNA was also used to conduct genetic studies on nondiabetic-related conditions such as schizophrenia, population inbreeding, and ethnic migration. This research was done without their consent and violated a number of tribal beliefs relating to the social stigma surrounding these issues. The negative consequences of this case were considerable: "The events surrounding . . . research on the Havasupai distilled existing distrust of medical researchers and discouraged tribe members from participating in further research, even that which might benefit the tribe. . . . Many tribes continue to refuse participation in genetic research" (Garrison 2013, 203).

Black people, Latino people, Indigenous peoples, the poor, the uneducated, and other groups, have all been victims of hideously unethical research practices. Thus, efforts by U.S. government agencies to ensure the adequate participation of underrepresented groups in clinical research have been seriously undermined by the unethical study practices approved and funded by some of these agencies (and mostly by white men).

Politics can sometimes give rise to suspicions that a new treatment might not work, potentially hindering participant recruitment in clinical trials. For example, on August 6, 2020, during an interview regarding the COVID-19 vaccine and its expedited development under Donald Trump, then former Vice President Joe Biden said, "If and when the vaccine comes, it's not likely to go through all the tests and the trials that are needed to be done" (Yahoo News 2020). Such concerns expressed by a respected politician may deter people not only from seeking treatment but also from participating in clinical trials of their efficacy.

Circumstances in Which Special Recruitment Efforts Are Not Necessary

Some studies are planned to involve relatively small numbers of people, say thirty or forty participants in each arm of a two-arm randomized experiment. For example, social work researchers might decide to dispense with recruiting participants from underrepresented groups in the initial stages of evaluating a new treatment. Once a pilot study or smaller-scale RCT shows that a treatment has promise, conducting a larger-scale study with a diverse sample of sufficient size to enable subgroup analyses is justified.

Sometimes an evaluation is undertaken of a *specific program's* outcomes, with no effort made to ensure findings have external validity. In such circumstances, the sample size is predetermined by a pool of existing participants, and no proactive recruitment is possible. The researchers must make do with the data made available by everyday agency operations. Such studies can help agencies determine whether the services *they* provide actually help *their* clients. The flow of clients at a given agency may give rise to naturally occurring wait-list control groups that permit an experimental investigation. Or an agency that provides two treatments, say individual counseling and group therapy, could decide to assess their comparative effectiveness. For example, after intake, prospective clients could be told of the two options and asked, with appropriate informed consent, if they would be willing to be randomly assigned to one treatment or the other. It would be explained that the agency believes both are useful treatments and they are trying to find out if one is better than the other. Those who refuse would be assigned to a treatment according to the agency's usual practice. Validated assessment measures could be completed pre- and posttreatment. By looking at differences in outcomes between groups posttreatment, legitimate (i.e., internally valid) conclusions could be drawn about the comparative effectiveness of the services offered by the agency. Similarly, an agency could compare the outcomes of psychosocial treatment versus medication or each treatment versus the combination of the two (therapy plus medication). Over time, each arm of the study could be populated as the agency takes on new clients. Even if only a few people each week are assigned to each condition, after sufficient time, say six months, the agency-based practitioner researchers would have completed data collection for a respectable number of participants, perhaps sufficient to yield an internally valid study or even a publication in a professional journal.

Some studies are focused on obtaining findings from only a *particular group*. For example, an intervention for sickle cell disease, a condition found almost exclusively among people of African descent, would be wasting resources to recruit white participants. A study of an educational intervention to help women to conduct more accurate breast self-examinations could rightly dispense with recruiting men. For a condition that is almost exclusively found among members of a relatively homogeneous group, it may be legitimate to discard conventional ideas about recruiting a diverse range of participants. But certain diversity considerations may still be relevant. For example, if prior research studies were conducted only with adolescent males, it may be useful to replicate the study with preteens or young men. If prior work was completed on highly educated people, it could be worth replicating the study with people who did not complete high school. There is always some way that clinical researchers can strive to produce findings that are more generalizable to a larger group and extend the external validity of prior conclusions.

In summary, there are at least three circumstances in which concerted efforts to recruit a highly diverse sample of participants are misplaced. One is when a planned study's sample will be so small that a subgroup analysis would not have sufficient statistical power to be worthwhile. Early small-scale trials of a newly developed treatment are one such circumstance. Statistically it may then be legitimate to deliberately recruit a homogeneous sample to enhance the likelihood of finding a treatment effect owing to the fact there is less "noise" or variance in the data. The second circumstance is when one is conducting a program evaluation of an agency's outcomes. Here the sample is predetermined by the people of who seek services at that agency. In this case, there is no recruitment per se and no concern with external validity. The point is to find out whether a particular agency's clients are benefiting from its services. The third circumstance is when a psychosocial or health problem occurs among a narrowly defined group of people. Women need not be recruited in a study of prostate cancer treatment, for example. But Black men have been terribly underrepresented in clinical trials on treatments for prostate cancer—from 1987 to 2016, white men composed 96 percent of participants in this type of research (see Jaklevic 2020). In this case, ignoring women and heavily recruiting Black men would be good practice with regard to addressing the disparity between Black and white participation in this type of study.

Circumstances in Which Special Recruitment Efforts Are Not Feasible

Some experimental studies are conducted in locations with very homogeneous populations and not enough members of other groups to make a study with a diverse sample feasible. A study being conducted in Chengdu, China, or New Delhi, India, for example, will be limited to recruiting Chinese or Indian participants. Similarly, a study undertaken in Montana whose population is about 1 percent Black might find it unfeasible to recruit large numbers of Black participants. In instances such as this, generalizability to other groups is demonstrated by replicating a study that used a very homogeneous sample in other settings where it is possible to recruit more diverse participants.

Replication studies specifically recruiting underrepresented groups are often a more practical approach to evaluating whether an intervention's effects are generalizable to groups of people not represented in earlier studies. Conducting a first investigation of a new treatment by attempting a mega-sized experiment can be fraught with peril, given the costs often associated with large-scale RCTs. Keep in mind that most newly proposed psychosocial interventions will be found not to be effective when evaluated, resulting in a squandering of the time and resources needed to conduct a large study. It is usually more practical to conduct smaller-scale experiments or even quasi-experimental outcome studies to see whether the results will be sufficiently promising to justify a larger trial. Even then, the field is replete with huge and expensive investigations of interventions that did not benefit participants more than credible placebo treatments.

Guidelines on Recruiting Participants from Underrepresented Groups

It is important that outcome studies be undertaken across diverse groups so that any conclusions regarding the effectiveness of an intervention can be shown to apply to many types of people. Establishing a therapy's external validity can be undertaken via two broad approaches. One is to undertake a number of studies evaluating the same treatment with different groups of people. Another is to conduct a large study that recruits a sufficient number of people representing diverse groups. Both approaches pose the challenge of how to recruit such people. Fortunately a large literature describes various methods that have been shown to be effective in recruiting participants representing diverse groups. Some of these guidelines address strategies related to specific groups. Examples include the following:

- Black people (Otado et al. 2015)
- Black children (Graves and Sheldon 2018)
- People from nondominant ethnic groups (Waheed et al. 2015)
- Older people from nondominant ethnic groups (Stahl and Vasquez 2004)
- Black women (Johnson et al. 2015)
- New mothers (Paquin et al. 2021)
- Black and Latino community residents (Sankaré et al. 2015)
- People from nondominant ethnic groups or with low socioeconomic status (Ejiogu et al. 2011)
- Older Mexican American people (Hazuda et al. 2000)

Generally, one can make use of various databases such as PsycINFO and government websites to locate participant recruitment information specific to the group or groups you need to recruit for your experiment. In addition, some more general guidelines provide useful recruitment strategies for intervention research. Examples include *Tips and Tricks for Successful Research Recruitment* (Kubicek and Robles 2016) and *Recruitment and Retention in Minority Populations* (Levkoff et al. 2000). The following are some strategies that clinical researchers have found useful in recruiting underrepresented groups:

- As soon as you begin planning a study, assemble a research advisory team including various stakeholders invested in the issue you are addressing. Include one or more people who represent the group you are hoping to recruit; for example, people who experienced homelessness or people with a history of substance abuse or mental illness. Such individuals have firsthand knowledge of the issue you are addressing and can provide invaluable help in deciding where and how to recruit participants, as well as other aspects of study design. The Latin phrase *Nihil de nobis, sine nobis* ("nothing about us without us") reflects this principle. This early European political slogan has been used by various disability rights groups around the world and has been widely adopted within the community of those conducting clinical trials in the areas of health and mental health. According to the Cochrane Collaboration standards, including individuals with lived experience is an important element to include in primary research studies and systematic reviews (Higgins et al. 2022). Including people with secondhand knowledge of the issue (e.g., victims of violence, parents of troubled teens, partners of people with alcoholism) is also a good practice.
- If your participants are from a group that is not your own, employ at least one person who is culturally and linguistically competent (if language is an issue) to work with them, ideally a person with demographic features similar to your research participants. It would be ill advised, for example, to undertake an RCT in Miami involving Haitians without having one or more Haitian

people on your advisory team. And in a study recruiting Spanish speakers, it would be important to ensure that at least one person on the research team who will be interacting with participants is fluent in the language.

- Be aware of the potential for substantial differences to exist *within* groups that may affect your recruitment efforts. For example, a person born and raised in Hong Kong may be fluent in Cantonese but unable to speak to a Beijing-born person who speaks only Mandarin. And there are many cultural differences, including aspects of language, between Cuban Americans and Puerto Rican Americans.

- Prepare outreach materials such as brochures and flyers with considerable input from the research advisory team. This team can also provide useful input regarding where recruitment materials should be placed or displayed. For example, posting recruitment flyers on college bulletin boards will likely be ineffective in reaching members of marginalized communities. Once drafted, have your outreach materials reviewed by members of the group from which you are hoping to recruit participants to ensure the content is appropriate. Materials to be provided in a language other than English should be drafted in that language, not translated from English.

- Place recruitment materials in sites frequented by potential research participants (e.g., hospitals, homeless shelters, mental health clinics, ethnic community festivals). The social work doctoral student Nicole Cesnales wished to undertake a community-based needs assessment among people who were HIV positive or had AIDS. She posted flyers on the bulletin boards of the local AIDS agency and provided them with the free bags of groceries given out weekly by the agency. When contacted, she offered to meet potential participants at a public venue of their choice; for example, a public library, coffee shop, or park (Cesnales et al. 2016). If wishing to recruit participants from the homeless community, visit homeless encampments, as many unhoused people prefer to avoid shelters.

- Provide modest incentives or gratuities to research participants following guidance from your local institutional review board. If too generous, the review board may suggest that the monetary value of the incentive could detract from potential participants' ability to freely choose whether to participate. If too small, your recruitment effort will not be effective.

- Offer to provide local agencies with free in-service training on the topic of your study, and at the end of training indicate that you are currently recruiting participants and would appreciate referrals.

- Advertisements about your study can be judiciously placed in ethnic or culturally specific newspapers, community flyers, church bulletins, and the like. Cultivating relationships with local members of the clergy can be fruitful. For example, one professor at my university encouraged several local churches in the Black community to host the health-and-wellness program she was evaluating based on her conversations with ministers. They were happy to provide classroom and gym space for the project free of charge.

- Consider covering the costs of transportation and/or childcare to make it easier for people to participate.
- In your recruitment efforts, avoid discussing controversial topics that are not germane to your project, such as political opinions or people's immigration status. Do weave into the conversation topics that might help establish rapport; for example, a shared experience like being a parent, a fellow veteran, or a fan of a local sports team.
- Speak to potential participants with respect, and avoid using overly familiar terms.
- Use plain language to explain the potential benefits and risks of participating, but make no promises. Even with the most effective therapies, not all people respond favorably.
- Pilot test all assessment methods and scales before using them to collect data. Ensure self-report measures are appropriate for all participants, and provide accommodations where needed (e.g., for participants not fluent in English, those who are illiterate, or those who need but do not have glasses because they cannot afford them).
- Offer to provide participants a summary of your project's findings when the study is completed, and provide the summary to those who want it. This is not a copy of your published article but a specially prepared document like an abstract that describes the study and its findings in plain language and is no more than two pages. Not all will want it, but at least make the offer. Do the same for stakeholders involved in any way with the project (e.g., local politicians, agency directors, service workers). For these individuals, also provide a copy of your publication. If you conducted an evaluation study at a particular agency and obtained positive results, the agency administrators will be pleased to receive such a report, as it may help them in their public relations and fundraising efforts. Consider also holding a wrap-up meeting with all agency staff involved with the study, describing what you found.
- Truthfully provide assurances of confidentiality, if not anonymity. Describe how the participants' data will be protected. This is especially important if participants are being recruited because of their involvement in something illegal or embarrassing. Examples include intervention research with sex workers, human traffickers, drug manufacturers or dealers, and undocumented immigrants. Undertaking clinical research intended to help such groups is a worthwhile undertaking. Treating them with respect, regardless of one's personal views or feelings, is consistent with the code of ethics of the National Association of Social Workers and a hallmark of being a true professional. If this is not possible, changing one's clinical research focus might be indicated.

Recruiting for Experimental Survey Studies

Experimental designs can also be used in the context of survey studies. A review of the experimental studies published by social workers in the appendix will reveal many such investigations. Recruitment in experimental surveys poses the challenges of obtaining enough respondents (to determine the internal validity) and adequate diversity among respondents (to determine external validity). As with outcome studies, surveys are usually made stronger by greater numbers of participants, as a larger sample size increases the statistical power of the analysis, enabling the researcher to obtain statistical significance with smaller differences between groups than with a smaller sample size.

It is a common practice for academic faculty to take advantage of the availability (and pliability) of students, using them as respondents for an experimental survey or correlational investigation. In experiments, various versions of a survey can be assigned randomly in class, one to each student. With this approach, it can be possible to obtain the necessary number of participants in a relatively brief period of time. While in some ways convenient and potentially yielding results with good internal validity, the external validity of student-based experimental surveys tends to be low. A survey conducted in one class (or several) may not yield results that can be legitimately extrapolated to other students in the same program, much less to students in other programs around the state or country. The ability to recruit a diverse sample is limited because of the circumscribed pool of potential participants available.

Given that social work is a practice profession, it makes more sense for social workers to undertake research studies on clients receiving social services or who are troubled by one or more psychosocial difficulties. Social work practitioners are sometimes the focus of an experimental vignette study, for example on the topic of clinical decision-making. Vignettes that differ by one or more factors are prepared and randomly distributed to and completed by selected respondents. With enough people completing the survey, differences in decision-making can reasonably be attributed to the factors manipulated in the survey. For example, consider a randomly assigned clinical vignette that purports to describe a person with a mental illness being considered for hospital admission, one version of which describes a Black person and the other a white person. If the recommendations for hospital admission (yes or no) do not differ by race, it can be said that race does not play a role in hospital admission decision-making. But if the recommendations do vary by race, then it appears that race does make a difference in admissions recommendations.

When conducting studies of clinical decision-making, it is best to use experienced clinicians (e.g., LCSWs) as respondents, as they possess greater familiarity with making clinical decisions in the real world than inexperienced students or others who do not routinely make such decisions. But then, we are faced with a conundrum: Use students and get a lot of responses quickly, or use experienced clinicians, who will be harder to reach and persuade to take the time to complete the survey.

A further issue to be considered is that reading a brief vignette and providing a yes-or-no recommendation for hospital admission is quite dissimilar from real-world decision-making. Decisions on hospital admissions in the real world involve clinical interviews and history-taking. One could improve the methodology by asking LCSWs not to read a vignette but to watch a video of a real clinical interview. Such a study would more closely reflect actual practice but at the cost of preparing the video and persuading LCSWs to watch it (it would take more time than reading a vignette). This methodological improvement would make recruitment harder. Vignette studies thus present the researcher with a series of challenges and choices: quick and easy with lots of respondents or long and time-consuming with fewer responses but greater connection to real-world practice.

A technical improvement that has facilitated the design and conduct of survey studies, both experimental and nonexperimental, is the availability of online platforms such as SurveyMonkey (https://www.surveymonkey.com) and Qualtrics (https://www.qualtrics.com). These platforms have made it much easier to reach a large number of people and a greater diversity of people. These platforms also allow the researcher to import the saved data into a suitable statistical program (e.g., R, SAS, SPSS) for analysis. This saves much time compared with manually transcribing data from a pencil-and-paper survey into the statistical program and reduces the risk of transcriber errors. Once the data are imported and clean, running the analysis to test your hypotheses is relatively easy. If you do not get enough participants in your initial round of data collection, you can simply extend the survey deadline or recruit participants from a different site. This is a great improvement over the survey methodologies of several decades ago.

One may also obtain data from the virtual equivalents of agency waiting rooms, hospitals, or social service agencies. By "virtual equivalent," I mean internet platforms such as Facebook pages dedicated to the group or groups you wish to recruit for your survey. Etiquette suggests contacting the Facebook page administrator, explaining your study, sharing your materials with them, and asking permission to post an invitation on the page to participate in the study. Your message can contain information about the study, its value, any incentives you will be providing, and the link to the survey. Virtually any constituency group, psychosocial problem, or shared interest is likely to have many dedicated Facebook pages. While preparing this chapter, I searched for the word "bipolar" on Facebook and found dozens of support groups for people with bipolar disorder and their families, one with more than sixty-three thousand members. Similar pages for people who have experienced domestic violence are also available. Recruiting participants for surveys was once a much more arduous process than it is now. Websites like Facebook have become one way researchers can recruit potential respondents.

Online surveys can be set up with initial questions that exclude respondents that are not of interest. For example, if you wished to survey Latino women over the age of thirty years who have been diagnosed with bipolar disorder, initial questions could ask about race, ethnicity, gender, and diagnosis. Those who do not meet these inclusion criteria will be excluded from further participation. Online surveys have greatly enhanced the ability of social workers conducting experimental surveys to selectively recruit people who are members of diverse or historically underrepresented groups. Surveys can remain open for however long is desired or reposted for different groups.

Keep in mind, however, that no matter how large your sample size is, how diverse your respondents are, or how many participants reflect historically underrepresented groups, the external validity of these studies, if conducted only once, will be low. As with live experiments, the generalizability of a one-off project is most legitimately obtained via probability sampling from a larger population of interest. And this is difficult. Even if you do have access to a population of interest, unless *everyone* in the group participates, your sample will not be completely random. It is not uncommon to have a low response rate, and the lower the rate, the more the randomness of your sample is compromised.

Summary

Obtaining a large sample of participants in experiments is a worthy goal. Historically and through to today, certain groups of people have been deliberately overlooked as research participants in important studies in health and psychosocial care. Sometimes this is because these groups have been seen as unimportant in society, because they represent a lower proportion of the population, or because they are not on the radar of social work and other experimentalist professionals, people whose features typically reflect those holding positions of power. Like attracts like, and it has been estimated that upward of 80 percent of research respondents in published studies come from WEIRD ("Western, Educated, Industrialized, Rich and Democratic") societies (Azar 2010). Most social work researchers are also WEIRD.

When people of color or those with a low socioeconomic status have gained the attention of researchers and been included in studies, it was often because of their marginalized status or relative lack of perceived value. Want to study the natural progression of syphilis? Let's use poor Black men living in rural Alabama. Want to find out if antibiotics are effective? Let's infect Guatemalans with venereal diseases and then provide antibiotic therapy. Want to study the genetics of schizophrenia? Use DNA samples from a small group of Native Americans who provided them for a study on diabetes.

Greater attention is now being paid to the importance of making legitimate conclusions about internal and external validity. The use of effect size calculations in addition to conventional p values helps attenuate the tendency to ascribe importance to benchmarks such as .05 or .01. In reality, statistically significant differences between treatments, while nontrivial, can sometimes be of little practical or clinical significance. The addition of effect size calculations promotes more accurate conclusions about the internal validity of a study.

Now that the importance of including sufficient numbers of participants from historically underrepresented groups has been recognized, this issue has become a matter of policy among federal research funders and other important stakeholders in the research community such as the Cochrane Collaboration. Although there are times when obtaining a diverse sample of participants is not feasible or not necessary, the default assumption today is that it *is* of vital importance and should be taken into account when designing experiments. Sometimes it seems that attention to diversity is more symbolic than practical. Although more than thirty years have elapsed since the NIH began mandating that sufficient numbers of underrepresented groups be included in its funded clinical trials, recent appraisals show little progress. According to a recent editorial in the *British Medical Journal* by Janice Hopkins Tanne (2022, 1),

> Underrepresentation of ethnic and racial groups in US research and clinical trials compounds the disparities in health outcomes in these groups and should be corrected urgently. . . . While progress has been made on some fronts, particularly with the participation of women in clinical trials and clinical research, participation has largely stalled on participation of racial and ethnic minority populations. . . . Not only is there a lack of participation by racial and ethnic minorities in clinical trials, but other patient groups including older people, pregnant and lactating people, LGBTQIA+ populations, and people with disabilities are underrepresented and even excluded.

Relatively new is the default position that people from the groups we wish to study—true stakeholders in other words—be involved from the beginning in the design and conduct of experimental outcome studies on social work policies and practice. External validity, which depends on the use of participants who are randomly selected from a larger population of interest, is often difficult to establish through the results of a single study. More common is the practice of replicating an investigation using participants from other groups. Similar findings across groups of people increase our confidence in the conclusion that a treatment or intervention has widespread applicability. Providing enhanced opportunities for social workers from underrepresented groups to obtain training in the design and conduct of experimental intervention studies is another underused approach to enhance the diversity of our doctoral students and the types of projects they undertake (Harrison and Thyer 1988; Schiele and Wilson 2001).

CHAPTER 9

ALTERNATIVES TO GROUP-RANDOMIZED DESIGNS FOR MAKING CAUSAL INFERENCES

Experimentation is the greatest science.

—Arabic proverb

I s experimental research as described thus far in this book considered the *only* legitimate way that science is capable of making causal inferences? Absolutely not. Across the scientific disciplines there are many different ways to infer causation. Chemistry, physics, geology, meteorology, and other disciplines all have their unique approaches to try to determine cause-and-effect relationships, and the randomized experiment is not usually among their methods. RCTs are much more common among the social and behavioral sciences because of the need for complex inferential statistics to tease out small changes and differences. Some effects are so obvious as not to require any type of formal experiment, as Jacob Cohen (1994) described in his classic paper "The Earth Is Round ($p < .05$)." And Smith and Pell (2003) illustrated the absurdity of using RCTs to demonstrate causation in their spoof paper titled "Parachute Use to Prevent Death and Major Trauma Related to Gravitational Challenge: Systematic Review of Randomized Trials." Using legitimate literature search processes, they were unable to identify any RCTs, published or unpublished, demonstrating that using parachutes saves lives. Of course, this does not mean that parachutes are ineffective. The authors suggested that "we accept that, under exceptional circumstances, common sense might be applied when considering the potential risks and benefits of interventions" (Smith and Pell 2003, 1460). This paper has been highly cited by both detractors and defenders of the presumptive ubiquitous need for RCTs to demonstrate the efficacy of interventions. It was correctly pointed out that the physics of gravity and parachutes are so compellingly clear that experimental evidence is not needed, and no promoter of evidence-based practice would claim otherwise. But biological, social, and psychological interventions typically exert highly variable effects, nowhere as compellingly clear as the value of parachutes, and in such circumstances, RCTs *are* often needed to tease out genuine effects.

Unlike launching a rocket, conducting a chemistry experiment, or sending drones to peer inside of the eye of a hurricane, social workers have investigatory tools that tend to provide less clear-cut results than those used in the natural sciences. As we have seen, RCTs are a legitimate and useful tool for examining the true effects of psychosocial, community, and policy-based interventions, but they are simply that: one tool. RCTs are not necessarily the only way to investigate treatment outcomes. This chapter will describe some useful alternatives to the randomized experiment that, under certain conditions, also permit legitimate causal inferences via the elimination of alternative explanations.

Pre-Experimental Designs

Pre-experimental and quasi-experimental studies are used much more often than randomized experiments in social work research and evaluation, according to content analyses of the types of papers published in our major research journals (e.g., Holosko 2009; Rosen, Proctor, and Staudt 1999; Rubin and Parrish 2007). A pre-experimental study evaluates the outcomes of social work practice using only *one group* of participants. This is done using a posttest-only design, diagrammed as $X - O_1$, or a pretest–posttest design, diagrammed as $O_1 - X - O_2$. (These designs can also be depicted in the manner shown in chapters 4, 5, and 6 to illustrate true experimental designs.) In the first example, a group of participants receive an intervention, and their functioning is assessed after treatment has concluded. Such designs can be valuable in answering limited forms of evaluation questions, such as the following:

- How satisfied are clients three months after receiving our agency's services?
- Did clients actually obtain the services our referral service recommended for them?
- How many social work graduates of our program are employed in a professional social work position one year after graduation?

- How do social work students rate a professor's teaching at the end of a course?
- How severe are the symptoms of PTSD among our clients three months after they were discharged from our program?
- What is the recidivism rate among ex-prisoners discharged from a halfway house program?

These are all important questions, but questions initially answered with the posttest-only design give rise to other questions, particularly, "In comparison to what?" Lacking a comparator condition, any attempt at *causal* inference is usually quite limited. Finding that client symptoms are low post-treatment is good, but without knowing the level of symptoms pretreatment, one cannot really claim the treatment was effective. Sometimes one can compare the results of an $X - O_1$ study against some sort of normative data, which can aid in the interpretation of the results. For example, a professor's student evaluations can be compared against the course evaluation data of other faculty who taught during the same term. A teacher who is consistently rated among the lowest may motivate administrators to check in with the faculty member to try to improve their teaching effectiveness. PTSD symptom ratings from a group of clients who completed a trauma-informed therapy for PTSD may be compared with published norms based on the scale used in the study so that agency administrators can see whether their clients' outcomes are similar to those seen by other agencies using the same treatment protocol. Published normative data are available for many outcome measures (see, for example, Fischer, Corcoran, and Springer 2020; Whisman and Richardson 2015; Thyer et al. 1981, 1985), and these have some limited value for use in appraising the results of a posttest-only study that used one or more such standardized measures.

The posttest-only design can be strengthened somewhat by adding multiple posttest assessments, as in $X - O_1 - O_2 - O_3 - \ldots O_k$, but additional posttest assessments enhance the ability to assess only the durability or maintenance of the results, not that the intervention caused these outcomes. Despite these limitations, Holosko (2009); Rosen, Proctor, and Staudt (1999); and Rubin and Parrish (2007) found the single-group posttest-only design to be used much more often than the more complex quasi-experimental evaluation or RCT. It is rare, however, that this design is useful for making legitimate causal inferences. A hypothetical example is a group of patients recently diagnosed with an incurable disease, one with a short life span once diagnosed. If prior research has shown that everyone with this disease dies soon after diagnosis, then an $X - O_1$ treatment study could be valuable if it were found that a meaningful proportion of patients were alive a year later. However, such uniformly irremediable conditions are uncommon in social work. Many of the psychosocial problems that our clients encounter wax and wane over time, and few interventions are extremely powerful. This is why evaluation designs with greater potential internal validity such as RCTs are needed to isolate the true effects of modestly effective therapies on clients' changeable conditions.

Researchers planning to use the $X - O_1$ design for preliminary outcome studies should be prepared for some pushback from some colleagues and funding agencies because these designs are commonly held in poor regard in relation to the idealized standards of rigorous science. Mislabeled (in my opinion) as a "one-shot case study" in the highly respected classic text by Campbell and Stanley (1963, 6), this design is readily confused with the narrative case study, which has long been favored by qualitative researchers (see Brandell and Varkas 2010) but is commonly seen as being of little value in making causal inferences by more quantitatively oriented methodologists. Campbell and Stanley (1963) were quite damning in their assessment of the value of the $X - O_1$ design, saying that "such studies have such a total absence of control as to be of almost no scientific value. . . . It seems well-nigh unethical at the present time to allow, as theses or dissertations in education, case studies of this nature" (i.e., involving a single group observed at one time only) (6–7). Similar negative pronouncements have been made by equally weighty authorities such as Boring (1954). As such, this design has become tainted as valueless or even misleading. My view is that the utility of the posttest-only design needs to be considered in terms of the question being asked. If it is a simple question, then the design may be suitable. For example, each semester my students complete a standardized course evaluation of my teaching. A measure called the Student Perception of Courses and Instructors (SPCI) is used, a predominantly quantitative scale that asks questions about the course and the instructor's teaching, with quantitative responses reported via a six-point Likert scale ranging from strongly agree to strongly disagree.

Each year during my annual evaluation, my dean summons me into his office to review my accomplishments in the areas of service, scholarship, and teaching, My scores on the SPCI are the major benchmark used to evaluate my teaching, particularly my "overall rating." If responses are mostly "excellent" and "above satisfactory," I get a cursory pat on the back, but if I get a number of "below satisfactory" or "poor" responses, woe betide me. I will be admonished and instructed to shape up. The dean's face will harden when I protest that this measure has no quantitative measures of reliability or validity. He will shake his head when I assert that I teach the most disliked courses in the curriculum (research classes, of course), and he will sigh when I explain that the SPCI is a poor measure of teaching effectiveness. He will correctly point out that the fact are the facts—these are the course evaluations my students gave me, and I alone am responsible for these ratings. In other words, for his purposes (and that of the larger institution), these SPCI scores are sufficient to answer the question asked by the university: "How do students evaluate Professor Thyer's teaching?" And the X – O_1 design ("X" being my teaching and "O_1" being the students' aggregated evaluations) is useful in this circumstance. We do not need any comparison groups, randomly assigned or not, to answer that simple question. We need no inferential statistics, no measures of teaching content or my instructional delivery methods. Similarly, the X – O_1 design is adequate to the task of answering the question, "What percentage of our 2019 MSW graduates obtained their licensure as clinical social workers by 2023?" One cannot obtain the LCSW qualification without earning an accredited MSW degree, so the causal relationship is clear. If postgraduation surveys find a high rate of licensure, our MSW program is doing a good job. If a high proportion of our clinical graduates fail the LCSW examination, we are clearly not fulfilling our mandate to produce skilled clinicians. So, let us not be so quick to dismiss the posttest-only design, as it has a valued role in answering simple questions of a noncausal nature.

The second form of pre-experimental design is the pretest–posttest design, or O_1 – X – O_2, more advanced than the posttest-only design because it permits a form of *comparison*, that all-important element in allowing for causal inference. In this instance, the comparison is within *one* group and usually consists of comparing posttest scores against pretest scores. Key features to the success of this design include having a sufficient number of participants, little attrition, the use of a reliable and valid outcome measure, a well-proceduralized intervention delivered by qualified people, using measures to ensure and document treatment fidelity, and the correct use of suitable inferential statistical tests. This approach can permit us to credibly document real changes in participants and in clinical settings can allow us to assert that participants who received a particular treatment showed improvements that were statistically and clinically significant. Professors can use this design to document student learning over the course of a term; clinicians can use it to see whether patients improved after treatment; and policy analysts can use it to ascertain whether a certain social problem was ameliorated after introducing a new policy.

This is all highly valuable information, as long as one is not tempted to exaggerate one's claims, which actually happens a lot in the social work literature, as documented by Rubin and Parrish (2007). These scholars evaluated the merits of the conclusions of 138 published outcome studies in social work and found that "70 percent used designs that do not warrant making conclusive causal inferences, and 60 percent of articles with those designs contained phrases that could be misconstrued or exploited as implying an inflated evidence-based status" (Rubin and Parrish 2007, 334). The authors provide dozens of direct quotes taken from published social work outcome studies that clearly state or imply a causal effect that is not warranted by the internal validity of the designs used. Even the best RCTs may not satisfactorily control for some threats to internal validity, indicating that some circumspection on the part of authors is needed before claiming that a therapy produced given outcomes. I was the editor of the journal in which Rubin and Parrish published their 2007 article, and I took quiet delight in my decision letter recommending a revision and in providing a direct quote from one of Rubin's previously published studies that contained a problematic phrase implying a stronger effect of treatment than was justified by the research design. To his credit, and as a testimony to his integrity as a scholar, Rubin included this quote as an example of such problematic phrases in the revised manuscript, which I was pleased to accept and publish. As an example of a legitimate conclusion that can be derived from a pretest–posttest study, I offer the following from a study by Buchanan, Dixon, and Thyer (1997) involving thirty military veterans treated with an inpatient psychiatric treatment program and assessed with a valid measure of mental health upon admission and at discharge. We found the veterans to be significantly improved over the course of treatment. Did we excitedly proclaim that the program was effective and had *caused* the patients to improve? No, we did not. Instead, we said the following:

> To determine whether these veterans improved following care, a simple pretest-posttest group design was employed, using the SCL-90 to assess psychiatric symptomatology before and after inpatient treatment. Both statistically significant and practically meaningful improvements in symptomatology were evident at discharge. *While the research design does not permit causal inference*, low-cost evaluations such as this one simply demonstrating that patients get better are important first steps in empirically demonstrating the efficacy of inpatient psychiatric services, and represent one means of demonstrating accountable practice [823, my emphasis]. . . . Thus the research design in this study is a pretest-posttest study (O-X-O) (Thyer 1992), consisting of obtaining measures of patient functioning before inpatient treatment begins (i.e., at admission), and readministering these measures at the time of the patient's discharge (i.e., post-treatment). Statistical analysis of the pretreatment and post-treatment data determines whether any meaningful change has occurred. This type of design is effective at answering the question "Do patients improve?," but it is not usually useful in proving that a given treatment *caused* any observed improvements. Given that most VA psychiatric services have no data to document simple improvements, it is suitable to begin evaluation research looking at outcomes alone, before undertaking the more sophisticated studies needed to isolate causal variables [856, emphasis in the original]. . . . It remains for more sophisticated studies, perhaps involving control groups and assessments conducted some months post-discharge, to prove that these changes are caused by psychiatric treatment, and that the improvements remain long after discharge.

(Buchanan, Dixon, and Thyer 1997, 823, 856–57)

I stand by these modest claims, based on the single-group pretest–posttest study we conducted. They illustrate the kind of useful information agencies can gather using their own resources. A finding of no improvement could inform agencies that all is not well and that a more careful examination of their services is indicated. We were unable to rule out many obvious threats to internal validity in our study. Perhaps simply providing the veterans with a vacation of several weeks away from home, free of familial stress or employment obligations, would have produced similar improvements (at far less cost). We had no resources to undertake this more sophisticated evaluation, which was an unfunded MSW student project conducted at his internship site. But this design *did* answer the question it was intended to. Our field needs more such simple studies of routinely provided health and social care services simply to see whether clients are improving.

Allen Rubin and his colleagues suggest that agencies can conduct single-group pretest–posttest pre-experimental studies and calculate the effect size on the standardized mean difference obtained for a group of clients with a specific condition treated with a well-established research-supported treatment. After doing so, agency staff could then compare the effect size obtained with their clients against the effect sizes obtained in previously published outcome studies of the same clinical problem treated with the same treatment. In this manner, they claim that the agency could determine whether they are obtaining clinical outcomes (as expressed by effect sizes) comparable to those found with similar clients at other agencies. Rubin and his colleagues have conveniently published what they call clinical benchmarks—that is, overall effect sizes—to use for this purpose (see Rubin, Parrish, and Washburn 2014; Rubin, Washburn, and Schieszler 2017; Rubin and Yu 2015). For example, Rubin, Washburn, and Schieszler (2017) found an effect size called the Hedges g of 0.50 for the effects of trauma-focused behavior therapy on traumatized children and adolescents on a widely used outcome measure called the Child Behavior Checklist (CBCL). What this means is that treated youth, on average, were 0.50 standard deviations better off following treatment. The authors contend that the staff at a given agency could do an uncontrolled outcome study using the $O_1 - X - O_2$ design, treating youth with trauma-focused cognitive behavioral therapy (TF-CBT) and using the CBCL as an outcome measure. If the effect size they obtain is in the vicinity of the 0.50 benchmark found by Rubin, Washburn, and Schieszler (2017) (derived from an analysis of the outcomes of seventeen previously published studies of the impact of TF-CBT on traumatized youth) compared with youth assigned to a waiting list or TAU, the agency could be sure the treatment they were providing was *better than an alternative*, in this case a waiting list or TAU, *had they had such a comparison group*.

The benchmarking approach is not yet widely employed, and its legitimacy remains undetermined. The agencies, clients, therapeutic staff, and circumstances surrounding the delivery of a given treatment in a published study no doubt vary widely from those of any one agency attempting to use the benchmarking approach; thus, comparisons would be misleading at best and perhaps invidious. A conservative perspective would contend that the only way to compare the outcomes of an experimental treatment against no treatment, TAU, or a credible placebo treatment is within the context of a *single* study comparing such treatments head-to-head in the *same* setting. At a professional conference, I had a friendly but critical discussion with Rubin and some colleagues about his benchmarking strategy (Rubin et al. 2019), and while I do not know if anyone's opinions were changed, I have devised the following newer approach to attempt to make meaningful comparisons of treatment outcomes in the absence of suitable comparison or control conditions in the interests of disseminating Rubin's novel ideas.

Quasi-Experimental Designs

If you review table 4.1, you will see a series of increasingly complex diagrams depicting various types of RCTs. Note that each arm of the study is preceded by the capital letter "R." This means that each group was deliberately created by the researchers and that participants were randomly assigned to each group. Sometimes events in life arrange for groups to be created randomly without deliberate manipulation by researchers, but these so-called natural experiments are relatively rare, and careful evaluations should be made to ensure that the assignments to conditions were truly random; that is, that each participant had an equal chance of being assigned to each group in advance of assignment. Such formalism distinguishes true random assignment techniques from methods of assignment that may look random but are in fact merely haphazard or wherein some underlying bias is present but disguised or hidden.

Now imagine table 4.1, and in your head erase the Rs preceding each group. You have created a chart of quasi-experiments, a large category of research designs that look identical, and indeed are identical, to true experiments, with the exception that in quasi-experiments groups are created not through random assignment but some other process. Creating groups using nonrandom methods is a less reliable way of ensuring that the groups are essentially equivalent on all relevant (and irrelevant) variables. Lacking random assignment methods, pre-intervention equivalence cannot be ensured, despite how similar the groups may appear. Even if after constructing groups nonrandomly, the researcher looks at relevant clinical and demographic variables and empirically determines that there are no statistically significant differences pretreatment, these findings hold only for the variables examined, not for the many others that were not checked.

For example, this term I am teaching two sections of the same MSW research course. One meets from 1 P.M. to 4 P.M. and the other from 5 P.M. to 8 P.M. on the same day. Both classes have twenty-five students. I could opt to evaluate a new method of instruction by introducing it to one section only and then looking at how each section performed on the standardized final exam at the end of the term. Let's call my regular teaching method "teaching as usual" (TAU) and the novel instruction method "instruction by shaming" (IBS, the details of which I will omit). I am equally skilled in both TAU and IBS and decide to offer TAU in my evening section and IBS in the afternoon class. I could diagram my research design as follows:

| Afternoon class, N = 25 | $X_{IBS} - O_1$ |
| Evening class, N = 25 | $X_{TAU} - O_1$ |

As a careful researcher, I look at the students' demographic variables in each section, factors such as age, gender, race, and GRE scores, and find the two sections are equivalent, with no significant differences between them. I then teach my two classes throughout the semester, being careful to not use any TAU in the IBS class or any IBS techniques in my TAU section. I give my standardized final exam to both classes under similar conditions and then grade each section. And I find that the students in the IBS section score an average of 92 percent and that the students in the TAU section scored an average of only 81 percent. I also find that this difference is statistically significant at $p < .05$. It appears that IBS is a superior method of teaching, assuming that the final exam was a valid measure of research knowledge, as demonstrated by this posttest-only alternative-treatment control-group quasi-experimental study. Am I ready to proclaim the pedagogical merits of IBS and try to publish my findings in a professional journal? After all, the groups were very similar at the beginning of the term. Can I conclude that any posttreatment differences were solely caused by the teaching methods? You might be able to come up with some threats to internal validity that this study did not control for. One obvious one (obvious to me after many years of teaching) is that students who take evening classes often have been hard at work all day before coming to school, unlike the afternoon students who come to my class well rested. My disparate results showing that the students taught using TAU performed more poorly *could be* due to TAU being a poorer method of instruction, *or* they could be due to the evening students simply being more fatigued. Or perhaps the difference was caused by *my* being more tired in the evening and thus teaching more poorly! This quasi-experimental design does not control for such possibilities. It would not be feasible to randomly assign all fifty students to the afternoon or evening section, and thus create a truly random experiment, wherein the student fatigue factor would be equally divided between the two sections and thus controlled for and removed as a compromising variable. It is practical constraints like this that render the quasi-experimental designs more widely used than true experimental designs. Random assignment is often just not possible; in such cases, quasi-experimental designs are seen as the best alternative option to true experiments.

Make no mistake, though. Quasi-experiments are a valuable tool for conducting evaluations of social work therapies, policies, teaching methods, and other aspects of our work, and I have extolled their virtues elsewhere (Royse, Thyer, and Padgett 2016; Thyer 2010, 2012; Thyer and Myers 2007). Even though randomized experiments are often viewed as inherently superior to quasi-experiments for evaluating the true outcomes of social work services by their ability to reduce the risk of bias and control for various threats to internal validity, this is too simplistic an appraisal. Although we tend to think of a study design in terms of the use or nonuse of random assignment and the arrangement of assessment and intervention periods (as exemplified by the diagrams of Os and Xs depicted in this book), this is too limited a view:

> The term *design* in its broadest sense refers to all the elements that go into creating and conducting a research study, features such as forming a broad research question; creating a specific, directional, and falsifiable hypothesis; selecting a sample of clients; choosing one or more outcome measures; developing a way to deliver the intervention in a credible manner; figuring out how to assess client functioning following (and sometimes before) receipt of the intervention; analyzing the results; and integrating the findings back into any relevant body of theory that your hypotheses were based upon (recognizing that not all hypotheses are based on an explicit behavioral or social science theory).
>
> (Thyer 2010, 183, emphasis in the original)

Although a modern computer is made up of many components, we commonly see the logic chip or "brain" of the computer as the most important one. But lots of things go into the smooth functioning of our computers, and if any is not working correctly, the computer is useless. If the keyboard or monitor is broken or the mouse is out of commission, this complex machine can't really do much. Similarly, a randomized experiment has a number of important elements, some of which are outlined in the previous quote, and if one or more of them are poorly chosen or poorly implemented, the RCT will not provide reliable information. If embedded into the most sophisticated of evaluation studies is an invalid outcome measure, the entire study breaks down. If interventions are administered ineptly, the statistics incorrectly chosen, or there is too much client attrition, the study is of poor internal validity. It may well be that a well-designed quasi-experimental study could yield superior results, in terms of learning about nature's truths, compared to a mediocre RCT. And, as noted by Cohen (1994) and others, some causal inferences are so glaringly self-evident that experimental studies are simply not needed. This notion was recognized by the founders of evidence-based practice when they noted that there are "interventions whose face validity is so great that randomized trials assessing their value were unanimously judged by the team to be both unnecessary and, if they involved placebo treatments, unethical" (Straus et al. 2019, 230).

The preference for randomized experiments over quasi-experimental studies was investigated empirically by William Shadish and his colleagues (Shadish, Clark, and Steiner 2008). While endorsing the general contention that RCTs are superior for making causal inferences about the effects of interventions, his empirical research has demonstrated that under certain conditions, the results of quasi-experimental outcome studies can approximate those of true experiments. Shadish's approach was quite clever. Using a large number of undergraduate student participants, his team randomly assigned half to participate in a true experiment. The students in this group were in turn randomized to receive mathematics *or* vocabulary training. The other half of the original participants were assigned to participate in a quasi-experiment with a nonrandom assignment method in which the students selected which training they received. Pretests and posttests were given to all participants in both vocabulary and math knowledge. In both the randomized experiment and the quasi-experiment, it was hypothesized that training in mathematics would improve posttest math scores (compared to pretest scores) but not vocabulary scores and that training in vocabulary would improve posttest vocabulary scores but not math scores. The authors then compared the results of the two types of study and found that "there is only borderline evidence indicating that the results from the nonrandomized experiment differ significantly different from those of the randomized experiment. . . . This study suggests that adjusted results from nonrandomized experiments can approximate results from randomized experiments" (Shadish, Clark, and Steiner 2008, 1339, 1341).

This study does not by itself indicate that RCTs have no value over quasi-experiments in terms of internal validity. Shadish, Clark, and Steiner (2008) conducted an analog study of college students subjected to an educational intervention, not a clinical or psychosocial treatment; therefore, extrapolation to real clients with the types of problems addressed by social workers cannot be assumed. Further, Shadish, Clark, and Steiner (2008) performed various feats of statistical sleight of hand to determine the equivalence of the two types of studies, using techniques such as ordinary least squares regression and propensity analysis, and they controlled for a variety of demographic variables. Still, under some circumstances it appears that quasi-experiments *can* yield internally valid results and are not always inferior to RCTs in this regard.

The findings of Shadish, Clark, and Steiner (2008) replicated and extended an earlier study (Heinsman and Shadish 1996). Thus, when faced with a practice environment in which legitimate randomization is not possible, conducting a more practical quasi-experiment may be a viable alternative that will not necessarily sacrifice the legitimacy of inferential outcomes.

However, one cannot simply conclude that the results of a given quasi-experimental study, say a posttest-only no-treatment control-group study, are just as valid as its randomized experimental equivalent. As Heinsman and Shadish (1996) assert, one must adequately control for a variety of factors before such equivalence can be found, factors such as the credibility of the placebo or alternative treatment, the levels of attrition across groups over the course of the study, pretest differences, and the accuracy of the effect size estimations, among others. But if one can do this, "nonrandomized experiments are more like randomized experiments, if one takes confounds into account" (Heinsman and Shadish 1996, 162). The problem is knowing *which* confounds are important. Theory may be informative in this regard, but data from prior similar studies are more useful. There is no justification for asserting that the findings of a typical quasi-experiment are as valid as those from its experimental equivalent. But lacking the ability to randomly assign individual participants or groups, a well-constructed quasi-experimental study may be useful.

Natural Experiments

Evaluation designs are sometimes used in what are called *natural experiments*, situations that approximate some aspects of random assignment. A good example of this is David Card's study investigating the effects of raising the minimum wage on unemployment, for which he was awarded half the 2021 Nobel Memorial Prize in Economic Sciences. Card took advantage of the increase in New Jersey's minimum wage in 1992 and compared the unemployment rates of New Jersey and Pennsylvania, which did not raise its minimum wage. Many researchers and politicians predict that a raise in the minimum wage will cause employers to lay off workers and thus increase unemployment. Card interviewed 410 fast-food restaurant managers in the two states one month before the passage of New Jersey's minimum wage increase and again eight months later. The independent variable was the increase in the minimum wage, and there were a variety of dependent variables (outcome measures), such as full-time-equivalent employment (number of full-time employees, including managers, plus 0.5 times the number of part-time employees) at each restaurant and the percentage of full-time employees. Table 9.1 shows the pretest and posttest data for each state.

TABLE 9.1 Pretest and posttest employment data in relation to a minimum wage increase in New Jersey but not Pennsylvania, 1992

State	Pretest (1 month before minimum wage increase)		Posttest (8 months later)	
	FTE[a]	Employees, N	FTE	Employees, N
New Jersey	20.4	32.8	21.0	35.9
Pennsylvania	23.3	35.0	21.2	30.4

Source: Card, D., and A. B. Krueger. 1994. "Minimum Wages and Employment: A Case Study of the Fast-Food Industry in New Jersey and Pennsylvania." *American Economic Review* 84, no. 4: 776.

[a]FTE: full-time-equivalent employment.

In contrast to what some would predict, employment in New Jersey increased after the minimum wage was increased, but it did not go up in Pennsylvania. In the authors' words, "Contrary to the central prediction of the textbook model of the minimum wage . . . we find no evidence that the rise in New Jersey's minimum wage reduced employment in fast-food restaurants in the state. . . . Finally, we find that prices of fast-food meals increased in New Jersey relative to Pennsylvania, suggesting that much of the burden of the minimum wage increase was passed on to consumers" (Card and Krueger 1994, 792). (This study illustrates the aphorism that there is no such thing as a free lunch!) Measures of the dependent variables were made only twice. If monthly data had been obtained before and after the minimum wage increase, this design could have been considered an interrupted time-series study, but as it is, it conformed to a pretest–posttest no-treatment control-group design. The Oregon Health Insurance Experiment described in chapter 5 is another example of a well-conducted natural experiment that permitted strong causal inferences about the effects of the intervention. Such studies are yet another tool in the research design armamentarium of social work experimentalists. The Nobel Prize committee has this to say in its announcement of the award to Card:

This year's Laureates—David Card, Joshua Angrist and Guido Imbens—have provided us with new insights about the labour market *and shown what conclusions about cause and effect can be drawn from natural experiments*. Their approach has spread to other fields and revolutionized empirical research. Many of the big questions in the social sciences deal with *cause and effect*. How does immigration affect pay and employment levels? How does a longer education affect someone's future income? These questions are difficult to answer because we have nothing to use as a comparison. We do not know what would have happened if there had been less immigration or if that person had not continued studying. However, this year's Laureates have shown that it is possible to answer these and similar questions using natural experiments. The key is to use situations in which chance events or policy changes result in groups of people being treated differently, in a way that resembles clinical trials in medicine. "Card's studies of core questions for society and Angrist and Imbens' methodological contributions have shown that *natural experiments are a rich source of knowledge. Their research has substantially improved our ability to answer key causal questions, which has been of great benefit to society,*" says Peter Fredriksson, chair of the Economic Sciences Prize Committee.

(RSAS 2021, my emphasis)

Clearly natural experiments can afford rich opportunities to make legitimate inferences about the true effects of social policies and psychosocial interventions. Obvious traditional randomized controlled trials are not the only legitimate research designs to permit causal inferences.

Time-Series Designs

Time-series designs were classified by Campbell and Stanley (1963) as a form of quasi-experimental investigation, and their use greatly predates the development and application of RCTs. The inferential logic is relatively simple. A dependent variable (an outcome of interest) is measured repeatedly over time. The data are graphed with the dependent variable on the vertical axis and time on the horizontal axis. The increments of time may be evenly spaced (as in consecutive days, weeks, months, or years) or not (as in sessions). The data points may be evenly spaced (e.g., with a data point for every day) or irregularly spaced (data may be missing or unavailable). But each data point should be properly placed in time on the graph. With this simple technique alone, one can make inferences regarding the future direction of data. The more data points, the better. Two data points can be connected with a straight line, but this is insufficient to legitimately infer anything about future data. It takes at least three data points to begin to see a trend, and one's confidence in a predicted trend is enhanced with more information. If the data are highly variable, with data points moving up and down erratically, predicting the future is more difficult than with consistent data, with data points that follow a straight line.

People use simple time-series data all the time in everyday life. A young professional trying to decide where to invest for retirement income can examine the performance of a mutual fund. Most investment websites allow one to see the performance (i.e., the rate of return) over periods of months and years.

A mutual fund that has shown steady high rates of return over ten years is likely to be preferred over one yielding lower rates. One can examine population growth in the United States over the past fifty years and confidently assert that next year will see another increase in the population. One does not need any type of statistical test to infer effects, just a pair of eyeballs! Of course, dramatic changes can happen. The stock market may crash and epidemics can ravage a country, but in general a prolonged trend in data heading in a particular direction is usually (though not always) a good predictor of the near future. Designs like this can be diagrammed as follows:

$$O_1 - O_2 - O_3 - O_4 - O_5 - O_6 - O_7 - O_8 - O_9 - O_{10} - O_{11} - O_k \ldots$$

Interrupted Time-Series Designs

Descriptive studies using a time-series design alone are not a tool for inferring the effects of a particular intervention, since there is no intervention, but they can be useful in areas such as epidemiological research, planning for future enrollments in a program, planning where to invest one's money, or predicting the trajectory of an ongoing epidemic. For evaluation purposes, the time-series design can be used if at some point in the data stream, a particular intervention is implemented. Such a study design can be diagrammed as follows:

$$O_1 - O_2 - O_3 - O_4 - O_5 - O_6 - O_7 - O_8 - O_9 - O_k - X - O_{k+1} - O_{k+2} - O_{k+3} - O_4 - O_{k+4} - \ldots$$

In this type of study, the design is transmogrified into what is called an interrupted time-series design, with "X" standing for an intervention. With this design, the researcher evaluates whether the data change after an intervention is implemented. Sometimes the data are so compelling that the conclusion almost jumps out at you. Cook and Shadish (1994) describe the inferential logic behind the interrupted time-series design as follows:

> In interrupted time series, the same outcome variable is examined over many time points. If the cause-effect link is quick acting or has a known causal delay, then an effective treatment should lead to change in the level, slope or variance of the time series at the point where treatment occurred. The test, then, is whether the obtained data show the change in the series at the pre-specified point. . . . Internal validity is the major problem, especially because of history (e.g., some other outcome-causing event occurring at the same time as the treatment) and instrumentation (e.g., a change of record keeping occurring with the treatment).
> (562)

One is looking for a *discontinuity*, or change, at or near the point of intervention; thus, these types of studies are sometimes called regression discontinuity studies. Consider a classic case study in medical research. Dr. Ignaz Semmelweis was a professor of obstetrics at the Vienna General Hospital in the 1840s. At the time, the infection rate of a life-threatening condition called childbed fever was high among women giving birth at obstetric hospitals but low among women who gave birth at home. This was decades before the development of the germ theory of infection by Pasteur and Lister, and Semmelweis, like his colleagues of the era, had no ready explanation for the high rates of infection. At a nearby clinic for pregnant women, pelvic exams were conducted by female midwives, who did not perform autopsies, and their patients' mortality rate was very low. A medical colleague of Semmelweis's died of an infection with similar symptoms to those of childbed fever after he was accidently cut with a scalpel while performing an autopsy on a woman who had died of childbed fever.

These facts led Semmelweis to develop the radical (for the time) notion that perhaps particles of cadavers were being transferred from the anatomy lab to the living patients by the medical students and that it was this inadvertent contamination that was causing childbed fever. To test this hypothesis, he imposed a rigid regimen requiring his students to wash their hands in a weak beach solution prior to conducting any pelvic examinations. The mortality rates dropped precipitously, supporting Semmelweis's hypothesis. His insistence on cleanliness as a means of preventing infection was met with scorn and ridicule at the time, and he eventually lost his position in Vienna. He published his theory and preventive methods, but these reports were largely ignored. It was not until twenty years later that the work of Pasteur in France vindicated Semmelweis's underappreciated discovery. One can Google "Semmelweis chart" to find examples of his use of an interrupted time-series design to demonstrate a plausible causal relationship between handwashing and the reduction in deaths. All without using an RCT design. However, there are several ways to enhance the validity of the interrupted time-series design.

One is replication. In the case of Semmelweis's experiment, his colleagues could have replicated his intervention at other hospitals. If independent investigators had found similar dramatic reductions in mortality following the introduction of the handwashing regimen, the evidence would have been strengthened. Thus, the replication of an initially strong finding is one good approach to help establish the effectiveness of a treatment.

In an interrupted time-series study, one uses the data from the baseline period, the period prior to the introduction of the intervention, to project or infer the future trend of the data. Once treatment is applied, one looks to see whether there is a meaningful change, deviation, or discontinuity in the *observed* posttreatment data relative to what could have been *predicted* from the pretreatment trend. If there is no evident change, one can fairly safely conclude that the intervention had no effect. If there *is* evident change, this would support the hypothesis that the independent variable caused the deviation in the data. Causal inference is strengthened if the baseline data are stable over a long period of time and if the dependent variable is highly resistant to change. Depression, for example, is a more labile clinical condition than the durable anxieties experiences by people with a specific phobia or the cognitive impairments and behavioral difficulties sometimes seen among people with autism spectrum disorder. An interrupted time-series study that found strong improvements on IQ test scores among a cohort of people with autism spectrum disorder tracked for many months before and after an intervention compared to a no-treatment group would been seen as more credibly yielding valid causal inferences than a similarly designed study involving people with moderate depression.

Causal inference in an interrupted time-series study is also strengthened by the absolute magnitude and rapidity of a change following an intervention, with a treatment being followed quickly by a dramatic change more likely to be seen as causing those improvements than a smaller change evident some considerable time following exposure to the treatment. The slope of a line of data can also be a factor in the strength of a causal inference; if a line of data that is slowly increasing begins to rise much more quickly immediately after treatment is implemented, a stronger causal inference can be inferred than with a less dramatic increase in slope. If a line of data is moving in the direction opposite to that predicted by an intervention (i.e., the problem is getting worse), causal inference may be stronger if the data change in the direction of improvement following treatment. *Variability* in the data may also indicate change. A treatment that dramatically reduces the highs and lows of the mood cycling experienced by people with bipolar disorder evens things out so to speak, may be seen as useful, even if the overall trend line does not change. All these factors can be qualitatively assessed via visual inspection, but they can also be evaluated using specialized statistics, as will be discussed.

Another way to enhance the internal validity of an interrupted time-series design is to continue to collect data after deliberately *removing* the intervention to see whether the data revert back to their original state. If they do, then one has two demonstrations of an effect: one when the intervention was introduced, and the problem improved, and the second when the intervention was removed, and the problem worsened. This, too, is a form of replication. The removal of an intervention can be deliberate or inadvertent, but the inference is made stronger if the introduction and removal are prospectively planned. When shifts in the data coincide with the introduction and removal of a treatment, causal inference is enhanced. This has long been recognized as a strong method for demonstrating causation. As Galileo stated, "That and no other is to be called a cause, at the presence of which the effect always follows, and at whose removal the effects disappear" (cited in Bunge 1959, 33). In many ways, this is simply applied common sense. If wearing a new pair of glasses is followed by a headache that continues only until the glasses are removed, one can fairly confidently infer that the new glasses caused the headache. However, this logic holds only when treatment effects are expected to be temporary, experienced only while an intervention is in effect. Interventions that produce permanent changes cannot be effectively evaluated in this manner. For establishing causal inference, the more data points, the better, both pre- and postintervention.

Removing a potentially effective intervention can pose an ethical problem if the result is a deterioration of psychosocial functioning or health. In cases where this could be a possibility, an interrupted time-series design would not deliberately be employed. If the problem is not severe, then it might be justifiable to remove a treatment that had been followed by improvement for the purpose of enhancing the experimental rigor of the study. If the removal of an intervention that had been followed by improvement results in deterioration, this enhances internal validity. This, in turn, can be further enhanced by reinstating the intervention. If the outcome measure improves a second time, we have three demonstrations of a potential treatment effect: the first when the data improved upon the introduction of the treatment, the second when the data reverted to the baseline level, and the third when the data improved upon the intervention being reinstated. A data pattern of this type effectively excludes many potential threats to internal validity, as it is extremely unlikely that some other factor just happened to coincide with the introduction and removal of the intervention three times in a row. In *Quasi-experimental Research Designs* (Thyer 2012), I describe a number of published examples of researchers who used time-series and interrupted time-series designs to investigate the effect of training alcohol servers to stop serving intoxicated people, the effect of raising the legal drinking age on teenage traffic accidents, and the effect of smoking bans in hospitals on reductions in psychiatric admissions.

Another way to increase the internal validity of interrupted time-series designs is to have a comparator condition and assess the same outcome measure in parallel across two or more situations. Let's say we wish to evaluate the effect of a new social policy introduced by a state that mandates parental consent before an adolescent can legally obtain an abortion with the intent of reducing the number of abortions among minors. We could call the state that introduced this policy the experimental state and a comparable state the control state. Data are first collected for the baseline period (say from 2019 to 2021), prior to the introduction of the policy, during which neither state requires parental consent. Once the policy is introduced in the experimental state at the end of 2021, data collection continues as before. If the experimental state experiences a decline in abortions from 2022 to 2024, these data alone are suggestive of a causal effect but by themselves are not solidly convincing. If, however, the rate of abortions in the control state remains unchanged, we have stronger grounds for concluding that the policy caused a reduction in adolescent abortions.

Another example is the evaluation of the effect of a new law requiring motorcycle riders to wear a helmet on motorcycle-related fatalities. Let's say that one state implements such a law, and another state does not. If the state that implemented the law saw a reduction in the monthly mortality rate among motorcycle riders, this alone suggests that the law caused the result in deaths. If there was no change in the monthly mortality rates of the comparator state, the strength of the causal inference is enhanced. This type of interrupted time-series design, with a no-treatment comparison condition, can be diagrammed as follows:

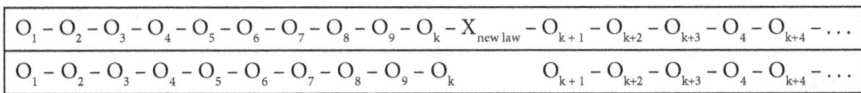

$$O_1 - O_2 - O_3 - O_4 - O_5 - O_6 - O_7 - O_8 - O_9 - O_k - X_{new\ law} - O_{k+1} - O_{k+2} - O_{k+3} - O_4 - O_{k+4} - \ldots$$

$$O_1 - O_2 - O_3 - O_4 - O_5 - O_6 - O_7 - O_8 - O_9 - O_k \qquad\qquad O_{k+1} - O_{k+2} - O_{k+3} - O_4 - O_{k+4} - \ldots$$

Again, causal inference is strengthened through further independent replications of original findings. Of course, new threats to internal validity can creep into a study or may have been present all along. If a state made a morning-after pill that induces miscarriage available at about the time a new parental consent law went into effect, the introduction of the pill would make inferring any changes caused by the new law problematic.

Another way to make inferences using interrupted time-series data is to apply suitable forms of inferential statistics. Typically, this requires a relatively large number of data points. The Box–Jenkins statistical test called time-series *analysis* (not to be confused with time-series *designs*) recommends at least fifty data points per phase of an interrupted time-series study (Box and Jenkins 1970). Latent growth-curve modeling is an alternative approach that does not require such a large number of data points for analysis (Duncan and Duncan 2004). Swanson (2016) outlines a number of methods of statistical inference that can be applied to time-series designs, including spectral analysis, differential equation modeling, phase space reception, recurrence quantification analysis, and autocorrelation/cross-correlation. Bernal, Cummins, and Gasparrini (2017) discuss the use of segmented regression methods. Although the data from time-series and interrupted time-series studies can be illustrated in simple line graphs and conclusions drawn solely through visual inspection, such studies with dense collections of data often use these advanced forms of statistical analysis. These types of analysis are particularly useful when the data lines are highly variable or when the independent variable effects are not very strong. Interrupted time-series designs have been described, recommended, and used by social work researchers when random assignment was not feasible but causal inferences were sought (see DiNitto 1983; DiNitto et al. 1986; Tripodi and Harrington 1979; Bowen and Farkas 1991).

The Regression Discontinuity Design

William Shadish and his colleagues have demonstrated that the results of some forms of quasi-experimental designs need not always be considered less valid than those obtained by randomized experiments. Shadish et al. (2011) conducted a randomized experiment on the effects of training undergraduate students in either vocabulary words or in mathematics skills. He wanted to compare the results obtained from a true RCT versus those obtained from a type of quasi-experiment called a regression-discontinuity design. Of an initial pool of 588 undergraduate students, 197 were randomly assigned to participate in a true experiment on the effects of this training, and 391 were assigned to participate in a quasi-experiment (QE) on the effects of the same training. In the QE, students who scored above a certain cutoff score on the pretest vocabulary test were *nonrandomly* assigned to get training in math, and those who scored lower got *nonrandomly* assigned to training in vocabulary. In the true experiment students were randomly assigned to either training. Both types of study obtained similar results—training in vocabulary improved vocabulary scores posttest, but not math scores, those who got trained in math improved in math but not vocabulary. Assignment to training in the QE based on pretest vocabulary scores reflects a form of nonrandom assignment, which defines this part of the study as a quasi-experiment, not a true RE. The authors concluded:

> It is less a matter of one design being better or worse than the other across the board and more a matter of understanding the competing strengths and weaknesses of the two designs. . . . The two estimates were quite concordant on the whole. . . . The estimates were not significantly different from each other when analyzed as usual. . . . REs [randomized experiments] are still preferable to RDDs [regression discontinuity designs] because they have more power and fewer assumptions. But researchers who need to use an RDD can . . . have reasonable confidence that they are getting an accurate estimate of the effects of treatments.
>
> (Shadish et al. 2011, 187, 189–90)

At the time of writing I was unable to locate any published social work-authored study that made use of this regression-discontinuity design. This presents a good opportunity for researchers to try and apply this type of QE to evaluating social work practice.

Single-Subject Experiments

If we shrink the units of analysis and logical inference used in interrupted time-series designs, we eventually emerge upon a research methodology called the single-subject research design. Instead of looking at aggregated statistics involving large numbers of people, single-subject research designs collect data from just *one* person. Under certain circumstances, these designs can so adequately control for threats to internal validity as to allow for causal inference at the level of the individual and thus be equivalent to experiments in terms of the strength of the causal inference that can be determined. Single-subject research designs have a long history of use in social work intervention research (see Thyer and Thyer 1992), as well as in many other disciplines. Claude Bernard ([1865] 1949) and Ivan Pavlov (Todes 2014) are two examples of experimentalists in the field of medicine who made use of this design to make great scientific contributions. Indeed, Pavlov received the Nobel Prize for Physiology or Medicine in 1904 for his work with individual subjects.

The logic of the single-subject research design is identical to that of the time-series design. Using a reliable and valid measure of functioning, the researcher repeatedly assesses the subject over time during a baseline period, implements an intervention, and then continues collecting data. In single-subject research designs, the baseline period is called the "A phase" and the period after the implementation of the intervention is the "B phase." A simple AB design does not usually possess sufficient internal validity to permit causal inference because of the many alternative explanations possible for changes seen after an intervention is applied. But by applying the techniques used in an interrupted time-series design, one can rule out some threats to internal validity. One variation is to remove an intervention, creating a third condition or second baseline phase, in an AB design. If the data show improvement after treatment is introduced and show a decline when treatment is withdrawn, causal inference is strengthened. If a second intervention phase follows an ABA design, resulting in an ABAB design, and three such discontinuities are observed in the data, causal inference is quite strong. Figure 9.1 provides an example of this type of design. Single-subject research studies involving several abrupt shifts in the data provide a substantial improvement in internal validity to the extent that they are called *experimental* studies by those who use them.

These designs can be very flexible, allowing for repeated baseline and intervention phases. Another form of single-subject research design that can permit causal inferences at the level of the individual is the multiple baseline design, of which there are at least three types.

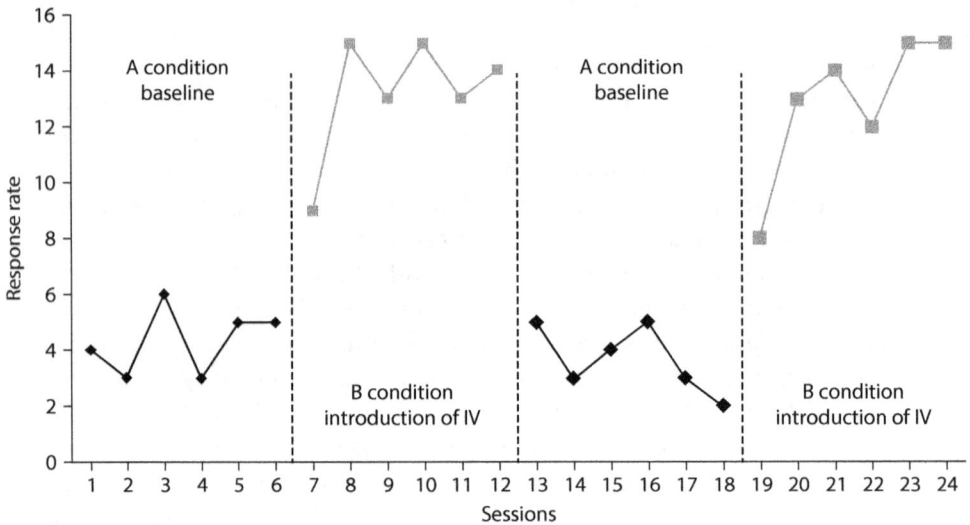

9.1 An example of the ABAB single-subject experimental research design.

Abbreviation: IV, intervention.

Multiple Baselines Across Participants

The multiple-baselines-across-participants design involves evaluating at least two participants being treated with the same intervention. The question attempting to be answered is, "Does the intervention cause improvements?" The limited internal validity of the AB design is improved upon here with replication by adding additional participants. Baselines of the same outcome measure are begun at the same time period for two or more participants. The intervention is then introduced to the first participant (usually depicted at the top of a graph illustrating a single-subject research design), and data collection continues with the first participant being treated and the second continuing in the baseline phase. If the intervention is effective, the first participant should experience an improvement, but the second should not. Treatment is then provided to the second participant. If this participant now improves, the researcher has replicated their finding with the first participant. Each additional participant added who demonstrates the same pattern increases internal validity, as each is another successful replication. The staggered baselines of differing lengths help control for threats to internal validity such as concurrent history, maturation, spontaneous improvement, and regression to the mean. Figure 9.2 provides an example of this type of design.

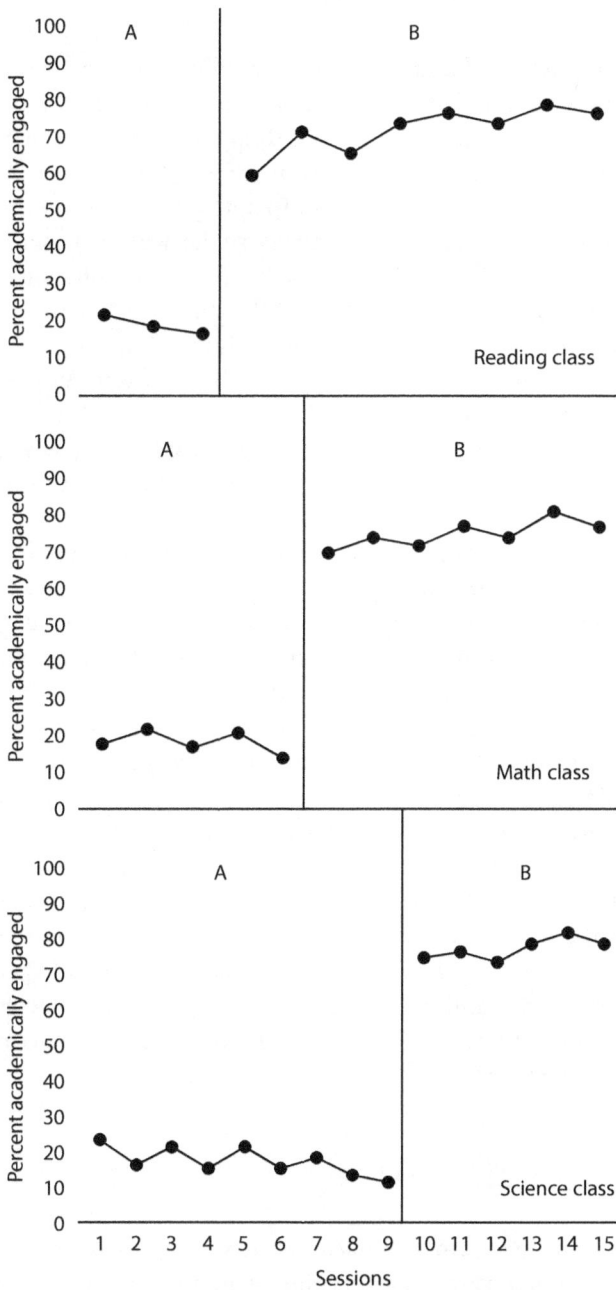

9.2 An example of the multiple-baselines-across-participants design.

Source: Maggin, D., B. Cook, and L. Cook. 2018. "Using Single-Case Research Designs to Examine the Effects of Interventions in Special Education." *Learning Disabilities Research and Practice* 33: 187.

Multiple Baselines Across Situations

The multiple-baselines design can also be used to evaluate whether an intervention caused observed improvements (i.e., to make a causal inference). The multiple-baselines-across-situations design requires *one* participant with *one* problem that occurs across *two or more* situations who is treated with *one* intervention. Say a child displays disruptive behavior at school in their reading, math, and science classes, and a social worker wishes to see if a program of reinforcing on-task behavior is effective at reducing disruptions. Separate baseline measurements of the child's behavior are recorded in each class at about the same time. The intervention is then implemented in one class only, while data collection continues in all three classes. Subsequently, the intervention is then implemented in the second class, and then again in the third class. If the intervention is effective, in terms of logical inference, we hope to see an improvement in each class but only after the intervention has been applied in that class.

Figure 9.3 provides an example of this type of design. From the data depicted in this figure, we could reasonably infer that it was the intervention that caused the child's improvements. Using staggered baselines of uneven length controls for some threats to internal validity such as concurrent history and passage of time. If the child's behavior had improved in all three classes when the intervention had been applied only in the first class (top graph in figure 9.3), the inferential integrity of the design is compromised, since this effect might mean that something else in the child's life had impacted their behavior generally (the threat of concurrent history). This multiple-baselines-across-situations design is not useful for evaluating interventions that produce broad effects. For example, if the intervention in the study of the child's behavior were a medication, the medication would have a systemic impact on the child, and improvements, if any, would be expected across all three settings at the same time. Similarly, if the child were taught behavioral self-control techniques, the effects of this intervention would be anticipated to be wide-ranging, not specific to a particular class.

Multiple Baselines Across Problems

The multiple-baselines-across-problems design can be used when you have *one* client with *two or more* problems that you intend to treat sequentially using the *same* psychosocial intervention. The intervention should be expected to exert a specific, not a broad, effect on client functioning. As an example, say you have a client with three discrete phobias: dogs, snakes, and cockroaches. You devise a method to validly measure features for each phobia stimulus. The Behavioral

Student performance

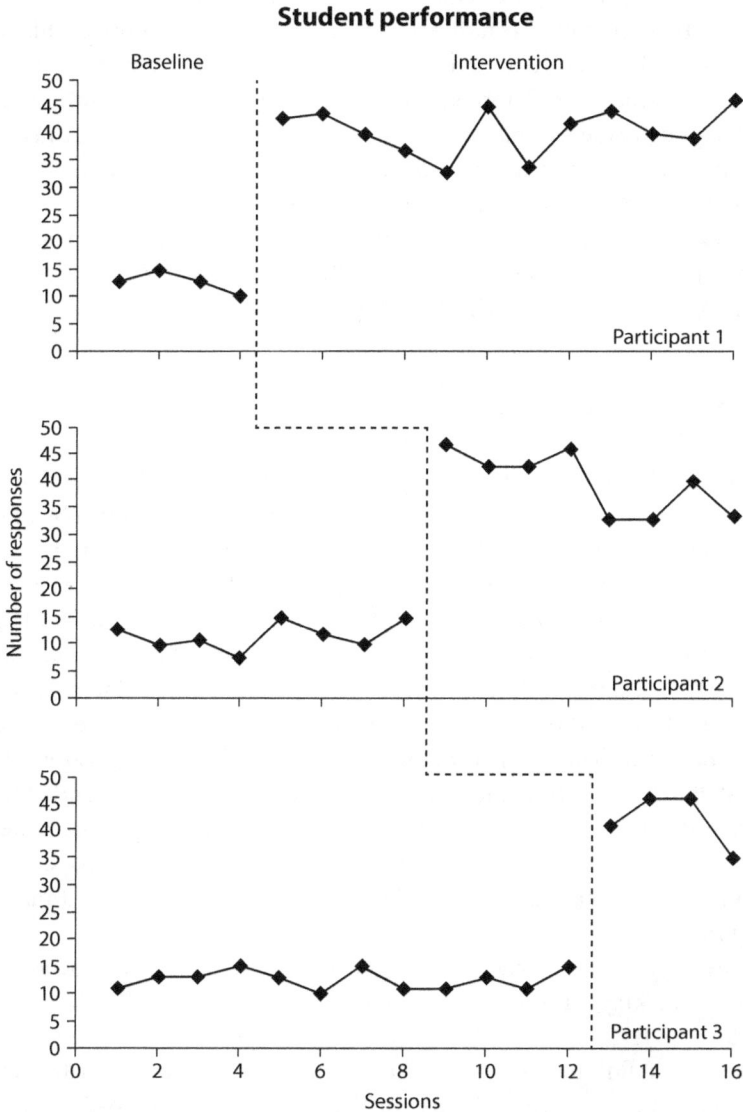

9.3 An example of the multiple-baselines-across-situations design.

Approach Test is one such standardized method for assessing clients with an anxiety disorder, as described by the social worker Gail Steketee and her colleagues (Steketee et al. 1996). Baseline measurements of each of the client's phobias are taken concurrently. Treatment is then implemented for one phobia, say dogs, but not for snakes or cockroaches, while data collection continues across all three phobias. The treatment is then implemented sequentially to address the second and third phobias. If we see an improvement in each phobia only after treatment has been directed to it, the internal validity of this design in demonstrating that treatment has caused the improvements is quite high. A single AB study can demonstrate improvement but not causation (e.g., it might be a coincidence that a client improves after receiving treatment). But replicating the effect of improvements experienced only after treatment has been applied tends to rule out most other plausible explanations.

The experimental logic of the multiple-baselines design used with one or very few participants is similar to that of the stepped-wedge RCT design used with many participants described in chapter 5.

N-of-One Randomized Trials

Readers familiar with the five-step process of clinical decision-making called evidence-based practice will know that the fifth step involves evaluating effectiveness and efficiency (Straus et al. 2019, 5). In the authoritative text on evidence-based practice, Straus and his colleagues discuss the use of a specialized form of single-subject research design called the n-of-one randomized trial used to assess the effects of treatment at the level of the individual. They describe this design as follows: "The n-of-1 trial applies the principles of rigorous clinical trial methodology . . . when trying to determine the best treatment for an individual patient. It randomizes time and assigns the patient (using concealed randomization and hopefully blinding of the patient and clinician) to active therapy or placebo at different times so that the patient undergoes cycles of experimental and control treatment resulting in multiple crossovers (within the same patient) to help decide on the best therapy" (Straus et al. 2019, 146).

An example may help clarify the logic of this design. Let's say a school social worker is working with a child diagnosed with attention deficit hyperactivity disorder (ADHD) for which the child's pediatrician has recommended medication. The child's parents do not believe that the medication will work and are reluctant to have their child take it. The social worker proposes an n-of-one randomized trial to empirically determine whether the medicine is effective. She asks the child's teachers to complete a valid measure of ADHD on a daily basis and begins baseline data collection. The social worker then arranges to get two bottles of identical-looking pills, one containing real medication (labeled "A") and the other placebo pills (labeled "B"). After a baseline period, the parents toss a coin each morning to determine which pill (A or B) to give their child that day. Neither the child nor the parents nor the teachers know which pill the child receives each day. The medication's effects are short lived, lasting eight to ten hours before wearing off. The teachers continue to record data.

After a period of time, say two weeks, the social worker plots the teachers' daily ratings on a graph. The data points for each day the child received the real medication are connected, as are those for each day the child received the placebo pill. If the teachers' evaluations are markedly better on the days the child received the real medication compared to the placebo days, the social worker has visually convincing evidence that the medication is effective—or not, as the case may be.

Figure 9.4 provides an example of the n-of-one randomized trial design. Here, the baseline ("nontreatment") data show the participant's levels of fatigue. The participant then randomly receives either treatment A or treatment B each day. The data in figure 9.4 appear to show that the participant experienced less fatigue on the days they received treatment B, thus enabling a more informed decision about which treatment to continue, A or B. For this design to work, the treatment must be fast acting and short lived. The stimulant medications used to treat ADHD fit this description, and clinicians working with such clients developed the n-of-one randomized trial design. This design was used by the social worker Stephen E. Wong to evaluate the usefulness of a checklist in helping a person with memory impairment self-assess her blood glucose levels (Wong, Seroka, and Ogisi 2000). In psychology, the n-of-one randomized trial is called the alternating-treatments design (see Barlow and Hayes 1979).

N-of-one randomized trials have been a part of the evidence-based practice model from its inception. As of 2014 more than two thousand such studies had been published in the medical literature, more than half of which used solely visual methods of drawing inferences (Kravitz and Duan 2014). The internal validity of these designs can be strong. According to Guyatt and Rennie (2002),

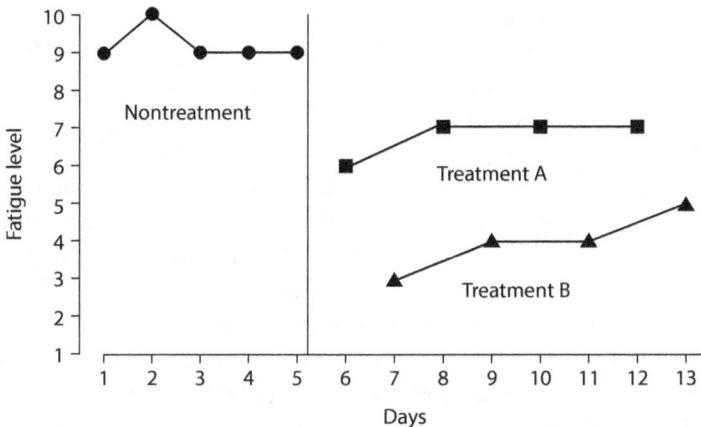

9.4 An example of the n-of-one randomized trial design. In this example, it appears that treatment B resulted in lower fatigue levels than did treatment A.

"When the conditions are right, N of 1 RCTs (a) are feasible, (b) *can provide definitive evidence of treatment effectiveness in individual patients,* and (c) may lead to long-term differences in treatment administration" (108, my emphasis). The authors note that this design is not suitable for assessing long-term outcomes, treatments that are curative, or problems that occur infrequently. And of course, the participant must be willing to subject themselves to this form of experimental evaluation. N-of-one randomized trials are widely used and highly recommended within the evidence-based practice community (Gabler et al. 2011; Guyatt et al. 1988). Qualitative studies have found that both patients and clinicians find the n-of-one randomized trial approach to be acceptable, with one patient noting they appreciated it "because it individualizes what's good for you, not for the percentage of the masses" (Kronish et al. 2017, 236). This brings to mind the dictum of the founder of social work, Mary Richmond: "In work with individuals, averages mean very little" ([1917] 1935, 163). A focus group study involving participants from nondominant racial and ethnic groups concluded that "personalized trials have the potential to change the way we deliver primary care and improve disparities for minorities" (Marrast et al. 2021, 1).

The Repeated Pretest–Posttest Experimental Single-Subject Design

When I worked in the anxiety disorders program of the Department of Psychiatry at the University of Michigan Medical School, I provided treatment to a large number of people who met the DSM criteria for what was then called simple phobia. The anxiety-evoking stimulus for people with simple phobia usually relates to specific situations, most commonly interactions with small animals like dogs, cats, or snakes; heights; or small, enclosed spaces. Fear of the sight of blood, needles or injections, or witnessing trauma are less common. One of the most research-supported treatments for simple phobia involves gradually exposing the client to their phobia in real life (Plaud and Vavrovsky 1997; Thyer 1983, 1987). Exposure therapy is a fairly effective treatment, and some improvements can usually be seen within an hour or two. Complete remission in ten to fifteen hours of treatment is not uncommon. As summarized by Barlow, Allen, and Basden (2007, 367), "A consensus has developed that the treatment of choice for specific phobias is exposure-based procedures, particularly in vivo exposure. Exposure has been shown to be effective for a wide spectrum of specific phobias . . . and in vivo exposure is generally accepted as the most powerful treatment for specific phobias." Not only does the treatment usually work rapidly but the effects are also typically enduring.

In my work with clients with specific phobia, I often used the Behavioral Approach Test (BAT), a structured method of assessment mentioned earlier.

One way to conduct this assessment is to have the object or animal that the client is afraid of available in another room. With the client's full and informed consent, they are asked to look into the room from a given distance and to rate their level of fear on a scale ranging from 0 (completely calm) to 100 (completely petrified). Their rating of fear at that distance is noted, and they are then asked to move closer by a foot or two. Their level of fear is then assessed at that distance. This process continues over ever shorter distances, with the client typically coming to a point at which their fear prevents them from moving any closer. Constructing a simple graph depicting the client's self-reported fear at each distance and the closest distance they could tolerate is one way to operationalize the construct of phobic anxiety. The comprehensiveness of the BAT can be enhanced by having the client wear a heart rate monitor on their finger and recording their heart rate, as well as subjective anxiety, at each increment of distance, thus providing a concurrent measure of behavior (closest distance tolerated), feelings (subjective anxiety score), and physiology (heart rate). Treatment is then provided, and when the client is successfully treated, the BAT is repeated. The posttreatment BAT assessment should show much different results from those of the pretreatment assessment. Behavioral avoidance should be virtually absent, heart rate should not be elevated, and subjective anxiety should be much lower. A comparison of pretreatment and posttreatment BAT data provides an excellent assessment of client improvements. Two cases in which I used this approach to assess treatment outcomes with clients with severe fears of the sight of blood and injections are reported in Thyer and Curtis (1983).

The use of just two measures of client functioning, one pretreatment and one posttreatment, is a simple form of single-subject research design, but such an approach cannot be called a true experiment since many threats to internal validity cannot be ruled out. Occasionally, however, I conducted a BAT assessment with a client with specific phobia before and after *each session* of exposure therapy. Typically, the first BAT indicated higher anxiety and the second one, after an hour or two of exposure, reflected lower anxiety. When the client returned a week or two later for another session, the pretreatment BAT might be a bit higher than the posttreatment BAT from the previous session but then reflect further improvements at the end of this additional session.

It occurred to me that this data pattern had the potential to rule out many threats to internal validity and come close to the power of a true experiment in permitting the conclusion not merely that the client got better but that they got better *because* of the treatment. Table 9.2 presents hypothetical data for a client receiving treatment for specific phobia. For simplicity, I have used BAT scores ranging from 0 (no fear) to 10 (terrified), rather than providing data for behavioral avoidance, subjective anxiety, and heart rate separately. Thus, we can see that at the beginning of the first session, the client's anxiety was very

TABLE 9.2 Hypothetical pre- and posttreatment BAT data for a client with specific phobia

Session	Pretreatment BAT score[a]	Posttreatment BAT score[a]
1	10	8
2	8	7
3	8	6
4	7	5
5	6	4
6	5	3
7	4	2
8	3	1
9	2	0
10	1	0

[a]For simplicity, the BAT data are depicted as ranging from 0 (no fear) to 10 (terrified).

high and had gone down a bit by the end of that session. This change reflects clinical improvement *within a single session*. Since only an hour or two separated the two BAT assessments, there are very few plausible explanations for the improvement apart from the provision of exposure therapy. At the beginning of the second session there were no further improvements, indicating that spontaneous remission of the problem had not occurred. In contrast, by the end of the second session, even greater improvements than those seen at the end of the first session were observed. Again, the most plausible explanation for these *within-session* improvements is the treatment itself, and the lack of improvement *between sessions* further suggests the causal influence of treatment. The consistent pattern of improvements within sessions and a lack of improvement between sessions effectively excludes other possible explanations for improvement.

I was so struck by the apparent effectiveness of this design that I coauthored "The Repeated Pretest-Posttest Single-Subject Experiment: A New Design for Empirical Clinical Practice" and published it in a psychiatric journal (Thyer and Curtis 1983). This design is suitable for experimentally evaluating treatments that have a fairly immediate effect and demonstrate durable improvements. Examples include tutoring, social skills training, and job-interviewing skills—knowledge or skills that can be quickly acquired yet not be expected to improve on their own, absent intervention. This design could be improved by having the pre- and posttreatment assessments conducted by a third party, not the researcher, and it does not do a good job of controlling for placebo effects. However, many client problems addressed by social workers are little affected by placebo factors; phobias are certainly not, and neither are mathematical abilities or social skills. The article by Thyer and Curtis (1983) provides actual BAT data from a client I worked with and does include each session's pre- and posttreatment data on behavioral avoidance, subjective anxiety, and heart rate.

Summary

This chapter has reviewed some plausible alternatives to randomized experiments: pre-experimental and quasi-experimental group designs that have high levels of internal validity. These include time-series and interrupted time-series designs; a variety of single-subject designs, including the ABA and ABAB designs; multiple-baseline designs; the n-of-one randomized trial; and the repeated pretest–posttest experimental single-subject design. I do not contend that these alternatives are replacements for randomized experiments with large numbers of participants. However, I agree with other research methodologists that randomized experiments are not always practical or possible undertake and that the alternatives presented in this chapter are often viable alternatives that possess strong internal validity absent randomization.

CHAPTER 10

ETHICAL CONSIDERATIONS FOR THE USE OF EXPERIMENTAL DESIGNS

We ought, in every instance, to submit our reasoning to the test of experiment, and never to search for truth but by the natural road of experiment and observation.

—Antoine-Laurent de Lavoisier

The field of social work has a long and admirable history of concern with ethical practice. Partially responding to Flexner's judgment that social work was not a true profession and recognizing that one of the hallmarks of established professions was a discipline-specific code of ethics, our field set about developing such a code. Hailman (1949) reviewed some of the nascent attempts to develop professional ethical standards for social workers, but it was not until the National Association of Social Workers (NASW) was created in 1955 that an encompassing umbrella organization existed with enough influence to develop a set of standards that would be widely adopted. Prior to this time, there was an awareness of the need for standards of ethical practice (e.g., Elliot 1931) but little that was formalized in an ethical code until the NASW adopted a one-page ethical code in 1960 (NASW 1965, 1027). However, no mention was made of ethical standards governing the conduct of research by social workers, and this lacuna remained for some years. Writing in 1974, Levy described the need for an expanded code of ethics to provide governance related to practitioners, clients, professional colleagues, and society. All well and good, but nary a mention was made of ethical standards surrounding the undertaking of social work research.

The need for ethical standards for social workers undertaking research was mentioned in the *Encyclopedia of Social Work* by Keith-Lucas: "Ethical problems may arise when one of the objects of the service is research or experimentation that may lead to advances in knowledge or skills. The obligation to not use clients for research purposes without their consent and without regard to their interests may be clear" (Keith-Lucas 1977, 355).

A small section dealing with research ethics finally appeared in the NASW *Code of Ethics* in 1980 (4), and an entry on ethical issues in research was included in the eighteenth edition of the *Encyclopedia of Social Work* (Gillespie 1987). The latter was a remarkably comprehensive analysis of important issues and encouraged more attention be paid to the topic of research ethics. The NASW *Code of Ethics* now contains a lengthy section on research and scholarship; box 10.1 lists some of its current guidelines. Among the points worthy of highlighting are the idea that evaluating our own practice, as individuals and as a discipline, is an important and ethical aspect of practice. We should contribute to the knowledge base of our field, and publishing articles in professional journals is one significant way of fulfilling this mandate. Any research project, evaluative or not, should obtain suitable measures of informed consent from participants. This is not always required, however, as some forms of research could not be undertaken if informed consent were mandatory. For example, hospital data or governmental records may not necessitate informed consent from individuals. When one provides informed consent to receive services at a hospital, buried within the verbiage is your permission for the hospital to make use of your information for research purposes. Facebook conducts experimental research on its users without their knowing it and justifies their actions by stating that Facebook users give consent for this data collection when they sign up for an account. If one is researching archival records on dead people or people for whom no personally identifiable information is available, informed consent is not possible, and some experimental studies do make use of such data.

Other notable elements of the NASW standards for ethical research are that clients must be told they can withdraw from participation in a study, experimental or not, without penalty and that their data will be kept confidential (if personally identifiable information is collected) or anonymous (if personally identifiable information is not collected). Researchers must protect participants from harm, although the possibility of harm cannot always be accurately foreseen. Although it might be thought that the potential for inadvertent harm is more likely in experimental evaluations, even seemingly benign studies such as surveys can cause harm. For example, at one school of social work I know of, a professor was conducting a study on adoptive parents who took in a child

Box 10.1 Selections from the Code of Ethics of the National Association of Social Workers

5.02 Evaluation and Research

(a) Social workers should monitor and evaluate policies, the implementation of programs, and practice interventions.

(b) Social workers should promote and facilitate evaluation and research to contribute to the development of knowledge.

(d) Social workers engaged in evaluation or research should carefully consider possible consequences and should follow guidelines developed for the protection of evaluation and research participants. Appropriate institutional review boards should be consulted.

(e) Social workers engaged in evaluation or research should obtain voluntary and written informed consent from participants, when appropriate, without any implied or actual deprivation or penalty for refusal to participate; without undue inducement to participate; and with due regard for participants' well-being, privacy, and dignity.

(h) Social workers should never design or conduct evaluation or research that does not use consent procedures, such as certain forms of naturalistic observation and archival research, unless rigorous and responsible review of the research has found it to be justified because of its prospective scientific, educational, or applied value and unless equally effective alternative procedures that do not involve waiver of consent are not feasible.

(i) Social workers should inform participants of their right to withdraw from evaluation and research at any time without penalty.

(k) Social workers engaged in evaluation or research should protect participants from unwarranted physical or mental distress, harm, danger, or deprivation.

(m) Social workers engaged in evaluation or research should ensure the anonymity or confidentiality of participants and of the data obtained from them.

(n) Social workers who report evaluation and research results should protect participants' confidentiality by omitting identifying information.

(o) Social workers should report evaluation and research findings accurately. They should not fabricate or falsify results and should take steps to correct any errors later found in published data using standard publication methods.

Source: NASW. 2021b. "NASW Code of Ethics: Ethical Standards—5. Social Workers' Ethical Responsibilities to the Social Work Profession." https://www.socialworkers.org/About /Ethics/Code-of-Ethics/Code-of-Ethics-English/Social-Workers-Ethical-Responsibilities -to-the-Social-Work-Profession.

from state custody. The study collected demographic information and surveyed parenting satisfaction with regard to the adopted child. Working with the state's Department of Children and Families, the professor obtained the names and addresses of people who had adopted a child within a certain time frame. With the university's institutional review board (IRB) approval, he mailed these adoptive parents a letter inviting them to participate in his study, with an opt-out proviso. If they did not want to participate, they could send back an enclosed postcard, and he would remove their names from the list of parents to be surveyed. After some time had passed, he mailed his survey to the parents who did not opt out. A few days later, the phones in the university president's office, the IRB, and the professor's office began ringing with calls from angry parents. It turns out that not all adoptive parents tell their child that they have been adopted. In some cases, older children had opened the survey package and inadvertently learned that they had been adopted. The university was irate, and the IRB shut the project down temporarily and forbade the professor access to data he had already collected. In time, he was allowed to modify his protocol so that surveys were sent only to adoptive parents who *opted in* to participation; that is, they agreed to be sent the survey. This case illustrates that almost any form of research has the potential to cause harm to participants. In this situation, even the a priori ethical oversight and approval from the university's IRB was not enough to foresee the possibility of the problem that arose. More on the role of IRBs later in this chapter.

It should be noted that adherence to the NASW *Code of Ethics* is agreed to when one joins the NASW. Also, some state licensing boards require their LCSWs to follow the NASW *Code of Ethics* regardless of whether they are members of the NASW. And some social work programs require that its enrolled students follow the NASW *Code of Ethics* even if they are not members. Curiously, these programs do not always require their program *faculty* to follow the NASW's ethical guidelines. That is the case in my home college of social work.

The NASW *Code of Ethics* is not the most effective instrument for promoting adherence to high ethical standards within the social work profession. For one thing, most social workers do not belong to the NASW. For another, in the rare event that an ethics complaint is filed with the NASW, the review that follows is intended to be primarily educational and constructive. Actual penalties are imposed only in instances of serious ethical violations (e.g., having had sex with a client, charging excessive fees). Such penalties may involve expulsion from the NASW, the association reporting the ethics finding to the state licensing board (if the individual is licensed) or to the person's employer, or publishing the name of the member who committed the violation. On its website, the NASW publishes such names on a page titled "Sanctions in Force," and when I checked this page in November 2022, it said "No current sanctions as of May 4, 2021." Thus, it appears that the association's list of ethics violators had not been updated for some time. It appears that they do not take this aspect of member services seriously.

Professional social workers sometimes have additional qualifications and join other associations with their own codes of ethics. For example, apart from being a social worker, I am also a psychologist and belong to the American Psychological Association (APA). As a member, I am obliged to adhere to the APA's code of ethics. Box 10.2 lists some of these standards that pertain to research. You can see that some of the issues addressed are similar to those addressed in the NASW *Code of Ethics*, such as informed consent, providing participants the opportunity to withdraw from research participation without penalty, protecting participants from harm, reporting findings accurately, avoiding plagiarism, and making use of IRBs when appropriate.

Apart from my LCSW credential, I also hold a board-certified behavior analyst practice credential, and I am thus voluntarily subject to the Behavior Analyst Certification Board's (BACB's) *Ethics Code for Behavior Analysts*, selections of which are provided in box 10.3. Again, we see familiar themes: obtaining IRB approval prior to data collection, informed consent, confidentiality, ensuring the accuracy of one's findings, and avoiding plagiarism. This code also includes a mandate that one conduct research only after having demonstrated competence in completing prior research studies under supervision. This strict standard is designed to protect participants from harm and is not found in the NASW or APA codes.

Box 10.2 Selections from the American Psychological Association's Ethical Principles of Psychologists and Code of Conduct

Section 8: Research and Publication

8.01 Institutional Approval

When institutional approval is required, psychologists provide accurate information about their research proposals and obtain approval prior to conducting the research.

8.02 Informed Consent to Research

(b) Psychologists conducting intervention research involving the use of experimental treatments clarify to participants at the outset of the research (1) the experimental nature of the treatment; (2) the services that will or will not be available to the control group(s) if appropriate; (3) the means by which assignment to treatment and control groups will be made; (4) available treatment alternatives if an individual does not wish to participate in the research or wishes to withdraw once a study has begun; and (5) compensation for or monetary costs of participating including, if appropriate, whether reimbursement from the participant or a third-party payor will be sought.

8.06 Offering Inducements for Research Participation

(a) Psychologists make reasonable efforts to avoid offering excessive or inappropriate financial or other inducements for research participation.

8.07 Deception in Research

(a) Psychologists do not conduct a study involving deception unless they have determined that the use of deceptive techniques is justified by the study's significant prospective scientific, educational, or applied value and that effective nondeceptive alternative procedures are not feasible.

8.10 Reporting Research Results

(a) Psychologists do not fabricate data.
(b) If psychologists discover significant errors in their published data, they take reasonable steps to correct such errors.

8.11 Plagiarism

Psychologists do not present portions of another's work or data as their own.

8.12 Publication Credit

(a) Psychologists take responsibility and credit, including authorship credit, only for work they have actually performed or to which they have substantially contributed.

8.13 Duplicate Publication of Data

Psychologists do not publish, as original data, data that have been previously published.

8.14 Sharing Research Data for Verification

(a) Psychologists do not withhold the data on which their conclusions are based from other competent professionals.

Source: APA. 2017. "Ethical principles of psychologists and code of conduct." https://www.apa.org /ethics/code.

Box 10.3 Selections from the Behavior Analyst Certification Board's Ethics Code for Behavior Analysts

---

Section 6—Responsibility in Research

6.02 Research Review

Behavior analysts conduct research, whether independent of or in the context of service delivery, only after approval by a formal research review committee.

6.03 Research in Service Delivery

Behavior analysts conducting research in the context of service delivery must arrange research activities such that client services and client welfare are prioritized.

6.04 Informed Consent in Research

Behavior analysts are responsible for obtaining informed consent (and assent when relevant) from potential research participants under the conditions required by the research review committee.

6.05 Confidentiality in Research

Behavior analysts prioritize the confidentiality of their research participants except under conditions where it may not be possible. They make appropriate efforts to prevent accidental or inadvertent sharing of confidential or identifying information while conducting research and in any dissemination activity related to the research (e.g., disguising or removing confidential or identifying information).

6.06 Competence in Conducting Research

Behavior analysts only conduct research independently after they have successfully conducted research under a supervisor in a defined relationship (e.g., thesis, dissertation, mentored research project).

6.07 Conflict of Interest in Research and Publication

When conducting research, behavior analysts identify, disclose, and address conflicts of interest (e.g., personal, financial, organization related, service related).

6.08 Appropriate Credit

Behavior analysts give appropriate credit (e.g., authorship, author-note acknowledgment) to research contributors in all dissemination activities.

6.09 Plagiarism

Behavior analysts do not present portions or elements of another's work or data as their own.

6.10 Documentation and Data Retention in Research

Behavior analysts must be knowledgeable about and comply with all applicable standards (e.g., BACB rules, laws, research review committee requirements) for storing, transporting, retaining, and destroying physical and electronic documentation related to research.

6.11 Accuracy and Use of Data

Behavior analysts do not fabricate data or falsify results in their research, publications, and presentations.

Source: BACB. 2020. *Ethics Code for Behavior Analysts*. Littleton, CO: BACB. https://www.bacb
    .com/wp-content/uploads/2022/01/Ethics-Code-for-Behavior-Analysts-220316-2.pdf.

A fourth organization worth mentioning is the American Evaluation Association (AEA), an interdisciplinary group (unlike the NASW, APA, and BACB) of about six thousand professionals. The AEA consists of subgroups called Topical Interest Groups (TIGs). Although there is one to accommodate almost every evaluation interest (e.g., Feminist Issues in Evaluation, Government Evaluation, Health Evaluation), two are particularly pertinent to social workers: the Human Service Evaluation TIG and the Social Work TIG. The Social Work TIG has several hundred members, and they sponsor a sequence of papers each year at the AEA annual conference. The AEA also has a comprehensive document called *Guiding Principles for Evaluators*, which is similar to a code of ethics, selections of which are provided in box 10.4.

Like the BACB, the AEA emphasizes research competence and admirably includes the importance of cultural competence in research, a recurrent theme in social work (e.g., Farmer and Bess 2010). Also discussed are the importance of honesty in interactions with research participants, accurate data collection and reporting, and reducing participants' risk of harm. Evaluation researchers must also acknowledge real or potential conflicts of interest (e.g., conducting an experimental evaluation of a therapy one invented or receiving financial benefit from conducting an experiment). The AEA also asks evaluators to promote social equity issues in their research, and randomized experiments are positioned to help fulfill this mandate. By conducting experimental evaluations of interventions using sufficient numbers of members of underrepresented groups and demonstrating that interventions benefit them, social work researchers are promoting social equity. This is particularly evident in RCTs intended to evaluate interventions designed to reduce unemployment, promote financial security, enhance educational attainment, reduce disease and housing disparities, racially biased police brutality, and psychosocial problems commonly experienced by underrepresented groups such as domestic violence. Well-crafted RCTs on the impact of Head Start programs for preschoolers from groups with low socioeconomic status exemplify the role researchers can play in reducing disadvantage and inequity (e.g., Feller et al. 2016). And by disseminating this evidence, they help ensure its application in real-world settings. A number of such studies are provided in the appendix. Using research evidence to promote social equity is being given increasing attention among social work researchers.

However, ethical standards and recommended research guidelines have meager enforceability. What other sources of influence does the social work profession have to promote the ethical design and conduct of experimental research? A few are addressed in the next section.

Box 10.4 Selections from the American Evaluation Association Guiding Principles for Evaluators

Principles

A. Systematic Inquiry: Evaluators conduct systematic, data-based inquiries.

1. Evaluators should adhere to the highest technical standards appropriate to the methods they use.
3. Evaluators should communicate their methods and approaches accurately and in sufficient detail to allow others to understand, interpret and critique their work.

B. Competence: Evaluators provide competent performance to stakeholders.

1. Evaluators should possess . . . the education, abilities, skills and experience appropriate to undertake the tasks proposed in the evaluation.
3. Evaluators should practice within the limits of their professional training and competence.

C. Integrity/Honesty: Evaluators display honesty and integrity in their own behavior, and attempt to ensure the honesty and integrity of the entire evaluation process.

1. Evaluators should negotiate honestly with clients and relevant stakeholders concerning the costs, tasks to be undertaken, limitations of methodology, scope of results likely to be obtained, and uses of data resulting from a specific evaluation.
5. Evaluators should not misrepresent their procedures, data or findings.
7. Evaluators should disclose all sources of financial support for an evaluation.

D. Respect for People: Evaluators respect the security, dignity and self-worth of respondents, program participants, clients, and other evaluation stakeholders.

2. Evaluators should abide by current professional ethics, standards, and regulations regarding risks, harms, and burdens that might befall those participating in the evaluation.
5. Where feasible, evaluators should attempt to foster social equity in evaluation, so that those who give to the evaluation may benefit in return.

E. Responsibilities for General and Public Welfare: Evaluators articulate and take into account the diversity of general and public interests and values that may be related to the evaluation.

2. Evaluators should consider not only the immediate operations and outcomes of whatever is being evaluated, but also its broad assumptions, implications and potential side effects.
5. Evaluators have obligations that encompass the public interest and good.

Source: AEA. 2004. *American Evaluation Association Guiding Principles for Evaluators.* Washington, DC: AEA. https://www.eval.org/Portals/0/Docs/gp.principles.pdf?ver =YMYJx_4-pquvpjg6RgNkeQ%3d%3d.

Promoting Ethical Experimental Research Practices

While most BSW, MSW, and doctoral programs provide exposure to the NASW *Code of Ethics*, little attention is paid to the ethics of conducting empirical research and still less to the design and conduct of experimental studies. A small body of useful literature is available on this topic (e.g., Burstrom 1975; Holosko, Thyer, and Danner 2009; Humphreys 2015; Phillips 2021), which could be judiciously integrated into professional curricula. For example, social work PhD and DSW programs could require a discussion of the ethical aspects of the research projects that form the focus of dissertations or capstone projects. Social work faculty and doctoral students could submit proposals to present papers or deliver workshops on the topic of experimental research ethics at the annual meetings of the NASW, the AEA, the Council on Social Work Education, and the Society for Social Work and Research, as well as other relevant groups of stakeholders. Many journals in our field would welcome competently written papers on the unique features of experimental social work research. Such journals include, for example, the *Journal of Social Work Values & Ethics*, *Research on Social Work Practice*, the *Journal of Evidence-Based Social Work*, and the *Child and Adolescent Social Work Journal*. In the interest of disclosing possible conflicts of interest, I acknowledge editing the latter three of these journals.

Research is sometimes published in our journals that reflects unethical practices. Such papers practically cry out for readers to submit a critical commentary or letter to the editor pointing out the ethical flaws and how they could have been avoided. Of course, faculty should be exemplary role models in terms of experimental research ethics.

Do not inappropriately coauthor student-written papers (Thyer 2013). Share authorship with students who make sufficient intellectual contributions to warrant the credit; don't fob them off with a mere footnote. Emphasize the importance of accuracy and reliability in student data collection by asking them to show you their spreadsheets and raw data. Scores on measures completed by participants should align with the data in the spreadsheet; if some do not, another person should recheck all the data. For manual data entry, having two people enter the data independently and then comparing their spreadsheets to check for discrepancies should be a standard practice.

Make sure that students' studies evaluate specific hypotheses and that they report the results for each one, whether supported or not. Urge them to refrain from reporting novel findings that are not clearly linked to specific hypotheses. Urge them to replicate their studies upon graduation to see whether they can replicate their findings. If this is successful, encourage them to prepare *one* paper reporting the *two* studies. Encourage your students to register study protocols with suitable clinical trial registries in advance of data collection, and make sure their final reports align with the essential aspects of the study described in the protocol. Ask them to register their data with a suitable data depository to allow others access to the data and permit reanalysis, extended analysis, and replication efforts by others. Make sure outliers in the data are not inappropriately discarded from students' data analysis and results. Impress upon students that the purpose of experimental research is to determine the effects of a given intervention or whether a particular hypothesis is supported. Intervention research is *not* about attempting to *prove* that an intervention works (or does not), or that a hypothesis is true (or not). By doing research, one is trying to determine nature's truths, not support one's preferences, difficult though this detached stance may be to take. Support studies that provide *robust* tests of interventions. Showing that an experimental treatment is better than no treatment is good. Showing that the experimental treatment is better than a credible placebo treatment or TAU is more difficult and is accordingly a more valuable finding. Showing that a novel treatment is better than TAU in the short run is good, but showing that it is better than TAU in the long run is better. Allowing students to design an experiment with weak or indirect dependent variables is no favor to the profession. Doing so enhances the likelihood of obtaining spurious findings. Encourage students to use stringent or conservative statistical analyses. Using a t-test to see whether posttreatment-only differences between two groups are statistically significant in the context of a pretest–posttest no-treatment control-group study is a weaker method of analysis than a two (groups) by two (assessment times) analysis of variance or analysis of covariance. Interventions that yield statistically significant but weak effects may well be publishable but are of little pragmatic value. Urge students not to prepare separate articles for each outcome measure in a study; it is more ethical to prepare one article for a study and include the results of all outcome measures.

Consider Using a Data Safety and Monitoring Board

In complex RCTs, it is recommended that the principal investigator arrange for the formation of a data safety and monitoring board (DSMB), a small group of patient advocates, statisticians, and clinicians who stay abreast of the ongoing progress of the study, paying specific attention to client safety, outcome data, and adherence to the study protocol (Slutsky and Lavery 2004). The DSMB should be independent of oversight from the principal investigator, the IRB, and other stakeholders on the research team. Its primary function is to stop the trial if significant harms, risks, or side effects become apparent. It also assesses the integrity and validity of the data being gathered. A DSMB is most commonly used in multisite RCTs in which the clinical services and data collection may be difficult for the principal investigator, located at just one site, to keep track of. Studies of long duration may plan on interim data analysis at multiple points throughout the study period. If substantial harms are detected, the study may be halted; but if the data are overwhelmingly favorable, the study may be stopped so that all participants in control arms (e.g., TAU, placebo, no treatment) can be offered the experimental treatment. This situation is more likely to occur in evaluations of suicide prevention programs, life-saving medicines, or vaccines than a trial of a new acne cream or a treatment for nail-biting.

The DSMB reports to the IRB and adheres to strict timelines for reporting deaths or serious adverse side effects. After each interim analysis, the DSMB decides to continue or discontinue the study. Apart from finding significant harms or very powerful positive effects, a study may be stopped if it is simply not progressing well. For example, this might happen if too few participants have been recruited and it is clear that the original protocol cannot be adhered to.

Participant safety is the key remit for DSMBs. DSMBs were first developed in the 1990s and adopted within medical RCTs in fields such as cancer and HIV prevention and treatment, and their use has gradually spread to other fields, such as psychopharmacological trials with youth (Carandang et al. 2007). Chandler et al. (2009) describe the lessons learned from the experiences of a DSMB overseeing a complex multisite RCT in the fields of criminal justice and drug abuse. This study was coauthored by the noted social work clinical researcher Nabila El-Bassel. Lewis, Calis, and DeMets (2016) further describe some lessons learned after years of evaluating the operations of DSMBs with the aim of enhancing their efficacy and independence. Web-based training is now available for prospective or current DSMB members (Zuckerman, van der Schalie, and Cahill 2015), which is valuable given that the uptake of DSMBs is increasing, although they are not yet required. Their increasing involvement with social work RCTs is another step toward enhancing the ethical standards of experimental investigations and minimizing potential harms.

Obtain Institutional Review Board Approval

In the United States, those wishing to undertake research are usually required to submit a protocol application to their host institution's IRB. The federal government requires all entities receiving federal dollars to maintain an interdisciplinary-member IRB consisting of individuals charged with reviewing all research applications originating from their institution. The U.S. Department of Health and Human Services defines "research" as "a systematic investigation, including research development, testing and evaluation, designed to develop or contribute to generalizable knowledge. Activities that meet this definition constitute research for purpose of this policy, whether or not they are conducted or supported under a program that is considered research for other purposes" (Office of Research Integrity n.d.). "Systematic" means that the research study is based on a written plan that is consistent with standard scientific methods and practices. "Generalizable" means an intent to publicly disseminate the findings, for example through journal or book publications or conference presentations. "Generalizable" here *does not* refer to the principle of external validity in a statistical sense. Many investigations do not fall under the definition of "research" used by the Department of Health and Human Services. Examples include the following:

- Those for which the researcher has no plan to publish or otherwise publicly share the findings
- Case reports or a small number of case series
- Educational presentations
- Quality improvement projects
- Projects using publicly available information with no personally identifiable data
- Historical research
- Most forms of journalistic reporting

Investigators should carefully review the guidelines and mandates of their home institution's IRB. These can be complex. Most IRBs require that researchers complete approved training programs in research and ethics, with the Collaborative Institutional Training Initiative (CITI) being the most common program (https://about.citiprogram.org). CITI offers an array of training programs, and IRBs typically require investigators to complete one or more of these and to provide a certificate of completion with their IRB application. IRBs can be helpful in providing things like sample informed consent forms for research with adults, informed assent forms for use with participants who are minors, and flowcharts and decision-tree diagrams to determine whether your project meets the federal definition for research. They can also tell investigators whether their applications will require a brief review, if the study is exempt from the need for IRB approval (see box 10.5), or requires review. (Examples of decision-tree diagrams can be found on the website of your local IRB.)

The policy that governs the protections of people participating in federally funded research, and thus pertains to IRB operations, is called the Revised Common Rule (CFR 2022). The Revised Common Rule defines a clinical trial as "a research study in which one or more human subjects are prospectively assigned to one or more interventions (which may include placebo or other

---

(1) Research, conducted in established or commonly accepted educational settings, that specifically involves normal educational practices that are not likely to adversely impact students' opportunity to learn required educational content or the assessment of educators who provide instruction. This includes most research on regular and special education instructional strategies, and research on the effectiveness of or the comparison among instructional techniques, curricula, or classroom management methods.

(2) Research that only includes interactions involving educational tests (cognitive, diagnostic, aptitude, achievement), survey procedures, interview procedures, or observation of public behavior (including visual or auditory recording) if at least one of the following criteria is met: (i) The information obtained is recorded by the investigator in such a manner that the identity of the human subjects cannot readily be ascertained, directly or through identifiers linked to the subjects; (ii) Any disclosure of the human subjects' responses outside the research would not reasonably place the subjects at risk of criminal or civil liability or be damaging to the subjects' financial standing, employability, educational advancement, or reputation; or (iii) The information obtained is recorded by the investigator in such a manner that the identity of the human subjects can readily be ascertained, directly or through identifiers linked to the subjects, and an IRB conducts a limited IRB review to make the determination required by § 46.111(a)(7).

(3) (i) Research involving benign behavioral interventions in conjunction with the collection of information from an adult subject through verbal or written responses (including data entry) or audiovisual recording if the subject prospectively agrees to the intervention and information collection and at least one of the following criteria is met: (A) The information obtained is recorded by the investigator in such a manner that the identity of the human subjects cannot readily be ascertained, directly or through identifiers linked to the subjects; (B) Any disclosure of the human subjects' responses outside the research would not reasonably place the subjects at risk of criminal or civil liability or be damaging to the subjects' financial standing, employability, educational advancement, or reputation; or (C) The information obtained is recorded by the investigator in such a manner that the identity of the human subjects can readily be ascertained, directly or through identifiers linked to the subjects. (ii) For the purpose of this provision, benign behavioral interventions are brief in duration,

harmless, painless, not physically invasive, not likely to have a significant adverse lasting impact on the subjects, and the investigator has no reason to think the subjects will find the interventions offensive or embarrassing. Provided all such criteria are met, examples of such benign behavioral interventions would include having the subjects play an online game, having them solve puzzles under various noise conditions, or having them decide how to allocate a nominal amount of received cash between themselves and someone else. (iii) If the research involves deceiving the subjects regarding the nature or purposes of the research, this exemption is not applicable unless the subject authorizes the deception through a prospective agreement to participate in research in circumstances in which the subject is informed that he or she will be unaware of or misled regarding the nature or purposes of the research.

(4) Secondary research for which consent is not required: Secondary research uses of identifiable private information or identifiable biospecimens, if at least one of the following criteria is met: (i) The identifiable private information or identifiable biospecimens are publicly available; (ii) Information, which may include information about biospecimens, is recorded by the investigator in such a manner that the identity of the human subjects cannot readily be ascertained directly or through identifiers linked to the subjects, the investigator does not contact the subjects, and the investigator will not re-identify subjects.

Source: CFR. 2022. "Title 45: Public Welfare—Part 46: Protection of Human Subjects." Last amended November 7, 2022. https://www.ecfr.gov/current/title-45/subtitle-A/subchapter-A/part-46 ?toc=1.

control) to evaluate the effects of the interventions on biomedical or behavioral health-related outcomes." Other important definitions are as follows:

Human subject means a living individual about whom an investigator (whether professional or student) conducting research: (i) Obtains information or biospecimens through intervention or interaction with the individual, and uses, studies, or analyzes the information or biospecimens; or (ii) Obtains, uses, studies, analyzes, or generates identifiable private information or identifiable biospecimens.

Intervention includes both physical procedures by which information or biospecimens are gathered (e.g., venipuncture) and manipulations of the subject or the subject's environment that are performed for research purposes.

Interaction includes communication or interpersonal contact between investigator and subject.

Private information includes information about behavior that occurs in a context in which an individual can reasonably expect that no observation or recording is taking place, and information that has been provided for specific purposes by an individual and that the individual can reasonably expect will not be made public (e.g., a medical record).

Identifiable private information is private information for which the identity of the subject is or may readily be ascertained by the investigator or associated with the information.

Research means a systematic investigation, including research development, testing, and evaluation, designed to develop or contribute to generalizable knowledge. Activities that meet this definition constitute research for purposes of this policy, whether or not they are conducted or supported under a program that is considered research for other purposes. For example, some demonstration and service programs may include research activities. For purposes of this part, the following activities are deemed not to be research: scholarly and journalistic activities (e.g., oral history, journalism, biography, literary criticism, legal research, and historical scholarship), including the collection and use of information, which focus directly on the specific individuals about whom the information is collected.

If this all seems overwhelming and confusing, you are right to feel that way because it is overwhelming. Working with an established colleague familiar with the IRB process is one way to become more comfortable with it, as is completing the training programs your IRB mandates. Most IRB staff are prepared to answer your questions, typically by email. The first time you complete an online IRB application is the toughest. The second time a bit less so, and so forth. The use of paper applications has largely been discarded, but your colleagues may be able to provide you with copies of previously approved IRB applications. Reviewing a completed application can take away much of the mystery from the process. And if you make mistakes, the IRB staff will be exceedingly happy to point them out to you and tell you what you need to do.

You do not need to be receiving federal funding yourself to be required to complete an IRB application; you need to complete one if your *institution* receives federal funding. Working on completely unfunded projects or projects funded with private grant money does not exempt you—if your institution receives federal funding, you must submit an IRB application. The consequences of undertaking and publishing research that should have been approved by an IRB can be severe for you, your career, and your institution. At one extreme, an entire university had all its federal funding frozen until IRB issues pertaining to only one program at the university were resolved (Grigsby and Roof 1993).

The best advice is that if you are in doubt as to whether you need to file an IRB application, check with your IRB staff. Do not decide on your own.

If this sort of stuff really interests you, consider volunteering to be a member of your institution's IRB. The experience will provide you with all the exposure and inside information you could possibly want on the topic, and you would be performing a valuable service to your institution and colleagues. And you might be able to negotiate some course release time or other reward for IRB service. Social workers sometimes not only serve on their university IRB but also chair the committee. Heaven has a special place for such saints.

Confrontation and Whistleblowing

The NASW *Code of Ethics* has this to say about the unethical conduct of colleagues (NASW 2021a):

2.10 Unethical Conduct of Colleagues

(a) Social workers should take adequate measures to discourage, prevent, expose, and correct the unethical conduct of colleagues, including unethical conduct using technology.

(b) Social workers should be knowledgeable about established policies and procedures for handling concerns about colleagues' unethical behavior. Social workers should be familiar with national, state, and local procedures for handling ethics complaints. These include policies and procedures created by NASW, licensing and regulatory bodies, employers, agencies, and other professional organizations.

(c) Social workers who believe that a colleague has acted unethically should seek resolution by discussing their concerns with the colleague when feasible and when such discussion is likely to be productive.

(d) When necessary, social workers who believe that a colleague has acted unethically should take action through appropriate formal channels (such as contacting a state licensing board or regulatory body, the NASW National Ethics Committee, or other professional ethics committees).

(e) Social workers should defend and assist colleagues who are unjustly charged with unethical conduct.

There is ample scope here for you to take action when you become aware of a social work colleague who is acting or has acted unethically with respect to the design, conduct, or reporting of an experimental study. First, it is obvious that taking such action is something we *should* do. It is not something that would be nice if we did; we are forthrightly told that we should do it. If your colleague is a member of the NASW, they are expected to abide by its code of ethics. After learning as much as possible about the situation, as well as the process the NASW asks us to follow, the first step is usually to meet individually with your colleague (let's call her Dr. Gauner) to discuss your concerns. Perhaps you misunderstand the situation or are acting on false or distorted information or rumor. Give your colleague the opportunity to correct your understanding if that is the case; for example, "I heard that you published an experimental study written by your doctoral student, Ms. Opfer, claiming that you were the sole author. I find it difficult to believe this, so I wanted to ask you about it in private." Let Gauner respond. Perhaps what you heard is incorrect. But if it is true, explain that you are acting in accordance with the NASW *Code of Ethics* by bringing your concern to her first, and you hope that she can come up with a way to resolve the problem. See what she suggests. Perhaps she could contact the publisher and ask them to correct the authorship of the article if it has not yet been published. If it has, Gauner could ask the journal to publish a correction. Once the correction is published, Ms. Opfer would be able to add the publication to her curriculum vitae (CV) and take legitimate credit for it.

This action may resolve that instance of research misconduct but provides no assurance that future offenses will not occur. If Dr. Gauner refuses to acknowledge wrongdoing and you have good reason to believe she acted unethically, tell her that you will be bringing the matter to the attention of an appropriate superior (e.g., departmental chair, dean, agency director), and then do so. You may be called upon to make a statement or provide evidence, such as emails to you from the aggrieved Ms. Opfer or draft manuscripts authored by Opfer. Let the internal mechanisms of your institution deal with the situation. If you find the process unsatisfactory, you can file a complaint with the NASW itself if Gauner is a member or with the state licensing board if she is licensed. These are all difficult things to undertake, but if you do not do so, who will? How many others may be taken advantage of by the Dr. Gauners of the world if no action is taken?

Similar steps can be taken in the case of a colleague suspected of committing plagiarism, data falsification, or even outright fabrication. Studies sometimes get published in reputable journals based on false data that were never collected. Some superstars in various medical, behavioral, and social sciences have built their careers on false studies and the exploitation of others (Crocker 2011). This hurts the reputation of science and injures both the profession and the institution with which the violator is affiliated. For a few egregious examples, Google the names Diederik Stapel (fraud in social psychology), Andrew Wakefield (fraud in autism research), Cyril Burt (fraud in intelligence research), and Stephen Breuning (fraud in drug testing). Lest you think that my recommending whistleblowing as one approach to deal with research misconduct is an extreme position, I refer you to Gibelman and Gelman (2001, 2005) who make a similar case, also citing our obligation to take action when we become aware of a colleague's unethical behavior according to the NASW *Code of Ethics*. The case for whistleblowing is made even stronger, in my opinion, when it occurs in experimental research on social work interventions because such interventions have the potential to harm clients. This step is not one to be taken lightly, however. Allegations of scientific misconduct can derail a person's career and reputation, and the possibility of retribution against the whistleblower by the perpetrator or their friends cannot be ignored.

Publish a Rebuttal

If you notice that a published paper is very similar to an earlier published work, either authored by the same author (self-plagiarism) or by someone else (plagiarism), you can use plagiarism detection software to empirically test the degree of overlap. If warranted, bring this finding to the attention of the journal's editor. No good editor wishes to publish an experimental study that is substantially similar to a work published earlier. That is why submitting authors need to attest that their manuscript has not been previously published and presents original data. If such a claim is made but later found to be false, the consequences can be dire for the offending author.

If you find serious problems in a newly published social work experiment, and the author refuses to engage you in a discussion of the possible problems, if you have the intestinal fortitude, you can choose to submit a letter to the editor or critical commentary to the journal in question. For example, you may note that a published RCT deviated substantially from its previously approved and published protocol. You can call attention to these discrepancies. You can ask why, for example, the protocol specified that the authors would use five outcome measures but the final report included only two, both coincidently supportive of the study's hypotheses. Perhaps there was good reason to leave out the other three outcomes, but the authors' failure to provide you with a convincing explanation in private should elevate your concern that they are engaging in selective reporting, presenting only positive results, not those that failed to support their hypotheses. Such an action is scientific misconduct and a violation of research ethics.

Retraction Watch

Retraction Watch is a service supported by the aptly named Center for Scientific Integrity, a nonprofit organization that attempts to enhance the reproducibility and openness of scientific research. Retraction is a step (rarely) undertaken by authors or journals when it becomes evident that a published paper had such serious flaws as to render its conclusions untenable, featured deliberate plagiarism or data falsification, or described a study that was made up entirely. Having a paper retracted by a journal has been likened to Winston Smith's use of the desktop incinerator to destroy original documents or rewrite history in George Orwell's dystopian novel *Nineteen Eighty-Four*. A retracted paper should not be cited. The publisher will remove the article from its online archives and publish a retraction notice with an explanation for its decision.

In more benign situations, an author may only belatedly become aware of serious problems in their published paper, such as a student or colleague falsifying quantitative data without the author's knowledge. When the author becomes aware of the problem and judges it to be of sufficient importance, they can request that the paper be retracted by the publisher.

Sometimes errors in published research appear to have been honest mistakes, and it is to an author's credit when they request a retraction and later submit a corrected revision of their work. Less creditable is when authors were dishonest from the beginning.

The infamous article by the physician Andrew Wakefield and colleagues (1998) claimed that a common early childhood vaccination caused autism. This report, based on twelve children and published in one of the world's leading medical journals, led to a sharp downturn in vaccinations among children and a subsequent increase in illnesses that vaccines can prevent, such as measles, mumps, and rubella. Childhood deaths from these illnesses also increased. Thanks to a whistleblowing investigative journalist, serious problems with the study came to light, both methodologically and in terms of undeclared financial conflicts of interest on the part of Wakefield, and the article was retracted by the journal. Why was it retracted? According to Stephen Barrett (2010), "The full retraction came five days after the British General Medical Council (GMC), which registers doctors in the United Kingdom, reported that Wakefield had acted dishonestly, irresponsibly, unethically, and callously in connection with the research project and its subsequent publication." Wakefield lost his medical license to practice and relocated to the United States, his legitimate career as a practicing physician and clinical researcher in ruins, but he continues to stoke pseudoscientific antivaccination theories.

An involuntary retraction of a paper, such as that experienced by Wakefield, is a truly damning indictment, and any social worker who is publicly outed as having committed scientific fraud or other unethical practices in this manner similarly risks professional ruin. Akin to the whistleblower process described earlier, if you become aware of serious ethical improprieties in published social work experiments, contacting Retraction Watch is a viable option, one much more likely to result in an appropriate response than filing a complaint with the impotent NASW ethics office. Remember, our professional code of ethics requires us to take action regardless of whether the issue is plagiarism, unwarranted authorship, excluding deserving collaborators from authorship, falsifying data, or publishing an article describing a fictitious study as if it really occurred. Retraction Watch serves as a repository for the retractions scattered across the literature and provides a searchable database of these. Thankfully, a search of "social work" finds only a few retractions.

In one instance, the social work professor and child welfare expert Richard Barth read a report on child mistreatment published by the prestigious RAND Corporation global policy think tank. Barth and his colleagues determined that the statistical modeling used in the report seriously underestimated the extent of child mistreatment in the United States (Drake et al. 2018). The RAND study authors reran their analysis and found out that Barth and his colleagues were correct. They retracted their paper and promised to republish it once their reanalysis was completed. This was done and is a good example of how science is supposed to work in a self-correcting manner and how ethical social work scientists such as Barth can take proactive steps to correct mistaken research findings published by others (https://retractionwatch.com/2017/12/22/rand-re-releases-withdrawn-report-modelling-child-mistreatment/).

Another social work example found on Retraction Watch was a paper wherein a professor took an MSW student's paper, revised it, and submitted it for publication in a social work journal as a coauthored paper, all without the student's knowledge. When she found out about this intellectual theft years later, she notified the journal, and the article was retracted (https://retractionwatch.com/?s=%22social+work%22).

The *Journal of Anxiety Disorders* also reported a retraction instigated by the authors of an article, one of whom was a social work faculty member, who found mistakes in their data analysis. They properly notified the journal, the article was retracted, and the authors planned to reanalyze their data and submit a revised article (Daundasekara et al. 2021). This, too, is an example of the self-correcting feature of science.

What *you* can do and should do if you become aware of an instance of scientific misconduct in a study, regardless of whether you are a practitioner, a social work student, or a faculty member, is document the incident and contact the journal's editor. Although it's hard to imagine, misconduct does occur. The study by Cha, Wirth, and Lobo (2001) describes a remarkable international experiment in which women attempting to become pregnant through in vitro fertilization (which has a low success rate) were randomly assigned to receive services from a prayer group or not receive such services (a no-treatment condition). The authors of this study reported that the rate of successful implantation increased by 100 percent among those in the prayer group compared with the no-treatment group. They also reported that the women being prayed for did not know they were being prayed for. This apparently miraculous study was published in a high-quality journal but raised eyebrows throughout the scientific community, even though one of the authors was the chair of reproductive medicine at Columbia University. Ultimately it was determined that there was no evidence that the study had even taken place. No records of university IRB approval, no data, no patient records, no confirmation from the hospitals where the study was said to have taken place. Nothing! The audacity of these authors is truly breathtaking. But again, this example illustrates that science can be self-correcting.

Blowing the whistle on a colleague, particularly if they are a senior and well-established social work experimental researcher, can be a difficult task to undertake. But, as noted, our code of ethics demands it of us, and if we fail to report instances of scientific misconduct and researchers get away with their unethical behavior, they may repeat such transgressions, surreptitiously eroding the confidence we have and the value we accord science as a means to advance the social work profession.

Advanced Ethical Guidelines for the Conduct of Experiments

In the evolution of professional codes of ethics, history has witnessed the gradual expansion and specialization of such guidelines. The one-page NASW *Code of Ethics* of 1960 has become much more extensive (NASW 1965, 1027). Ethical guidelines for research are also slowly being developed. One earlier admirable standard, the *Berlin Code of Ethics* (also known as the *Prussian Code*) was created in 1900 and in effect until 1930. Its creation was stimulated by unethical research undertaken in Germany involving deliberately infecting female sex workers with syphilis to determine the natural course of the illness. The *Berlin Code* states that "all medical interventions for other than diagnostic, healing and immunization purposes, regardless of other legal or moral authorization are excluded under all circumstances if (1) the human subject is a minor or not competent due to other reasons; (2) the human subject has not given his unambiguous consent; (3) the consent is not preceded by a proper explanation of the possible negative consequences of the intervention" (AHRP 2022).

This sounds . . . sound, right? In 1931, the German government replaced the *Berlin Code* with *Directives for New Therapies and Experiments in Humans*. This document stated that "it was forbidden to experiment on patients who were dying, poor or socially disadvantaged. It also stated the proportionality of risk and benefit must be respected and that experiments should first be done on animals" (Sierra 2011, 396). This too sounds sound, right? It was, but these noble guidelines began to be derailed in 1933 when Hitler assumed power and newer guidelines were issued, ones that removed many protections and indeed were used to justify cruel and inhuman practices and experiments. For example, things took an ethical downturn when German "hospitals" were created for the chronically mentally ill, those with severe disabilities, the intellectually disabled, and people with alcoholism, among others, in which practices such as deliberately providing poor diets were instituted, resulting in high mortality when diseases such as influenza swept the wards. Later, the practice of proactive euthanasia was instituted in the name of "racial health." Such civilian-based initiatives in the 1930s led to the medical horrors of the concentration camps.

The public disclosure of the atrocities committed by German medical doctors in the war crimes trials after World War II led to the establishment in 1947 of the *Nuremberg Code*, which reestablished discarded standards and created new ones governing experimental research on human beings (see Lifton 2017; Mitscherlich and Mielke 1949). Among these were the following:

- Voluntary informed consent was reestablished.
- An experiment should be expected to produce beneficial results sufficient to justify the study.
- Unnecessary injury and suffering should be minimized.
- Risks should be proportionate to benefits.
- Researchers should be scientifically qualified.
- Preparations should be made to terminate the experiment if unforeseen risk of injury or death becomes evident.

Again, these principles sound good, right? Well, sadly, the *Nuremberg Code* proved insufficient to ensure ethical research practices, and since its publication, unethical experimental research continued to be conducted and published, including many studies by American researchers.

Thus, in 1974, the U.S. government published the *Belmont Report*, a more expansive set of ethical principles intended to govern the design and conduct of research on human beings (NCPHS 1979). Among its fundamental principles are respect for persons, beneficence, and justice, each of which was elaborated upon. Specific guidelines are provided pertaining to the need for informed consent based on participants' truly understanding the purpose of a study, the voluntary nature of participating in a research study, an assessment of risks and benefits of participating in a given project, the just selection of potential participants, and the need for special protections for vulnerable populations being recruited for research. Interestingly, the final paragraph of the venerable *Belmont Report* says this: "Because the problems related to social experimentation may differ substantially from those of biomedical and behavioral research, the Commission specifically declines to make any policy determination regarding such research at this time. Rather, the Commission believes that the problem ought to be addressed by one of its successor bodies."

To my knowledge no such successor bodies have tackled the issue of developing research guidelines specific to social experiments, which of course social workers frequently undertake. It is time for such an interdisciplinary initiative. Existing guidelines for research such as the APA's Journal Article Reporting Standards and the EQUATOR Network's CONSORT-SPI checklist and associated standards focus on the niceties of doing high-quality *research*, with little attention given to the ethical principles specific to experimental studies. Indeed, the term "informed consent" does not even appear in the APA manual's index (APA 2020, see 415). It goes without saying that for an experimental investigation to be ethical, it must have sufficient scientific rigor, but high-quality scientific rigor does not always mean that a study is ethical (Trace and Kolstoe 2018).

Although greater attention is being paid to the topics addressed in the NASW *Code of Ethics* and related guidelines, it is usually of a generic nature (e.g., Clark 2009; Ferguson and Clark 2018). There are a number of discussions of the ethics of conducting certain types of social work research, such as the design and conduct of qualitative social work research (Peled and Leichtentritt 2002), research with participants who identify as lesbian, gay, or bisexual (Tufford et al. 2012), and the comparative study of social work ethical codes across countries (Gallagher et al. 2016). But again, a focus on ethical guidance for conducting experimental studies is generally lacking.

Discussions of ethical practices specific to conducting experimental research and intervention studies are rare (see Holosko, Thyer, and Danner 2009). Other examples include discussions of ethical issues related to conducting online experiments (Benbunan-Fich 2017) and the ethical implications of clinical trials in low- and middle-income countries (Bittker 2021). The American Evaluation Association has offered webinars with titles such as "Exploring Feminist Monitoring, Evaluation and Learning in Practice," "How to Collect LGBTQ Inclusive Data," and "Evaluate with Pride: Culturally Responsive Learning Strategies for LGBT+ Evaluation," but these were focused more on methods than discussions of experimental research ethics (AEA n.d.). An excellent video titled "Emerging Ethics Challenges for Experimental Social Science: Exploring Ethics" is available on YouTube (UCTV 2019). It addresses experimental ethics in general but not specifically related to randomized experimental evaluations of interventions.

Experimental investigations of psychosocial or medical interventions possess unique features that other forms of experimental research such as surveys and vignette studies typically lack. Risks and benefits are usually a greater consideration, as are the protection of human rights, the use of deception or placebo treatments, the ability of participants to provide truly informed consent, cultural differences, avoiding inappropriately influencing or incentivizing vulnerable people, and conflicts of interest. All these issues require greater attention in our professional literature. Bloom and Orme (1993) are two social workers who have provided some ethical principles for conducting evaluations of practice, but their focus was single-subject research designs, not group-based randomized experiments. Cox et al. (2022) recently published an entire book on the topic of the ethics of conducting experimental single-case studies. Something similar, even if incomplete or imperfect, focused on experimental evaluations using large groups of participants, would be a good start to help fill this gap in our professional ethical guidelines.

Summary

The topic of ethical principles specific to the design and conduct of social work experiments is underdeveloped. Our existing social work code of ethics focuses on practice situations and provides only generic guidelines with regard to undertaking research. It says nothing about the special considerations that go into the conduct and reporting of experimental investigations. Despite this lack, there are various extradisciplinary ways to promote ethical practices. Some other disciplines have developed such guidelines that can be consulted, and the special protections afforded by establishing a data safety and monitoring board can be valuable. Institutional review boards provide extra scrutiny to experimental proposals, especially if studies involve recruiting members of vulnerable and protected populations. Individual social workers can be whistleblowers if they become aware of unethical experimental practices, and external entities such as state licensing boards, the NASW Office of Ethics and Professional Review, and Retraction Watch can be used to investigate, report, and halt the conduct of unsafe studies. There is a need for the profession of social work to expand upon existing ethical research standards to take into account the unique features of experimental studies.

REFERENCES

Chapter 1

Angell, R. C. 1954. "A Research Basis for Welfare Practice." *Social Work Journal* 35, no. 4: 145–48, 169–171.

APA (American Psychological Association). 2012. "Our Members." https://www.apa.org/about/apa.

——. 2013. "Your Career." https://www.apa.org/action/careers/facts.

——. 2020. "Definition of Psychology." Last modified January 2022. https://www.apa.org/about.

APNA (American Psychiatric Nurses Association). 2022. "About Psychiatric-Mental Health Nursing." https://www.apna.org/m/pages.cfm?pageID=3292#1.

Austin, D. M. 1998. *A Report on Progress in the Development of Research Resources in Social Work*. University of Texas at Austin.

Barker, R. L., ed. 2014. *The Social Work Dictionary*, 6th ed. NASW.

Bhuga, D. 2016. "Social Discrimination and Social Justice." *International Review of Psychiatry* 28, no. 4: 336–41.

Blenkner, M., M. Bloom, and M. Nielsen. 1971. "A Research and Demonstration Project of Protective Services." *Social Casework* 52, no. 8: 483–99.

Bonell, C., A. Fletcher, M. Morton, T. Lorene, and L. Moore. 2012. "Realist Randomised Controlled Trials: A New Approach to Evaluating Complex Public Health Interventions." *Social Science and Medicine* 75, no. 12: 2299–306.

Brandell, J. R., ed. 2021. *Theory and Practice in Clinical Social Work*, 3rd ed. Cognella.

Brennen, W. C. 1973. "The Practitioner as Theoretician." *Journal of Education for Social Work* 9: 5–12.

Brewer, C., and J. Lait. 1980. *Can Social Work Survive?* Temple Smith.

Burns, B. H. 1966. "Causation in Mental Illness: A Developmental Approach." *British Journal of Psychiatric Social Work* 8, no. 4: 28–32.

Cabot, R. C. 1931. "Treatment in Social Case Work and the Need of Criteria and Tests of Its Success or Failure." *Proceedings of the National Conference of Social Work*, 435–53. Columbia University Press.

Chan, C., and M. Holosko. 2016. "An Overview of the Use of Mechanical Turk in Behavioral Sciences: Implications for Social Work." *Research on Social Work Practice* 26, no. 4: 441–48.

——. 1957. "Researchers Disagree." *Social Work* 2, no. 1: 119.

Cockerill, E. E., L. J. Lehrman, P. Sacks, and I. Stamm. 1952. *A Conceptual Framework for Social Casework*. University of Pittsburgh Press.

Cotton, H. A. 1922. "The Etiology and Treatment of the So-Called Functional Psychoses. Summary of Results Based Upon the Experience of Four Years." *American Journal of Psychiatry* 79, no. 2: 157–210.

Coyle, G. L. 1958. *Social Science in the Professional Education of Social Workers*. CSWE.

CSWE (Council on Social Work Education). 2021. *Annual Report: 2020–2021*. CSWE. https://www.cswe.org/CSWE/media/CSWEAnnualReports/CSWE_2020-2021_AnnualReport.pdf.

Dawes, R. M. 1994. *House of Cards: Psychology and Psychotherapy Built on Myth*. Free Press.

Dixon, J., N. Biehal, J. Green, I. Sinclair, C. Kay, and E. Parry. 2014. "Trials and Tribulations: Challenges and Prospects for Randomised Controlled Trials of Social Work with Children." *British Journal of Social Work* 44, no. 6: 1563–81.

Eaton, J. W. 1956. "Whence and Whither Social Work: A Sociological Analysis." *Social Work* 1, no. 1: 11–26.

Ell, K. 1996. "Social Work Research and Health Care Practice and Policy: A Psychosocial Research Agenda." *Social Work* 41, no. 6: 583–92.

Fals-Stewart, W., and G. R. Birchler. 2000. "Behavioral Couples Therapy with Alcoholic Men and Their Intimate Partners: The Comparative Effectiveness of Bachelor's- and Master's-Level Counselors." *Behavior Therapy* 33, no. 1: 123–47.

Festinger, L. 1957. *A Theory of Cognitive Dissonance*. Row Peterson.

Fischer, J. 1973. "Is Casework Effective? A Review." *Social Work* 18, no. 1: 5–20.

——. 1976. "The End of Social Casework or the Beginning?" In *The Effectiveness of Social Casework*, edited by J. Fischer, 311–42. Charles C. Thomas.

Flexner, A. ([1915] 2000). "Is Social Work a Profession?" *Research on Social Work Practice* 11, no. 2: 152–65. It originally appeared in "National Conference on Charities and Corrections." 1915. *Proceedings of the National Conference of Charities and Corrections* at the Forty-Second Annual Session, Baltimore, MD, May 12–19.

Florida Legislature. 2022a. "Title XXII: Regulation of Professions and Occupations, chapter 490, Psychological Services." http://www.leg.state.fl.us/statutes/index.cfm?App_mode=Display_Statute&Search_String=&URL=0400-0499/0490/Sections/0490.003.html.

——. 2022b. "Title XXII: Regulation of Professions and Occupations, chapter 491, Clinical, Counseling, and Psychotherapy Services, paragraph 8." http://www.leg.state.fl.us/statutes/index.cfm?App_mode=Display_Statute&Search_String=&URL=0400-0499/0491/Sections/0491.003.html.

Gartlehner, G., R. A. Hansen, D. Nissman, K. N. Lohr, and T. S. Carey. 2006. *Criteria for Distinguishing Effectiveness from Efficacy Trials in Systematic Reviews*. AHRQ Publication No. 06-00-46. Research Triangle Park: RTI International, University of North Carolina Evidence-Based Practice Center.

Gelles, R. 1996. *The Book of David: How Family Preservation Services Can Cost Children's Lives*. Basic Books.

Gerber, A. S., and D. P. Green. 2012. *Field Experiments: Design, Analysis, and Interpretation*. Norton.

Gibbs, A. 2001. "The Changing Nature and Context of Social Work Research." *British Journal of Social Work* 31, no. 5: 687–704.

Glueck, S., and E. Glueck. 1930. *Five Hundred Criminal Careers*. Knopf.

Greenwood, E. 1957. "Social Work Research: A Decade of Reappraisal." *Social Service Review* 31, no. 3: 311–20.

Griesinger, W. 1867. *Mental Pathology and Therapeutics*, translated by C. L. Robinson and J. Rutherford. New Sydenham Society.

Grunebaum, H. 1986. "Harmful Psychotherapy Experience." *American Journal of Psychotherapy* 40, no. 2: 165–76.

Hartman, A. 1971. "But What Is Social Casework?" *Families in Society* 52, no. 7: 411–19.

Heineman, M. 1981. "The Obsolete Scientific Imperative in Social Work Research." *Social Service Review* 55, no. 3: 371–97.

Henning, S. 2018. "Psychiatric Social Work Training: Justifying a Profession." *Practice: Social Work in Action* 30, no. 4: 239–56.

Hewes, A. 1930. *The Contributions of Economics to Social Work*. Columbia University Press.

Holden, G., and K. Barker. 2018. "Should Social Workers Be Engaged in These Practices?" *Journal of Evidence-Based Social Work* 15, no. 1: 1–13.

Holland, M. L., S. Groth, J. A. Smith, Y. Meng, and H. Kitzman. 2018. "Low Birthweight in Second Children After Nurse Home Visiting." *Journal of Perinatology* 38, no. 12: 610–19.

Hollis, E. V., and A. L. Taylor. 1951. *Social Work Education in the United States: The Report of a Study Made for the National Council on Social Work Education*. Columbia University Press.

Holosko, M. J., W. A. Hamby, and J. A. Pettus. 2013. "Social Work Research Designs: Let's Stop Apologizing!" Paper presented at the annual convention of the Campbell Collaboration, Chicago, IL, 2013.

Hull-House, Residents of. 1895. *Hull-House Maps and Papers: A Presentation of Nationalities and Wages in a Congested District of Chicago, Together with Comments and Essays on Problems Growing Out of the Social Conditions*. T. Y. Crowell.

Jaggers, J. W., and A. M. Loomis. 2020. "Research at Work: Sampling, Central Tendency, and Causation." *Families in Society* 101, no. 4: 539–46.

Jansen, J. I. 1972. "The Death of a Profession." *British Journal of Psychiatry* 120: 647–49.

Johnson, C. V., H. L. Friedman, J. Diaz, Z. Franco, and B. K. Nastasi, eds. 2014. *The Praeger Handbook of Social Justice and Psychology*. Praeger.

Johnstone, L. 1989. *Users and Abusers of Psychiatry: A Critical Look at Traditional Psychiatric Practice*. Routledge.

Karger, H. J. 1983. "Science, Research, and Social Work: Who Controls the Profession?" *Social Work* 28, no. 3: 200–205.

Kennedy, R., and J. R. Kennedy. 1942. "Sociology in American Colleges." *American Sociological Review* 7, no. 5: 661–75.

Kerlinger, F. N. 1973. *Foundations of Behavioral Research*, 2nd ed. Holt, Rinehart & Winston.

Kolevzon, M. S. 1977. "Negative Findings Revisited: Implications for Social Work Practice and Education." *Clinical Social Work Journal* 5: 210–18.

Lilienfeld, S. O. 2007. "Psychological Treatments That Cause Harm." *Perspectives on Psychological Science* 2, no. 1: 53–70.

Lilienfeld, S. O., L. A. Ritschel, S. J. Lynn, R. L. Cautin, and R. D. Latzman. 2014. "Why Ineffective Psychotherapies Appear to Work: A Taxonomy of Causes of Spurious Therapeutic Effectiveness." *Perspectives on Psychological Science* 9, no. 4: 355–87.

Lorand, S., and M. Balint, eds. 1956. *Perversions, Psychodynamics and Therapy*. Random House.

Lowery, L. G. 1949. *Psychiatry for Social Workers*. Columbia University Press.

Lymbery, M. (2019). "The Slow Death of Social Work with Older People." In *What Is the Future of Social Work?*, edited by M. Lavalette, 39–56. Policy.

MacDonald, M. E. 1957. "Research in Social Work." In *Social Work Year Book, 1957*, 13th issue, edited by Russell H. Kurtz, 489–500. NASW.

——. 1966. "Reunion at Vocational High: An Analysis of 'Girls at Vocational High: An Experiment in Social Work Intervention.'" *Social Service Review* 40, no. 2: 175–89.

Marx, D. M., S. J. Ko, and R. A. Friedman. 2009. "The 'Obama Effect': How a Salient Role Model Reduced Race-Based Performance Differences." *Journal of Experimental Social Psychology* 45, no. 4: 953–56.

Mercer, J., L. Sarner, and L. Rosa. 2003. *Attachment Therapy on Trial: The Torture and Death of Candace Newmaker*. Praeger.

Meyer, H. J., E. F. Borgatta, and W. C. Jones. 1965. *Girls at Vocational High: An Experiment in Social Work Intervention*. Russell Sage Foundation.

Miller, R. R. 1960. "Statistical Analysis of Data." In *Social Work Research*, edited by N. Polansky, 167–86. University of Chicago Press.

Montgomery, E. C., M. E. Kunik, N. Wilson, M. A. Stanley, and B. Weiss. 2010. "Can Paraprofessionals Deliver Cognitive-Behavioral Therapy to Treat Anxiety and Depressive Symptoms?" *Bulletin of the Menninger Clinic* 74, no. 1: 45–61.

Mor Barak, M. E., and J. S. Brekke. 2014. "Social Work Science and Identity Formation for Doctoral Scholars within Intellectual Communities." *Research on Social Work Practice* 24, no. 5: 616–24.

Mullen, E. 1995. "A Review of Research Utilization in the Social Services." *Social Work* 40: 282–83.

NASW (National Association of Social Workers). 2015. *Sexual Orientation Change Efforts (SOCE) and Conversion Therapy with Lesbians, Gay Men, Bisexuals and Transgender Persons*. NASW.

——. 2017. "Read the Code of Ethics." NASW. https://www.socialworkers.org/About/Ethics/Code-of-Ethics/Code-of-Ethics-English.

Olds, D. L., H. Kitzman, M. D. Knudtson, E. Anson, J. A. Smith, and R. Cole. 2014. "Effect of Home Visiting by Nurses on Maternal and Child Mortality. Results of a 2-Decade Follow-Up of a Randomized Clinical Trial." *Archives of Pediatrics and Adolescent Medicine* 166, no. 9: 800.

Pearson, G. S. 2012. "The Concept of Social Justice for Our Psychiatric Nursing Practice." *Perspectives in Psychiatric Care* 48, no. 4: 185–86.

Petersen, A., and J. I. Olsson. 2015. "Calling Evidence-Based Practice into Question: Acknowledging Phronetic Knowledge in Social Work." *British Journal of Social Work* 45, no. 5: 1581–97.

Pratt, A. B. 1921. "The Relation of the Teacher and the Social Worker." *Annals of the American Academy of Political and Social Science* 98, no. 1: 90–96.

Rosen, A., E. K. Proctor, and M. M. Staudt. 1999. "Social Work Research and the Quest for Effective Practice." *Social Work Research* 23, no. 1: 4–14.

Rosenberg, M. L., and R. Brody. 1974. "The Threat or Challenge of Accountability." *Social Work* 19, no. 3: 344–50.

Ross, C. A., and A. Pam. 1995. *Pseudoscience in Biological Psychiatry: Blaming the Body*. Wiley.

Rubin, A., and D. E. Parrish. 2012. "Comparing Social Worker and Non-social Worker Outcomes: A Research Review." *Social Work* 57, no. 4: 309–20.

Rushton, A., and E. Monck. 2009. *Enhancing Adoptive Parenting: A Test of Effectiveness*. British Association for Adoption and Fostering.

Saari, C. 1994. "An Exploration of Meaning and Causation in Clinical Social Work." *Clinical Social Work Journal* 22, no. 3: 251–61.

Salander, P. 2011. "It's Futile to Believe that RCT Studies Will Steer Us to Godot." *Psycho-Oncology* 20, no. 3: 333–34.

Saleebey, D. 1979. "The Tension Between Research and Practice: Assumptions of the Experimental Paradigm." *Clinical Social Work Journal* 7: 267–84.

Saunders, B. N. 1986. Introduction to *Studies of Research on Social Work Practice: A Bibliography*, edited by L. Videka-Sherman, 1–3. NASW.

Segal, S. P. 1972. "Research on the Outcome of Social Work Therapeutic Interventions: A Review of the Literature." *Journal of Health and Social Behavior* 13, no. 1: 3–17.

Seligman, M. E. 1995. "The Effectiveness of Psychotherapy: The Consumer Reports Study." *American Psychologist* 50, no. 12: 965–74.

Sheldon, B. 1984. "Evaluation with One Eye Closed: The Empiricist Agenda in Social Work Research: A Reply." *British Journal of Social Work* 45, no. 5: 1581–97.

Singal, A. G., P. D. R. Higgins, and A. K. Waljee. 2014. "A Primer on Effectiveness and Efficacy Trials." *Clinical and Translational Gastroenterology* 5, no. 1: e45.

Sobell, L. C., M. B. Sobell, and W. C. Christelman. 1972. "The Myth of One Drink." *Behaviour Research and Therapy* 10, no. 2: 119–23.

Specht, H., and M. Courtney. 1994. *Unfaithful Angels: How Social Work Has Abandoned Its Mission*. Free Press.

Staff. 1949. "A Review of *Social Work as Human Relations: The Family in a Democratic Society*." *Journal of Consulting and Clinical Psychology* 13, no. 5: 384–85.

Stein, D. M., and M. J. Lambert. 1995. "Graduate Training in Psychotherapy: Are Therapy Outcomes Enhanced?" *Journal of Consulting and Clinical Psychology* 63, no. 2: 182–96.

Strupp, H. H., and S. W. Hadley. 1979. "Specific vs. Nonspecific Factors in Psychotherapy: A Controlled Study of Outcome." *Archives of General Psychiatry* 36, no. 10: 1125–36.

Stuart, R. B. 1970. *Treat or Treatment: How and When Psychotherapy Fails*. Research Press.

SWRG (Social Work Research Group). 1955. *The Function and Practice of Research in Social Work (Unpublished Reports, 1951, 1952, 1953)*. NASW.

Theis, S. V. S. 1924. *How Foster Children Turn Out*. State Charities Aid Association.

Thiery, M. 1998. "Battey's Operation: An Exercise in Surgical Frustration." *European Journal of Obstetrics, Gynecology, and Reproductive Biology* 81, no. 2: 243–46.

Thomas, E. J. 1960. "Field Experiments and Demonstrations." In *Social Work Research*, edited by N. A. Polansky, 273–97. University of Chicago Press.

Thyer, B. A. 2002. "Developing Discipline-Specific Knowledge for Social Work: Is It Possible?" *Journal of Social Work Education* 38, no. 1: 101–13.

——. 2012. *Quasi-experimental Research Designs*. Oxford University Press.

——. 2013. "Unwarranted Social Work Authorships: A Partial Solution Is at Hand." *Social Work Research* 37, no. 1: 14–15.

——. 2015. "A Bibliography of Randomized Controlled Experiments in Social Work (1949–2013): *Solvitur Ambulando*." *Research on Social Work Practice* 25, no. 7: 753–93.

——. 2017. "It Is Time to Delink Psychodynamic Theory from the Definition of Clinical Social Work." *Clinical Social Work Journal* 45, no. 4: 364–66.

Thyer, B. A., R. T. Parrish, G. C. Curtis, R. M. Nesse, and O. G. Cameron. 1985. "Ages of Onset of DSM-III Anxiety Disorders." *Comprehensive Psychiatry* 26, no. 2: 113–22.

Thyer, B. A., and M. G. Pignotti. 2015. *Science and Pseudoscience in Social Work Practice*. Springer.

Triseliotis, J. 1998. "When Is Evaluation a Scientific Activity, When Is It Not?" *Scandinavian Journal of Social Welfare* 7, no. 2: 87–93.

Turner, F. J. 2017. *Social Work Treatment: Interlocking Theoretical Approaches*, 6th ed. Oxford University Press.

Tyson, K. B. 1992. "A New Approach to Relevant Scientific Research for Practitioners: The Heuristic Paradigm." *Social Work* 37, no. 6: 541–56.

Valenstein, E. 1986. *Great and Desperate Cures: The Rise and Decline of Psychosurgery and Other Radical Treatments for Mental Illness*. Basic Books.

Van Kleeck, M., and G. R. Taylor. 1922. "The Professional Organization of Social Work." *Annals of the American Academy of Political and Social Science* 101, no. 1: 158–69.

Videka-Sherman, L. 1988. "Metaanalysis of Research on Social Work Practice in Mental Health." *Social Work* 33, no. 4: 325–38.

Vigilante, J. L. 1974. "Between Values and Science: Education for the Profession During a Moral Crisis or Is Proof Truth?" *Journal of Education for Social Work* 10, no. 3: 107–15.

Washington, F. B. 1925. "What Professional Training Means to the Social Worker." *Annals of the American Academy of Political and Social Sciences* 121: 165–69.

Wasserman, S. 1960. "Casework Treatment of a Homosexual Acting-Out Adolescent in a Treatment Center." *Mental Hygiene* 44: 18–29.

Watson, M. F. 2019. "Social Justice and Race in the United States: Key Issues and Challenges for Couple and Family Therapy." *Family Process* 58, no. 1: 23–33.

Wayland, H. L. 1894. "A Scientific Basis of Charity." *Charities Review* 3, no. 6: 263–74.

Webb, S. 2002. "Evidence-Based Practice and Decision Analysis in Social Work." *Journal of Social Work* 2, no. 1: 45–63.

Webber, M., ed. 2015. *Applying Research Evidence in Social Work Practice*. Palgrave MacMillan.

Whitaker, R. 2015. "Chemical Imbalances: The Making of a Societal Delusion." In *The Science and Pseudoscience of Children's Mental Health: Cutting Edge Research and Treatment*, edited by S. Olfman, 11–22. Praeger.

Witkin, S. L. 2001. "Complicating Causes." *Social Work* 46, no. 3: 197–201.

Witkin, S. L., and W. D. Harrison. 2001. "Whose Evidence and for What Purpose?" *Social Work* 46, no. 4: 293–96.

Wood, K. M. 1978. "Casework Effectiveness: A New Look at the Evidence." *Social Work* 23, no. 6: 437–58.

Wootton, B. 1959. *Social Science and Social Pathology*. Macmillan.

Yin-Bun, C. 1998. "The Use of Experimental Design in Social Work Evaluation." *Asia Pacific Journal of Social Work and Development* 8, no. 2: 77–87.

Young, A. R. 2002. "Freud's Friend Fliess." *Journal of Laryngology and Otology* 116, no. 12: 5.

Zlotnik, J. L., and C. Galambos. 2004. "Evidence-Based Practice in Health Care: Social Work Possibilities." *Health & Social Work* 29, no. 4: 259–62.

Chapter 2

Abbott, E. 1931. *Social Welfare and Professional Education*. University of Chicago Press.

AMA (American Medical Association). 2022. "Code of Medical Ethics Opinion 2.1.4." https://www.ama-assn.org/delivering-care/ethics/use-placebo-clinical-practice.

AMA Council on Ethical and Judicial Affairs. 2013. "Opinion 8.20: Invalid Medical Treatment." *Virtual Mentor* 15, no. 11: 943–44. https://journalofethics.ama-assn.org/article/ama-code-medical-ethics-opinions-patient-requests-and-use-non-prescribed-treatments/2013-11.

Barker, R. L., ed. 2014. *The Social Work Dictionary*, 6th ed. NASW.

Blenkner, M. 1962. "Control Groups and the 'Placebo Effect' in Evaluative Research." *Social Work* 7, no. 1: 52–58.

Blenkner, M., M. Bloom, and M. Nielsen. 1971. "A Research and Demonstration Project of Protective Services." *Social Casework* 52, no. 8: 483–99.

Bloom, M., J. Fischer, and J. G. Orme. 2006. *Evaluating Practice: Guidelines for the Accountable Professional*, 5th ed. Pearson.

Bruno, F. J. 1964. *Trends in Social Work 1874–1956: A History Based on the Proceedings of the National Conference of Social Work*. Columbia University Press.

Cahill, S. P., M. H. Carrigan, and B. C. Frueh. 1999. "Does EMDR Work? And If So, Why? A Critical Review of Controlled Outcome and Dismantling Research." *Journal of Anxiety Disorders* 13, nos. 1–2: 5–33.

Chapin, F. S. 1917. "The Experimental Method and Sociology." *Scientific Monthly* 4: 133–44.

——. 1942. "Preliminary Standardization of a Social Insight Scale." *American Sociological Review* 7, no. 2: 214–25.

Coelho, H. F., P. H. Canter, and E. Ernst. 2008. "The Effectiveness of Hypnosis for the Treatment of Anxiety: A Systematic Review." *Primary Care & Community Psychiatry* 12, no. 2: 49–63.

Colosetti, S. D., and B. A. Thyer. 2000. "The Relative Effectiveness of EMDR Versus Relaxation Training with Battered Women Prisoners." *Behavior Modification* 24: 719–39.

Corcoran, K., and A. R. Roberts. 2015. *Social Workers' Desk Reference*, 3rd ed. Oxford University Press.

Corsini, R. 2002. *The Dictionary of Psychology*. Brunner-Routledge.

Dawes, R. M. 1994. *House of Cards: Psychology and Psychotherapy Built on Myth*. Free Press.

Eckmanns, T., J. Bessert, M. Behnke, P. Gastmeier, and H. Ruden. 2006. "Compliance with Antiseptic Hand Rub Use in Intensive Care Units: The Hawthorne Effect." *Infection Control and Hospital Epidemiology* 27: 931–34.

Fischer, J., K. Corcoran, and D. Springer. 2020. *Measures for Clinical Practice and Research*, 6th ed. Oxford University Press.

Franklin, B., G. de Bory, A. Lavoisier, J. S. Bailly, S. Majault, J. D'Arcet, J. Guillotin, and J. B. LeRoy. (1795) 1996. "Report of the Commission Charged by the King to Examine Animal Magnetism." *Skeptic* 4: 66–83.

Franklin, C., and C. Jordan, eds. 2021. *Clinical Assessment for Social Workers*, 5th ed. Oxford University Press.

Freeman, W. 1962. "Lobotomy After 65." *Geriatrics* 17: 15–19.

Garb, H. N., and P. A. Boyle. 2003. "Understanding Why Some Clinicians Use Pseudoscientific Methods: Findings from Research on Clinical Judgement." In *Science and Pseudoscience in Clinical Psychology*, edited by S. O. Lilienfeld, S. J. Lynn, and J. M. Lohr, 17–38. Guilford.

Greenwald, A. G., E. R. Spangenberg, A. R. Pratkanis, and J. Eskenazi. 1991. "Double-Blind Tests of Subliminal Self-Help Audiotapes." *Psychological Science* 2, no. 2: 119–22.

Grinnell, R. M., and Y. A. Unrau. 2008. *Social Work Research and Evaluation*, 8th ed. Sage.

Gunter, R. W., and G. E. Bodner. 2009. "EMDR Works. . . . But How? Recent Program in the Search for Treatment Mechanisms." *Journal of EMDR Practice and Research* 3, no. 3: 161–68.

Hartman, A. 1990. "Many Ways of Knowing." *Social Work* 35: 3–4.

Haygarth, J. 1800. *Of the Imagination, as a Cause and as a Cure of Disorders of the Body; Exemplified by Fictitious Tractors, and Epidemical Conclusions*. Ecco.

Holosko, M. J., and B. A. Thyer. 2011. *Pocket Glossary for Commonly Used Research Terms*. Sage.

Hunt, J. M., M. Blenkner, and L. S. Kogan. 1950. "A Field Test of the Movement Scale." *Social Casework* 31: 267–77.

Hyer, L., and J. Brandsma. 1997. "EMDR Minus Eye Movements Equals Good Psychotherapy." *Journal of Traumatic Stress* 10, no. 3: 515–22.

Ioannidis, J. P. A. 2005. "Why Most Published Research Findings Are False." *PLoS Medicine* 2, no. 8: e124.

Karls, J. M., and K. E. Wandrei. 1994. *Person-in-Environment System: The PIE Classification System for Social Function Problems*. NASW.

Leykin, Y., and R. J. DeRubeis. 2009. "Allegiance in Psychotherapy Outcomes Research: Separating Association from Bias." *Clinical Psychology: Science and Practice* 16, no. 1: 54–65.

Lilienfeld, S., J. Marshall, J. Todd, and H. Shane. 2014. "The Persistence of Fad Interventions in the Face of Negative Scientific Evidence: Facilitated Communication for Autism as a Case Example." *Evidence-Based Communication Assessment and Intervention* 8, no. 2: 62–101.

Lopes-Júnior, L. C., L. A. da Cruz, V. C. Leopoldo, F. R. de Campos, A. M. de Almeida, and R. C. Silveira. 2016. "Effectiveness of Traditional Chinese Acupuncture Versus Sham Acupuncture: A Systematic Review." *Revista Latino-Americana de Enfermagem* 24: e2762.

MacDonald, M. E. 1957. "Research in Social Work." In *Social Work Year Book, 1957*, 13th issue, edited by Russell H. Kurtz, 489–500. NASW.

Madrigal, A. 1995. "Interview with the Author—Autistic Girl Becomes Her Mother's Spirit Guide. Through 'Facilitated Communication,' She Tells Her Mom About Past Lives." *SFGate*. October 15, 1995. https://www.sfgate.com/books/article/INTERVIEW-WITH-THE -AUTHOR-Autistic-Girl-3022198.php.

Margolin, A., R. D. Kelber, S. K. Avants, J. Konefal, F. Gawin, E. Stark, J. Sorensen, E. Midkiff, E. Wells, T. R. Jackson, M. Bullock, P. D. Culliton, S. Boles, and R. Vaughan. 2002. "Acupuncture for the Treatment of Cocaine Addiction: A Randomized Controlled Trial." *Journal of the American Medical Association* 287: 55–63.

McCambridge, J., J. Witton, and D. R. Elbourne. 2014. "Systematic Review of the Hawthorne Effect: New Concepts Are Needed to Study Research Participation Effects." *Journal of Clinical Epidemiology* 67: 267–77.

McConkey, K. M., and C. Perry. 2002. "Benjamin Franklin and Mesmerism Revisited." *International Journal of Clinical and Experimental Hypnosis* 50, no. 4: 320–31.

McNeil, D., and M. J. Zvolensky. 2000. "Systematic desensitization." In *Encyclopedia of Psychology*, edited by A. E. Kazdin, 533–35. American Psychological Association.

Mu, J., A. D. Furlan, W. Y. Lam, M. Y. Hsu, Z. Ning, and L. Lao. 2020. "Acupuncture for Chronic Nonspecific Low Back Pain." *Cochrane Database of Systematic Reviews* 12, no. 12: CD013814.

Munafo, M. R., and J. Flint. 2010. "How Reliable Are Scientific Studies?" *British Journal of Psychiatry* 197: 257–58.

Newman, T., and H. Roberts. 1997. "Assessing Social Work Effectiveness in Child Care Practice: The Contribution of Randomized Controlled Trials." *Child: Care, Health, and Development* 23: 287–96.

Pignotti, M. 2005. "Thought Field Therapy Voice Technology vs. Random Meridian Point Sequences: A Single-Blind Controlled Experiment." *Scientific Review of Mental Health Practice* 4, no. 1: 38–47.

Prioleau, L., M. Murdock, and N. Brody. 1983. "An Analysis of Psychotherapy Versus Placebo Studies." *Behavioral and Brain Sciences* 6, no. 2: 275–310.

Roberts, A. R., and K. R. Yeager, eds. 2004. *Evidence-Based Practice Manual: Research and Outcome Measures in Health and Human Services*. Oxford University Press.

Rosen, S., and N. A. Polansky. 1975. "Observation of Social Interaction." In *Social Work Research*, rev. ed., edited by N. A. Polansky, 154–81. University of Chicago Press.

Rosenthal, D., and J. D. Frank. 1956. "Psychotherapy and the Placebo Effect." *Psychological Bulletin* 53: 294–302.

Schlosser, R. W., S. Balandin, B. Hemsley, T. Iacono, P. Probst, and S. von Tetzchner. 2014. "Facilitated Communication and Authorship: A Systematic Review." *Augmentative and Alternative Communication* 30, no. 4: 359–68.

Sherry, M. 2016. "Facilitated Communication, Anna Stubblefield and Disability Studies." *Disability & Society* 31, no. 7: 974–82.

Solomon, R. L. 1949. "An Extension of Control Group Design." *Psychological Bulletin* 46: 137–50.

Strupp, H. H., and S. W. Hadley. 1979. "Specific vs. Nonspecific Factors in Psychotherapy: A Controlled Study of Outcome." *Archives of General Psychiatry* 36, no. 10: 1125–36.

Taylor, J. A., W. Weber, L. Standish, H. Quinn, J. Goesling, M. McGann, and C. Calabrese. 2003. "Efficacy and Safety of Echinacea in Treating Upper Respiratory Tract Infections in Children: A Randomized Trial." *Journal of the American Medical Association* 290, no. 21: 2824–30.

Thomas, E. J. 1960. "Field Experiments and Demonstrations." In *Social Work Research*, edited by N. A. Polansky, 273–97. University of Chicago Press.

Thyer, B. A. 1989. "First Principles of Practice Research." *British Journal of Social Work* 19, no. 4: 309–23.

Tryon, W. 2005. "Possible Mechanisms for Why Desensitization and Exposure Therapy Work." *Clinical Psychology Review* 25, no. 1: 67–95.

Wartolowska, K., A. Judge, S. Hopewell, G. S. Collins, B. J. Dean, I. Rombach, D. Brindley, J. Savulescu, D. J. Beard, and A. J. Carr. 2014. "Use of Placebo Controls in the Evaluation of Surgery: Systematic Review." *British Medical Journal* 348: g3253.

Wechsler, M. W., J. M. Kelley, I. O. Boyd, S. Dutile, G. Marigowda, I. Kirsch, E. Israel, and T. J. Kaptchuk. 2011. "Active Albuterol or Placebo, Sham Acupuncture, or No Intervention in Asthma." *New England Journal of Medicine* 365, no. 2: 119–26.

Wikipedia. 2022. "List of Abuse Allegations Made Through Facilitated Communication." Last modified July 3, 2022, 13:46. https://en.wikipedia.org/wiki/List_of_abuse_allegations _made_through_facilitated_communication.

Witkin, S. L. 1991. "Empirical Clinical Practice: A Critical Analysis." *Social Work* 36, no. 2: 158–63.

Wolman, B. B. 1973. *Dictionary of Behavioral Science*. Van Nostrand Reinhold.

Wolpe, J. 1958. *Psychotherapy by Reciprocal Inhibition*. Stanford University Press.

Chapter 3

Anastas, J. W. 2012. "From Scientism to Science: How Contemporary Epistemology Can Inform Social Work Practice Research." *Clinical Social Work Journal* 40: 157–65.

Anastas, J. W., and M. L. MacDonald. 1994. *Research Design for Social Work and the Human Services*. Jossey-Bass.

APA (American Psychological Association). 2020. *Publication Manual of the American Psychological Association*, 7th ed. APA.

Atherton, C. R. 1993. "Empiricists Versus Social Constructivists: Time for a Cease-Fire." *Families in Society* 74, no. 10: 617–24.

BACB (Behavior Analyst Certification Board). 2014. *Professional and Ethical Compliance Code for Behavior Analysts*, section 2.09. BACB. https://www.bacb.com/wp-content /uploads/2020/05/BACB-Compliance-Code-english_190318.pdf.

Barker, R. L., ed. 2014. *The Social Work Dictionary*, 6th ed. NASW.

Barney, D. D., and L. E. Dalton. 2008. "Social Work Under Nazism." *Journal of Progressive Human Services* 17, no. 2: 43–62.

Bisman, C. D., and D. A. Hardcastle. 1999. *Integrating Research Into Practice: A Model for Effective Social Work*. Brooks/Cole.

Bisno, H. 1952. *The Philosophy of Social Work*. Public Affairs.

Blau, J. 2017. "Science as a Strategy for Social Work." *Journal of Progressive Human Services* 28, no. 2: 73–90.

Bolland, K., and C. Atherton. 2002. "Heuristics Versus Logical Positivism: Solving the Wrong Problem." *Families in Society* 83, no. 1: 7–13.

Boynton, J. 2012. "Facilitated Communication—What Harm It Can Do: Confessions of a Former Facilitator." *Evidence-Based Communication Assessment and Intervention* 6, no. 1: 3–13.

Bruno, F. 1936. *The Theory of Social Work*. D. C. Heath.

Burghardt, S. 1996. "A Materialist Framework for Social Work Theory and Practice." In *Social Work Treatment*, 4th ed., edited by F. Turner, 409–33. Free Press.

Chapman, D. P., S. R. Dube, and R. F. Anda. 2007. "Adverse Childhood Events as Risk Factors for Negative Mental Health Outcomes." *Psychiatric Annals* 37, no. 5: 359–64.

Chein, I. 1959. "On Some of the Difficulties of Doing Social Welfare Research." *Jewish Social Service Quarterly* 120–29.

Cohen, N. E. 1958. *Social Work in the American Tradition*. Holt, Rinehart & Winston.

Corsini, R. 2002. *The Dictionary of Psychology*. Brunner-Routledge.

Daston, L., and Galison, P. 2007. *Objectivity*. Zone.

Davis, L. V. 1994. "Is Feminist Research Inherently Qualitative and Is It a Fundamentally Different Approach to Research?" In *Controversial Issues in Social Work Research*, edited by W. W. Hudson and P. Nurius, 63–74. Allyn & Bacon.

Deming, W. E. 1975. "The Logic of Evaluation." In *Handbook of Evaluation Research*, edited by E. L. Struening and M. Guttentag, 53–68. Sage.

Dick, P. K. 1978. *How to Build a Universe That Doesn't Fall Apart Two Days Later*. https://urbigenous.net/library/how_to_build.html.

Dong, M., R. F. Anda, S. R. Dube, W. H. Giles, and V. J. Felitti. 2003. "The Relationship of Exposure to Childhood Sexual Abuse to Other Forms of Abuse, Neglect, and Household Dysfunction During Childhood." *Child Abuse & Neglect* 27: 625–39.

Drisko, J. W. 2004. "Common Factors in Psychotherapy Outcome: Meta-analytic Findings and Their Implications for Practice and Research." *Families in Society* 85, no. 1: 81–90.

Edmonds, D. 2020. *The Murder of Professor Schlick: The Rise and Fall of the Vienna Circle*. Princeton University Press.

Epstein, R. 1984. "The Principle of Parsimony and Some Applications in Psychology." *Journal of Mind and Behavior* 5, no. 2: 119–30.

Fischer, J., K. Corcoran, and D. Springer. 2020. *Measures for Clinical Practice and Research*, 6th ed. Oxford University Press.

Freedman, A., H. L. Kaplan, and B. J. Sadock, eds. 1976. *Modern Synopsis of Comprehensive Textbook of Psychiatry, II*, 2nd ed. Williams & Wilkins.

French, D. G. 1952. *An Approach to Measuring Results in Social Work*. Columbia University Press.

Garven, S., J. M. Wood, and R. S. Malpass. 2000. "Allegations of Wrongdoing: The Effects of Reinforcement on Children's Mundane and Fantastic Claims." *Journal of Applied Psychology* 85, no. 1: 38–49.

Glashow, S. 1989. "Positivism Lives: We Believe That the World Is Knowable." *New York Times,* October 22, 1989, 24E.

Goldstein, H. 1992. "If Social Work Hasn't Made Progress as a Science, Might It Be an Art?" *Families in Society* 73, no. 1: 48–55.

Gorenstein, E. E. 1986. "On the Distinction Between Science and Valuation in the Mental Health Field." *American Psychologists* 41: 588–90.

Guild, J. P., and A. A. Guild. 1936. *Handbook on Social Work Engineering.* Whittet & Shepperson.

Hall, R. E. 2010. *An Historical Analysis of Skin Color Discrimination in America.* Springer.

Hardy, M. 2014. "To Good to Be True? Reckoning with Realism." *Qualitative Social Work* 13, no. 4: 584–92.

Harrison, D. F., and B. A. Thyer. 1988. "Doctoral Research on Social Work Practice: A Proposed Agenda." *Journal of Social Work Education* 24: 107–14.

Hartman, A. 1990. "Many Ways of Knowing." *Social Work* 35: 3–4.

Haskell, T. L. 1997. *The Emergence of Professional Social Science: The American Social Science Association.* University of Illinois Press.

Heineman, M. 1981. "The Obsolete Scientific Imperative in Social Work Research." *Social Service Review* 55, no. 3: 371–97.

Hewes, A. 1930. *The Contributions of Economics to Social Work.* Columbia University Press.

HHS (U.S. Department of Health and Human Services). n.d. "Commission on Evidence-Based Policymaking (CEP)." https://www.acf.hhs.gov/opre/project/commission-evidence-based-policymaking-cep#:~:text=The%20Commission%20on%20Evidence%2DBased,Obama%20on%20March%2030%2C%202016.

Hill, B. 1965. "The Environment and Disease: Association or Causation?" *Proceedings of the Royal Society of Medicine* 58, no. 5: 295–300.

Hodge, D. R. 2007. "A Systematic Review of the Empirical Literature on Intercessory Prayer." *Research on Social Work Practice* 17, no. 2: 174–87.

Hollis, F. 1964. *Casework: A Psychosocial Therapy.* Random House.

Houdini, E. 1924. *A Magician Among the Spirits.* Harper and Brothers.

Hsiao, F.-H., G.-M. Jow, W.-H. Kuo, K.-J. Chang, Y.-F. Liu, R. T. H. Ho, S.-M. Ng, C. L. W. Chan, Y.-M. Lai, and Y.-T. Chen. 2012. "The Effects of Psychotherapy on Psychological Well-Being and Diurnal Cortisol Patterns in Breast Cancer Survivors." *Psychotherapy and Psychosomatics* 81, no. 3: 173–82.

Hudson, W. H. 1978. "First Axioms of Treatment." *Social Work* 23, no. 1: 65–66.

——. 1986. "The Proof Is in the Pudding." *Social Work Research and Abstracts* 22: 2.

Hume, D. 1748. *An Essay Concerning Human Understanding.* A. Millar.

Hunt, J. M., and L. S. Kogan. 1950. *Measuring Results in Social Casework.* Family Service Association of America.

Jayaratne, S., and R. L. Levy. 1979. *Empirical Clinical Practice.* Columbia University Press.

Kassan, P. 2021. "Disillusioned: Why Time, Consciousness, the Self and Free Will Are Not Illusions." *Skeptic Magazine* 26, no. 1: 50–59.

Kelvin, Lord. n.d. "Lord Kelvin Quotes." AZ Quotes. https://www.azquotes.com/author/7873-Lord_Kelvin.

Kunstreich, T. 2003. "Social Welfare in Nazi Germany." *Journal of Progressive Human Services* 14, no. 2: 23–52.

LDS (Church of Jesus Christ of Latter-Day Saints). n.d. "Articles of Faith." https://www.churchofjesuschrist.org/study/manual/gospel-topics/articles-of-faith?lang=eng.

Levitt, E. E. 1959. "The Basic Philosophy of Experimentation." *Smith College Studies in Social Work* 30, no.1: 63–72.

Lifton, R. J. 2017. *The Nazi Doctors: Medical Killing and the Psychology of Genocide*. Basic Books.

Lyon, J. 1985. "Benny Goodman." *Chicago Tribune*. July 8, 1985. https://www.chicagotribune.com/news/ct-xpm-1985-07-08-8502140129-story.html.

McMillen, A. W. 1930. *Measurement in Social Work: A Statistical Problem in Family and Child Welfare and Allied Fields*. University of Chicago Press.

Merckelbach, H., P. de Jong, P. Muris, and M. A. van den Hout. 1996. "The Etiology of Specific Phobias: A Review." *Clinical Psychology Review* 16, no. 4: 337–61.

Mill, J. S. 1843. *A System of Logic*. John Parker.

Mowbray, D. 2017. "Greatest Scientific Discoveries That Were Made in Dreams." Mattress Online. https://www.mattressonline.co.uk/blog/sleep-science/greatest-scientific-discoveries-that-were-made-in-dreams/.

Mullen, E. J., and J. L. Magnabosco, eds. 1997. *Outcomes Measurement in the Human Services*. NASW.

Myers, L. L., and B. A. Thyer. 1997. "Should Social Work Clients Have the Right to Effective Treatment?" *Social Work* 42: 288–98.

NASW (National Association of Social Workers). 1996. *Code of Ethics of the National Association of Social Workers*, section 4.01(c). NASW. https://naswor.socialworkers.org/Portals/31/Docs/Code_of_Ethics%20(1).pdf?ver=2019-02-14-113753-927.

Nathan, D. 2011. *Sybil Exposed: The Extraordinary Story Behind the Famous Multiple Personality Case*. Free Press.

NBC News. 2005. "Hurricane Katrina: Wrath of God?" October 5, 2005. https://www.nbcnews.com/id/wbna9600878.

Nezu, A. M., G. F. Ronan, E. A. Meadows, and K. S. McClure, eds. 2000. *Practitioner's Guide to Empirically Based Measures of Depression*. Springer.

Ormsby, R. 1951. "Measurement: A Valuable Contribution to Casework." *Smith College Studies in Social Work* 21: 85–93.

Paris, J. 2019. "Dissociative Identity Disorder: Validity and Use in the Criminal Justice System." *BJPsych Advances* 25, no. 5: 287–93.

Peck, M. S. 2005. *Glimpses of the Devil: A Psychiatrist's Personal Accounts of Possession, Exorcism, and Redemption*. Free Press.

Pickering, M. 1993. *Auguste Comte: An Intellectual Biography*, vol. 1. Cambridge University Press.

Pieper, M. H. 1985. "The future of social work research." *Social Work Research and Abstracts* 21, no. 4: 3–11.

——. 1986. "The Author Replies." *Social Work Research and Abstracts* 22: 2.

Pignotti, M. 2007. "Thought Field Therapy: A Former Insider's Experience." *Research on Social Work Practice* 17, no. 3: 392–407.

Pignotti, M., and B. A. Thyer. 2009. "Some Comments on 'Energy Psychology: A Review of the Evidence': Premature Conclusions Based on Incomplete Evidence?" *Psychotherapy: Theory, Research, Practice, Training* 46, no. 2: 257–61.

Polansky, N. A. 1975. "Theory Construction and the Scientific Method." In *Social Work Research*, edited by N. A. Polansky, 18–37. University of Chicago Press.

Randi, J. 1989. *The Faith Healers*. Prometheus.

Reamer, F. G. 1993. *The Philosophical Foundations of Social Work*. Columbia University Press.

Reid, W. J. 1997. "Evaluating the Dodo's Verdict: Do All Interventions Have Equivalent Outcomes?" *Social Work Research* 21, no. 7: 5–15.

Reynolds, B. C. 1942. *Learning and Teaching in the Practice of Social Work*. Farrar & Rinehart.

Richmond, M. (1917) 1935. *Social Diagnosis*. Russell Sage Foundation.

Robbins, S. P., P. Chatterjee, and E. R. Canda. 1999. "Ideology, Scientific Theory, and Social Practice." *Families in Society* 80, no. 4: 374–84.

Rubin, A., and E. R. Babbie. 2008. *Research Methods for Social Work*. Brooks/Cole.

Rudd, G. L. 1995. *Pure Religion: The Story of Church Welfare Since 1930*. Church of Jesus Christ of Latter-Day Saints.

Sablan, J. R. 2019. "Can You Really Measure That? Combining Critical Race Theory and Quantitative Methods." *American Educational Research Journal* 56, no. 1: 178–203.

Schreiber, F. R. 1973. *Sybil: The Classic True Story of a Woman Possessed by Sixteen Separate Personalities*. Warner.

Schünemann, H., S. Hill, G. Guyatt, E. A. Akl, and F. Ahmed. 2011. "The GRADE Approach and Bradford Hill's Criteria for Causation." *Journal of Epidemiology and Community Health* 65, no. 5: 392–95.

Sidman, M. 1960. *Tactics of Scientific Research*. Basic Books.

Steketee, G., and K. White. 1990. *When Once Is Not Enough: Help for Obsessive Compulsives*. New Harbinger.

Thyer, B. A. 1987. *Treating Anxiety Disorders*. Sage.

——. 2012. "The Scientific Value of Qualitative Research for Social Work." *Qualitative Social Work* 11: 115–25.

——. 2015. "A Bibliography of Randomized Controlled Experiments in Social Work (1949–2013): *Solvitur Ambulando*." *Research on Social Work Practice* 25, no. 7: 753–93.

Thyer, B. A., and M. G. Pignotti. 2015. *Science and Pseudoscience in Social Work Practice*. Springer.

Towle, C. 1930. "Changes in the Philosophy of Social Work." *Mental Hygiene* 14: 341–68.

Tripodi, T. 1983. *Evaluative Research for Social Workers*. Prentice Hall.

Turner, F. J. 1996. "Theory and Social Work Treatment." In *Social Work Treatment: Interlocking Theoretical Approaches*, 4th ed., edited by F. J. Turner, 1–17. Free Press.

Tutty, L. 1990. "The Response of Community Mental Health Professionals to Clients' Rights: A Review and Suggestions." *Canadian Journal of Community Mental Health* 9: 1–24.

Warner, A. G. 1930. *American Charities and Social Work*. Thomas Y. Crowell.

Welch, M. 2017. "Doing Special Things to Special People in Special Places: Psychologists in the CIA Torture Program." *Prison Journal* 97, no. 6: 729–49.

Witkin, S. L. 1991. "Empirical Clinical Practice: A Critical Analysis." *Social Work* 36, no. 2: 158–63.

Wittgenstein, L. 1922. *Tractatus Logico-Philosophicus*, translated by C. K. Ogden. Routledge & Kegan Paul.

Wolf, D. B., and N. Abell. 2003. "Examining the Effects of Meditation Techniques on Psychosocial Functioning." *Research on Social Work Practice* 13, no. 1: 27–42.

Wyatt, W. J. 2002. "What Was Under the McMartin Preschool? A Review and Behavioral Analysis of the 'Tunnels' Find." *Behavior and Social Issues* 12, no. 1: 29–39.

Zane, M. 1984. "Psychoanalysis and Contextual Analysis of Phobias." *Journal of the American Academy of Psychoanalysis* 12, no. 4: 553–68.

Chapter 4

Allen, H., K. Baicker, A. Finkelstein, S. Taubman, B. Wright, and the Oregon Health Study Group. 2010. "Introduction to the Oregon Health Study: A Medicaid Expansion Experiment." *Health Affairs* 29, no. 8: 1498–1506.

Allen, H., B. Wright, and L. Broffman. 2018. "The Impacts of Medicaid Expansion on Rural Low-Income Adults: Lessons from the Oregon Health Insurance Experiment." *Medical Care Research and Review* 75, no. 3: 354–83.

Arntz, K. J., H. Merckelbach, and P. de Jong. 1993. "Opioid Antagonist Affects Behavioral Effects of Exposure In Vivo." *Journal of Consulting and Clinical Psychology* 56, no. 2: 287–91.

Barlow, D. H., L. B. Allen, and S. L. Basden. 2007. "Psychological Treatments for Panic Disorders, Phobias, and Generalized Anxiety Disorder." In *A Guide to Treatments That Work*, 3rd ed., edited by P. E. Nathan and J. M. Gorman, 351–94. Oxford University Press.

Bernard, C. (1865) 1949. *An Introduction to the Principles of Experimental Medicine*. Adelard /Shuman.

Bertrand, M., and S. Mullainathan. 2003. *Are Emily and Greg More Employable Than Lakisha and Jamal? A Field Experiment on Labor Market Discrimination*. National Bureau of Economic Research. https://www.nber.org/papers/w9873.

Bhatt, A. 2010. "Evolution of Clinical Research: A History Before and After James Lind." *Perspectives in Clinical Research* 1, no. 1: 6–10.

Blenkner, M., M. Bloom, and M. Nielsen. 1971. "A Research and Demonstration Project of Protective Services." *Social Casework* 52, no. 8: 483–99.

Boynton, K. E., and B. A. Thyer. 1994. "Behavioral Social Work in the Field of Oncology." *Journal of Applied Social Sciences* 18: 189–97.

Caddick, B. 1994. "The 'New Careers' Experiment in Rehabilitating Offenders: Last Messages from a Fading Star." *British Journal of Social Work* 24, no. 4: 449–60.

Campbell, D. T., and M. J. Russo. 1999. *Social Experimentation*. Sage.

Carmack, H. J., B. R. Bates, and L. M. Harter. 2008. "Narrative Constructions of Health Care Issues: The Case of President Clinton's Apology-by-Proxy for the Tuskegee Syphilis Experiment." *Journal of Medical Humanities* 29: 89–109.

Case, L. P., and N. B. Lingerfelt. 1974. "Name-Calling: The Labeling Process in the Social Work Interview." *Social Service Review* 48, no. 1: 75–86.

Chapin, F. S. 1917. "The Experimental Method and Sociology." *Scientific Monthly* 4: 133–44.

Crane, J. 1998. *Social Programs That Work*. Russel Sage Foundation.

Davidson, J. R. 2009. "First-Line Pharmacotherapy Approaches for Generalized Anxiety Disorder." *Journal of Clinical Psychiatry* 70: 25–31.

De Araujo, L. A., L. Ito, I. M. Marks, and A. Deale. 1995. "Does Imagined Exposure to the Consequences of Not Ritualizing Enhance Live Exposure for OCD: A Controlled Study I. Main Outcome." *British Journal of Psychiatry* 167, no. 1: 65–70.

de Wit, H., E. H. Uhlenhuth, D. Hedeker, S. G. McCracken, and C. E. Johanson. 1986. "Lack of Preference for Diazepam in Anxious Volunteers." *Archives of General Psychiatry* 43: 533–41.

DeRubeis, R. J., M. D. Evans, S. D. Hollon, M. J. Garvey, W. M. Grove, and V. B. Tuason. 1990. "How Does Cognitive Therapy Work? Cognitive Change and Symptom Change in Cognitive Therapy and Pharmacotherapy for Depression." *Journal of Consulting and Clinical Psychology* 58, no. 6: 862–69.

Eack, S. M. 2010. "In Memoriam: Gerard Hogarty, MSW (1935–2006)." *Research on Social Work Practice* 20, no. 3: 341–42.

Egan, K., J. E. Carr, D. D. Hunt, and R. Adamson. 1988. "Endogenous Opiate System and Systematic Desensitization." *Journal of Consulting and Clinical Psychology* 56, no. 2: 287–91.

Fischer, J. 1971. *Interpersonal Helping: Emerging Approaches for Social Work Practice*. Charles C. Thomas.

Floyd, M., and F. Scogin. 1998. "Cognitive Behavior Therapy for Older Adults: How Does It Work?" *Psychotherapy: Theory, Research, Practice* 35, no. 4: 459–63.

Flynn, M., J. S. Brekke, and H. Soydan. 2008. "The Hamovitch Research Center: An Experiment in Collective Responsibility for Advancing Science in the Human Services." *Social Work Research* 32, no. 4: 260–68.

Freshour, J. S., A. B. Amspoker, M. Yi, M. E. Kunik, N. Wilson, C. Kraus-Schuman, J. A. Cully, E. Teng, S. Williams, N. Masozera, M. Horsfield, and M. Stanley. (2016). "Cognitive Behavior Therapy for Late-Life Generalized Anxiety Disorder Delivered by Lay and Expert Providers Has Lasting Benefits." *International Journal of Geriatric Psychiatry* 31, no. 11: 1225–32.

Gerber, A. S., and D. P. Green. 2012. *Field Experiments: Design, Analysis, and Interpretation.* Norton.

Goldman, S. K., and D. C. Mutz. 2008. *The Obama Effect: How the 2008 Campaign Changed White Racial Attitudes.* Russell Sage Foundation.

Grant, S., E. Mayo-Wilson, P. Montgomery, G. Macdonald, S. Michie, S. Hopewell, D. Moher; on behalf of the CONSORT-SPI Group. 2018. "CONSORT-SPI 2018 Explanation and Elaboration: Guidance for Reporting Social and Psychological Intervention Trials." *Trials* 19, no. 1: 406.

Hargreaves, W. A., J. Showstack, R. Flohr, C. Brady, and S. Harris. 1974. "Treatment Acceptance Following Intake Assignment to Individual Therapy, Group Therapy, or Contact Group." *Archives of General Psychiatry* 31: 343–49.

Harter, L. M., R. J. Stephens, and P. M. Japp. 2000. "President Clinton's Apology for the Tuskegee Syphilis Experiment: A Narrative of Remembrance, Redefinition, and Reconciliation." *Howard Journal of Communications* 11: 19–34.

Hogarty, G. E., C. M. Anderson, D. J. Reiss, S. J. Kornblith, D. P. Greenwald, C. D. Javna, and M. J. Madonia. 1986. "Family Psychoeducation, Social Skills Training, and Maintenance Chemotherapy in the Aftercare Treatment of Schizophrenia." *Archives of General Psychiatry* 43, no. 7: 633–42.

Hoppe, B. S., R. C. Nichols, R. H. Henderson, C. G. Morris, C. R. Williams, J. Costa, R. B. Marcus Jr., W. M. Mendenhall, Z. Li, and N. P. Mendenhall. 2012. "Erectile Function, Incontinence, and Other Quality of Life Outcomes Following Proton Therapy for Prostate Cancer in Men 60 Years Old and Younger." *Cancer* 118, no. 18: 4619–26.

Hyde, A. B., and J. Murphy. 1955. "An Experiment in Integrative Learning." *Social Service Review* 29: 358–71.

Katzmann, J., A. Goertz-Dorten, C. Hautmann, and M. Doepfner. 2019. "Social Skills Training and Play Group Intervention for Children with Oppositional-Defiant Disorders/Conduct Disorder: Mediating Mechanisms in a Head-to-Head Comparison." *Psychotherapy Research* 29, no. 6: 784–98.

Kirk, S. A. 1974. "The Impact of Labeling on Rejection of the Mentally Ill: An Experimental Study." *Journal of Health and Social Behavior* 15, no. 2: 108–17.

Kirk, S. A., and D. K. Hsieh. 2004. "Diagnostic Consistency in Assessing Conduct Disorder: An Experiment on the Effects of Social Context." *American Journal of Orthopsychiatry* 74, no. 1: 43–55.

Klerman, G. L., M. M. Weissman, B. Rounsaville, and E. S. Chevron. 1984. *Interpersonal Psychotherapy of Depression.* Basic Books.

Kuyken, W., E. Watkins, E. Holden, K. White, R. S. Taylor, S. Byford, A. Evans, S. Radford, J. D. Teasdale, and T. Dalgleish. 2010. "How Does Mindfulness-Based Cognitive Therapy Work?" *Behaviour Research and Therapy* 48, no. 11: 1105–12.

Maurer, L. F., C. A. Espie, and S. D. Kyle. 2018. "How Does Sleep Restriction Therapy for Insomnia Work?" *Sleep Medicine Reviews* 42: 127–38.

McCord, J., and W. McCord. 1959. "A Follow-Up Report on the Cambridge-Somerville Youth Study." *Annals of the American Academy of Political and Social Science* 322: 89–96.

McGrath, R. D. 2021. "The Deliberate Infection Myth of the Tuskegee Syphilis Study." *Chronicles.* June 1, 2021. https://www.chroniclesmagazine.org/the-deliberate-infection-myth -of-the-tuskegee-syphilis-study/.

Moss, E., and S. Davidson. 1982. "The Community-Based Group Home: Experiment in Psychiatric Rehabilitation." *International Journal of Partial Hospitalization* 1, no. 2: 105–17.

Neilson, W. A. 1919. "The Smith College Experiment in Training for Psychiatric Social Work." *Mental Hygiene* 3: 59–64.

Pecukonis, E., E. Greeno, M. Hodorowicz, H. Park, L. Ting, T. Moyers, C. Burry, D. Linsen-meyer, F. Strieder, K. Wade, and C. Wirt. 2016. "Teaching Motivational Interviewing to Child Welfare Social Work Students Using Live Supervision and Standardized Clients: A Randomized Controlled Trial." *Journal of the Society for Social Work and Research* 7, no. 3: 479–505.

Powers, E. 1949. "An Experiment in Prevention of Delinquency." *Annals of the American Academy of Political and Social Sciences* 261: 77–88.

Reid, W. J., and A. W. Shyne. 1969. *Brief and Extended Casework.* Columbia University Press.

Richards, K., and B. A. Thyer. 2011. "Does Individual Development Account Participation Help the Poor? A Review." *Research on Social Work Practice* 21: 348–62.

Rizzo, V. M., and J. M. Rowe. 2006. "Studies of the Cost-Effectiveness of Social Work Services in Aging: A Review of the Literature." *Research on Social Work Practice* 16, no. 1: 67–73.

Rossi, P. H., and W. Williams. 1972. *Evaluating Social Programs.* Seminar.

Royse, D., B. A. Thyer, and D. K. Padgett. 2016. *Program Evaluation: An Evidence-Based Approach*, 6th ed. Cengage.

Simon, H. A., W. R. Divine, E. M. Cooper, and M. Chernin. 1941. *Determining Work Loads for Professional Staff in a Public Welfare Agency.* Bureau of Public Administration, University of California, Berkeley.

Smith, M. J., J. D. Smith, M. F. Fleming, N. Jordan, C. H. Brown, L. Humm, D. Onsen, and M. D. Bell. 2017. "Mechanism of Action for Obtaining Job Offers with Virtual Reality Job Interview Training." *Psychiatric Services* 68, no. 7: 747–50.

Solomon, P., M. Cavanaugh, and J. Draine. 2009. *Randomized Controlled Trials: Design and Implementation for Community-Based Psychosocial Interventions.* Oxford University Press.

Sowers-Hoag, K., and B. A. Thyer. 1985. "Teaching Social Work Practice: A Review and Analysis of Empirical Research." *Journal of Social Work Education* 21, no. 3: 5–15.

Stoesz, D. 2020. *Building Better Social Programs: How Evidence Is Transforming Public Policy.* Oxford University Press.

Sugerman, D. T., and E. Livingston. 2014. "Proton Beam Therapy for Prostate Cancer." *Journal of the American Medical Association* 311, no. 14: 1462.

Tennille, J., P. Solomon, E. Brusilovskiy, and D. Mandell. 2016. "Field Instructors Extending EBP Learning in Dyads (FIELD): Results of a Pilot Randomized Controlled Trial." *Journal of the Society for Social Work and Research* 7, no. 1: 1–22.

Thyer, B. A. 2012. "Respondent Learning Theory." In *Human Behavior in the Social Environment: Theories for Social Work Practice*, edited by B. A. Thyer, C. N. Dulmus, and K. M. Sowers, 47–81. Wiley.

Thyer, B. A., M. Baum, and L. D. Reid. 1988. "Exposure Techniques in the Reduction of Fear: A Comparative Review of the Procedures in Animals and Humans." *Advances in Behaviour Research and Therapy* 10: 105–27.

Thyer, B. A., and J. Mathews. 1986. "The Effect of Phobic Anxiety on Plasma Beta-Endorphin: A Single-Subject Experiment." *Behaviour Research and Therapy* 24: 237–41.

Wallace, M. P., J. S. Weiner, R. Pekmezaris, A. Almendral, R. Cosiquien, C. Auerbach, and G. Wolf-Klein. 2007. "Physician Cultural Sensitivity Training in African American Advance Care Planning: A Pilot Study." *Journal of Palliative Medicine* 10, no. 3: 721–27.

Washburn, M., A. Rubin, and S. Zhou. 2016. "Benchmarks for Outpatient Dialectical Behavioral Therapy for Adults with Borderline Personality Disorder." *Research on Social Work Practice* 28, no. 8: 895–906.

Watson, J. P., R. Gaind, and I. M. Marks. 1971. "Prolonged Exposure: A Rapid Treatment for Phobias." *British Medical Journal* 1, no. 5739: 13–15.

Webb, A., J. Vincent, G. Wistow, and K. Wray. 1991. "Developmental Social Care: Experimental Handicap Teams in Nottinghamshire." *British Journal of Social Work* 21, no. 5: 491–513.

Wodarski, J. S., B. A. Thyer, J. D. Iodice, and R. G. Pinkston. 1991. "Graduate Social Work Education: A Review of Empirical Research." *Journal of Social Service Research* 14, nos. 3–4: 23–44.

Yelick, A., and B. A. Thyer. 2020. "The Effects of Family Structure and Race on Decision Making in Child Welfare." *Journal of Public Child Welfare* 14, no. 3: 336–56.

Yesberg, J. A., and D. L. Polaschek. 2019. "How Does Offender Rehabilitation Therapy Actually Work? Exploring Mechanisms of Change in High-Risk Treated Parolees." *International Journal of Offender Therapy and Comparative Criminology* 63, nos. 15–16: 2672–92.

Young, L., K. W. Johnson, and D. Bryant. 2002. "Conducting a Therapeutic Community Training Experiment in Peru: Research Design and Implementation Issues." *Journal of Social Work Research and Evaluation* 3, no. 1: 89–102.

Chapter 5

Allen, H., B. Wright, and L. Broffman. 2018. "The Impacts of Medicaid Expansion on Rural Low-Income Adults: Lessons from the Oregon Health Insurance Experiment." *Medical Care Research and Review* 75, no. 3: 354–83.

Baicker, K., H. L. Allen, B. J. Wright, and A. N. Finkelstein. 2017. "The Effect of Medicaid on Medication Use Among Poor Adults: Evidence from Oregon." *Health Affairs* 36, no. 12: 2110–14.

Baicker, K., H. L. Allen, B. J. Wright, S. L. Taubman, and A. N. Finkelstein. 2018a. "The Effect of Medicaid on Dental Care of Poor Adults: Evidence from the Oregon Health Insurance Experiment." *Health Services Research* 53, no. 4: 2147–64.

——. 2018b. "The Effect of Medicaid on Management of Depression: Evidence from the Oregon Health Insurance Experiment." *Milbank Quarterly* 96, no. 1: 29–56.

Baicker, K., S. L. Taubman, H. L. Allen, M. Bernstein, J. H. Gruber, J. P. Newhouse, E. C. Schneider, B. J. Wright, A. M. Zaslavsky, A. N. Finkelstein, and the Oregon Health Study Group. 2013. "The Oregon Experiment—Effects of Medicaid on Clinical Outcomes." *New England Journal of Medicine* 368, no. 18: 1713–22.

Blake, W. 1973. "The Influence of Race on Diagnosis." *Smith College Studies in Social Work* 43, no. 3: 184–92.

Campbell, D. T., and J. C. Stanley. 1963. *Experimental and Quasi-experimental Designs for Research*. Rand McNally.

Canady, K., and B. A. Thyer. 1990. "Promoting Voting Behavior Among Low Income Black Voters Using Reminder Letters: An Experimental Investigation." *Journal of Sociology and Social Welfare* 17, no. 4: 109–16.

Carpenter-Aeby, T., D. Xiong, and V. G. Aeby. 2014. "Comparing the Health Locus of Control Among Caucasian and Hmong College Students." *Journal of Human Behavior in the Social Environment* 24, no. 5: 635–42.

Curry, A. 1968. "The Negro Worker and the White Client: A Commentary on the Treatment Relationship." In *Differential Diagnosis and Treatment in Social Work*, edited by F. Turner, 544–51. Free Press.

Despard, M., M. Grinstein-Weiss, A. deRuyter, S. Gu, J. E. Oliphant, and T. Friedline. 2018. "Effectiveness of a Randomized Tax-Time Savings Intervention on Savings Account Ownership Among Low- and Moderate-Income Households." *Journal of Financial Counseling and Planning* 29, no. 2: 219–32.

Finkelstein, A., S. Taubman, B. Write, M. Bernstein, J. Gruber, J. P. Newhouse, H. Allen, K. Baicker, and the Oregon Health Study Group. 2012. "The Oregon Health Insurance Experiment: Evidence from the First Year." *Quarterly Journal of Economics* 127, no. 3: 1057–1106.

Fischer, J. 1973. "Is Casework Effective? A Review." *Social Work* 18, no. 1: 5–20.

Greene, S. V. 2009. "Social Workers' Experience of Implementing Therapeutic Touch: A Hermeneutic Study." (Master of social work thesis, Augsburg College). https://idun.augsburg.edu/cgi/viewcontent.cgi?article=1812&context=etd.

Hastings, C. 1943. "Review of the Book *Determining Work Loads for Professional Staff in a Public Welfare Agency* by H. A. Simon, W. R. Divine, E. M. Cooper & M. Chernin." *Journal of the American Statistical Association* 38, no. 221: 132–33.

Hays, K., and M. Aranda. 2015. "Faith-Based Mental Health Interventions with African-Americans." *Research on Social Work Practice* 26, no. 7: 777–89.

Hemming, K., and M. Taljaard. 2016. "Sample Size Calculations for Stepped Wedge and Cluster Randomised Trials: A Unified Approach." *Journal of Clinical Epidemiology* 69: 137–46.

Hodge, D. R. 2007. "A Systematic Review of the Empirical Literature on Intercessory Prayer." *Research on Social Work Practice* 17, no. 2: 174–87.

Holden, G., and K. Barker. 2018. "Should Social Workers Be Engaged in These Practices?" *Journal of Evidence-Based Social Work* 15, no. 1: 1–13.

Hussey, M. A., and J. P. Hughes. 2007. "Design and Analysis of Stepped Wedge Cluster Randomized Trials." *Contemporary Clinical Trials* 28: 182–91.

Kroenke, K., T. W. Strine, R. L. Spitzer, J. B. W. Williams, J. T. Berry, and A. H. Mokdad. 2009. "The PHQ-8 as a Measure of Current Depression in the General Population." *Journal of Affective Disorders* 114, nos. 1–3: 163–73.

Laird, J. 1984. "Sorcerers, Shamans and Social Workers: The Use of Ritual in Social Work Practice." *Social Work* 29, no. 2: 123–29.

Lee, M.-J., W.-C. Wu, H.-C. Chang, H.-J. Chen, W.-S. Lin, J. Y. Feng, and T. S.-H. Lee. 2020. "Effectiveness of a School-Based Life Skills Program on Emotional Regulation and Depression Among Elementary School Students: A Randomized Study." *Children and Youth Services Review* 118: 105464.

Lee, M. Y., C. H. Chan, C. L. Chan, S. Ng, and P. P. Leung. 2018. *Integrative Body-Mind-Spirit Social Work: An Empirically Based Approach to Assessment and Treatment*, 2nd ed. Oxford University Press.

Lee, S., and F. K. O. Yuen. 2003. "Hmong Americans' Changing Views and Approaches Towards Disability: Shaman and Other Helpers." In *International Perspectives on Disability Services: The Same But Different*, edited by F. K. O. Yuen, 121–32. Haworth.

Meuche, G. 2015. "Embracing the Oneness of All Things: A Personal Reflection on the Implications of Shamanism for Social Work Practice in End-of-Life and Palliative Care." *Journal of Social Work in End-of-Life and Palliative Care* 11, no. 1: 3–5.

Palmer, G. T. 1942. "Review of the Book *Determining Work Loads for Professional Staff in a Public Welfare Agency* by H. A. Simon, W. R. Divine, E. M. Cooper & M. Chernin." *American Journal of Public Health* 32, no. 6: 660.

Pignotti, M., and B. A. Thyer. 2009. "The Use of Novel Unsupported and Empirically Supported Therapies by Licensed Clinical Social Workers: An Exploratory Study." *Social Work Research* 33: 5–17.

——. 2012. "Novel Unsupported and Empirically Supported Therapies: Patterns of Usage Among Licensed Clinical Social Workers." *Behavioural and Cognitive Psychotherapy* 40: 331–49.

Rosa, L., E. Rosa, L. Sarner, and S. Barrett. 1998. "A Closer Look at Therapeutic Touch." *Journal of the American Medical Association* 279, no. 13: 1005–10.

Scarlett, M. 1942. "Review of the Book *Determining Work Loads for Professional Staff in a Public Welfare Agency* by H. A. Simon, W. R. Divine, E. M. Cooper & M. Chernin." *Social Service Research* 15, no. 4: 780–81.

Schinke, S. P., M. A. Orlandi, G. J. Botvin, L. D. Gilchrist, J. E. Trimble, and V. S. Locklear. 1988. "Preventing Substance Abuse Among American-Indian Adolescents: A Bicultural Competence Skills Approach." *Journal of Counseling Psychology* 35, no. 1: 87–90.

Segal, S. P. 1972. "Research on the Outcome of Social Work Therapeutic Interventions: A Review of the Literature." *Journal of Health and Social Behavior* 13, no. 1: 3–17.

Simon, H. A., W. R. Divine, E. M. Cooper, and M. Chernin. 1941. *Determining Work Loads for Professional Staff in a Public Welfare Agency*. Bureau of Public Administration, University of California, Berkeley.

Taubman, S. L., H. L. Allen, B. J. Write, K. Baicker, and A. N. Finkelstein. 2014. "Medicaid Increased Emergency Department Use: Evidence from Oregon's Health Insurance Experiment." *Science* 343, no. 6168: 263–68.

Thompson, J. A., K. Fielding, J. Hargreaves, and A. Copas. 2016. "The Optimal Design of Stepped Wedge Trials with Equal Allocation to Sequences and a Comparison to Other Trial Designs." *Clinical Trials* 14, no. 6: 339–47.

Thyer, B. A. 2015. "A Bibliography of Randomized Controlled Experiments in Social Work (1949–2013): *Solvitur Ambulando*." *Research on Social Work Practice* 25, no. 7: 753–93.

Thyer, B. A., and M. G. Pignotti. 2015. *Science and Pseudoscience in Social Work Practice*. Springer.

Thyer, B. A., and M. Pignotti. 2016. "The Problem of Pseudoscience in Social Work Continuing Education." *Journal of Social Work Education* 52: 136–46.

Walton, E. 2001. "Combining Abuse and Neglect Investigations with Intensive Family Preservation Services: An Innovative Approach to Protecting Children." *Research on Social Work Practice* 11: 627–44.

Wolf, D. B., and N. Abell. 2003. "Examining the Effects of Meditation Techniques on Psychosocial Functioning." *Research on Social Work Practice* 13, no. 1: 27–42.

Wright, B. J., A. K. Conlin, H. L. Allen, J. Tsui, M. J. Carlson, and H. F. Li. 2016. "What Does Medicaid Expansion Mean for Cancer Screening and Prevention? Results from a Randomized Trial on the Impacts of Acquiring Medicaid Coverage." *Cancer* 122: 791–97.

Zatzick, D., G. Jurkovich, P. Heagerty, J. Russo, D. Darnell, L. Parker, M. K. Roberts, R. Mood-liar, A. Engstrom, J. Wang, E. Bulger, L. Whiteside, D. Nehra, L. A. Palinkas, K. Moloney, and R. Maier. 2021. "Stepped Collaborative Care Targeting Posttraumatic Stress Disorder Symptoms and Comorbidity for US Trauma Care Systems: A Randomized Clinical Trial." *JAMA Surgery* 156, no. 5: 430–42.

Chapter 6

Bass, J. K., J. Annan, S. M. Murray, D. Kaysen, S. Griffiths, T. Cetinoglu, K. Wachter, L. K. Murray, and P. A. Bolton. 2013. "Controlled Trial of Psychotherapy for Congolese Survivors of Sexual Violence." *New England Journal of Medicine* 368, no. 23: 2182–91.

Cukrowicz, K. C., K. A. Timmons, K. Sawyer, K. M. Caron, H. D. Gummelt, and T. E. Joiner Jr. 2011. "Improved Treatment Outcome Associated with the Shift to Empirically Supported Treatments in an Outpatient Clinic Is Maintained Over a Ten-Year Period." *Professional Psychology: Research and Practice* 42, no. 2: 145–52.

Cukrowicz, K. C., B. A. White, L. R. Reitzel, A. B. Burns, K. A. Driscoll, T. S. Kemper, and T. E. Joiner. 2005. "Improved Treatment Outcome Associated with the Shift to Empirically Supported Treatments in a Graduate Training Clinic." *Professional Psychology: Research and Practice* 36, no. 3: 330–37.

de Felice, G., A. Giuliani, S. Halfon, S. Andreassi, G. Paoloni, and F. F. Orsucci. 2019. "The Misleading Dodo Bird Verdict. How Much of the Outcome Variance Is Explained by Common and Specific Factors?" *New Ideas in Psychology* 54: 50–55.

El-Bassel, N., T. McCrimmon, G. Mergenova, M. Chang, A. Terlikbayeva, S. Primbetova, A. Kuskulov, B. Baiserkin, A. Denebayeva, K. Kurmetova, and S. S. Witte. 2021. "A Cluster-Randomized Controlled Trial of a Combination HIV Risk Reduction and Microfinance Intervention for Female Sex Workers Who Use Drugs in Kazakhstan." *Journal of the International Aids Society* 24, no. 5: e25682.

Fischer, J., K. Corcoran, and D. Springer. 2020. *Measures for Clinical Practice and Research*, 6th ed. Oxford University Press.

Flora, D. B. 2020. "Thinking About Effect Sizes: From Replication Crisis to a Cumulative Psychological Science." *Canadian Psychology* 16, no. 4: 318–30.

Goldberg, S. B., S. U. Lam, W. B. Britton, and R. J. Davidson. 2022. "Prevalence of Meditation-Related Adverse Effects in a Population-Based Sample in the United States." *Journal of Psychotherapy Research* 32, no. 3: 291–305.

Heidenreich, T., J. Gebrande, J. Renz, A. Noyon, M. Zinnöcker, and M. Hautzinger. 2021. "Improving Social Functioning in Depressed Mothers: Results from a Randomized Controlled Trial." *European Journal of Social Work* 24, no. 1: 109–22.

Hilliard, R. E. 2001. "The Effects of Music Therapy-Based Bereavement Groups on Mood and Behavior of Grieving Children: A Pilot Study." *Journal of Music Therapy* 38: 291–306.

——. 2007. "The Effects of Orff-Based Music Therapy and Social Work Groups on Childhood Grief Symptoms and Behaviors." *Journal of Music Therapy* 44, no. 2: 123–38.

Hong, P. Y. P., S. Choi, and R. Hong. 2020. "A Randomized Controlled Trial Study of Transforming Impossible Into Possible (TIP) Policy Experiment in South Korea." *Research on Social Work Practice* 30, no. 6: 587–96.

Hsiao, F.-H., G.-M. Jow, Y.-M. Lai, Y.-T. Chen, K.-C. Wang, S.-M. Ng, R. T. H. Ho, C. L. W. Chan, and T.-T. Yang. 2011. "The Long-Term Effects of Psychotherapy Added to Pharmacotherapy on Morning to Evening Diurnal Cortisol Patterns in Outpatients with Major Depression." *Psychotherapy and Psychosomatics* 80: 166–72.

Iyer, P. 1988. "Tibet's Living Buddha." *Time*. April 11, 1988, 58–60.

Kane, J. M. 2016. "Comprehensive Versus Usual Community Care for First-Episode Psychosis: 2-Year Outcomes from the NIMH RAISE Early Treatment Program." *American Journal of Psychiatry* 173, no. 4: 362–72.

Karsch-Völk, M., B. Barrett, D. Kiefer, R. Bauer, K. Ardjomand-Woelkart, and K. Linde. 2014. "Echinacea for Preventing and Treating the Common Cold." *Cochrane Database of Systematic Reviews*, Issue 2. Art. No.: CD000530.

Larkin, R., and B. A. Thyer. 1999. "Evaluating Cognitive-Behavioral Group Counseling to Improve Elementary School Students' Self-Esteem, Self-Control and Classroom Behavior." *Behavioral Interventions* 14: 147–61.

Lilienfeld, S. O. 2014. "The Dodo Bird Verdict: Status in 2014." *Behavior Therapist* 37, no. 4: 91–95.

McDonell, M. G., K. A. Hirchak, J. Herron, A. J. Lyons, K. C. Alcover, J. Shaw, G. Kordas, L. G. Dirks, K. Jansen, J. Avey, K. Lillie, D. Donovan, S. M. McPherson, D. Dillard, R. Ries, J. Roll, D. Buchwald; HONOR Study Team. 2021. "Effect of Incentives for Alcohol Abstinence in Partnership with 3 American Indian and Alaska Native Communities: A Randomized Clinical Trial." *JAMA Psychiatry* 78, no. 6: 599–606.

Novoa, M. P., and D. S. Cain. 2014. "The Effects of Reiki Treatment on Mental Health Professionals at Risk for Secondary Traumatic Stress: A Placebo Control Study." *Best Practices in Mental Health* 10, no. 1: 29–46.

O'Rourke, K., and J. C. Worzbyt. 1996. *Support Groups for Children*. Accelerated Development.

Pignotti, M. 2005. "Thought Field Therapy Voice Technology vs. Random Meridian Point Sequences: A Single-Blind Controlled Experiment." *Scientific Review of Mental Health Practice* 4, no. 1: 38–47.

Pignotti, M., and B. A. Thyer. 2009. "Some Comments on 'Energy Psychology: A Review of the Evidence': Premature Conclusions Based on Incomplete Evidence?" *Psychotherapy: Theory, Research, Practice, Training* 46, no. 2: 257–61.

Prisco, M. K., M. C. Jecmen, K. J. Bloeser, K. K. McCarron, J. E. Akhter, A. D. Duncan, M. S. Balish, R. Amdur, and M. J. Reinhand. 2013. "Group Auricular Acupuncture for PTSD-Related Insomnia in Veterans: A Randomized Trial." *Medical Acupuncture* 25, no. 6: 407–22.

Reid, W. J. 1997. "Evaluating the Dodo's Verdict: Do All Interventions Have Equivalent Outcomes?" *Social Work Research* 21, no. 7: 5–15.

Robertson, L., P. Mushati, J. W. Eaton, L. Dumba, G. Mavise, J. Makoni, C. Schumacher, T. Crea, R. Monasch, L. Sherr, G. P. Garnett, C. Myamukapa, and S. Gregson. 2013. "Effects of Unconditional and Conditional Cash Transfers on Child Health and Development in Zimbabwe: A Cluster Randomized Trial." *Lancet* 381: 1283–92.

Rosenzweig, S. 1936. "Some Implicit Common Factors in Diverse Methods of Psychotherapy." *American Journal of Orthopsychiatry* 6: 412–15.

Safford, F., and B. Baumel. 1994. "Testing the Effects of Dietary Lecithin on Memory in the Elderly: An Example of Social Work/Medical Research Collaboration." *Research on Social Work Practice* 4, no. 3: 349–58.

Schinke, S. P., and B. J. Blythe. 1981. "Cognitive-Behavioral Prevention of Children's Smoking." *Child Behavior Therapy* 3, no. 4: 25–42.

Schinke, S. P., B. J. Blythe, and L. D. Gilchrist. 1981. "Cognitive-Behavioral Prevention of Adolescent Pregnancy." *Journal of Counseling Psychology* 28, no. 5: 451–54.

SEED (Stockton Economic Empowerment Demonstration). 2019. *Our Vision for SEED: A Discussion Paper*. SEED. https://static1.squarespace.com/static/6039d612b17d055cac14070f/t/605029ab52a6b53e3dd38cf8/1615866284641/10+-+SEED+Discussion+Paper.pdf.

Solomon, R. L. 1949. "An Extension of Control Group Design." *Psychological Bulletin* 46: 137–50.

Suomi, A., N. Lucas, M. McArthur, C. Humphreys, T. Dobbins, and S. Taplin. 2020. "Cluster Randomized Controlled Trial (RCT) to Support Parental Contact for Children in Out-of -Home Care." *Child Abuse & Neglect* 209: 104708.

Tackett, J. L., C. M. Brandes, M. King, and K. E. Markon. 2019. "Psychology's Replication Crisis and Clinical Psychological Science." *Annual Review of Clinical Psychology* 15: 579–604.

Taylor, J. A., W. Weber, L. Standish, H. Quinn, J. Goesling, M. McGann, and C. Calabrese. 2003. "Efficacy and Safety of Echinacea in Treating Upper Respiratory Tract Infections in Children: A Randomized Trial." *Journal of the American Medical Association* 290, no. 21: 2824–30.

Thomas, E. J. 1960. "Field Experiments and Demonstrations." In *Social Work Research*, edited by N. A. Polansky, 273–97. University of Chicago Press.

Thyer, B. A., and M. G. Pignotti. 2015. *Science and Pseudoscience in Social Work Practice*. Springer.

Thyer, B. A., and M. Pignotti. 2016. "The Problem of Pseudoscience in Social Work Continu- ing Education." *Journal of Social Work Education* 52: 136–46.

Tolin, D. F. 2014. "Beating a Dead Dodo Bird: Looking at Signal vs. Noise in Cognitive- Behavioral Therapy for Anxiety Disorders." *Clinical Psychology: Science and Practice* 21, no. 4: 351–62.

Towfighi, A., E. M. Cheng, M. Ayala-Rivera, F. Barry, H. McCreath, D. A. Ganz, M. L. Lee, N. Sanossian, B. Mehta, T. Dutta, A. Razmara, R. Bryg, S. S. Song, P. Willis, S. Wu, M. Ramirez, A. Richards, N. Jackson, J. Wacksman, B. Mittman, J. Tran, R. R. Johnson, C. Ediss, T. Sivers-Teixeira, B. Shaby, A. L. Montoya, M. Corrales, E. Mojarro-Huang, M. Castro, P. Gomez, C. Muñoz, D. Garcia, L. Moreno, M. Fernandez, E. Lopez, S. Valdez, H. R. Haber, V. A. Hill, N. M. Rao, B. Martinez, L. Hudson, N. P. Valle, B. G. Vickrey; Sec- ondary Stroke Prevention by Uniting Community and Chronic Care Model Teams Early to End Disparities (SUCCEED) Investigators. 2021. "Effect of a Coordinated Community and Chronic Care Model Team Intervention vs Usual Care on Systolic Blood Pressure in Patients with Stroke or Transient Ischemic Attack: The SUCCEED Randomized Clinical Trial." *JAMA Network Open* 4, no. 2: e20366227.

USC (University of Southern California Suzanne Dworak-Peck School of Social Work). 2019. "Countertransference: Preventing Compassion Fatigue and Improving Your Prac- tice Along the Way." https://dworakpeck.usc.edu/news/countertransference-preventing -compassion-fatigue-and-improving-your-practice-along-the-way.

——. 2020. "Social Work and Me: Restoration Through Relationships." https://dworakpeck .usc.edu/events/social-work-me-restoration-through-relationships.

Wechsberg, W. M., W. A. Zule, N. El-Bassel, I. A. Doherty, A. M. Minnis, S. D. Novak, B. Myers, and T. Carney. 2016. "The Male Factor: Outcomes from a Cluster Randomized Field Experiment in a Couple-Based HIV Prevention Intervention in a South African Township." *Drug and Alcohol Dependence* 161: 307–15.

Weintraub, S., M. M. Mesulam, R. Auty, R. Baratz, B. N. Cholakos, L. Kapust, B. Ransil, J. G. Tellers, M. S. Albert, S. LoCastro, and M. Moss. 1983. "Lecithin in the Treatment of Alz- heimer's Disease." *Archives of Neurology* 40, no.8: 527–28.

West, S., A. Castro Baker, S. Samra, and E. Coltera. 2021. *Preliminary Analysis: SEED's First Year*. SEED. https://socialprotection.org/discover/publications/preliminary-analysis-seed %E2%80%99s-first-year.

Wolf, D. B., and N. Abell. 2003. "Examining the Effects of Meditation Techniques on Psychosocial Functioning." *Research on Social Work Practice* 13, no. 1: 27–42.

Wong, D. F. K., T. K. Ng, X. Y. Zhuang, P. W. C. Wong, J. T. Y. Leung, I. K. M. Cheung, and P. C. Kendall. 2020. "Cognitive-Behavior Therapy with and Without Parental Involvement for Anxious Chinese Adolescents: A Randomized Controlled Trial." *Journal of Family Psychology* 34, no. 3: 353–63.

Xia, J. 2022. *Predatory Publishing*. Routledge.

Chapter 7

Abell, N., D. W. Springer, and A. Kamata. 2009. *Developing and Validating Rapid Assessment Instruments*. Oxford University Press.

Adetugbo, K., and H. Williams. 2000. "How Well Are Randomized Controlled Trials Reported in the Dermatological Literature?" *Archives of Dermatology* 136, no. 3: 381–85.

Al-Jundi, A., and S. Sakka. 2016. "Protocol Writing in Clinical Research." *Journal of Clinical & Diagnostic Research* 10, no. 11: ZE10–13.

American Psychiatric Association. 2013. *Diagnostic and Statistical Manual of Mental Disorders*, 5th ed. American Psychiatric Association.

APA (American Psychological Association). 2020a. *JARS–Quant Table 2: Reporting Standards for Studies with an Experimental Manipulation—Module C: Reporting Standards for Studies Involving Clinical Trials*. APA. https://apastyle.apa.org/jars/quant-table-2c.pdf.

——. 2020b. *Publication Manual of the American Psychological Association*, 7th ed. APA.

Barbee, A. P., B. Antle, C. Langley, M. R. Cunningham, D. Whiteside, B. K. Sar, A. Archuleta, E. Karam, and K. Borders. 2021. "How to Ensure Fidelity in Implementing an Evidence Based Teen Pregnancy Prevention Curriculum." *Children and Youth Services Review* 129: 106175.

Barker, R. L., ed. 2014. *The Social Work Dictionary*, 6th ed. NASW.

Bhatt, M., L. Zielinski, N. Sanger, I. Shams, C. Luo, B. Bantoto, H. Shahid, G. Li, L. P. F. Abbade, I. Nwoso, Y. Jin, M. Wang, Y. Chang, G. Sun, L. Mbusgbaw, M. A. H. Levine, J. D. Adachi, L. Thabane, and Z. Samaan. 2018. "Evaluating Completeness of Reporting in Behavioral Interventions Pilot Trials: A Systematic Survey." *Research on Social Work Practice* 28, no. 5: 577–84.

Bobo, H.-P., A. Y. Chow, D. K. F. Wong, J. S. Chan, C. H. Y. Chan, R. T. Ho, T.-S. So, T.-C. Lam, V. H.-F. Lee, A. W. M. Lee, S. F. Chow, and C. L. W. Chan. 2018. "Study Protocol of a Randomized Controlled Trial Comparing Integrative Body–Mind–Spirit Intervention and Cognitive Behavioral Therapy in Fostering Quality of Life of Patients with Lung Cancer and Their Family Caregivers." *Journal of Evidence-Informed Social Work* 15, no. 3: 258–76.

Chan, A. W., and D. G. Altman. 2005. "Epidemiology and Reporting of Randomised Trials Published in PubMed Journals." *Lancet* 365: 1159–62.

Drisko, J. 2012. "Standards for Qualitative Studies and Reports." In *Qualitative Research in Social Work*, 2nd ed., edited by R. Fortune, W. Reid, and R. Miller, 1–34. Columbia University Press.

Fischer, J., K. Corcoran, and D. Springer. 2020. *Measures for Clinical Practice and Research*, 6th ed. Oxford University Press.

Fisher, S., and R. P. Greenberg, eds. 1989. *The Limits of Biological Treatments for Psychological Distress: Comparisons with Psychotherapy and Placebo*. Lawrence Erlbaum.

Fung, Y. L., B. H. Lau, M. Y. Tam, Q. Xie, C. L. W. Chan, and C. H. Y. Chan. 2019. "Proto-col for Psychosocial Interventions Based on Integrative Body-Mind-Spirit (IBMS) Model for Children with Eczema and their Parent Caregivers." *Journal of Evidence-Based Social Work* 16, no. 1: 36–56.

Gadaire, D. M., and R. P. Kimler. 2020. "Use of the Template for Intervention Description and Replication (Tidier) Checklist in Social Work Research." *Journal of Evidence-Based Social Work* 17, no. 2: 137–48.

Grant, S., E. Mayo-Wilson, P. Montgomery, G. Macdonald, S. Michie, S. Hopewell, D. Moher; on behalf of the CONSORT-SPI Group. 2018. "CONSORT-SPI 2018 Explanation and Elaboration: Guidance for Reporting Social and Psychological Intervention Trials." *Trials* 19, no. 1: 406.

Greenwald, A. G. 1975. "Consequences of Prejudice Against the Null Hypothesis." *Psychological Bulletin* 82: 1–20.

Harrison, B. A., and E. Mayo-Wilson. 2014. "Trial Registration: Understanding and Preventing Reporting Bias in Social Work Research." *Research on Social Work Practice* 24, no. 3: 372–76.

Himle, M. B. 2015. "Let Truth Be Thy Aim, Not Victory: Comment on Theory-Based Exposure Process." *Journal of Obsessive-Compulsive and Related Disorders* 6: 183–90.

Hoffman, T., C. Erueti, and P. Glasziou. 2008. "Poor Description of Non-pharmacological Interventions: Analysis of a Consecutive Sample of Randomized Trials." *British Medical Journal* 336: 1472–74.

Hoffmann, T., P. Glasziou, I. Boutron, R. Milne, R. Perera, D. Moher, D. Altman, V. Barbour, H. Macdonald, M. Johnston, S. Lamb, M. Dixon-Woods, P. McCulloch, J. Wyatt, A. Chan, and S. Michie. 2014. "Better Reporting of Interventions: Template for Intervention Description and Replication (TIDieR) Checklist and Guide." *British Medical Journal* 348: g1687.

Holden, G., B. A. Thyer, J. Baer, J. Delva, C. Dulmus, and T. Williams. 2008. "Suggestions to Improve Social Work Journal Editorial and Review Processes." *Research on Social Work Practice* 18: 66–71.

Holosko, M. J. 2006a. *A Primer for Critiquing Social Research: A Student Guide.* Brooks/Cole.

——. 2006b. "A Suggested Author's Checklist for Submitting Manuscripts to *Research on Social Work Practice*." *Research on Social Work Practice* 16, no. 4: 449–54.

Howard, M. O., and J. Jenson. 2003. "Clinical Practice Guidelines: Should Social Work Develop Them?" *Research on Social Work Practice* 9, no. 3: 283–301.

ICMJE (International Committee of Medical Journal Editors). 2022. "Clinical Trials: Registration." https://www.icmje.org/recommendations/browse/publishing-and-editorial-issues/clinical-trial-registration.html.

LeCroy, C. W. ed. 1994. *Handbook of Child and Adolescent Treatment Manuals.* Simon & Shuster.

——. ed. 2008. *Handbook of Evidence-Based Treatment Manuals for Children and Adolescents,* 2nd ed. Oxford University Press.

Littrell, J. L., and J. R. Lacasse. 2012. "The Controversy Over Antidepressant Drugs in an Era of Evidence-Based Practice." *Social Work in Mental Health* 10, no. 6: 445–63.

Moher, D. 1998. "CONSORT: An Evolving Tool to Help Improve the Quality of Reports of Randomized Controlled Trials." Consolidated Standards of Reporting Trials. *Journal of the American Medical Association* 279: 1489–91.

Moher, D., S. Hopewell, K. F. Schulz, V. Montori, P. C. Gotzsche, P. J. Devereaux, D. Elbourne, M. Egger, and D. G. Altman. 2010. "CONSORT 2010 Explanation and Elaboration: Updated Guidelines for Reporting Parallel Group Randomized Trials." *British Medical Journal* 340: c869.

Montgomery, P., S. Grant, E. Mayo-Wilson, G. Macdonald, S. Michie, S. Hopewell, and D. Moher, on behalf of the CONSORT-SPI Group. 2018. "Reporting Randomised Trials of Social and Psychological Interventions: The CONSORT-SPI 2018 Extension." *Trials* 19: 407.

NIH (National Institutes of Health). 2017. "Does Your Human Subjects Research Study Meet the NIH Definition of a Clinical Trial?" https://grants.nih.gov/ct-decision/index.htm.

Nugent, W. R. 1987. "Information Gain Through Integrated Research Approaches." *Social Service Review* 61: 337–64.

Rice, E., A. Yoshioka-Maxwell, R. Petering, L. Onasch-Vera, J. Craddock, M. Tambe, A. Yadav, B. Wilder, D. Woo, H. Winetrobe, and N. Wilson. 2018. "Piloting the Use of Artificial Intelligence to Enhance HIV Prevention Interventions for Youth Experiencing Homelessness." *Journal of the Society for Social Work and Research* 9, no. 4: 551–73.

Rosen, A., and E. K. Proctor, eds. 2003. *Developing Practice Guidelines for Social Work Intervention: Issues, Methods, and Research Agenda.* Columbia University Press.

Rubin, A. 2000. "Standards for Rigor in Qualitative Inquiry." *Research on Social Work Practice*, 10, no. 2: 1730178.

Schoech, D., H. Jennings, L. Schkade, and C. Hooper-Russell. 1985. "Expert Systems: Artificial Intelligence for Professional Decisions." *Computers in Human Services* 1, no. 1: 81–115.

Shamseer, L., S. Hopewell, D. G. Altman, D. Moher, and K. F. Schulz. 2016. "Update on the Endorsement of CONSORT by High Impact Factor Journals: A Survey of Journal 'Instructions to Authors' in 2014." *Trials* 17, no. 1: 301.

Shera, W. 2001. "Guidelines for Quality Social Work Dissertations." *Arete* 25, no. 1: 103–14.

Simera, I., and D. G. Altman. 2009. "Writing a Research Article That Is 'Fit for Purpose': EQUATOR Network and Reporting Guidelines." *Evidence-Based Medicine* 14, no. 5: 132–34.

Slayter, E. M. 2021. "Want to Be Evidence-Based? Here's a Literature Review Hack That Will Help Get You There." *New Social Worker.* https://www.socialworker.com/feature-articles/practice/want-to-be-evidence-based-literature-review-hack/.

Sloan, D. M., and B. P. Marx. 2019. *Written Exposure Therapy for PTSD: A Brief Treatment Approach for Mental Health Professionals.* APA.

Soifer, S., G. Zgouridges, and J. Himle. 2020. *The Secret Social Phobia: Shy Bladder Syndrome,* 2nd ed. New Harbinger.

Steketee, G., and K. White. 1990. *When Once Is Not Enough: Help for Obsessive Compulsives.* New Harbinger.

Thyer, B. A. 1989. "First Principles of Practice Research." *British Journal of Social Work* 19, no. 4: 309–23.

——. 1991. "Guidelines for Evaluating Outcome Studies in Social Work." *Research on Social Work Practice* 1: 76–91.

——. 2002. "How to Write Up a Social Work Outcome Study for Publication." *Journal of Social Work Research and Evaluation* 3, no. 2: 215–24.

——. 2003. "Social Work Should Help Develop Interdisciplinary Evidence-Based Practice Guidelines, Not Discipline-Specific Ones." In *Developing Practice Guidelines for Social Work Intervention: Issues, Methods, and Research Agenda,* edited by A. Rosen and K. Proctor, 128–39. Columbia University Press.

——. 2012. "The Scientific Value of Qualitative Research for Social Work." *Qualitative Social Work* 11: 115–25.

——. 2014a. "Evolving Reporting Guidelines for Social Work Research." *Nordic Social Work Research* 4, no. 1: 1–4.

——. 2014b. "Improving Publication Standards for Psychotherapy Outcome Studies." *Journal of Evidence-Based Psychotherapies* 14, no. 2: 25–28.

——. 2017. "Suggested Reporting Guidelines to Improve Health-Related Social Work Research." *Health and Social Work* 42, no. 4: 195–98.

——. 2020. "30 Years Plus of *Research on Social Work Practice*: Past Accomplishments and Future Directions." *Research on Social Work Practice* 31, no. 1: 3–5.

Thyer, B. A., and G. C. Curtis. 1984. "The Effects of Ethanol Intoxication on Phobic Anxiety." *Behaviour Research and Therapy* 22: 599–610.

Tolin, D. F., R. O. Frost, and G. Steketee. 2014. *Buried in Treasures: Help for Compulsive Acquiring, Saving, and Hoarding*, 2nd ed. Oxford University Press.

Tripodi, T., P. Fellin, and H. J. Meyer. 1969. *The Assessment of Social Research: Guidelines for Use of Research in Social Work and Social Science*. F. E. Peacock.

Turner, L., L. Shamseer, D. G. Altman, L. Weeks, J. Peters, T. Kober, S. Dias, K. F. Schulz, A. C. Plint, and D. Moher. 2012. "Consolidated Standards of Reporting Trials (CONSORT) and the Completeness of Reporting of Randomised Controlled Trials (RCTs) Published in Medical Journals." *Cochrane Database of Systematic Reviews* 11, no. 11: MR000030.

UK EQUATOR Centre. n.d. "What Is a Reporting Guideline?" https://www.equator-network .org/about-us/what-is-a-reporting-guideline/.

Van Hasselt, V. B., and M. Hersen, eds. 1996. *Sourcebook for Psychological Treatment Manuals for Adult Disorders*. Plenum.

Westhuis, D. J., and B. A. Thyer. 1989. "Development and Validation of the Clinical Anxiety Scale: A Rapid Assessment Instrument for Empirical Clinical Practice." *Educational and Psychological Measurement* 49: 153–63.

Whitaker, R. 2019. *Mad in America: Bad Science, Bad Medicine, and the Enduring Mistreatment of the Mentally Ill*. Basic Books.

Wilhelm, S., and G. S. Steketee. 2006. *Cognitive Therapy for Obsessive-Compulsive Disorder: A Guide for Professionals*. New Harbinger.

Wong, S. E., and R. P. Liberman. 1996. "Behavioral Treatment and Rehabilitation for Persons with Schizophrenia." In *Sourcebook for Psychological Treatment Manuals for Adult Disorders*, edited by V. B. van Hasselt and M. Hersen, 233–56. Plenum.

Zarin, D. A., and A. Kesselman. 2007. "Registering a Clinical Trial in ClinicalTrials.gov." *Chest* 131, no. 3: 909–12.

Chapter 8

Azar, B. 2010. "Are Your Findings 'WEIRD'?" *Monitor on Psychology* 41, no. 5: 11.

Cesnales, N. I., B. A. Thyer, D. L. Albright, and N. E. Neujahr. 2016. "Health-Related Quality of Life Among People Living with HIV/AIDS." *Journal of HIV/AIDS & Social Services* 15: 202–15.

Ejiogu, N., J. H. Norbeck, M. A. Mason, B. C. Cromwell, A. B. Zonderman, and M. K. Evans. 2011. "Recruitment and Retention Strategies for Minority or Poor Clinical Research Participants: Lessons from the Healthy Aging in Neighborhoods of Diversity Across the Lifespan." *Gerontologist* 51, no. S1: S33–45.

Friedman, S., L. C. Smith, B. Halpern, C. Levine, C. Paradis, R. Viswanathan, B. Trappler, and R. Ackerman. 2003. "Obsessive-Compulsive Disorder in a Multi-ethnic Urban Outpatient Clinic: Initial Presentation and Treatment Outcome with Exposure and Ritual Prevention." *Behavior Therapy* 34, no. 3: 397–410.

Garrison, N. A. 2013. "Genomic Justice for Native Americans: Impact of the Havasupai Case on Genetic Research." *Science, Technology & Human Values* 38, no. 2: 201–23.

Graves, D., and J. P. Sheldon. 2018. "Recruiting African American Children for Research: An Ecological Systems Theory Approach." *Western Journal of Nursing Research* 40, no. 10: 1489–1521.

Harrison, D. F., and B. A. Thyer. 1988. "Doctoral Research on Social Work Practice: A Proposed Agenda." *Journal of Social Work Education* 24: 107–14.

Hazuda, H. P., M. Gerety, J. W. Williams, V. Lawrence, W. Calmbach, and C. Mulrow. 2000. "Health Promotion Research with Mexican American Elders: Matching Approaches to Settings at the Mediator- and Micro-levels of Recruitment." In *Recruitment and Retention in Minority Populations: Lessons Learned in Conducting Research on Health Promotion and Minority Aging*, edited by S. E. Levkoff, T. R. Prohaska, P. F. Weitzman, and M. G. Ory, 79–90. Springer.

Higgins, J. P. T., J. Thomas, J. Chandler, M. Cumpston, T. Li, M. J. Page, and V. A. Welch, eds. 2022. *Cochrane Handbook for Systematic Reviews of Interventions*, version 6.3. Cochrane Collaboration. https://www.training.cochrane.org/handbook.

Hill, L. D., S. Avenevoli, and J. A. Gordon. 2022. "The Role of the National Institute of Mental Health in Promoting Diversity in Psychiatric Research." *Psychiatric Clinics of North America* 45, no. 2: 303–12.

Himle, J., J. R. Muroff, R. J. Taylor, R. E. Baser, J. M. Abelson, G. L. Hanna, J. L. Abelson, and J. S. Jackson. 2008. "Obsessive-Compulsive Disorder Among African Americans and Blacks of Caribbean Descent: Results from the National Survey of American Life." *Depression and Anxiety* 25, no. 12: 993–1005.

Jaklevic, M. C. 2020. "Researchers Strive to Recruit Hard-Hit Minorities Into COVID Vaccine Trials." *Journal of the American Medical Association* 324, no. 9: 826–28.

Johnson, D. A., and Y. A. Joosten, C. H. Wilkins, and C. A. Shibao. 2015. "Case Study: Community Engagement and Clinical Trial Success: Outreach to African American Women." *Clinical and Translational Research* 8, no. 4: 388–90.

Kara, Y., and V. Duyan. 2022. "The Effects of Emotion-Based Group Work on Psychosocial Functions of LGBT People." *Social Work with Groups*. https://doi.org/10.1080/01609513.2022.2027851.

Kubicek, K., and M. Robles. 2016. *Tips and Tricks for Successful Research Recruitment: A Toolkit for a Community-Based Approach*. Southern California Clinical and Translational Science Institute grant UL1TR001855. https://sc-ctsi.org/uploads/resources/recruitment_retention_toolkit.pdf.

Levkoff, S. E., T. R. Prohaska, P. F. Weitzman, and M. G. Ory, eds. 2000. *Recruitment and Retention in Minority Populations: Lessons Learned in Conducting Research on Health Promotion and Minority Aging*. Springer.

Medical Research Council. 1948. "Streptomycin Treatment of Tuberculous Meningitis." *Lancet* 1, no. 6503: 582–96.

NIH (National Institutes of Health). 2022. "Inclusion of Women and Minorities as Participants in Research Involving Human Subjects." https://grants.nih.gov/policy/inclusion/women-and-minorities.htm.

Otado, J., J. Kwagyan, D. Edwards, A. Ukaegbu, F. Rockcliffe, and N. Osafo. 2015. "Culturally Competent Strategies for Recruitment and Retention of African American Populations Into Clinical Trials." *Clinical and Translational Science* 8, no. 5: 160–66.

Paquin, R. S., M. A. Lewis, B. A. Harper, R. R. Moultrie, A. Gwaltney, L. M. Gehtland, H. L. Peay, M. Duparc, M. Raspa, A. C. Wheeler, C. M. Powell, N. M. King, S. M. Shone, and

D. B. Bailey Jr. 2021. "Outreach to New Mothers Through Direct Mail and Email: Recruitment in the Early Check Research Study." *Clinical and Translational Science* 14, no. 3: 880–89.

Reverby, S. M. 2001. "More Than Fact and Fiction: Cultural Memory and the Tuskegee Syphilis Study." *Hastings Center Reports* 31: 22–28.

Sankaré, I. C., R. Bross, A. F. Brown, H. E. del Pino, L. F. Jones, D. M. Morris, C. Porter, A. Lucas-Wright, R. Vargas, N. Forge, K. C. Norris, and K. L. Kahn. 2015. "Strategies to Build Trust and Recruit African American and Latino Community Residents for Health Research: A Cohort Study." *Clinical and Translational Science* 8, no. 5: 412–20.

Schiele, J., and R. G. Wilson. 2001. "Guidelines for Promoting Diversity in Doctoral Social Work Education." *Arete* 25, no. 1: 53–66.

Stahl, S. M., and L. Vasquez. 2004. "Approaches to Improving Recruitment and Retention of Minority Elders Participating in Research." *Journal of Aging and Health* 16, no. 5: 9S–17S.

Tang, W.-J., and Y.-C. Yang. 2012. "Theory and Practice of Exposure and Response/Ritual Prevention for Obsessive-Compulsive Disorder: A Review." *Chinese Mental Health Journal* 26, no. 7: 520–24.

Tanne, J. H. 2022. "US Must Urgently Correct Ethnic and Racial Disparities in Clinical Trials, Says Report." *British Medical Journal* 377: 01292.

Waheed, W., A. Hughes-Morley, A. Woodham, G. Allen, and P. Bower. 2015. "Overcoming Barriers to Recruiting Ethnic Minorities to Mental Health Research: A Typology of Recruitment Strategies." *BMC Psychiatry* 15, no. 101: 1–11.

Yahoo News. 2020. "Newsmaker Plenary with Former Vice President Joe Biden." YouTube video, 59:33. Uploaded August 6, 2020. https://www.youtube.com/watch?v=iCpyx2T-lDA&t=863s.

Young, D. K. W., P. Y. N. Ng, P. Corrigan, R. Chiu, and S. Yang. 2020. "Self-Stigma Reduction Group for People with Depression: A Randomized Controlled Trial." *Research on Social Work Practice* 30, no. 8: 846–57.

Chapter 9

Barlow, D. H., L. B. Allen, and S. L. Basden. 2007. "Psychological Treatments for Panic Disorders, Phobias, and Generalized Anxiety Disorder." In *A Guide to Treatments That Work*, 3rd ed., edited by P. E. Nathan and J. M. Gorman, 351–94. Oxford University Press.

Barlow, D. H., and S. C. Hayes. 1979. "Alternating Treatments Design: One Strategy for Comparing the Effects of Two Treatments in a Single Subject." *Journal of Applied Behavior Analysis* 12, no. 2: 199–210.

Bernal, J. L., S. Cummins, and A. Gasparrini. 2017. "Interrupted Time Series Regression for the Evaluation of Public Health Interventions: A Tutorial." *International Journal of Epidemiology* 46, no. 1: 348–55.

Bernard, C. (1865) 1949. *An Introduction to the Principles of Experimental Medicine*. Adelard/Shuman.

Boring, E. G. 1954. "The Nature and History of Experimental Control." *American Journal of Psychology* 67, no. 4: 573–89.

Bowen, G. L., and G. Farkas. 1991. "Application of Time-Series Designs to the Evaluation of Social Services Program Initiatives: The Recycling Fund Concept." *Social Work Research and Abstracts* 27, no. 3: 9–15.

Box, G., and G. Jenkins. 1970. *Time Series Analysis: Forecasting and Control*. Holden-Day.

Brandell, J. R., and T. Varkas. 2010. "Narrative Case Studies." In *Handbook of Social Work Research Methods*, 2nd ed., edited by B. A. Thyer, 376–96. Sage.

Buchanan, J. P., D. R. Dixon, and B. A. Thyer. 1997. "A Preliminary Evaluation of Treatment Outcomes at a Veterans' Hospital Inpatient Psychiatry Unit." *Journal of Clinical Psychology* 53, no. 8: 853–58.

Bunge, M. A. 1959. *Causality: The Place of the Causal Principle in Modern Science*. Harvard University Press.

Campbell, D. T., and J. C. Stanley. 1963. *Experimental and Quasi-experimental Designs for Research*. Rand McNally.

Card, D., and A. B. Krueger. 1994. "Minimum Wages and Employment: A Case Study of the Fast-Food Industry in New Jersey and Pennsylvania." *American Economic Review* 84, no. 4: 772–93.

Cohen, J. 1994. "The Earth Is Round ($p < .05$)." *American Psychologist* 49, no. 12: 997–1003.

Cook, T. D., and W. R. Shadish. 1994. "Social Experiments: Some Developments Over the Past 15 Years." *Annual Review of Psychology* 45: 545–80.

DiNitto, D. 1983. "Time-Series Analysis: An Application to Social Welfare Policy." *Journal of Applied Behavioral Science* 19: 507–18.

DiNitto, D., R. R. McDaniel, T. W. Ruefli, and J. B. Thomas. 1986. "The Use of Ordinal Time-Series Analysis in Assessing Policy Inputs and Impacts." *Journal of Applied Behavioral Science* 22: 77–93.

Duncan, T. E., and S. C. Duncan. 2004. "An Introduction to Latent Growth Curve Modeling." *Behavior Therapy* 35: 333–63.

Fischer, J., K. Corcoran, and D. Springer. 2020. *Measures for Clinical Practice and Research*, 6th ed. Oxford University Press.

Gabler, N. B., N. Duan, S. Vohra, and R. L. Kravitz. 2011. "N-of-1 Trials in the Medical Literature: A Systematic Review." *Medical Care* 49, no. 8: 761–68.

Guyatt, G., and D. Rennie, eds. 2002. *Users' Guides to the Medical Literature: Essentials of Evidence-Based Clinical Practice*. AMA.

Guyatt, G., D. Sackett, J. Adachi, R. Roberts, J. Chong, D. Rosenbloom, and J. Keller. 1988. "A Clinician's Guide for Conducting Randomized Trials in Individual Patients." *Canadian Medical Association Journal* 139, no. 6: 497–503.

Heinsman, D. T., and W. R. Shadish. 1996. "Assignment Methods in Experimentation: When Do Nonrandomized Experiments Approximate Answers from Randomized Experiments?" *Psychological Methods* 1, no. 2: 154–69.

Holosko, M. J. 2009. "What Types of Designs Are We Using in Social Work Research and Evaluation?" *Research on Social Work Practice* 20, no. 6: 665–73.

Kravitz, R. L., and N. Duan, eds., and the DEcIDE Methods Center N-of-1 Guidance Panel. 2014. *Design and Implementation of N-of-1 Trials: A User's Guide*. AHRQ Publication No. 13(14)-EHC122-EF. Agency for Healthcare Research and Quality. www.effectivehealthcare. ahrq.gov/N-1-Trials.cfm.

Kronish, I. M., C. Alcantara, J. Duer-Hefele, T. St. Onge, K. W. Davidson, E. J. Carter, V. Medina, E. Cohn, and N. Moise. 2017. "Patients and Primary Care Providers Identify Opportunities for Personalized (N-of-1) Trials in the Mobile Health Era." *Journal of Clinical Epidemiology* 89: 236–37.

Marrast, L., J. Conigliaro, C. Chan, E. J. Kim, J. Duer-Hefele, M. A. Diefenbach, and K. W. Davidson. 2021. "Racial and Ethnic Participation in N-of-1 Trials: Perspectives of Healthcare Providers and Patients." *Personalized Medicine* 18, no. 4. https://doi.org/10.2217/pme-2020-0166.

Plaud, J. J., and K. G. Vavrovsky. 1997. "Specific and Social Phobias." In *Handbook of Empirical Social Work Practice*, vol. 1, *Mental Disorders*, edited by B. A. Thyer and J. S. Wodarski, 327–41. Wiley.

Richmond, M. (1917) 1935. *Social Diagnosis*. Russell Sage Foundation.

Rosen, A., E. K. Proctor, and M. M. Staudt. 1999. "Social Work Research and the Quest for Effective Practice." *Social Work Research* 23, no. 1: 4–14.

Royse, D., B. A. Thyer, and D. K. Padgett. 2016. *Program Evaluation: An Introduction to an Evidence-Based Approach*, 6th ed. Cengage.

RSAS (Royal Swedish Academy of Sciences). 2021. "Press Release: The Prize in Economic Sciences 2021." NobelPrize.org. https://www.nobelprize.org/prizes/economic-sciences/2021 /press-release/.

Rubin, A., and D. Parrish. 2007. "Problematic Phrases in the Conclusions of Published Outcome Studies: Implications for Evidence-Based Practice." *Research on Social Work Practice* 17: 334–47.

Rubin, A., D. E. Parrish, and M. Washburn. 2014. "Outcome Benchmarks for Adaptations of Research-Supported Treatments for Adult Traumatic Stress." *Research on Social Work Practice* 26, no. 3: 243–59.

Rubin, A., B. A. Thyer, J. Yaffe, and D. Parrish. 2019. "Utility of Benchmarking to Evaluate the Implementation of Research Supported Interventions." Roundtable discussion presented at the annual conference of the Society for Social Work and Research, San Francisco, CA, January 18, 2019.

Rubin, A., M. Washburn, and C. Schieszler. 2017. "Within-Group Effect-Size Benchmarks for Trauma-Focused Cognitive Behavioral Therapy with Children and Adolescents." *Research on Social Work Practice* 27, no. 7: 789–801.

Rubin, A., and M. Yu. 2015. "Within-Group Effect-Size Benchmarks for Problem-Solving Therapy for Depression in Adults." *Research on Social Work Practice* 27, no. 5: 552–60.

Shadish, W. R., M. H. Clark, and P. M. Steiner. 2008. "Can Nonrandomized Experiments Yield Accurate Answers: A Randomized Experiment Comparing Random and Nonrandom Assignments." *Journal of the American Statistical Association* 103, no. 484: 1334–43.

Shadish, W. R., R. Galino, V. C. Wong, P. M. Steiner, and T. D. Cook. 2011. "A Randomized Experiment Comparing Random and Cutoff-Based Assignment." *Psychological Methods* 16, no. 2: 179–91.

Smith, G. C. S., and J. P. Pell. 2003. "Parachute Use to Prevent Death and Major Trauma Related to Gravitational Challenge: Systematic Review of Randomised Controlled Trials." *British Medical Journal* 327: 1459–61.

Steketee, G., D. L. Chambless, G. Q. Tran, H. Worden, and M. M. Gillis. 1996. "Behavioral Approach Test for Obsessive Compulsive Disorder." *Behaviour Research and Therapy* 34, no. 1: 73–83.

Straus, S. E., P. Glasziou, W. S. Richardson, and R. B. Haynes. 2019. *Evidence-Based Medicine: How to Practice and Teach EBM*, 5th ed. Elsevier.

Swanson, T. 2016. "Time-Series Methods in Experimental Research." *APS Observer*, November 30, 2016. https://www.psychologicalscience.org/observer/time-series-methods -in-experimental-research.

Thyer, B. A. 1983. "Treating Anxiety Disorders with Exposure Therapy." *Social Casework* 64: 77–82.

——. 1987. *Treating Anxiety Disorders*. Sage.

——. 1992. "Promoting Evaluation Research in the Field of Family Preservation." In *Advancing Family Preservation Practice*, edited by E. S. Morton and R. K. Grigsby, 131–49. Sage.

——. 2010. "Pre-experimental and Quasi-experimental Research Designs." In *Handbook of Social Work Research Methods*, 2nd ed., edited by B. A. Thyer, 183–204. Sage.

——. 2012. *Quasi-experimental Research Designs*. Oxford University Press.

Thyer, B. A., and G. C. Curtis. 1983. "The Repeated Pretest-Posttest Single-Subject Experiment: A New Design for Empirical Clinical Practice." *Journal of Behavior Therapy & Experimental Psychiatry* 14, no. 4: 311–15.

Thyer, B. A., and L. L. Myers. 2007. *A Social Worker's Guide to Evaluating Practice Outcomes*. Council on Social Work Education.

Thyer, B. A., J. D. Papsdorf, D. Himle, and H. Bray. 1981. "Normative Data on the Rational Behavior Inventory." *Educational and Psychological Measurement* 41: 757–60.

Thyer, B. A., and K. B. Thyer. 1992. "Single-System Research Designs in Social Work Practice: A Bibliography from 1965 to 1990." *Research on Social Work Practice* 2, no. 1: 99–116.

Thyer, B. A., P. Tomlin, G. C. Curtis, O. G. Cameron, and R. M. Nesse. 1985. "Diagnostic and Gender Differences in the Expressed Fears of Anxious Patients." *Journal of Behavior Therapy and Experimental Psychiatry* 16, no. 2: 111–15.

Todes, D. P. 2014. *Ivan Pavlov: A Russian Life in Science*. Oxford University Press.

Tripodi, T., and J. Harrington. 1979. "Use of Time-Series for Formative Program Evaluation." *Journal of Social Service Research* 3, no. 1: 67–78.

Whisman, M. A., and E. D. Richardson. 2015. "Normative Data on the Beck Depression Inventory—Second Edition (BDI-II) in College Students." *Journal of Clinical Psychology* 71, no. 9: 898–907.

Wong, S. E., P. L. Seroka, and J. Ogisi. 2000. "Effects of a Checklist on Self-Assessment of Blood Glucose Level by a Memory-Impaired Woman with Diabetes Mellitus." *Journal of Applied Behavior Analysis* 33, no. 2: 251–54.

Chapter 10

AEA (American Evaluation Association). n.d. "Digital Knowledge Hub: By Evaluators for Evaluators." https://www.pathlms.com/aea/courses?page=2.

——. 2004. *American Evaluation Association Guiding Principles for Evaluators*. AEA. https://www.eval.org/Portals/0/Docs/gp.principles.pdf?ver=YMYJx_4-pquvpjg6RgNkeQ%3d%3d.

AHRP (Alliance for Human Research Protection). 2022. "1900–1930: Berlin Code of Ethics." https://ahrp.org/1900-1930-berlin-code-of-ethics/.

APA (American Psychological Association). 2017. "Ethical Principles of Psychologists and Code of Conduct." https://www.apa.org/ethics/code.

——. 2020. *Publication Manual of the American Psychological Association*, 7th ed. APA.

BACB (Behavior Analyst Certification Board. 2020. *Ethics Code for Behavior Analysts*. BACB. https://www.bacb.com/wp-content/uploads/2022/01/Ethics-Code-for-Behavior-Analysts-220316-2.pdf.

Barrett, S. 2010. "Lancet Retracts Wakefield Paper." *Autism Watch*. May 29, 2010. https://quackwatch.org/autism/news/lancet/.

Benbunan-Fich, R. 2017. "The Ethics of Online Research with Unsuspecting Users: From A/B Testing to C/D Experimentation." *Research Ethics* 13, nos. 3–4: 200–18.

Bittker, B. M. 2021. "The Ethical Implications of Clinical Trials in Low- and Middle-Income Countries." *Human Rights* 46, no. 4. https://www.americanbar.org/groups/crsj/publications/human_rights_magazine_home/the-truth-about-science/the-ethical-implications-of-clinical-trials/.

Bloom, M., and J. Orme. 1993. "Ethics and the Single-System Design." *Journal of Social Service Research* 18: 161–80.

Burstrom, H. G. 1975. "Ethics of Experimental Research." *Dialectica* 29, no. 4: 237–47.

Carandang, C., D. Santor, D. M. Gardner, N. Carrey, and S. Kutcher. 2007. "Data Safety Monitoring Boards and Other Study Methodologies That Address Subject Safety in 'High-Risk' Therapeutic Trials in Youths." *Journal of the American Academy of Child and Adolescent Psychiatry* 46, no. 4: 489–92.

CFR (Code of Federal Regulations). 2022. "Title 45: Public Welfare—Part 46: Protection of Human Subjects." Last amended November 7, 2022. https://www.ecfr.gov/current/title-45/subtitle-A/subchapter-A/part-46?toc=1.

Cha, K. Y., D. P. Wirth, and R. R. Lobo. 2001. "Does Prayer Influence the Success of In Vitro Fertilization-Embryo Transfer?" *Journal of Reproductive Medicine* 46: 781–87.

Chandler, R. K., M. L. Dennis, N. El-Bassel, R. P. Schwartz, and G. Field. 2009. "Ensuring Safety, Implementation and Scientific Integrity of Clinical Trials: Lessons from the Criminal Justice Abuse Treatment Studies Data and Safety Monitoring Board." *Journal of Experimental Criminology* 5: 323–44.

Clark, J. J. 2009. "Why Social Work Practitioners Need Research Ethics Knowledge." *Social Work* 54, no. 1: 5–7.

Cox, D. J., N. Y. Syed, M. T. Brodhead, and S. P. Quigley, eds. 2022. *Research Ethics in Behavior Analysis: From Laboratory to Clinic and Classroom*. Academic.

Crocker, J. 2011. "The Road to Fraud Starts with a Single Step." *Nature* 479: 151.

Daundasekara, S. S., B. R. Schular, and D. C. Hernandez. 2021. "RETRACTED: Independent and Combined Association of Intimate Partner Violence and Food Insecurity on Maternal Depression and Generalized Anxiety Disorder." *Journal of Anxiety Disorders* 81: 102409.

Drake, B., E. Putnam-Hornstein, M. Jonson-Reid, C. Wildeman, H. Kim, B. Needell, J. Fluke, and R. Bartch. 2018. "RAND's Recently Released Child Welfare System Simulation: Revisions Are Needed." Retraction Watch.

Elliott, L. J. 1931. *Social Work Ethics*. American Association of Social Workers.

Farmer, A. Y., and D. Bess. 2010. "Gender, Ethnicity, and Racial Issues." In *Handbook of Social Work Research Methods*, 2nd ed., edited by B. A. Thyer, 579–90. Sage.

Feller, A., T. Grindal, L. Miratrix, and L. C. Page. 2016. "Compared to What? Variation in the Impacts of Early Childhood Education by Alternative Care Type." *Annals of Applied Statistics* 10, no. 3: 1245–85.

Ferguson, A., and J. J. Clark. 2018. "The Status of Research Ethics in Social Work." *Journal of Evidence-Informed Social Work* 15, no. 4: 351–70.

Gallagher, B., A. H. Berman, J. Bieganski, A. D. Jones, L. Foca, B. Raikes, and J. Schiratzki. 2016. "National Human Research Ethics: A Preliminary Comparative Case Study of Germany, Great Britain, Romania, and Sweden." *Ethics and Behavior* 26, no. 7: 586–606.

Gibelman, M., and S. R. Gelman. 2001. "Learning from the Mistakes of Others: A Look at Scientific Misconduct in Research." *Journal of Social Work Education* 37, no. 2: 241–54.

——. 2005. "Scientific Misconduct in Social Welfare Research: Preventive Lessons from Other Fields." *Social Work Education* 24, no. 3: 275–95.

Gillespie, D. F. 1987. "Ethical Issues in Research." In *Encyclopedia of Social Work*, 18th ed., edited by A. Minahan, 503–12. NASW.

Grigsby, R. K., and H. Roof. 1993. "Federal Policy for the Protection of Human Subjects: Applications to Research on Social Work Practice." *Research on Social Work Practice* 3: 448–61.

Hailman, D. E. 1949. "A Code of Ethics for Social Workers." *Social Work Journal* 30: 44–50.

Holosko, M. J., B. A. Thyer, and J. E. H. Danner. 2009. "Ethical Guidelines for Designing and Conducting Evaluations of Social Work Practice." *Journal of Evidence-Based Social Work* 6: 348–60.

Humphreys, M. 2015. "Reflections on the Ethics of Social Experimentation." *Journal of Globalization and Development* 6, no. 1: 87–112.

Keith-Lucas, A. 1977. "Ethics in Social Work." In *Encyclopedia of Social Work*, 17th ed., edited by J. B. Turner, 350–55. NASW.

Levy, C. S. 1974. "On the Development of a Code of Ethics." *Social Work* 39: 207–16.

Lewis, R. J., K. A. Calis, and D. L. DeMets. 2016. "Enhancing the Scientific Integrity and Safety of Clinical Trials: Recommendations for Data Monitoring Committees." *Journal of the American Medical Association* 316, no. 22: 2359–60.

Lifton, R. J. 2017. *The Nazi Doctors: Medical Killing and the Psychology of Genocide*. Basic Books.

Mitscherlich, A., and F. Mielke. 1949. *Doctors of Infamy: The Story of the Nazi Medical Crimes*. Schuman.

NASW (National Association of Social Workers). 1965. "Code of Ethics." In *Encyclopedia of Social Work*, edited by H. L. Lurie, 1027. NASW.

——. 1980. *Code of Ethics*. NASW.

——. 2021a. "NASW Code of Ethics: Ethical Standards—2. Social Workers' Ethical Responsibilities to Colleagues." NASW. https://www.socialworkers.org/About/Ethics/Code-of-Ethics/Code-of-Ethics-English/Social-Workers-Ethical-Responsibilities-to-Colleagues.

——. 2021b. "NASW Code of Ethics: Ethical Standards—5. Social Workers' Ethical Responsibilities to the Social Work Profession." NASW. https://www.socialworkers.org/About/Ethics/Code-of-Ethics/Code-of-Ethics-English/Social-Workers-Ethical-Responsibilities-to-the-Social-Work-Profession.

NCPHS (National Commission for the Protection of Human Subjects of Biomedical and Behavioral Research). 1979. *Belmont Report: Ethical Principles and Guidelines for the Protection of Human Subjects of Research*. Department of Health, Education, and Welfare. https://www.hhs.gov/ohrp/sites/default/files/the-belmont-report-508c_FINAL.pdf.

Office of Research Integrity. n.d. "Protection of Human Subjects." https://ori.hhs.gov/content/chapter-3-The-Protection-of-Human-Subjects-45-crf-46102-protection-human-subjects.

Peled, E., and R. Leichtentritt. 2002. "The Ethics of Qualitative Social Work Research." *Qualitative Social Work* 1, no. 2: 145–69.

Phillips, T. 2021. "Ethics of Field Experiments." *Annual Review of Political Science* 24: 277–300.

Sierra, X. 2011. "Ethics in Medical Research in Humans: A Historical Perspective." *Actas Dermo-Sifiliográficas* 102, no. 6: 395–401.

Slutsky, A. S., and J. V. Lavery. 2004. "Data Safety and Monitoring Boards." *New England Journal of Medicine* 350, no. 11: 1143–47.

Thyer, B. A. 2013. "Unwarranted Social Work Authorships: A Partial Solution Is at Hand." *Social Work Research* 37, no. 1: 14–15.

Trace, S., and S. Kolstoe. 2018. "Reviewing Code Consistency Is Important but Research Ethics Committee Must Also Make a Judgement on Scientific Justification, Methodological Approach and Competency of the Research Team." *Journal of Medical Ethics* 44, no. 12: 874–75.

Tufford, L., P. A. Newman, D. J. Brennan, S. L. Craig, and M. R. Woodford. 2012. "Conducting Research with Lesbian, Gay, and Bisexual Populations: Navigating Research Ethics Board Reviews." *Journal of Gay and Lesbian Social Services* 24: 221–40.

UCTV (University of California Television). 2019. "Emerging Ethics Challenges for Experimental Social Science: Exploring Ethics." YouTube video, 57:28. Uploaded May 30, 2019. https://www.youtube.com/watch?v=pnj9MTJts7w.

Wakefield, A. J., S. H. Murch, A. Anthony, J. Linnell, D. M. Casson, M. Malik, M. Berelowitz, A. P. Dhillon, M. A. Thomson, P. Harvey, A. Valentine, S. E. Davies, and J. A. Walker-Smith. 1998. "Ileal-Lymphoid-Nodular Hyperplasia, Non-specific Colitis, and Pervasive Developmental Disorder in Children." *Lancet* 351, no. 9103: 637–41.

Zuckerman, J., B. van der Schalie, and K. Cahill. 2015. "Developing Training for Data Safety Monitoring Board Members." *Clinical Trials* 12, no. 6: 688–91.

INDEX

GPSR Authorized Representative: Easy Access System Europe, Mustamäe tee
50, 10621 Tallinn, Estonia, gpsr.requests@easproject.com

www.ingramcontent.com/pod-product-compliance
Lightning Source LLC
Chambersburg PA
CBHW021845020426
42334CB00013B/194